THE CHAIRMAN'S LOUNGE

THE INSIDE STORY OF HOW QANTAS SOLD US OUT

JOE ASTON

SCRIBNER

SCRIBNER

First published in Australia in 2024 by Scribner,
an imprint of Simon & Schuster (Australia) Pty Limited
Level 4, 32 York St, Sydney NSW 2000

Simon & Schuster: Celebrating 100 Years of Publishing in 2024.
New York Amsterdam/Antwerp London Toronto Sydney New Delhi
Visit our website at www.simonandschuster.com.au

SCRIBNER and design are registered trademarks of The Gale Group, Inc.,
used under licence by Simon & Schuster LLC.

10 9 8 7 6 5

© Joe Aston 2024

A catalogue record for this
book is available from the
National Library of Australia

9781761429767 (paperback)
9781761632617 (hardback)
9781761429774 (ebook)

Cover design by Luke Causby
Cover image: Unsplash/Fajri Hafizh
Author photo: Stephen Blake
Typeset in 11.5/16 pt Adobe Caslon Pro by Midland Typesetters, Australia
Printed and bound in Australia by Griffin Press

The paper this book is printed on is certified against the
Forest Stewardship Council® Standards. Griffin Press holds
chain of custody certification SCS-COC-001185. FSC®
promotes environmentally responsible, socially beneficial
and economically viable management of the world's forests.

For Annabelle,
the best wife in Australia by the length of a straight

Disclosure

For reasons that will become obvious, it is right I declare that in my early years as a journalist, I accepted complimentary upgrades and free flights on many occasions from various airlines, including Air New Zealand, Emirates, Etihad, Qantas and Virgin Australia. None of these were in the past five years.

Since 2018 I have been a member of Virgin Australia's invite-only lounge, Beyond (formerly called the Club). Anyone who suspects this has made me soft on Virgin need only google 'Rear Window + Jayne Hrdlicka'.

I am not – *quelle surprise* – a member of the Chairman's Lounge.

Statement from Alan Joyce

I asked Alan Joyce to speak to me for this book but he declined to do so. Instead, he offered the following statement on the condition that it be published in its entirety:

I retired from the Qantas Group at the end of 2023 on good terms.

From a personal perspective, during my 15 years as CEO, Qantas achieved great things despite many challenges, not least navigating the unprecedented impact of the COVID-19 pandemic on the airline industry internationally.

As Qantas chairman Richard Goyder commented at the time, I always put the best interests of Qantas front and centre. Together with the management team, I believe we delivered great value to the business, its shareholders and most importantly, its customers.

Due to my ongoing obligations of confidentiality to Qantas, I am unable to comment further on the subject of this book. As such, I have serious reservations about whether it will provide readers with an accurate, fair and balanced account of my tenure at Qantas.

The author in September 2008, then Qantas corporate communications senior adviser, awaiting the arrival of the first Qantas A380 in Sydney airport's hangar 96.

Contents

Preface   1

Introduction   3
2006–2017

Eleven Weeks from Bankruptcy   17
Nov 2019–March 2020

Reality on an Underlying Basis   42
April–Oct 2020

Transport Workers' Union v. Qantas   54
Nov 2020–July 2021

Crossing the Rubicon   82
Sept 2020–Nov 2022

Not Match Fit   112
April–July 2022

The Best CEO in Australia   135
July–Sept 2022

Joyce 1.0   150
2008–2022

Fighting the Facts   168
Dec 2022–March 2023

Simon the Likeable   187
30 March–15 May 2023

Alan's Enchanted Spectacles   206
19 May–26 July 2023

A Very Valued Benefit 226
   2–27 Aug 2023

Grand Theft Aero 250
   28 Aug–5 Sept 2023

Captain, You Must Listen! 270
   1 Sept–3 Nov 2023

Feel the Difference? 296
   Oct 2023–Oct 2024

Afterword 321
   30 Sept 2023

Notes 323
Acknowledgements 349
Index 350

Preface

On a drizzly Monday in August 2024, five weeks before officially assuming his new role as the chairman of Qantas, John Mullen meets me for lunch in Sydney. Days earlier, the reconfigured Qantas board had stripped $9 million worth of bonuses from former CEO Alan Joyce, following an array of legal and customer service failures that had consumed the airline in the previous eighteen months.

At the same time, the board also published an independent report into the governance of the airline, and its findings were scathing: Joyce had a 'command and control' leadership style, and this was a 'root cause' of the events that led to the collapse of public trust in Qantas. His underlings were too afraid to speak up, and the board itself was too deferential to Joyce, failing to challenge him. Qantas, the report found, had prioritised its financial performance over the interests of its customers and employees.

These were accusations I'd made repeatedly in dozens of columns in the *Australian Financial Review* between August 2022 and October 2023, and which were flatly rejected by Mullen's predecessor, Richard Goyder. In response, Qantas boycotted the *AFR* and Goyder declared Joyce to be 'the best CEO in Australia by the length of a straight'.

When I ask John Mullen what he thinks of that claim, he says, 'I think Joyce was a very effective CEO in earlier times. He did a good job, investors liked him. But no, I don't think you could possibly call him the best in Australia. If he was, then much of this would not have happened.'

This book is a chronicle of Joyce's dramatic fall from Australian business legend to outcast. It is a tale of total dominance by one individual and the failure of a whole system; a parable of imbalance whereby loyal customers and staff were sacrificed at the altar of shareholder returns. It is the story of how a century-old company went from being one of Australia's most successful and beloved to a national pariah, over the course of just three and a half years. And it is above all a cautionary tale about power: the wielding of power from the shadows, the blinding power of money, and the soothing power of self-delusion.

The elite Qantas Chairman's Lounge came to symbolise the way that power works in this country. Its invitation-only membership opens an unmarked sliding door the rest of us aren't supposed to even know exists. Behind it: a world of preferential treatment, murmured conversations and favours traded. So sought after is Chairman's Lounge access among businesspeople and government officials that it distorts public policy and private contracts like a black hole bends light. It is the ultimate loyalty program.

And the Chairman's Lounge has another meaning. In the time of Alan Joyce, it might be said that the Qantas chairman had been catatonic on a lounge of his own, neglecting to manage an undoubtedly talented but increasingly disinhibited CEO as he veered disastrously off course.

Introduction

2006–2017

My involvement with Qantas began tangentially, in 2006, when I landed a job in the office of federal Liberal MP Bruce Baird.[1] Baird was Scott Morrison's predecessor as the member for Cook, the electorate encompassing the eastern half of Sydney's Sutherland Shire, stretching across Botany Bay from Sydney airport's north–south runways.

Bruce was known – only half jokingly – as the member for Qantas. More Qantas employees lived in Cook than in any other electorate, and he advocated fiercely for their interests. He was chairman of the Coalition's parliamentary Friends of Tourism group, a lunch club of government MPs and senators who were wined, dined and lobbied intensely by airlines, airports, hotel groups, travel agents, cruise ship companies, and even Morrison, then Tourism Australia's managing director, before he was sacked in July 2006.

Baird maintained an incredibly close relationship with Qantas chief executive Geoff Dixon. The two men had been friends since the mid-1970s, when they were colleagues in the Australian consulate in New York. Baird had an open line to Dixon's VIP coordinator in Canberra. Departing flights had been known to wait for him. Free flights were extracted for countless charity auctions, and Baird was not shy about requesting complimentary upgrades for himself, his family, his staff (including me), and others in his professional and social networks. Many of Baird's party room colleagues treated him as a conduit to the airline and its largesse. MPs turned to him with their travel problems, like feudal lords petitioning the royal court.

A career in representative politics presents a conundrum. It affords MPs a degree of celebrity, considerable power and relatively grand resources – multiple offices, a coterie of personal staff, limousines and, yes, membership of the Qantas Chairman's Lounge. Federal politicians work in the cosseted style of ASX 100 CEOs yet are paid like middle managers. In 2006, members of the Australian parliament were the nation's only professional cohort being chauffeured between TV studios and waited on by advisers while earning a base salary of just $127,060 per year. MPs are entitled and accustomed to travelling at the front of the plane on work trips (and as numerous travel expenses scandals have shown, a business purpose can often be interpolated on a leisure trip) but, unlike CEOs, most MPs can't afford to pay for that luxury in their personal lives. So when it came to the family trip to Europe or America, could they really be expected to endure the indignities of economy class when their habitual comforts might be just one beseeching phone call away?

Bruce was part travel agent, part priest in the confessional, part Santa Claus. He was certainly an unofficial arm of the Qantas influence machine and he seemed to thrive on his role as gatekeeper of these opaque privileges. This was consistent with his motivations, in that he was always uncommonly generous in expending any of his power, in any field, on others' behalf, from refugees and the homeless right through to his fellow parliamentarians en route to Disneyland.

He was a vocal human rights advocate, chairing the Amnesty International parliamentary group. His opposition to the asylum seeker policies of the Howard government left him deeply out of favour with John Howard, who entered political folklore by winning the 2001 election promising, 'We will decide who comes to this country and the circumstances in which they come.' In the Howard government's final term, Baird's twin pet policy fields of aviation and human rights happened to dovetail. He had campaigned relentlessly in 2005 for a stay of execution on behalf of Australian citizen Van Nguyen, who had been convicted of smuggling heroin through

Singapore the previous year and sentenced to death. At the same time, Singapore Airlines was seeking approval from the Howard government to launch flights on the Pacific route between Australia and the United States.

The trans-Pacific was utterly dominated by Qantas. Its only competitor was a weak one: United Airlines, still in Chapter 11 bankruptcy. And it was highly lucrative, at the time accounting for around 15 per cent of Qantas' entire annual earnings. Tourism minister Fran Bailey was strongly in favour of opening up the route. But on the eve of Van Nguyen's execution, Baird urged Howard's cabinet to consider Singapore's refusal of clemency when deciding on these air rights for Singapore Airlines.

While the decision was technically at the sole discretion of the transport minister – a line we heard ad nauseum from Albanese and his ministers during the Qatar Airways imbroglio eighteen years later – Howard (unlike Albanese) did not feign personal distance from it. 'There are arguments for and against,' Howard said. 'One of the arguments people put against it is that whereas Qantas is operating as a fully independent, freestanding company without any government support or subsidy, that is not always the case with foreign airlines, including Singapore Airlines.'

Singapore Airlines was (and remains) majority government-owned. There was nevertheless some irony in the prime minister citing Qantas' commendable self-reliance as his justification for shielding it from the competition of an open market. As Qantas chairwoman Margaret Jackson put it privately to one of Howard's most senior ministers, the government could grant Singapore access to the Pacific, but then the government would have to 'explain to people in Tamworth why they have to catch a bus to Sydney'.

The decision was made in February 2006 to block Singapore's request. It was an early taster of how Qantas' influence worked: independent when it suited them, quasi-sovereign when that was advantageous; with friends in high places who appreciated the largesse it could bestow.

While the formidable – perhaps even peerless – lobbying duo of Dixon and his chair Margaret Jackson killed Singapore's bid for market access on Qantas' eastern flank, they were also battling Dubai's state-owned carrier Emirates to the west. They turned to the same playbook.

Emirates' explosive growth at that time terrified every legacy airline the world over. When Emirates applied to double its flights to Australia from forty-two to eighty-four per week, Jackson described the request as 'not only extravagant, but flies in the face of fair competition'. Not for the first time, she accused the Gulf carrier of benefiting from government subsidies. 'To suggest that Emirates is competing on similar terms as commercially run airlines like Qantas is, quite frankly, fiction,' she said.

Emirates vice-chairman Maurice Flanagan had a riposte: 'Government protection is the most powerful subsidy of them all,' he replied. 'Qantas is one of the world's most anti-competitive airlines and customers are paying higher prices as a result. Their calls for protection belong in another era.'

Slowing down Emirates proved beyond even the awesome powers of the Qantas influence machine. In the high-stakes game of regulatory capture, Emirates was no slouch itself – and certainly streets ahead of Singapore. By 2006 it was already sponsor of the Melbourne Cup, where its trackside marquee was the most sought-after ticket in the Birdcage at Flemington, teeming each November with politicians (and journalists, including me in later years) gorging themselves on free champagne.

It didn't hurt that Deputy Prime Minister and Minister for Transport Mark Vaile had struck up a friendship with Sheikh Mohammed bin Rashid Al Maktoum, Dubai's ruler and Emirates' proprietor. When Vaile took the transport portfolio in 2006, he had been trade minister for the prior seven years. All up, he made an estimated twenty ministerial visits to the United Arab Emirates.[2]

On a visit to Canberra, Sheikh Ahmed bin Saeed Al Maktoum, chairman of Emirates and the uncle of Dubai's ruler Sheikh Mohammed, addressed the Coalition Friends of Tourism. Emirates had already announced it was building a luxury eco-resort in New South Wales' Wolgan Valley, which was big news in the Australian tourism industry. Sheikh Ahmed told the gathered MPs that Wolgan Valley might be the first of several such hotels and that Emirates was very interested in their input as to suitable locations. Marginal seat-holders rushed at the Gulf royal with topographical maps of their electorates. In March 2007, just thirteen months after the Howard government blocked Singapore Airlines, Vaile granted Emirates the doubling of rights it had requested.

Emirates' longstanding Australian adviser was public affairs firm Parker & Partners, whose principal Andrew Parker well understood, as did Dixon and Jackson, the shortest route to politicians' hearts. In 2009, Parker moved to Dubai as the airline's global government affairs boss, reporting to Emirates CEO Tim Clark.

By 2012 the barrage of insults between Qantas and Emirates was forgotten and their blood enmity buried. With its international arm haemorrhaging money, Qantas effected a complete volte-face: it leapt into bed with Emirates, striking a comprehensive alliance that still stands today. But rather than a defeat for Qantas, this was a strategic victory. With this deal, Qantas neutralised the only industry player capable of coming close to its influence over Australian policymakers. The lobbying power behind Qantas and its objectives had now effectively doubled. It was unstoppable.[3]

In 2014, Parker left Emirates with Clark's blessing to be Qantas CEO Alan Joyce's chief lobbyist.[4]

Rival airlines weren't the only threats to Qantas in 2006. In December of that year, demented by the froth of the pre-GFC credit boom, a consortium of financiers from Macquarie Bank, Texas Pacific Group (TPG) and the now-defunct Allco Finance attempted an $11 billion leveraged buyout of Qantas. The consortium called itself Airline Partners Australia (APA). And fatefully, the transaction was supported by Geoff Dixon's management team and Margaret Jackson's board of directors.

John Howard's government still needed to approve the deal, and in the early weeks of 2007, APA's principals haunted the corridors of Parliament House.⁵ On 25 January, for John Howard's opening address of the parliamentary year, TPG's Australian head, Ben Gray – son of former Tasmanian Liberal premier Robin Gray – hosted Bruce Baird on his table at the National Press Club. During the following sitting fortnight of parliament, Baird convened a meeting of around forty government MPs at which Dixon and the APA bosses made their pitch and fielded questions.

My job was to meet the APA delegation at the House of Representatives entrance, sign them in and escort them to Baird's office. For me, this initial meeting defined the whole period. In the room was Bruce and me; Gray and his colleague Simon Harle; Macquarie's Geoff Joyce; the consortium's lobbyist Lynton Crosby; and Allco's Peter Yates, a former CEO of the Packer family's Publishing and Broadcasting Limited. Nowadays, when it comes to egomaniacal financiers, I've just about seen it all. Back then, however, I was an unworldly young man and really hadn't been exposed to this variety of the human animal.

Yates came on strong in the meeting, including – apropos of absolutely nothing – complaining to Baird that Kerry Packer had only paid him $11 million in his final year at PBL. The meeting ended courteously but Baird was seriously unimpressed. I called Lynton Crosby later that day to share my boss' stupefaction at his client's command performance, suggesting that a little less Yates in Canberra might be in the consortium's best interests. Crosby seemed grateful for the feedback but already highly attuned to his key man vulnerability.⁶

The thing to understand about Liberal politicians – and even some Labor ones – is that absolutely nothing irks them more than business leaders earning ten or in some cases even a hundred times more money than they do. And no politician of that day carried this resentment more fervently than Peter Costello, the federal treasurer, whose explicit approval the Qantas deal required. In the event, however, Costello did not block the deal, waving it through the foreign investment review process on 7 March 2007.

By 4 May, when the APA takeover of Qantas fell narrowly short of shareholder approval – in dramatic circumstances – I'd left Baird's office and returned to the office of Joe Hockey, the minister responsible for WorkChoices, for the final chaotic months of the Howard government, which was turfed from office on 24 November.

And so, by the end of that year, I started a new job at – of all places – Qantas.

———

When I landed in Qantas' corporate communications department, right after Christmas of 2007, I was twenty-four years old and had never worked for a large company. But I had been schooled in the deranged ways of politics, with its ludicrous bureaucracy and its dubious standards of accountability and personal conduct. The transition was seamless.

Although less than two decades ago, this was truly a different era. Dixon had only recently fathered a child with his secretary, an open secret. Chairwoman Margaret Jackson had resigned over her advocacy – extending well beyond dispassionate recommendation – of the APA takeover bid, and been succeeded by Leigh Clifford at the annual general meeting the previous month. It was clear Dixon's days were also numbered, and media conjecture about CEO succession was in overdrive.

Qantas had never (and still hasn't) hired a CEO from outside the organisation. The three candidates being canvassed publicly were all internal: chief financial officer Peter Gregg; executive general manager John Borghetti; and Jetstar CEO Alan Joyce, considered the rank outsider around the water coolers at Qantas headquarters.

Clifford, however, had very quickly decided there was 'daylight' between Joyce and the others. 'I interviewed all the internal candidates, one other Australian and several overseas and I came to the conclusion that Alan was head and shoulders above the rest,' Clifford told me in 2024. He was particularly impressed with Joyce's numeracy, aviation knowledge and 'what I would call his strategic view of the industry'. Joyce was the only candidate invited to present to the Qantas board – not even Peter Gregg was extended that courtesy, and he was a *member* of the board.

The Qantas head office, inherited from Australian Airlines in their 1992 merger, was one of the ugliest places I'd ever seen, exuding all the aesthetic charm of a Centrelink branch on the Gold Coast. Floor upon floor of beige cubicles and frayed grey carpet sat beneath pitiless tube lights. This pallid bureau rose out of industrial Mascot – trucks rumbling below – near Sydney airport; through the filthy external windows we could glimpse Sydney's gleaming CBD in the distance.[7]

The work practices matched the decor. Joyce, when he was appointed, inherited an incredibly overweight and hierarchical organisation. (To his credit, he did drag the company into the modern age; swingeing managerial redundancies began almost immediately.) But even though many staff were set in their ways, or enslaved to obsolete processes, there was no questioning the industry expertise and the wholeheartedness of Qantas people, their consideration of the airline's customers and their staunch adherence to the safety ethos. What particularly struck me was how besotted staff were with the company. People really loved working there (or at the very least loved to hate working there), almost to the point of fixation. Indeed, many employees had never worked anywhere else. This made the culture terrifically insular – something of a paradox given how multicultural the workforce was.

I was self-evidently far too cynical to slide into a cult-like trance upon induction. I was also fortunate enough to meet and share a cheerless nook with Lucinda Holdforth, an author and former diplomat who was Dixon's and Jackson's (and then Clifford's and Joyce's) speechwriter. Lucinda introduced me to obscure pearls of the literary canon, to books which I suspect altered my life's trajectory, and together we found bleak humour in the crushing smallness of our professional lives.[8]

The first half of 2008, as Qantas waited on the announcement of its new CEO, was a bizarre period around the office. Every time I turned a corner, executives would abruptly break off their hushed conversations; doors were invariably closed and every rendezvous was analysed for potential significance. One particularly fraught morning, John Borghetti wandered into our department, entered the office of PR chief Belinda de Rome, and shut the door. While pretending to work but actually attempting to read a magnificent opus of nineteenth-century French nihilism, I watched Borghetti gesticulating through the glass. Barely thirty minutes after he'd left, Joyce appeared, entered de Rome's office and shut the door. A heavy silence fell upon the entire department. The intrigue was scintillating. For me, it was almost a return to regular transmission. Only months earlier I'd been similarly agog as Peter Costello, Alexander Downer and sundry other ministers had traipsed in and out of Joe Hockey's office as they plotted to depose John Howard.

Joyce was named CEO designate on 28 July 2008, with the handover to occur at the AGM on 28 November. Gregg resigned on the spot and Borghetti left in April 2009, becoming CEO of Virgin Blue in May 2010 and setting off a capacity war between Australia's two major domestic airlines. A fortnight before taking the reins from Dixon, Joyce replaced de Rome with David Epstein, then Prime Minister Kevin Rudd's outgoing chief of staff. Epstein wandered the corridors speaking in riddles whose meanings we spent hours failing to surmise. In July 2009 he hired Olivia Wirth, and while Epstein left soon after, Wirth quickly became Joyce's right-hand woman.[9]

Plenty was happening at Qantas in 2008 besides CEO succession. To great fanfare, the company took delivery of the first A380s: bigger, quieter and more luxurious, these were absolute game-changers to the amenity of international flying. Less welcome, in May, the licensed aircraft engineers launched rolling strikes in support of a 5 per cent pay increase. Dixon refused to budge from 3 per cent, famously telling the *Australian Financial Review*, 'The management of this company has contributed far more to its wellbeing and success than any bloody union has.' (We in the airline's PR team first learned about this interview when it peered up at us from the next morning's paper).[10]

Having moved from selling WorkChoices (not that anybody was buying it) to industrial relations pugilism at Qantas, I had incredibly jejune, almost cartoonish, ideas of good and evil in public life. Trade unions were pernicious. Union officials were devil spawn. Tony Sheldon, national secretary of the Transport Workers' Union (TWU), which represented Qantas baggage handlers, was Lucifer himself. Fifteen years later, it felt quite surreal to be in absolute lockstep with Sheldon in the vanguard of those attacking Qantas for its pernicious conduct. We all ripen. But back then, Qantas' position was a bit easier to defend: it was a formidable industrial relations opponent but had yet to cross the line into unapologetic law-breaking.

Qantas reached agreement with the engineers' union on 18 July. One week later, and just three days before the succession announcement, an oxygen tank exploded on the Qantas Boeing 747 operating flight QF30 an hour out of Hong Kong, blowing a 3-metre hole in the fuselage. The pilots diverted to Manila and landed safely.

Up to that point, I'd thought that Coalition campaign headquarters during a federal election represented the height of operational bedlam, but that was nothing on an airline's communications department after an in-flight accident in the same week as the announcement of a new CEO.

And then on 7 October, malfunctioning cockpit computers on a Qantas A330 seized control from the pilots on flight QF72 from Singapore to Perth, forcing the plane to suddenly and repeatedly pitch down, seriously injuring twelve people on board. The crew made an emergency landing at Learmonth airport, near Exmouth in Western Australia.

Notwithstanding the life-saving professionalism of both flight crews, Qantas' hard-won global reputation for safety after two accidents in less than three months was abruptly under the microscope.

But the most memorable incident of all occurred the following year, when four baby pythons escaped from their container in the freight hold of a Qantas 737 flying from Alice Springs to Melbourne and slithered deep into the aircraft's interior – beyond the reach of airport staff. The press quickly found out and the phones started ringing. 'Snakes on a Plane' was any news desk's dream headline.[11] After getting the full run-down from Qantas' integrated operations centre (IOC), I was able to assure multiple media outlets – who duly reported it – that the aircraft had been fumigated to kill the pythons before it was loaded with passengers and flown to Sydney.

The next morning, the ramp supervisor phoned me and apologised for not returning my call the previous day. I told him I'd spoken to the IOC and there was nothing to worry about; the pythons had been eliminated. The bemused ramp supervisor told me I'd been misinformed: in fact, when they couldn't locate the reptiles, ground staff had sent the plane on its way regardless, confident the (harmless) pythons would perish on the next leg. There was a negligible chance, the supervisor assured me, that one of the little suckers would crawl out of the dunny and nibble a passenger on the arse. I exercised my discretion not to update the media.

One of my regular tasks at Qantas was to produce the daily press clippings for the CEO and the executive leadership team. This comically antiquated process was one which, despite my bleating, none of my superiors would countenance ushering into the twenty-first century. When my turn on the roster came up, I would arrive at the office by 7am to cut every Qantas-related article out of that morning's newspapers. Then, I would sticky-tape them onto blank A4 pages, make ten photocopies, and walk up to the executive floor to distribute them no later than 7:30am.[12]

I regularly hand-delivered the press clippings to Joyce at his desk. He knew me by name and was genial towards me, but I was too junior to have any meaningful working relationship with him. Neither of us could have imagined that fifteen years later, the most trenchant, scathing newspaper articles about him would most days be written by me.

I left Qantas late in 2009. On my final day at the company, I was due to attend a black-tie function immediately after work, and for some inexplicable reason I had bought a traditional bow tie. I had no conception of how to tie it, and nobody in my department possessed this bygone skill either. A call went around the office and soon my desk phone rang. It was Kate Hogg, the chairman's executive assistant. Come upstairs, she said, the chairman would be all too happy to help. As a secondary problem, I was sporting a rather striking black eye after an unseemly altercation with a taxi driver in the early hours of that morning. Lucinda hurriedly caked my shiner in foundation before I shuffled upstairs for my formative – and farewell – life lesson from big Leigh Clifford.

Rummaging through a box of old paraphernalia recently, I came upon a faded copy of the December 2008 edition of 'Qantas News', the company's in-house monthly newspaper for its (then) 37,000 staff. The page one splash proclaimed, 'Re-Joyce: Alan takes the reins ... by Joe Aston'. Fifteen years later, on 6 September 2023, the front pages of real newspapers coast to coast – from the *West Australian* to Sydney's *Daily Telegraph* – deployed the same 'Re-Joyce' pun as they trumpeted the early resignation, in disgrace, of Qantas' veteran chief executive.

———

Aviation is a tiny industry. Straight out of Qantas, I briefly worked for a communications firm, CPR, where my major client was Air New Zealand. My main contact, and the carrier's boss in Australia at that time, was Cam Wallace, who in 2023 was appointed by Alan Joyce to run Qantas' international division. Then, in 2010, I was (again briefly) employed as a speechwriter for Etihad Airways' garrulous CEO, James Hogan, based in Abu Dhabi. While I was there, Etihad struck a comprehensive alliance with the newly rebranded Virgin Australia, inadvertently pushing Qantas into the arms of Emirates two years later. Virgin's PR boss at the time was Danielle Keighery, who in 2024 was hired by new Qantas CEO Vanessa Hudson to help her rehabilitate the airline's ravaged reputation.

In November 2011, I joined the *Australian Financial Review*. It was quite an anomaly for someone in corporate PR with negligible experience in journalism to score a senior staff role at a national newspaper. Plenty of my new colleagues were bemused. It was also an inversion of the curious (and oft remarked upon) tradition of *Financial Review* reporters defecting to Qantas. The *AFR*'s aviation reporter, Jane Boyle, joined Qantas in 2003, running investor relations before landing a plum posting in LA just as Geoff Dixon was retiring. In 2006, another *AFR* aviation reporter, Tansy Harcourt, joined Qantas in a strategy role, then was posted to London. She left Qantas in 2008, also just before Dixon retired, and returned to the *AFR* for several years. Both Boyle and Harcourt were personally close to Dixon. And then in 2013, yet another *AFR* aviation reporter, Andrew Cleary, went to work for Qantas, also in investor relations.

The Qantas–*AFR* symbiosis – or at least revolving door – became a running joke in the media industry, making their great schism of 2023 the more remarkable. My own relationship with Qantas as a newspaper columnist was initially wary: I was naturally distrusted, having spent the prior eighteen months at Etihad, by then Virgin's major international partner (Qantas and Virgin were, at the time, locked in a domestic capacity war of profound enmity). This was not helped when in November 2012, I published the immortal gossip item that Olivia Wirth, the dark arts operator behind the union-busting Qantas CEO, had hooked up with Australian Workers' Union secretary Paul Howes.

But relations ultimately defrosted. At Lachlan Murdoch's Christmas party in December 2015, Joyce and conservative News Corp columnist Miranda Devine had a heated argument about gay marriage. Devine started it, but Joyce gave as good as he got, and it was so hostile that Lachlan; his wife Sarah; the *Daily Telegraph*'s editor, Paul Whittaker; and News Corp Australia CEO Peter Tonagh were all involved in attempting to de-escalate the feud. When some months later Devine launched into Joyce in the *Tele*, suggesting he was 'doing a pretty good impersonation of an authoritarian dictator with his demands that corporate Australia promote same-sex marriage', which Joyce wasn't demanding at all, I weighed in on Joyce's side and reported the argument in my column.

Devine and I then became entangled in a nine-month feud of our own, with me in Joyce's corner. It ran right up to the next Murdoch Christmas party, in 2016, from which Devine was a last-minute withdrawal. Only the week before, she had written, 'Joyce accosted me at a party once to rant furiously', but 'I can handle myself just fine against angry leprechauns'.

There was a further rapprochement in 2016, when Qantas approached me to write an in-depth feature on its plans to launch direct flights from Perth to London in 2018. I experienced the Qantas star treatment at its highest wattage. I was given wide-ranging access to the company's executives and big-name collaborators, and was flown to Japan with celebrity chef Neil Perry and industrial designer David Caon, who at the Noritake factory in Nagoya selected the new inflight crockery for Qantas' international flights. I interviewed Joyce at Mascot, and we photographed Joyce, Perry, fashion designer Martin Grant, and industrial designer Marc Newson on the Sydney airport runway in matching black suits, *Reservoir Dogs*-style.[13] When the story appeared on the cover of the *AFR Magazine* in February 2017, Miranda Devine was – perhaps justifiably – unimpressed.

But the affair continued. In October 2017, I was one of twenty-five journalists Joyce invited to Seattle to collect Qantas' first 787-9 Dreamliner from Boeing's immense Everett factory and fly on it home to Australia. The first Qantas representative to greet me in Seattle was Annabelle Cottee, a PR manager in the airline's Los Angeles office who is now my wife.[14] Yes, I even have Alan Joyce to thank for my marriage.

The 787-9 was perfectly capable of flying non-stop from Seattle to Sydney but we nevertheless overnighted in Hawaii to prolong the festivities. A photograph of Joyce, Perry and me alighting on the tarmac at Honolulu airport, arms linked and draped in leis, subsequently made multiple appearances on ABC's *Media Watch*. The travelling party was conveyed to the Royal Hawaiian, the famous 'Pink Palace' on the beach at Waikiki, which had a tremendous mai tai bar. It was a boisterous occasion, I dimly recall. And I'm fairly sure that was the very last time I ever saw or spoke to Alan Joyce.

Eleven Weeks
from Bankruptcy
Nov 2019–March 2020

As 2019 drew to a close, it must have seemed for all the world to Alan Joyce like he was nearing the summit of Mount Everest. Only five years earlier, he had been begging the federal government for a $3 billion debt guarantee and was rebuffed, had then embarked upon a defining restructure, shedding fifty aircraft and five thousand jobs, and handed down a whopping $4 billion loss for 2014.

Now, the Qantas share price, having plumbed the depths of 97 cents in 2012 and 2013, was soaring at a record high of $7.40. The company had generated $1.3 billion of annual pre-tax profit for the 2019 financial year, Qantas' fourth successive year of profits greater than $1 billion. The airline was again paying shareholders respectable dividends, and since 2015 had handed them a further $3.2 billion in share buy-backs.[1] Eight years since Joyce abruptly grounded the Qantas fleet to break rolling industrial action by his pilots, engineers and baggage handlers, industrial peace – or at least subjugation – now reigned across the highly unionised airline. In November 2019, research company Roy Morgan placed Qantas at seven in Australia's top ten most trusted brands, while the company's own research found that 'half of Australians claim Qantas as the #1 business supporting the Australian community'.[2]

Joyce, therefore, had finagled the holy trinity of Qantas shareholders, employees and customers into a satisfied balance. This was 'very unique', according to Qantas' largest shareholder, Australian fund manager Pendal. As Crispin Murray, Pendal's head of equities, put it then, 'The position of the business in terms of the product and the trust in the brand, that's actually improved despite rationalisation and restructuring, and [Joyce has] restored employees' belief in the company and engagement.'

And on 2 November 2019, Joyce married his long-term partner Shane Lloyd on the roof of the Museum of Contemporary Art at Sydney's Circular Quay.

But although things were very, very good in 2019, a reasonable argument could be mounted that 2017 was actually Joyce's personal *annus mirabilis*. That year, he helped lead (and finance) the successful campaign for gay marriage in Australia. He was made a Companion of the Order of Australia, the nation's highest civil honour.[3] The *Australian Financial Review* named Joyce its businessperson of the year, while *GQ* named him its man of the year. He was paid a record $24 million. So by 2019 his accomplishments had set in the national psyche like dye: deliverer of an historic corporate turnaround, redeemer of a broken national icon, the cultural significance of which could not be overstated. His personal stock was in the clouds, a hero to economic conservatives for his hard-line industrial relations tactics, and adored by progressives over marriage equality. Market research by leading pollster JWS Research conducted in July 2019 identified Joyce as Australia's fourth most recognised businessperson, after Rupert Murdoch, James Packer and Gina Rinehart, all of whom were billionaire proprietors, not company managers; Joyce stood alone as the nation's singular celebrity CEO.

And he was rich. In just four years, he'd been paid an extraordinary $58 million. These were truly Joyce's halcyon days.

Ahead of him was the 'final frontier' of aviation, a pioneering ambition which Qantas codenamed Project Sunrise: to transform long-haul international travel with non-stop commercial flights from Sydney to London and New York, to launch in 2023. Crispin Murray hoped 'that this doesn't become a project that's the final trophy at the end of the tenure of the CEO'.

On 15 November 2019, the newly married Joyce stepped off a 19½-hour test flight from London Heathrow into hangar 96 at Sydney airport. At that stage, it was all just a PR stunt – a joy ride on a near-empty 787 Dreamliner, a plane that can't fly the route bearing a full load of passengers. The aircraft that could – either the Boeing 777X or the A350-1000ULR – hadn't been built yet and Qantas hadn't even placed an order for it. As US aviation journalist Brian Sumers put it, 'They weren't testing anything except the appetite of media to take free flights and write gushing stories.' The arrival reception, like the media coverage, bordered on ecstatic. Joyce was met by a cheering 1,200-strong crowd, including Prime Minister Scott Morrison and opposition leader Anthony Albanese, as a white-smocked children's choir belted out their well-worn rendition of 'I Still Call Australia Home'. This was rapture not seen again at the airport until Taylor Swift touched down in 2024 for her Eras tour; the launch of a real flight could only be imagined.

Within the company, Joyce's power was unchallenged. His original chairman, Leigh Clifford, had retired the previous year after a decade standing immovably behind Joyce's leadership, even as Joyce grasped around for a plausible strategy in the early years and stumbled to that record $4 billion loss in 2014. Clifford's successor, the affable Richard Goyder, was only twelve months into the job. With the benefit of hindsight, it would be too generous to say Goyder was still finding his feet, because he never found them. There was no question around the boardroom table, or the investment market, who was responsible for the tremendous shape the airline was in.

There was not even a plausible successor to Joyce. Just six months earlier, the untimely departure of Qantas International head Alison Webster had necessitated a reshuffle of Joyce's senior team, with Vanessa Hudson promoted to chief financial officer. At the same time, the board asked Joyce to stay on for another three years until 'at least' 2022.[4]

Had Joyce declined that request and called time in 2019 on his eleven-year tenure, he'd have retired a hero, an Australian business legend. Today, he'd be the chairman of a major bank or a mining giant, a person of uninterrupted high status. Instead, Alan Joyce became the most hated businessman in Australia, virtually forced to leave the country when he resigned in September 2023, two months before his scheduled retirement. The same month, a Senate committee threatened to throw him in jail. Having fled the Australian mob, he hid out with his elderly mother in Dublin, where he was chased to the local shops by paparazzi.[5]

What happened in those four years is the focus of this book. Of course, nobody in their wildest imaginings could have foreseen the coronavirus pandemic that would paralyse the global aviation industry just weeks after Qantas' December 2019 high, let alone predict Joyce's response to it and the spectacular unravelling of Qantas as it emerged from the pandemic in 2022 and 2023.

In a bizarre accident of timing, Joyce sat for the cover story of the March 2020 issue of the *Australian Financial Review Magazine*, published as the virus first seeped into the country. 'The most frequent failing of a successful long-term chief executive is not recognising when things start to go wrong,' the profile foreshadowed. 'Or more precisely, that moment when people become unwilling to challenge the all-powerful hero boss ... Can Joyce avoid falling into the trap?'

———

In Ernest Hemingway's first novel, *The Sun Also Rises*, Bill asks Mike, 'How did you go bankrupt?' The immortal response: 'Two ways. Gradually and then suddenly.'

In the opening weeks of the year 2020, the novel coronavirus seemed to be approaching Australia gradually. On 22 January, Flight Centre founder Graham 'Skroo' Turner said, 'At the moment I'm not too worried. People just get a bit excited about these things.' Three days later, Australia had its first confirmed coronavirus infection.

Australia shut its borders to China on 1 February, and on behalf of the Department of Foreign Affairs and Trade (DFAT), Qantas operated two rescue flights from Wuhan to Australia early that same month, by which time Australia had just fifteen confirmed cases. The next week, Beijing's top medical adviser predicted the outbreak would be over by April.

On 18 February, a third DFAT flight operated by Qantas evacuated 180 people stranded at Yokohama port in Japan on board COVID-stricken cruise ship the *Diamond Princess*.

Qantas announced its first-half results on 20 February like a company well accustomed to what Joyce's predecessor Geoff Dixon labelled 'constant shock syndrome'. Joyce took some modest evasive measures in reaction to the virus ('Calmly tweaking the dials', according to the *AFR*'s Chanticleer column): grounding eighteen jets, reducing flights to Asia by 15 per cent (equivalent to 5 per cent of Qantas' total international flights) and forecasting a profit hit of $125 million. 'It could get better, it could get worse, but we are projecting what we can see today,' Joyce told the media. Qantas shares rose 5 per cent to $6.67.

'This will be a short-term issue,' Sydney Airport CEO Geoff Culbert said the same day.

In the first week of March, Australia reported its first two coronavirus deaths and closed its borders to Iran and South Korea. Qantas shares fell 16 per cent to $4.66.

On 10 March, with 110 reported coronavirus cases in Australia and three deaths, and with Italy now in a national lockdown, Qantas announced what, briefly, seemed like radical measures. Joyce grounded a further thirty-eight aircraft (including eight A380s), reduced international seats by 23 per cent and domestic seats by 5 per cent. Two thousand staff were asked to take annual or unpaid leave. Joyce and Goyder both elected to work without pay until 30 June and executive bonuses were zeroed out for the financial year.

On 11 March, the World Health Organization designated COVID-19 a pandemic. Australian shares sunk officially into a bear market, down 20 per cent in three weeks flat. Qantas shares fell 9 per cent to $4.04 and another 10 per cent the next day to $3.64.

Panic was accelerating. On 13 March, Qantas shares fell 13 per cent to $3.18 as US president Donald Trump banned flights from Europe, and the Australian Grand Prix in Melbourne was cancelled mere hours before the Friday practice laps were scheduled to begin. When on 15 March the Morrison government introduced mandatory fourteen-day self-quarantine for all passengers arriving from overseas, it was obvious that international flying at scale had been rendered unworkable.

On 17 March, Qantas cut its international seats by 90 per cent and domestic seats by 60 per cent. That meant grounding another 150 aircraft, including the entire wide-body fleet.[6] Qantas and Jetstar customers were given the option of cancelling any existing flight booking and converting the value of their ticket to a travel credit. The process could be completed online at qantas.com, and customers were asked not to contact the airline's deluged call centres. On 18 March, Qantas emailed ticketholders saying, 'We strongly encourage customers to retain the value of your upcoming flight to a Qantas flight credit' via qantas.com.

Bear in mind that when Qantas cancelled a flight due to 'events beyond [its] control', customers were unambiguously entitled to a full refund.[7] Qantas' conditions of carriage, which was the legal contract between the airline and its ticketholders, stated that 'if we are unable to rebook you on services acceptable to you, we will refund the applicable fare'. And yet here was Qantas urging ticketholders to accept a flight credit and omitting any mention of their entitlement to a refund. In multiple further emails and public announcements, Qantas continued to hard-sell flight credits to its customers without ever mentioning the 'r' word.

'It's now fair to call this the single biggest shock that global aviation has ever experienced,' Joyce said on 17 March. 'We can't shy away from the fact we have a very tough journey ahead of us. But we will get through.' Nobody was seriously questioning whether Qantas would get through. For its domestic rival, Virgin Australia, however, that was fast becoming a matter of febrile speculation.

As he responded to each of Qantas' capacity announcements with his own, Virgin Australia's chief executive, Paul Scurrah, only twelve months into the job after succeeding Joyce's archrival John Borghetti, was desperately broadcasting the fact he had $1.1 billion cash in the bank and no major debt maturities for eighteen months. But Virgin was plainly in trouble. It was loaded with $4.3 billion of net debt, and in the six months to 31 December 2019 – when operating conditions were peachy – it had generated barely enough cashflow ($199 million) to cover the interest payments on that debt ($172 million).[8] In November, maxed out with its banks and shareholders, the company had raised a fresh $325 million by issuing ASX-listed debt notes (offering an 8 per cent interest rate). That cash was used to buy back the 35 per cent stake in the Velocity frequent flyer program that Virgin had sold to private equity in 2014. Those notes were issued at $100 but by 17 March were trading below $42, well into distressed territory.[9]

There was no prospect of tapping shareholders for new equity capital. Eighty per cent of Virgin Australia's shares were owned by four foreign airlines – Etihad Airways, Singapore Airlines, and China's HNA Group and Nanshan Group – while another 10 per cent was owned by Richard Branson's Virgin Group. Each of them was in its own sea of red ink.[10]

On 17 March, the Morrison government announced support measures for the aviation industry, with a headline value of $715 million. Yet upon closer inspection, the package was largely a waiver of fees and taxes that grounded airlines wouldn't accrue anyway. Treasurer Josh Frydenberg described the package as 'a down payment'. 'It will help, undoubtedly,' Scurrah said on 18 March as he grounded his international fleet and cut domestic capacity in half, but he added that 'everybody in our industry may need further government support'. Scurrah was walking a fine line. On the one hand he needed Commonwealth cash and needed to exert pressure on Canberra to provide it. On the other hand he was reassuring his lenders and customers that 'We have a solid position' and that Virgin would be 'in a strong position at the other side of this crisis'.

On 19 March, the government announced that Australia's borders would close to all non-citizens or non-residents at 9pm the following day. That same morning, Qantas announced the suspension of its entire international network and the deferral of its dividend (conserving $200 million). It also took the radical but patently necessary step of standing down two-thirds of its workforce – some 20,000 people – until at least the end of May. While those affected could draw on any paid leave they had, they were otherwise without pay, released into an economy in freefall.[11]

Mass stand-downs are permitted by the Fair Work Act under certain circumstances, including 'a stoppage of work for any cause for which the employer cannot reasonably be held responsible'. Qantas was the first company to avail itself of this clause. 'We're in a strong financial position right now, but our wages bill is more than $4 billion per year,' Joyce said. 'With the huge drop in revenue we're facing, we have to make difficult decisions to guarantee the future of the national carrier.'

'To avoid further inconvenience', Qantas announced on 19 March, it would unilaterally convert into flight credits all bookings on the thousands of flights it had just cancelled. What had been an option for customers now became compulsory. This was patently contrary to Qantas' legal obligation to refund the applicable fare.

And there was still no honesty with customers about their right to a refund. Qantas' flight credit confirmation email, sent to all credit-holders, was thoroughly misleading.[12] Some customers who miraculously managed to reach a Qantas agent by telephone reported being told – wrongly – that they weren't entitled to a refund. A button to request a refund instead of a flight credit was removed from qantas.com on 27 March.

Qantas had succeeded, by breathtakingly sharp practice, in preventing crushing – and rapid – cash outflows. Over the next several weeks, the company shifted $1.6 billion of ticket sales into flight credits, which were utterly useless to home-confined (and in many cases, abruptly unemployed) customers for the foreseeable future. In the laundry list of almost unthinkable steps the airline took in March 2020, this one was most central to Qantas' reputational inferno, and Joyce's downfall, three and a half years later.

At a press conference with Joyce on 19 March, CFO Vanessa Hudson told the media she was confident of unlocking more cash by taking out new loans against Qantas' youngest aircraft, its 787-9 Dreamliners, which had been purchased outright between 2017 and 2019. She expected to finalise an agreement with Qantas' banks the following week. And on 25 March, Qantas did indeed announce that it had raised a fresh $1 billion of debt by mortgaging seven of its eleven 787-9s. The ten-year package was secured at the attractive interest rate of 2.75 per cent and, critically, had no financial covenants.[13]

Qantas now had $3 billion of cash, another $1 billion sitting in an undrawn facility, $3.5 billion of unencumbered assets it could still borrow against, and 20,000 employees whose salaries it was no longer paying. It had $5.1 billion of net debt, still at the low end of its target range, and no major debts maturing until June 2021.[14]

Qantas shares had their best day in almost two decades, regaining 26 per cent. Investors' confidence in the company's future had found a floor. Qantas, the market believed, was going to make it.

———

At a sold-out Victorian Chamber of Commerce luncheon on 5 April 2022, as Qantas was bungling its surge out of fitful COVID hibernation, Joyce presented a very different picture of those weeks in 2020.

In the intervening two years, nothing had changed in Qantas call centres. The average wait time for customers was ninety minutes, something for which Joyce apologised to the 400-strong crowd at Melbourne's Convention Centre. And he planted the seed of a whole new idea: that when COVID hit in March 2020, 'We had eleven weeks of cash left and we were dead, bankrupt.'

This was reported cursorily by the *Herald Sun*, but the phrase must have pleased Joyce's ears as it fell from his lips, because three weeks later, he floated it again. At a press conference to unveil a major new aircraft order on 2 May 2022, he told the press, 'We were eleven weeks from bankruptcy.' The idea began to catch on among Joyce's lieutenants: two and a bit months later, with operational chaos continuing and Joyce in Europe on extended vacation, Qantas' acting CEO, Andrew David, wrote an opinion piece in Sydney's *Daily Telegraph* trying to explain the airline's acute disruption, and repeating, 'Early in the pandemic we were 11 weeks from bankruptcy.' Then on 1 September 2022, a Qantas spokesman told the *Daily Telegraph*, 'During the early stages of the pandemic we were 11 weeks from bankruptcy ...' Back in Australia, Joyce addressed another business lunch on 24 October, this one hosted by AmCham at the Four Seasons hotel in Sydney. 'I think people forget how low everything was back in March, April, May, June 2020,' he said. 'There was no vaccine, there was no hope it could be as effective as it was. We had to stare into this eleven weeks of survival.'

Joyce may well have been familiar with the illusory truth effect, which is the tendency for people to believe that a false piece of information is correct after they hear it repeatedly. Once he'd concocted his idea, he stuck with it. 'We were burning a lot of cash, we had eleven weeks to survive,' Joyce told journalists on the day his retirement was announced, 2 May 2023, and he repeated the line at his final results briefing in August. And the effect worked. Hours later, the *Financial Review*'s esteemed Chanticleer column reported as fact that 'the pandemic left the airline just 11 weeks from bankruptcy'. A hagiography of Joyce written by aviation analyst Peter Harbison and published in October 2023 even contained a chapter entitled 'Eleven Weeks Left'. 'We figured that we had eleven weeks left of cash before we'd go bankrupt,' Joyce told Harbison. This was the same Harbison who told the *AFR* on 19 March 2020 that Qantas was 'probably the financially safest airline in the world'.

At first glance, this might look like a small loose thread, but it's by picking at threads like this – evidence of a careless alteration – that the bigger Joyce story of these final years at Qantas can be unravelled. The 'eleven weeks from bankruptcy' delusion represents the first example – and it's a powerful one – of Joyce's malfunctioning behaviour and thinking. His implausible public assertions and rewriting of history became a drumbeat in 2023 that was central to the disintegration of his credibility, and it makes a fascinating psychological study of how power can send leaders mad. We will encounter several others.

The words 'eleven weeks from bankruptcy' never appeared in any of Qantas' multiple disclosures to the Australian Securities Exchange in March or April 2020, nor in any of its public commentary. Rather, Joyce told the ASX on 10 March 2020, 'We're in a good position to ride this out,' and he told the media later that day, 'Qantas is probably the most fit, the airline most capable of being able to manage this. This will be the survival of the fittest.'

Nine days later, when the government announced the closure of Australia's borders, Qantas, after grounding 150 planes and standing down 20,000 staff, saw its shares close at $2.14, down 70 per cent in two months. Yet Joyce remained unequivocal. 'Qantas will not be going under – I think the lenders know that. We have one of the healthiest balance sheets out there so we will have plenty of liquidity to last a very, very long time.' He backed that up the next day, 20 March, telling Sky News, 'We've built up a good reserve of cash, we've built up a large number of aircraft, $4.9 billion worth, that we can secure financing on, so we've got plenty of bandwidth to last a very, very long time.'

I asked Qantas in 2023 to explain how, and from exactly what date, it had calculated that it was eleven weeks from death, but the company flatly refused to do so. Under new management in 2024, Qantas was willing to say that it had been 'our expected weekly cash burn in March 2020 compared to our available cash balance if we did not raise debt or equity'. So the premise was absurd from the outset. If you were running out of cash, and you owned billions of dollars of assets, why wouldn't you raise debt or equity?

Nevertheless, let's unpack the calculation on that basis. Based on the previous six months, Qantas' expenditure, excluding fuel (which you self-evidently don't need to buy once your airline is grounded), was $253 million per week – or, to adopt Joyce's time period, $2.8 billion per eleven weeks. As of 10 March 2020, Qantas had access to $2.9 billion of cash and open credit, so that would just about match up.

However, on 10 March, Qantas hadn't yet been grounded. Cash was still coming through the door. The airline's drastic capacity cuts only came into effect at the end of March. By then (thanks to the $1 billion Hudson raised against the 787s), Qantas was packing $4 billion of cash and open credit. Also by the end of March, Qantas' costs had fallen considerably: it had stood down two-thirds of its employees without pay, which was saving it another $55 million per week.[15] The last day of March also marked the hasty introduction of the JobKeeper program, under which Qantas received $20 million per week. Initially, Qantas paid $15 million directly to stood-down employees and banked the rest as a subsidy.[16] So by 31 March, now at a burn rate of less than $195 million per week, Qantas had roughly twenty weeks' cash remaining, not eleven.

Of course, these assessments of head room are based on a plainly flawed assumption: that Qantas would take no further protective action during those eleven (or twenty) weeks, watching the remaining cash fly out the door as it settled every outstanding invoice, continued paying major overheads like rent, and even maintained its regular outgoings on inflight catering – at a grounded airline. That is what Joyce in 2022 and 2023 was asking his audiences to believe.

Has any company in the history of the world, faced with the sudden and almost total evaporation of its revenue, elected to do nothing? Joyce was offering a false dichotomy. In late March 2020, every business in the economy was scrambling to negotiate – or simply impose – standstill agreements on its liabilities. Qantas was no different. By the first week of April, it had already sparked a brawl with major airports by withholding rent and aeronautical charges that were due, plus it had found an innovative way to prevent its customers from getting their money back for their cancelled tickets.[17]

By 5 May (five to six weeks into the mythical eleven-week period), Qantas unlocked another $550 million of cash by mortgaging three more 787-9 aircraft, and told the ASX it had 'sufficient liquidity to respond to a range of scenarios, including one where the current trading conditions persist until at least December 2021'.[18] This was the first time Qantas had quantified its financial head room in calendar terms, and its assessment wasn't eleven weeks, it was eighteen months! Indeed, Joyce boasted, 'At the start of the crisis we said this was about survival of the fittest. In practical terms that means the carriers around the world that can survive for long periods with very little cash coming through the door. By that measure, Qantas is one of the fittest airline groups in the world.' And it would get fitter: he flagged that by 30 June, the airline's cash burn rate would fall to just $40 million per week – an extraordinary feat of contraction.[19]

Beyond the logical and arithmetical defects, the other problem with Joyce's 'eleven weeks' narrative was that it conflated running out of cash with being bankrupt. Companies don't go bankrupt, only individuals do. Companies become insolvent, then enter administration, receivership or liquidation. The fact that Joyce didn't even use the correct terminology – terminology he was all too familiar with – shows how nakedly he was playing to a retail audience with his fable. This is the real tell that the 'eleven weeks' yarn was spun not for the financial community or even readers of a book like this, but for breakfast television and talkback radio, where every day, without challenge, implausible things are asserted to be true, where glib lines are king, where the illusory truth effect prevails.[20] *Eleven* weeks – not twelve weeks or three months – also gilded the idea with an overtone of precision, making the lie sound credible.

Even if Qantas had effected no changes to its balance sheet or its rate of expenditure, and eleven weeks into the COVID shutdown had zero cash left, that still is not insolvency. And it is certainly not 'death'. A company is insolvent only if it cannot meet its debts as and when they fall due. Qantas had repeatedly advised the market that its debts were free of financial covenants and that its next debt maturity was not until June 2021. It also still owned $3.5 billion of aircraft assets it could securitise for more cash, or it could raise equity through a share issue.

Not only could Qantas do both of those things, Qantas *did* do both of those things. After the $1.6 billion of debt it raised in two tranches against the 787-9 fleet, the airline then raised $1.4 billion in new Qantas shares in June 2020, and a further $500 million of debt via a bond issue in September. It was able to do all of that because its balance sheet was in tremendous shape. That is to Joyce's great credit. His statements boasting of Qantas' balance sheet fitness were intended to calm his investors during a crisis with no historical equal. They also happened to be true.

In the years preceding the pandemic, Joyce had prioritised the airline's financial muscle above all else. Qantas was in such good shape that it could afford to pay $3.2 billion to shareholders in buy-backs (on top of dividends), largely at the expense of buying new planes or investing in technology. The Qantas balance sheet was also blessed with natural advantages.

As at 31 December 2019, a whopping $4.3 billion, or 24 per cent of the company's total liabilities, was in fact revenue received in advance, also known as unearned revenue – either cash paid for unflown trips or unredeemed frequent flyer points. This was the very best kind of liability – entirely different, for instance, to owing a bank $4.3 billion – because Qantas had significant discretion over when (and indeed whether) these could be recouped. Qantas could deflate the liability by, say, radically devaluing frequent flyer points. It could remove or severely limit the availability of Classic Reward redemptions, which offers business class seats to London for 144,000 points, and it could force members into the Points Plus Pay option, where the same seat costs 1.5 million points. It could also defer the liability by denying passengers cash refunds for cancelled flights in favour of flight credits. Better yet, it could even convert the liability into pure profit by making those flight credits expire.

Given Qantas' later conduct in relation to flight credits, to which we will return (not to mention the inflation of frequent flyer points in line with the Argentinian peso), you have to wonder if, at some point in 2020, Joyce and Hudson asked themselves, and each other: How real are these liabilities, really?

It was scarcely an accident that Joyce first alighted upon, then leaned into, his 'eleven weeks' tale just as Qantas was coming under huge public pressure over its dismal performance in the Great COVID Reopening of 2022. The tale was both self-congratulatory for rescuing Qantas from near-death and a self-justification for everything that was now quite unexpectedly going wrong.

But which Joyce are we to believe? Alan Joyce in the eye of the storm or Alan Joyce after the fact, looking back at his heroics through his enchanted spectacles? Were Joyce a Hemingway character and Bill asked him, 'How did you go bankrupt?' Joyce could've responded, 'Only in retrospect.'

———

There is another glaring problem with the *post hoc* notion that Qantas was careering towards insolvency. Why was Joyce arguing fiercely against Qantas receiving financial assistance from the federal government? Qantas shares closed on Thursday 19 March at $2.14, as low as they would go, but Joyce had clearly made a calculation of how to use this crisis to his advantage. Qantas could survive for many months – probably multiple years – in total hibernation. Virgin Australia, however, could not.

'Alan is quite an opportunist,' Virgin Australia's then CEO, Paul Scurrah, told me. Remembering March 2020, he says, 'I think Alan had one eye on survival and one eye on opportunity, whereas I just had both eyes on survival.'

Joyce well understood the huge windfall potential of Virgin failing. Having defected from Ansett in 2000 to lead Qantas' network planning function, he had seen up close the overnight structural dominance that accrued to Qantas upon Ansett's collapse in 2001. Qantas' domestic market share vaulted from 54 per cent to 90 per cent, and with that came enormous pricing power.[21] Qantas printed strong profits in 2001 and 2002 – even as the global airline industry lost more than US$30 billion in the wake of the September 11 terrorist attacks – and again in 2003 and 2004 during the SARS epidemic.[22] If Joyce played COVID the right way, he might well recapture those boom times for Qantas.

On Friday 20 March, the day after Qantas' share price nadir, *The Australian* published a column headlined 'PM looks to nationalise failing firms', by its political editor Simon Benson. Benson was carrying on a co-dependent relationship with the prime minister of the day, Scott Morrison; his reporting was uncritical and his commentary was unctuous, and by no coincidence he metronomically broke news of the government's decisions prior to their announcement.[23] It was widely understood by anyone inside the beltway of Australian politics that Benson's words were transcribed directly from the prime minister's mouth. Joyce must've broken into hives.

'Scott Morrison is heading down a road that may require him to do what was politically unimaginable only three weeks ago. Some companies may end up having to be nationalised, if even only temporarily,' Benson's column began. 'There are privately run bus services, even airports and airlines and basic economic infrastructure that, if they are about to fail in the hands of private enterprise, may ultimately have to be transferred into taxpayers' hands for a time.'

Benson's article continued: 'Virgin could be one example of a company, if it were to go to the wall, that the government might consider a "strategic" priority. There is no way it will allow Australia to return to a virtual single-carrier environment in a post-virus world.'

Clearly blindsided, Joyce immediately hurled himself into the fray, live on Sky News from the lobby of Qantas' Mascot headquarters early that morning; the window behind him showed that it was still pitch-black outside. Nationalising Virgin Australia, he said, would be 'completely unfair to our sector of the economy. It would mean that we are competing against the Australian government and Qantas couldn't do that. That would be a completely unbalanced competitive environment.'

Joyce was right and his alarm was justified. The Business Council of Australia's chief executive, Jennifer Westacott, hit the airwaves the same morning, saying, 'The problem with nationalisation is what Alan Joyce said: it's about picking winners. What we need to come out of this crisis is a modern market economy, not an economy that looks like something out of the 1950s.' Westacott was also right.[24]

The alarm in Joyce's voice was the first hint of something that would only be revealed to the Australian public much later – indeed, something that will be a major theme of this book. The competitive environment in aviation was *already* completely unbalanced – often secretly – in Qantas' favour. The enormous commercial advantages Qantas had extracted over decades from the Australian government would be compromised, if not reversed, by Virgin becoming a government business.

Joyce was explicit in his Sky News interview: the Morrison government 'can't pick winners and losers', and since Qantas didn't need a cash injection, Virgin must be allowed to fail. The government 'has to allow the healthy companies like Qantas to look after itself ... and not look after the badly managed companies that have been badly managed for ten years that have [*sic*] resulted in them being very weak.'

Joyce the formidable campaigner emerged. Later that Friday, he addressed an all-hands conference call with Qantas staff (twenty-four hours since announcing most of them were being stood down without pay). He urged employees to contact their federal MPs and lobby them against any government financial assistance for Virgin Australia beyond what was offered to Qantas. 'It is in your interest to make sure your member of parliament, if Scott Morrison is your member of parliament, to make it clear that you expect equal treatment for the airlines in this country ... I'd ask you for a call for action to make your point very clear to every politician in this country.' He also strayed into jingoism, saying that Australian 'governments are not there to support a company that's owned by Singaporeans, Chinese, Abu Dhabi and a British billionaire. They are there to do what's best for Australia.' Revealingly oblivious to the 10,000 Australians employed by Virgin, his pitch was also faintly ironic, considering Joyce had campaigned for years – unsuccessfully – to have the federal government remove the 49 per cent foreign ownership cap on Qantas. Indeed, Qantas was itself 36 per cent foreign owned at that time, and the dollar value of those foreign-owned Qantas shares far exceeded the value of all the shares in Virgin Australia.

There was also a strange echo of his own unfair treatment: although Joyce had taken citizenship nearly twenty years earlier, whenever he was in for criticism, Joyce was pejoratively Irish to the Australian public.

Virgin's Scurrah responded with dismay. 'We all need to remember we're in a national crisis at the moment and now is not the time for rivalry, for these unhelpful comments. This is not a game of *Survivor*. It's a global pandemic creating unprecedented challenges that require unprecedented decisions. We should see people joining arms and pulling each other through this. We see that as the Australian way and that's what we're doing.'

Scurrah wasn't the only person who seemed to have a different point of view. Three weeks later, Qantas chairman Richard Goyder was asked, in his capacity as AFL chairman, to reflect on the comparative survival prospects of the country's COVID-shuttered football codes, Aussie rules and rugby league. 'This is not a time to pick fights,' he said. 'It's also a time where you look inward a little and just try to manage your own affairs.' Many took this as an implicit rebuke of Joyce's *Hunger Games* tactics towards Virgin, though if that really was Goyder's intention, it was the only time he ever showed any stomach for moderating Joyce's worst instincts.

The eruption of the Virgin–Qantas brawl ended a defining week in which both airlines' shares lost another quarter of their value, and the true impact of COVID-19 on Australian society became frightfully clear. Goyder had at least found himself a silver lining. He told the *AFR*, 'You wouldn't wish this on anyone, but it's been quite invigorating.'

Nobody was invigorated on Monday 23 March as the Morrison government ordered all pubs, clubs, cinemas, gyms, and even places of worship to close indefinitely at noon, and interminable queues snaked out of Centrelink offices around the country.

Virgin Australia had used the weekend to lodge a complaint with the Australian Competition and Consumer Commission against Joyce's commentary, and even accused Qantas of spreading misinformation to damage Virgin. 'We have received reports of Qantas briefing journalists on the false pretence that Virgin Australia cash reserves are running out within days and that Virgin Australia has appointed administrators,' the letter said.[25] Qantas denied being the source of rumours that were undeniably circulating the investment market. But Virgin had found a sympathetic ear in ACCC chairman Rod Sims. 'It's obviously a serious matter,' Sims told the *Financial Review*. 'At a time of crisis when so many companies are working to ... keep Australia afloat if you like, to have comments about "survival of the fittest" and implications publicly made to allow Virgin to go under, I just think that's unhelpful.'

The complaint was never heard about again, dropped by Sims on closer inspection due to a lack of evidence.

Behind the scenes, the government had already been taking discreet soundings about Virgin. Assistant Treasurer Michael Sukkar approached prominent private equity investor Ben Gray around 20 March for advice on structuring a potential bailout facility for distressed Australian companies, to be modelled on the US government's GFC-era Troubled Asset Relief Program (TARP). In particular, Sukkar wanted Gray's take on Virgin Australia. This is the same Ben Gray who, with sidekick Simon Harle, had turned up in Canberra in 2007 as part of a consortium seeking to privatise Qantas; in 2017, Gray established BGH Capital with Harle and former gun Macquarie banker Robin Bishop.[26]

After running its ruler over Virgin, BGH considered the airline to be insolvent and its equity to be worthless. Gray went back to Sukkar to warn him against pouring public money into a company whose only real survival prospect was a balance sheet restructure through receivership. Thus an arguably more rational – albeit for Gray, self-interested – alternative to nationalising or bailing out Virgin was sown with the Morrison government.

The debate over government financial support continued through-out the final week of March. Deputy Prime Minister and Minister for Transport Michael McCormack announced a suite of funding assistance for regional airlines, including a $100 million program of untied cash grants, on 28 March. In microcosm, this was an illustra-tion of what could go wrong with subsidies.

Of this money, $54 million was awarded to another airline, Regional Express (or Rex).[27] There was no requirement to maintain any air services for regional communities and the money was not repayable. While small compared to the billions Qantas and Virgin were talking in, $54 million was a stupendous bequest because Rex was a tiny airline. Its total passenger revenue in the previous year was only $278 million, so McCormack had gifted Rex 20 per cent of its annual turnover, or the equivalent of two years' pre-COVID profit, no questions asked. The equivalent grant of free cash to Qantas would've been $3 billion, or $1 billion to Virgin.[28] This was the subject of mild uproar, given the political links between McCormack, the leader of the Nationals, and Rex's deputy chairman, John Sharp, a longstanding official of the National Party and himself a former transport minister.

Labor's transport spokesperson, Catherine King, wrote to the Commonwealth auditor general, Grant Hehir, asking him to examine the program's design. His report, delivered in 2022, revealed that McCormack's department had 'received a letter on 20 March 2020 from a regional airline indicating that it proposed to suspend operations in the absence of government support'. No prizes for guessing which regional airline that was. Nevertheless, Hehir found that the design of all support measures had been 'effective'.

Another emergency subsidy gave preferential treatment to Rex (which, like Virgin, was majority foreign-owned).[29] In a second, $198 million scheme to maintain regional flights through the pandemic, Rex was awarded 35 per cent of that money, despite operating only 2.5 per cent of the available seat kilometres on regional routes.[30] Off the back of this, Rex did something extraordinary: less than two months later, in May 2020, the airline announced it would lease 737-800 jets to launch services between capital cities.[31] Up to that point, Rex had solely operated a fleet of aged Saab turboprops to or from regional airports. As Scurrah recalls, 'They went from being on the brink of bankruptcy to being probably the only airline in the world that expanded in the pandemic. You do the maths.'

———

The government's intentions in relation to Virgin had become no clearer, at least publicly, by 30 March, a week after the nationwide physical shutdown, when Morrison and Frydenberg announced their flagship economic stimulus program, a $130 billion wage subsidy called JobKeeper.[32]

Joyce had flagged the Morrison government's consideration of such a scheme in the pitch-black early hours of 20 March, in his 'winners and losers' diatribe. He didn't want sovereign lines of credit to keep other airlines afloat, but he *was* open to a subsidy of his own costs. And any subsidy designed per head would benefit Qantas more than anyone else, because Qantas was the largest employer. New Zealand had introduced its wage subsidy scheme three days before, and JobKeeper was a direct copy. Qantas would ultimately be Australia's single largest JobKeeper recipient, receiving $856 million.

Administered by the Australian Taxation Office, the original version of JobKeeper paid employers $750 per week, per employee (no matter their position), for six months.[33] Employers had to satisfy a revenue test, though it was barely a test at all: to qualify, a company with over $1 billion of annual revenue could show the ATO an actual monthly revenue decline of greater than 50 per cent versus the previous year; or, alternatively, that business could elect to merely *predict* that its future revenue would fall by more than 50 per cent. No data was required to support the prediction, and should it fail to occur, the business still got to keep the money. In that sense, JobKeeper was an honesty box, but instead of twenty-cent pieces, it was full to overflowing with signed blank cheques.

So what did Australian businesses do? They submitted terribly gloomy forecasts! Only days into the shutdown, negative sentiment was of course justified, but as Charlie Munger's famous adage goes, 'Show me the incentive and I'll show you the outcome.'[34]

There was never any question that the airlines were eligible for JobKeeper. The scheme was intended and designed for the businesses most affected by government-mandated shutdowns, and the travel industry was more exposed than any other. The way JobKeeper worked, however, meant that it was never going to help Virgin Australia survive the early weeks of COVID, when virtually all of its staff were stood down. That's because when a company's workers were stood down without pay, JobKeeper accrued directly to those workers. As it should have. But when employees were working, their JobKeeper accrued to their employer. Of the $856 million Qantas received in JobKeeper over twelve months, about half went to staff on leave without pay, while the other half was retained by the company as a subsidy.

It was immediately clear that JobKeeper wouldn't save Virgin. On the same day that the PM and treasurer unveiled the scheme, *The Australian* reported that Scurrah had formally requested a $1.4 billion loan from the government. Under its proposed terms, the loan would convert to an equity stake in Virgin if not repaid within two or three years.

The leak of Scurrah's proposal had come from the government side, and initially Virgin interpreted this as a sign that Morrison and Frydenberg were softening the ground to lend Virgin the money. 'My instant thought was that the government had leaked it to gauge sentiment, to see if there'd be a major backlash or not,' Scurrah told me. 'But in a nanosecond, they were out criticising us – and it almost seemed scripted.'

Finance minister Mathias Cormann, a key figure on the expenditure review committee of cabinet, told the ABC on 31 March, 'It is not our plan to take a stake in an airline.' Privately, Cormann had argued vehemently against lending to a company which, he observed publicly, already 'had serious challenges prior to the coronavirus pandemic'.

Qantas was straight out of the blocks the same day, insisting that if Virgin got $1.4 billion, Qantas would need a $4.2 billion loan of its own.[35] By lunchtime, Virgin was forced by the ASX to confirm *The Australian*'s report.

According to Scurrah, 'The government and Qantas were both using the same language, which was that the government "shouldn't pick winners and losers". I don't blame Qantas for using its connections in Canberra for its own benefit – everyone tries to do that. It's the extent to which the government fell for it that disappoints me the most.'

By 2 April, the government had plainly decided to forsake Virgin. Ministers were spinning a new line to the Canberra Press Gallery that access to the domestic market could be facilitated for a new carrier if Virgin failed.

That week, Scurrah railed desperately against the dangers of a Qantas monopoly, while opposition leader Anthony Albanese called for the government to buy an emergency stake in Virgin, but the cause was all but lost. On 14 April, Virgin's shares entered a trading halt on the ASX. The airline had been given one month's grace by its lenders to obtain government support, which Scurrah relayed to the Prime Minister's Office and senior ministers. The government was unmoved.

Two weeks earlier, Scurrah was being coached by the government's most senior mandarins on how to maximise government support. 'Then suddenly it all changed,' he told me. 'That was the impact of Qantas' lobbying, but then also, other parties close to the government smelled a carcass and an opportunity. There were the really good bones of a product at Virgin they wanted to get for a bargain.'

Behind the scenes, Frydenberg had been engaging with BGH Capital. On his knees begging Frydenberg for a loan, Scurrah now also engaged with BGH. Only then, Scurrah says, did senior government figures begin referring publicly to 'a market-led solution' to Virgin's financial infirmity, as opposed to a taxpayer bailout. 'Their language around a market solution – we read that to mean BGH.'

Ben Gray and Robin Bishop had a phone hook-up with Morrison, Frydenberg and Cormann to discuss a potential takeover of Virgin. BGH took verbal assurances from that meeting that the government would provide a new Virgin owner with competition guarantees and material sweeteners. Virgin established a data room and over the weekend of 17–19 April, BGH conducted limited due diligence on the airline. Macquarie AirFinance also had a look but immediately walked away.

After three days of intensive meetings with BGH, Virgin management pushed the private equity firm for a $200 million bridging loan to tide them over. BGH baulked and negotiations ended. Forty-eight hours later, completely out of options, Scurrah tipped over his king. In Australian aviation's game of *Survivor*, Virgin had been voted off the island. The airline fell into voluntary administration, with the board of directors appointing Deloitte as administrator.

BGH, according to Scurrah, aggressively sought to pre-empt any competitive auction and negotiate a quick sale, painting themselves as the only serious bidder. 'Ben Gray said to [Deloitte administrator] Vaughan Strawbridge and I, "There are no fairies at the bottom of the garden; you do know this, don't you?"' But Deloitte did proceed with an auction and BGH was knocked out of the process on 2 June. After Virgin was sold to rival private equity firm Bain Capital, Gray sent a self-deprecating email to Strawbridge saying, 'What do you know, there are fairies at the bottom of the garden.'

On the face of it, the prime minister's position on Virgin changed radically between 19 and 31 March, but twelve days in March 2020 was the equivalent of twelve months in normal times. Morrison, his senior ministers and advisers were making decisions under extremely low forward visibility, rapidly shifting operating assumptions, and with demands for budget-smashing expenditures flying in every direction.

The $64,000 question is: who, if anyone, convinced Morrison not to extend a lifeline to Virgin Australia? Was it Alan Joyce or was it Ben Gray? 'It has to be a combination of both,' Scurrah surmised to me. 'I think for the government not to ultimately support us, they needed a reason other than Qantas, and I think Ben Gray became their reason. It made it easier for the politicians to do what they did to us because they could credibly claim that Qantas had nothing to do with it.'

The 'market-based' rationale provided by Morrison, Frydenberg and Cormann was consistent and reasonably persuasive. But the poison in their supposed philosophical purity was their egregious cash giveaway to the National Party's airline of choice, Rex. This made a bald-faced lie of Morrison's claim of solely 'sector wide' decisions. The rigour of policymaking in those days of radical uncertainty was a victim of its required speed. JobKeeper's architectural flaws were a prime example. But the cover of emergency was also used to allocate money in improper ways, and to act improperly – Morrison's secret self-appointment to additional ministries being the standout example. In the context of $320 *billion* of emergency measures being rushed out of the cabinet room that month, McCormack's $71 million fund (as window-dressing for a $54 million handout) was small beer. This is perhaps why McCormack thought he could get away with it; and he was right.

McCormack was a vaguely decent and not very clever fellow who had risen to the high office of deputy prime minister owing to the poverty of talent in the Nationals' ranks. The parliament was packed to the gunwales with intellectually meagre representatives, but the Nats supplied almost every dunce in the class. In 2020 they made up 20 per cent of the Morrison cabinet. As well as a lack of rigour, some tribal favours – especially when they could be dressed up as support for 'the regions' – were inevitable. The adage *never let a good crisis go to waste* was a common refrain at the time, and many people did not.

By 2023 another adage might have occurred to Joyce: *be careful what you wish for*. As his troubles mounted, he could have wistfully imagined a world in which Virgin had been extended government support and continued to limp along under a mountain of debt and a bloated cost base. Most likely, Virgin would still have collapsed, just six or nine months later than it actually did. Instead, the operating economics of Virgin Australia were rejuvenated substantially in Deloitte's restructuring process between April and November 2020, and after a bitter contest between private equity barbarians, Bain Capital emerged with a lean business poised to annex a respectable piece of the profit pool when normal conditions returned.

Four years later, however, Australian travellers were still awaiting normality.

Reality on an
Underlying Basis
April–Oct 2020

After Virgin Australia's tumble into administration on 21 April 2020, the nation spent the subsequent two months growing accustomed to its new life in lockdown.

While Qantas had ceased all international passenger flights for the first time since World War II, its foreign rivals stepped up to fill the breach. For the nearly two years that Qantas International was grounded (besides the occasional charter flight paid for by the Department of Foreign Affairs and Trade, and ably milked by the Qantas PR department), four other airlines maintained continuous – if radically reduced – passenger and freight services to and from Australia: Air New Zealand, Qatar Airways, Singapore Airlines and United Airlines. In the month of April, Qatar had a massive 45 per cent market share to/from Australia, followed by Air New Zealand and United with 5 per cent each. Qatar hoped that playing a lead and visible role in repatriating Australians from overseas after the national carrier had packed up and gone home would create lasting goodwill for the Gulf airline in Canberra. That turned out to be a miscalculation, to which we will return.

On the domestic front, Qantas was operating just 5 per cent of its usual seats in April and early May. By mid-June, it was 15 per cent.

With enough cash and open credit to last 'until at least December 2021' in almost total hibernation, Alan Joyce and his executives spent the autumn developing a plan to redesign the airline for the other side of the pandemic: in May 2020, the aviation industry's modelling was for global travel to take until 2023 to return to pre-pandemic levels, and for that recovery to be led by domestic or short-haul travel. Long-haul traffic, the International Air Transport Association forecast, would not reach pre-COVID levels until 2024. That meant, frankly, shrinking Qantas.

For example, would Qantas ever fly its A380s again? The official line was that it would, but these twelve aircraft were already ten to twelve years into their expected service life of twenty years and Joyce had them parked in the Mojave Desert 'for at least three years' of their remaining time. With societies worldwide in varying states of closure, and global airlines operating around 5 per cent of their usual international seats, it was courageous to imagine once again filling a 485-seat aircraft with intercontinental travellers on a daily basis.

Joyce had a plan but he'd need at least $1 billion to implement it. The money was for redundancies, because the plan was to permanently eliminate a significant proportion of the Qantas workforce. Radical cuts were a necessity, of course, but they were also a rare opportunity.

And so on 25 June, Joyce unveiled his three-year vision for Qantas, through to the expected resumption of normal travel in 2023. The airline said it would make 6,000 employees redundant – although the number would ultimately be 10,000 – while extending the stand-down of 15,000 more staff. It would retire the last six 747s in the fleet and defer the delivery of twenty-one new aircraft to Qantas and Jetstar. It would write down the value of the company's assets by around $1.3 billion, mostly an impairment in the value of the A380 fleet mothballed for a large part, if not the entirety, of their remaining useful lives.

But Qantas would also, over three years, shear enough costs out of its daily operations – 'through productivity improvements' – to save $1 billion per year by 2023. As Chanticleer pointed out that day, the sheer number of redundancies 'suggest the airline was looking for an opportunity for operational efficiencies irrespective of COVID-19'.

Here was the next phase in Joyce's exploitation of the pandemic. Having seen off Virgin Australia, he had decided to seize the once-in-a-generation chance to wield his scythe. What he was proposing was to use the cover of COVID to massively increase the structural profit margin of the company. Virgin was still in administration, but it was already apparent that Qantas' primary domestic competitor would end up in the hands of private equity toe-cutters. Virgin's cost base would be slashed, and to remain competitive, Qantas needed to respond in kind.

Joyce was a veteran of these cost reduction programs. Between 2009 and 2013, he had removed more than $2 billion of permanent costs by offshoring heavy maintenance of Qantas aircraft, increasing aircraft utilisation, tweaking the route network and schedule, and overhauling sales, procurement and IT. After Qantas' record $4 billion loss in 2014, Joyce pulled another $2 billion of costs (and 5,000 jobs) out of the company between July 2014 and June 2017, then another $1 billion between July 2017 and December 2019. He'd done that, as Qantas' largest shareholder, Pendal, had marvelled, all while improving both customer satisfaction and staff engagement.

But how much was too much? It was one thing saving money by retiming flights and reducing aircraft turnarounds, or by replacing airport check-in staff with faster machines. It was another entirely when the only remaining 'fat' had to be sliced from customer-facing services – and from customers who, incidentally, were being charged airfares at least 20 per cent higher than any other airline's.

It's unclear what, if any, serious consideration Joyce gave in the winter of 2020 to the impact on customer satisfaction of, say, permanently serving Jetstar-standard meals to Qantas' premium customers. In the prevailing uncertainty and fear, things like service standards might have felt like very distant concerns. Three years later they would become more pressing. At the time, though, the fund managers who owned the vast majority of Qantas shares loved it, of course, and its effect on their model of future cash flows made it a key reason to sign up for Joyce's equity raising, which Qantas also announced that June day.

Astutely, Joyce had raised $1.6 billion of debt while the Qantas share price was most severely depressed, and he waited until shares were back above $4 before tapping the market for equity. To pay for the mass redundancies, he sold \$1.36 billion of new Qantas shares to institutional investors, and raised another \$71 million via a share purchase plan for retail investors.[1]

The airline also announced that 'at the board's request', Joyce had agreed to remain as CEO until 'at least' June 2023, to see the three-year plan through. While this sounded like a three-year extension, it was actually just twelve months, given that in 2019 the board had already asked Joyce to stay until 'at least' 2022. Joyce would stay at the helm of Qantas as he'd always intended to, and his price would be handsome. If he could fatten the airline's profit margins with unsparing cost cuts, then launch straight into a period of 'huge pent-up demand for travel' (his own words the following month), plus grow the domestic market share from 60 to 70 per cent against a smaller, downmarket Virgin, well, what would that do to the share price? Joyce was already Qantas' largest individual shareholder, and that shareholding would grow further with each year's prodigious allotment of bonus shares. It was unambiguously in his own economic interests to stick around.

The day after Qantas' suite of announcements, Virgin Australia's administrator Deloitte responded: it was selling the restructured airline to Bain Capital. The US private equity firm would pay \$730 million but also assume responsibility for the airline's reduced debts of around \$1.8 billion. Virgin would be smaller, at least initially, have significantly lower costs, and prioritise profitability over market share. Cognisant of the potential for predatory conduct as Qantas and Virgin prepared to resume battle for their respective pieces of a recast domestic market, Treasurer Josh Frydenberg directed the ACCC to monitor and regularly report to the government on competition in the domestic aviation market for a period of three years. When those three years expired in June 2023, the need for regulatory super-vision had never been greater. However, as we shall see, the transport minister had other ideas.

By no coincidence, Frydenberg's direction came immediately after an ACCC investigation into the terms and conditions of Qantas' flight credits, which was itself triggered by hundreds of complaints to the regulator from Qantas customers. For the shortest moment, it looked like the airline's $1.6 billion confidence trick had caught up with it.

The ACCC's public statement on 19 June was as unambiguous as Qantas' conditions of carriage. 'From the outset, Qantas did not communicate clearly with customers about their rights and, in a large number of cases, simply omitted they were entitled to a refund,' ACCC chairman Rod Sims said. 'We do appreciate that the airline industry globally is significantly impacted by the global COVID-19 pandemic, but I think that customers can and should expect better from Qantas, particularly when many of those customers may be out of work or experiencing financial hardship.'[2]

As a result, Qantas was forced to email all credit-holders advising them of 'added flexibility ... following customer feedback'. But Qantas didn't place their right to a refund in the subject line or bolded in red type at the top of the email. More than 200 words into the update, Qantas merely included 'a reminder that your other options include a refund. If this is your preferred option, contact us on 13 13 13.'[3] Resignedly, the ACCC conceded that 'even [Qantas'] most recent communication is not particularly clear'. Far from raising the white flag, Qantas was thumbing its nose at the authorities, something that emerges in this book as a pattern of behaviour – right through to 2023, when Qantas' heedless appetite for legal risk finally brought it unstuck.

In outlining his three-year plan on 25 June, Joyce flagged returning to '40 per cent of our pre-crisis domestic flying during July and hopefully more in the months that follow'. These plans went out the window a mere five days later when swathes of suburban Melbourne were placed in lockdown. On 9 July, Greater Melbourne was plunged into a 111-day lockdown whose long tail of restrictions ran through to November. Melbourne–Sydney flights did not resume until 23 November. In the end, Qantas' July domestic capacity was just 19 per cent of the previous year's traffic.[4]

None of this dented Joyce's belief in Qantas' path out of the crisis. 'We are confident about the medium-term and the long-term future,' he told a speaking event in Brisbane on 30 July. 'I think people are getting more confident about a vaccine and treatments.'

———

There's a fine line between optimism and delusion.

On 20 August, Joyce unveiled Qantas' accounts for the twelve months to 30 June. In the airline's first COVID-affected year, it reported a $2.7 billion statutory loss. That figure included a $1.4 billion write-down of the value of Qantas' assets ($1.1 billion of which was the A380 fleet), $575 million in redundancies, $228 million in restructuring/transformation costs, and $570 million in fuel-hedging losses. Qantas, therefore, declared it had posted an *underlying* profit for the year of $124 million.

What is 'underlying profit', exactly? The *AFR*'s aviation reporter at the time, Lucas Baird, described it quite perfectly as 'a figure calculated in-house to show what a company believes is a more accurate reflection of the result'.

That is to say, underlying or 'adjusted' profit is whatever management would like it to be. It is a magical number, a stranger to International Financial Reporting Standards, and is arrived at by excluding from a company's legal profit any major items of expenditure the company deems 'one-off', 'non-recurring', 'significant', 'extraordinary', 'abnormal', 'exceptional' or just plain inconvenient. The former prime minister John Howard might have regarded them as 'non-core'. The cricketing equivalent would be if David Warner could exclude from his career batting average every Test series he ever played outside Australia, in which case 57.85 would be his *underlying* batting average. Warner was Sir Garfield Sobers on an underlying basis.

This accounting sleight was pioneered by King Louis XVI's finance minister, Jacques Necker, who in 1780 was quite adamant that the French Crown was in annual surplus, having excluded from his calculation the cost of funding the American Revolutionary War. When the true state of France's finances became apparent, another revolution transpired, this one much closer to home.

You can't pay shareholders their dividends with an underlying profit, of course, any more than I can pay my mortgage with an underlying salary. Yet the artifice was indulged by major shareholders and swallowed whole by most journalists.

For the first ninety years of its existence and its first fourteen as a public company, Qantas simply reported its statutory profits and losses. It was only in 2010, Joyce's second financial year as CEO, that the company introduced its 'underlying' measure of profit. This didn't make Qantas unique – indeed, quite the opposite. The usage was (and remains) customary for publicly listed companies in Australia, while in the United States, 'adjusted earnings' accounting is more pervasive than televangelism or the M16 assault rifle.

In the years preceding COVID-19, however, Qantas had been making a bad joke of the practice. Keep in mind that excluded items are supposed to be unusual or non-recurring, not the everyday costs of running the business. Excluding – or 'adding back' – a major asset write-down (such as the A380s parked in the desert) or the freak unravelling of a hedging position is at least arguable. But in 2020, Qantas excluded tens of millions of dollars in 'discretionary bonuses to non-executive employees' for the fifth year in a row! Qantas also added back $161 million in 'transformation costs' in 2020, $218 million in 2019, $162 million in 2018, $142 million in 2017, $183 million in 2016, and $91 million in 2015. When a restructuring program was eternal, how was it outside the company's 'underlying' performance?

Significant Qantas investors were bemused by these recurrent exclusions and even raised their objections with the company. Right before COVID hit, Qantas had promised to clean up its act on this front.

These weren't grave or even sophisticated tricks, but they might have been lead indicators of the way Qantas had begun to deviate, not from generally accepted accounting principles, but from the generally accepted corporate objective of believability. Qantas had posted an annual underlying profit only three months since it was eleven weeks from bankruptcy. I mean, which one was it?

CEOs trumpet their underlying profits, according to 2018 qualitative research by the US Center for Audit Quality, out of the 'desire to tell the company's story'. Joyce was an assiduous storyteller, and in him that desire was compulsive. His problems really began in 2022 and 2023 when his stories became increasingly implausible, and he proved impervious to the corresponding collapse in his public credit.

———

The Monday following the annual results announcement, Qantas announced that Tino La Spina, the boss of Qantas International, would leave the company. With the international division completely shuttered 'until at least mid-2021', there was no job for La Spina to do. His position would be eliminated and its responsibilities absorbed by Qantas Domestic boss, Andrew David.[5]

La Spina's departure had signal value. This was Joyce and the board demonstrating that the top brass was not immune (pardon the pun) to the pain being felt by 6,000 redundant employees or 20,000 stood-down staff. Qantas' top executives also forewent their base pay between April and June, though Joyce's direct reports were awarded 50 per cent of their long-term bonuses for 2020. Joyce was awarded his long-term bonus of 343,500 share options, but 'offered, and the board agreed, to defer the decision of whether [it] will be forfeited or allowed to convert to shares until at least August 2021'. This was another decision that would come home to roost in 2023.

Joyce wasted no time cashing any credit he felt he'd banked from sacrificing one of his own. The very next day, Qantas announced its intention to make a further 2,500 employees redundant – in addition to the original 6,000 – by outsourcing all of its, and Jetstar's, baggage handling and aircraft cleaning jobs.[6] This would produce savings of $100 million per year and also avoid $80 million of capital expenditure on new equipment. Qantas would pay for ground handling on a per aircraft basis: when no aircraft needed to turn, as in a pandemic, Qantas' ground handling costs would fall to virtually zero. While Qantas' collective agreement with its ground handling employees required the company to consider staff counter-proposals for savings, there was no real prospect that any proposal could compete with a third-party ground handling firm whose labour and equipment was scaled across multiple airline customers at the same airports. Jetstar had no such obligation to consult, and their 370 ground handling staff were let go immediately.

Predictably, a war of words ensued. Transport Workers' Union secretary Michael Kaine called for Joyce's resignation. He also claimed that Qantas was abusing the spirit of the JobKeeper program, whose stated purpose was maintaining the connection between stood-down workers and their employers. Qantas had received five months of JobKeeper payments for these workers before proposing to eliminate their roles.[7] 'Mr Joyce has abused that system today and he has abused the trust of the Australian people,' Kaine told reporters, demanding that Qantas repay the $267 million of total JobKeeper payments it had disclosed in its financial result the previous week.

Andrew David dismissed Kaine's demand as 'not worthy of a response'. And this was indeed cute of Kaine, given that Virgin Australia had in August resolved to make 3,000 employees redundant only after their JobKeeper benefits expired in October, a plan the TWU had actually supported.

The company did, however, deign to respond, in a letter to the union the following week. 'Qantas has become accustomed to the TWU's use of "alternative facts" in public debate,' came the haughty rebuke from general counsel Andrew Finch (not to be confused with Andrew David).[8] 'Having their representatives saying things they know to be false is not only unfair to our people but is also an unhelpful distraction from dealing with the challenges that they, and their company, face.'

Qantas' chief lawyer berating others for making false statements is, with the full benefit of hindsight, quite a delicious irony.

Michael Kaine's public pressure inspired another financial innovation from Qantas. When he put the airline on the defensive over the $515 million of Australian government subsidies it had collected in the first three and a half months of the pandemic (including JobKeeper, fees for international repatriation flights, and underwritten domestic and freight services), Jetstar's chief executive Gareth Evans responded, 'The actual margin ... or the profit – if you like – that the group made out of that government assistance was $15 million. That's what those numbers really mean.' Qantas would continue to advance this curious rationalisation for the next three years: that the amount of money the government paid Qantas was irrelevant; that only the profit Qantas was able to generate from that money was relevant.

This was convenient, because its profit margin was completely unverifiable. Qantas didn't put any of this in its financial accounts, naturally, so the number wasn't audited. There was no breakout of the cost allocations. The company just had to be taken at its word. And voila, Qantas had turned the *meaning* of $500 million of taxpayer money into just $15 million – a meagre quantum of assistance, wouldn't you agree?

Except that even then, it was an insane construction. It begged the question of why Qantas *should* be making a profit on government subsidies. Call me old-fashioned, but I would've thought the appropriate profit margin on government crisis funding was zero. This was the corporate equivalent of Work for the Dole. Canberra's objective was never for Qantas to generate a commercial return on the funding, only to enable the airline to continue operating parts of its business at no loss: to keep employees working, aircraft flying, and other equipment turning over when there was little commercial revenue.[9] Roughly half of the $515 million was JobKeeper, the intended benefit of which was keeping stood-down employees connected to the company (as Qantas discovered in 2022, rehiring and retraining thousands of workers is hard, and expensive). And the amount Qantas received for repatriation flights had multiple benefits beyond the profit motive. For example, Qantas told the ASX in Feb 2021 that repatriation flights 'reduces cost and lead time for re-activating the international network'. Getting paid by the government to operate a bunch of flights and breaking even on them – that was a massive gain versus losing money by doing nothing.

Joyce himself articulated the benefits of zero-profit flights in October 2020, when trying to stimulate passenger demand for domestic travel. 'We would rather have an aircraft in the air than on the ground – making a dollar in the air rather than losing a dollar on the ground, which means we're covering our cash cost.' His strategy was explicitly to pursue profitless revenue growth (by offering bargain basement fares): 'That is the right business decision for probably a number of years,' Joyce said. 'I think the next few years are going to be very good for consumers.'[10]

If Qantas was renouncing profit margin in its commercial operations, why on earth would profit margin be relevant to its fully subsidised operations? Especially when the repatriation flights Qantas operated on behalf of the government came with the added, incalculable benefit of the goodwill they generated. At a time of extreme fear, punters at home saw tearful footage of Aussies being rescued from virus-ridden India, South Africa and Latin America by gleaming Qantas aircraft tails. This was publicity money could not buy. Qantas' Sydney Olympics-era TV commercials of child choristers singing 'I Still Call Australia Home' in sumptuous locations around the globe, created by Geoff Dixon and ad man John Singleton, are some of the greatest television ads ever made. Period. They secured a soaring place for Qantas in the national psyche that no other Australian company had ever held a candle to. Qantas got to occupy that hallowed position by virtue of being seen to step up in times of conflict and strife. During the pandemic, Qantas had yet again come to the rescue of the Australian people in the average viewer's mind; but in reality, these were government flights, since Qantas had actually closed its international network and left 100,000 Australians to find their way home on foreign airlines.[11]

For Qantas to argue, then, that the benefit it received from all of these subsidies in financial 2020 was just $15 million was laughable. And in the airline's next set of accounts – for the six months to 31 December – Qantas disclosed $699 million of Australian government subsidies and another paltry profit margin on them of $14 million. But anyone who read the fine print learned that the $14 million was calculated not from the full $699 million, but from a handpicked $174 million of the $699 million, which – surprise, surprise – excluded

$460 million of JobKeeper. This must have been Qantas' *underlying* profit margin! There was no explanation for this change of methodology, of course, but quite plainly, Qantas excluded JobKeeper (which it *had* included in the calculation of profit margin in the previous accounts) because, with 11,000 staff back at work, the company's profit margin on the JobKeeper money was in the vicinity of $200 million. If Qantas' purpose was to inform its investors, not mislead them, about the bottom line drop-through of subsidies, how did JobKeeper not count? *Any* numbers that jarred with the exemplary self-narratives of Qantas management, with their heroic versions of themselves, well, they were just delete-able. It was an extraordinary fudge, the kind of thing you'd expect from mining or biotech small caps, not blue-chip companies, and it set an expectation for the investment market that any unaudited figures Qantas presented might just be bullshit.

Qantas' justifications were laughable but they were also revealing. This was the defective output of the Qantas brains trust, the way Joyce and his lieutenants looked at the world and their special place in it. In their minds, Qantas was an enviably fit and strong airline in August 2020 by virtue of its peerless leadership, not thanks to any subsidies. Here were the early indications that reality appeared very different from inside Qantas' Mascot headquarters looking out than it did to the rest of us peering in.

Transport Workers' Union v. Qantas

Nov 2020–July 2021

Qantas confirmed the decision to outsource its ground handling workforce on 30 November 2020. The Transport Workers' Union sued Qantas in the Federal Court on 9 December, with Maurice Blackburn's Josh Bornstein – who made his name acting for the Maritime Union of Australia in the 1998 waterfront dispute against Patrick Corporation – leading the union's case.

'We knew there was longstanding animosity to the union, we knew they were desperate to get rid of the TWU from their operations and we knew there was some skullduggery in [Qantas'] clandestine meetings with labour hire agencies,' Bornstein recalled in 2024. 'Those were the key factors that informed our decision to start, but that's a long way short of having a compelling case.

'It was a very big call for the union to commence this action. There were a lot of naysayers, and huge cost. We didn't have any documents, we didn't have any of the evidence you now see.'

The TWU and its legal team also knew that Qantas was, according to Bornstein, 'the most formidable industrial relations opponent in the country because they will just keep throwing millions and millions [of dollars] at lawyers to delay and fight cases, with a strong record of success.'

Before commencing action, TWU secretary Michael Kaine had consulted widely among the industrial relations club, an eccentric corner of Australia's legal profession. In the absence of any evidence to the contrary, he was advised that a judge would most likely see

Qantas' outsourcing as a normal commercial decision. 'It was difficult for me to disagree with that, yet we *knew* that the company had done this to take the opportunity to de-unionise, to get the TWU out of Qantas, because they'd been speaking about it for years,' Kaine told me. An internal presentation by Qantas Airports in 2010, for instance, had outlined the company's vision for the year 2020.[1] Its first point was '[below the wing] ground handling exited'.[2]

'It's not a state secret that they wanted to do this, but they couldn't because they knew the response [in normal times] would've been industrial action,' says Kaine. 'So COVID was the opportunity for them to do it, and they did it. We knew that, but we didn't have the evidence. These cases are incredibly difficult to win but we made the decision that so long as we had an arguable case, then it needed to be run.'

Qantas, meanwhile, exuded its customary high-handed confidence. 'We recognise that this is a difficult decision which impacts a lot of our people,' a company spokesman said, 'but outsourcing this work to specialist ground handlers who already do this work for us in other cities across the country is not unlawful.'

Time makes fools of us all.

———

Labour is by far the largest controllable cost in the fragile economics of any airline. Between December 2008 and December 2019, Joyce kept annual growth in Qantas' personnel expenses well below an historically low inflation rate of 2.1 per cent, while increasing flying by 20 per cent. He did that in large part by growing low-wages Jetstar and shrinking high-wages Qantas.[3]

From the perspective of Qantas shareholders, this was a superb exploit. The perspective of many employees was very different, and that's what the case of the Transport Workers' Union of Australia v. Qantas Airways Limited sheds fascinating light on.

The case went to trial in the Federal Court on 12 April 2021 and ran the course of twelve days. Acting for the union alongside Josh Bornstein was Senior Counsel Mark Gibian.[4] Qantas instructed corporate solicitors Herbert Smith Freehills and Senior Counsel

Neil Young, who had recently acted for casino operator Crown Resorts in the New South Wales government's Bergin Inquiry.

Presiding in this matter was Justice Michael Lee, a judge of burgeoning public renown, especially in defamation cases. Five months earlier, his Honour had sat in Stead v. Fairfax Media Publications, in which the venture capital director of failed Brisbane asset manager Blue Sky Alternative Investments, Elaine Stead, successfully sued the *Australian Financial Review* and me for defamation.[5] Justice Lee also sat in the absurd defamation suit (and counter-suit) between mining billionaire Clive Palmer and Western Australian Premier Mark McGowan in 2022 ('The game has not been worth the candle,' he wrote at the outset of his judgment) and in Bruce Lehrmann's 'omnishambles' defamation trial against Network Ten's *The Project* and its host Lisa Wilkinson in 2023. At Justice Lee's welcome ceremony in 2017, the Commonwealth attorney-general who appointed him, George Brandis, observed that Lee 'eloquently demonstrates that the legal tradition in Australia still retains a degree of thespian flair', and speculated – prophetically, as it turned out – that he 'would not be surprised if in the fullness of time [Lee's judgments] would have developed something of a cult following, at least among aficionados of the idiosyncratically erudite'.

The case of TWU v. Qantas, simply put, hinged on whether Qantas had made its outsourcing decision for a prohibited reason under the Fair Work Act. The key facts in dispute were:

1. The identity of the Qantas decision-maker
2. Who else at Qantas had a material effect on the decision
3. Whether any prohibited reasons were in the minds of those materially involved persons.

The Act has a reverse onus of proof; that is, Qantas was required to *disprove* that the prohibited reasons alleged by the TWU were a 'substantial and operative part' of its reasons for outsourcing. These two alleged prohibited reasons were: a) that the employees were union members, and/or b) to prevent the employees from exercising their workplace rights.

Justice Lee was determined, as per precedent, to place 'little if any reliance at all on witnesses' recollections of what was said in meetings and conversations, and to base factual findings on inferences drawn from the documentary evidence'. Qantas had done its level best to minimise the available documentary evidence, having, according to Justice Lee, 'always believed that any decision it made to outsource would be the subject of intense scrutiny by way of legal challenge'. The company had taken specialist legal advice by May 2020, nearly six months before the outsourcing occurred. 'Even early on,' his Honour noted, 'there was an awareness that any business record created may end up being subject to subsequent critical scrutiny.'

Still, as the trial started, a very limited paper trail started to materialise. And while these records were slight, they turned out to be pivotal indicators of what was missing.

The first significant document emerged in pre-trial discovery. Written advice provided to Qantas by its IR adviser, Oldmeadow Consulting, confirmed to the TWU that its suspicions about the airline's prohibited motives were well founded. 'It wasn't the document that really helped our case,' Kaine now concedes (those documents were to emerge later), 'but it proved they looked at this in intense detail. It gave us confidence that we could give their witnesses a really tough time on the stand.'

The Oldmeadow advice, received by Qantas on 11 June 2020, emphasised:

> Should a decision be made to outsource all of the below wing operation, this would represent the largest compulsory redundancy program of a single blue collar work group and the largest outsourcing program ever undertaken by Qantas ... The TWU has nothing to lose in taking [Qantas] on over outsourcing and in the current environment may well win significant public sympathy.
>
> Ultimately if the legal and commercial reasons support outsourcing all the below wing in [Qantas], then it will succeed.

However, the environment in which any outsourcing takes place needs to be carefully considered, both in terms of the impact on the timing of achieving the outsourcing, and current government and public attitudes.

Paul Jones, Qantas Domestic chief operating officer, received a draft of this advice, then spoke to both Oldmeadow advisers – Ian and his wife Justine – by phone. Under cross-examination, Jones revealed that Ian Oldmeadow had given him verbal advice that the outsourcing proposal was 'high risk'. Jones told the court that Ian Oldmeadow was 'very concerned about the overall risks and so was a proponent of other ways of reducing risk'. These concerns led to Jones considering a scaled-back, or partial, outsourcing proposal, achieving lower savings and affecting fewer than half the number of employees. That option was ultimately rejected by Qantas because the savings attached to the full outsourcing were so much greater.

Two months later, on 11 August, Oldmeadow had attended a dedicated session of the Alan Joyce-chaired group management committee (GMC) on the outsourcing proposal.[6] Qantas Domestic CEO Andrew David gave evidence to the court that Oldmeadow was such a longstanding fixture at Qantas that he, David, considered him to be part of the airline's IR team. In his judgment, Justice Lee was nonplussed that 'negative advice, highlighting the industrial risks of a proposal for outsourcing, was given by Qantas' external industrial relations adviser orally and this apparently valued adviser attended a number of relevant meetings of which there is no contemporaneous record of any of his oral representations'. His Honour expressed 'a sense of disquiet that I do not fully understand the true extent and nature of the dealings between Oldmeadow Consulting and Mr Jones or others during this period and, in particular, what precisely was said by Mr Oldmeadow and to whom about the risks and rewards of outsourcing (or alternate) options and when it was said'.

So who was this mysterious Qantas ornament, Ian Oldmeadow?

An assistant secretary of the Australian Council of Trade Unions in its Accord years under the Hawke government, Oldmeadow defected to Ansett in 1987 to become Sir Peter Abeles' IR director. Most notably, he prevailed in the 1989 pilots' strike, one of the most dramatic industrial disputes in Australian history.[7] 'We're always subtle about this [in the labour movement],' Kaine remarks drily. 'We call them turncoats.'

Oldmeadow moved to Qantas in 1994 (the same year that 24-year-old Vanessa Hudson joined Qantas as an internal auditor) to run airports and operations, reporting directly to CEO James Strong. He left in 1997 and with Justine established Oldmeadow Consulting, becoming Qantas' primary IR strategy consultant; his own lucrative sale-and-leaseback arrangement which endured for more than twenty years. 'He's very well known in aviation and his views about unions are highly valued within corporate Australia,' Bornstein says. 'He's taken seriously because he knows a lot about them. I take him seriously.'

In those two decades, Oldmeadow gave a single media interview – to me, published in the *AFR* right after the infamous Qantas grounding of 2011. He was an extremely reluctant participant. A lifelong back-room operator (and compulsive Nicorette chewer), he was dragged to our sit-down at Sydney's Sofitel Wentworth by Qantas' then corporate affairs chief, Olivia Wirth. There was little prospect of a beaming smile when my snapper took his photo.

Over the years, Oldmeadow and Joyce had become incredibly close; Joyce's long-time executive assistant, Jenny Borden, had even previously been Oldmeadow's EA. 'Oldmeadow came in under Strong as this integrity-filled person who understood workers and, you know, a handshake was a handshake,' Kaine says. 'The problem was, he was very adept at winning over union officials with these promises and these handshake arrangements. Some union officials were captured by him and that is responsible for the deals that ended up in fragmentation,' Kaine argues. 'He worked with Joyce to design the disaggregation of the workforce.'

Disaggregation was Qantas' practice from around 2007 of engaging incoming employees not directly under the parent company, Qantas Airways Limited (QAL) – where employees received legacy pay and conditions – but under new subsidiaries which offered inferior pay and conditions. Over time, the company's legacy labour costs would naturally be extinguished by attrition and retirement. Today, only half of the Qantas Group's operational employees are directly employed by QAL, while the other half are employed by one of seventeen subsidiary companies. For instance, any flight attendant wearing a Qantas uniform might be employed directly by Qantas or by any one of six Qantas subsidiaries or two external labour hire firms.

This strategy also had the 'advantage' of dividing and conquering the specialist workforces, which could no longer take protected industrial action as one group. One of the first groups to be targeted was the baggage handlers, who in 2009 began to be employed by a subsidiary entity called Qantas Ground Services (QGS), not covered by QAL's enterprise bargaining agreement with its baggage handlers, and on inferior pay and conditions. 'It was a dedicated strategy to unpick the system,' Kaine says. '[Oldmeadow] was the one who ripped the fabric of the system apart. He searched for the weak seams and he found them first [by creating] QGS.'

Another motive for establishing QGS was that the TWU had agreed pay deals with Virgin Blue and Jetstar, under which its airport staff earned 15 or even 20 per cent less than Qantas airport staff. To be competitive, Qantas needed its workers on those lower rates too.

Union anger over QGS provided the lead-in to the most dramatic IR showdown in Qantas' history, a taste of Joyce with the gloves off: his decision to paralyse the nation on 28 October 2011 by locking out his baggage handlers, pilots and engineers, and grounding the airline. The TWU had set about building its membership among the fledgling QGS workforce and took what Kaine characterises as 'very minor industrial action'. But it was enough to provoke the nuclear option from Joyce. Industrial action spread to the aircraft engineers, whose secretary Steve Purvinas advised the public not to fly Qantas and pledged to 'slow bake' the airline. Purvinas was cast in the mould of infamous United Airlines pilots' union boss, Rick Dubinsky, who a decade earlier had told United CEO James Goodwin, 'We don't want to kill the golden goose, we just want to choke it by the neck until it gives us every last egg.' The pilots' union was stunned to be 'really just sucked into the maelstrom of events', according to vice-president Richard Woodward. 'The word "strike" had not even entered our lexicon – we'd only ever worn red ties.'

Joyce was hostage to three critical workforces in an open bargaining period at the same time. Only drastic action would prevent Qantas from huge operational disruption or yielding to hefty pay demands, or both. In the Qantas war room in the hours before Joyce made his radical call, Oldmeadow entreated him, 'We have to jam them before they rat-fuck us.'

According to Kaine, Joyce deliberately escalated the situation, raising the stakes to the point where the Gillard government had to intervene. Kaine says Joyce 'closed down the company to inflict the very damage [the government] needed as evidence for the [Fair Work] Commission to cancel the industrial action. Talk about loopholes – that was completely gaming the system.'

This was only after transport minister Anthony Albanese had personally sought to broker a deal between Qantas and the TWU in secret meetings between Albanese, Joyce, and Kaine's predecessor as TWU national secretary, Tony Sheldon (now a Labor senator), held in Albanese's Sydney office. Why those negotiations for a new enterprise bargaining agreement (EBA) between Qantas and the TWU broke down before the grounding is highly disputed even today. Those on the Qantas side say they tabled an offer whereby the company would continue to directly hire baggage handlers under the QAL agreement and introduce a limit on the size of the QGS workforce relative to the QAL workforce, and that this offer was rejected by Sheldon. But Sheldon insists no such offer was ever made, and that, had it been, he would've grabbed it with both hands.

The Fair Work Commission terminated the industrial action three days after the grounding, on 31 October 2011, and forced Qantas' ground handling staff back to work immediately. In a determination handed down in August 2012, the Commission granted the workers a 3 per cent pay rise but none of the job security guarantees they had been seeking. As Wayne Mader, the TWU's Victorian state secretary at the time, lamented to me, 'History will show that moment as the end of the industrial strength of the TWU within Qantas.' The arbitration was a circuit breaker for Qantas management, enabling it to impose sweeping wage freezes on its frontline staff. 'They buttressed these wage freezes by promising a bonus at the end of three years, as long as you didn't take industrial action,' Kaine recalls. 'So when we came into post-grounding territory, there was very little appetite to fight.'

It took until 2019 before the TWU was ready to fight again. With their EBA open, 94 per cent of Jetstar ground crew voted to strike that December, taking protected action nationwide right through the summer (and costing Jetstar $33 million) before narrowly voting in a new deal on 2 March, right as COVID descended.[8] Six months later, Jetstar sacked them all.

Oldmeadow, of course, warned against the mass sackings at Qantas, with striking foresight. 'His advice was that this could backfire legally, politically and reputationally,' Bornstein says, 'and in the end, he was right.'

Kaine concedes, 'He had a good understanding of what [our] response was going to be, in detail, right down to our public messaging. I wouldn't suggest that means he deserves any credit, because it's really the height of hypocrisy; he's the one who unleashed this downward spiral. I actually think that he might have foreseen that if this goes south, the reputation of the company would be completely trashed and it could even be the tipping point of the IR system. He was perhaps, in Qantas, uniquely placed to be able to perceive that.'

This leads to the central question: if Qantas' master industrial relations strategist was warning that outsourcing was high risk, how did it proceed anyway? Given Oldmeadow and Joyce were so close, why did Joyce fail to heed his trusted adviser's warnings?

Purvinas, secretary of the aircraft engineers' union, reflected in 2024, 'There were a couple of years there where I think Joyce was disregarding the IR advice of long-term experts who had kept a steady hand on the ship over many years, and preferring hardliners who didn't necessarily give advice consistent with workplace laws.'

TWU v. Qantas shows us exactly how that played out in practice.

———

Despite Qantas' attempts to keep the paper trail cold, several internal documents produced in evidence were devastating to its case. As Josh Bornstein recalls, 'Our case got stronger and stronger as it progressed, because once we saw the documents, that gave us a real fillip, and then, of course, the witnesses started to fall apart in cross-examination.'

The first key document was from a meeting of the GMC on 1 May 2020 that discussed 'operational transformation' priorities. The presentation slides referred to a 'vanishing window of opportunity' for the potential implementation of an alternative 'ground handling model/ outsourcing approach'. Then, in notes prepared for a presentation to the GMC on 15 June on the potential 'full exit from ground handling', Qantas executive manager of airports Colin Hughes expanded on these timing considerations.

The legacy workforce employed by QAL was virtually all full-time employees and card-carrying TWU members. Anyone employed after 2009, however, was employed by QGS on inferior pay and conditions and almost exclusively on a part-time basis. Union membership among QGS workers was also much lower, at around 50 per cent. The QGS pay deal, or enterprise agreement, expired in September 2020, at which time those employees would be permitted to take protected strike action in support of a new agreement.[9] But a strike during COVID by a part-time, semi-unionised workforce would fail to cause much inconvenience to Qantas.

The advancing danger for Qantas was the expiry of the QAL agreement on 31 December. 'The QAL EA opens in [*sic*] 1 January 2021 and there is a risk of two agreements that are open simultaneously,' Hughes wrote. 'That would concentrate power back into the TWU early in the new calendar year when we would be growing domestic demand back and Virgin is potentially up on its feet.

'If we do not make the decision to exit at this time,' Hughes advised, 'it is hard to see the conditions in which we would ever have the opportunity to execute [a] full exit again.'

That a 'vanishing window of opportunity' existed to get rid of workers before they could exercise their rights to protected strike action was clearly an illegal consideration under the legislation. This was one smoking gun.

Another piece of documentary evidence, also prepared for the GMC, proved decisive. In late May, Paul Jones had scribbled notes on a document prepared by a subordinate, Paul Nicholas.[10] Searching for radical cost savings in the autumn of 2020, Nicholas and Hughes had recommended that Qantas' airport customer service staff should be reduced but kept in-house, while the entire ground handling workforce should be outsourced.[11] Jones and his boss Andrew David were due to present the idea to the GMC on 29 May. Jones' handwritten notes on Nicholas' document read:

Voice-over
> labour [sic] Gov lock in benefits
+ open EBA's 2020 DEC?

Jones conceded under cross-examination that 'voice-over' meant that the two points beneath it were to be spoken at the GMC meeting and not written into the presentation slides. Justice Lee later found, 'I consider it more likely than not that the use of the "voice over" expedient was an attempt to prevent [Jones'] real views being recorded in a contemporaneous document likely to be preserved.'

It was also put to Jones in cross-examination that 'the need to lock in [outsourcing] benefits in advance of a potential future Labor government was something that you were taking into account'. Jones denied that was the intended meaning of his notes, yet at the same time claimed he couldn't recall his intended meaning. Jones further conceded that 'open EBA's 2020 DEC' was a reference to the expiry of the QAL enterprise agreement, after which those employees would be permitted to take protected – and potentially highly disruptive and expensive – industrial action. He admitted that he was aware of those facts at the time he wrote his notes, but claimed those facts were not in his mind when he wrote his notes.

Justice Lee found that Jones was 'an unimpressive witness', which might well be the least devastating reflection upon Jones' credibility contained in his Honour's judgment:

> I have come to the conclusion that Mr Jones was feigning a lack of recollection as to what was in his mind when he made the hand-written annotations and was also pretending a lack of recollection as to what was discussed in the meeting [with Colin Hughes] when the words were [written] and whether he later conveyed to GMC (by way of 'voice over') comments consistent with his annotations.
>
> I am satisfied that Mr Jones was willing to fashion his evidence to suit what he perceived to be the forensic advantage of his erst-while employer.[12] After observing him closely in the witness box and reflecting upon his evidence generally ... I do not consider it is safe to place any significant reliance upon his evidence.

Bornstein watched Jones' cross-examination via Microsoft Teams from Melbourne, while TWU secretary Michael Kaine was in the courtroom in Sydney. 'When [Jones] stepped from the witness box,' says Bornstein, 'Michael and I exchanged very excited messages to the effect that, "That was a debacle; he's been completely discredited."'

———

After announcing its proposed outsourcing on 25 August and before making its final decision on 30 November, Qantas was required under the terms of the QAL enterprise agreement to consider an in-house bid from its ground handling workforce against the bids of the external ground handling companies.

In the trial, much evidence relating to the in-house bid (IHB) supported the notion that Qantas ran a token process. Indeed, only after the TWU lodged an initial complaint in the Fair Work Commission did Qantas push the 9 October deadline on the union's bid deep into November.

Unsurprisingly, the TWU took the IHB process very seriously, engaging consulting firm EY to assist. To develop its proposal, however, the TWU needed information from Qantas: the same information that had been provided to the external bidders. This proved difficult to obtain, much to the frustration of the TWU. 'Employees cannot properly formulate an IHB that has a prospect of saving their jobs without this information,' the union wrote to Qantas on 17 September.

In a rather blithe reply, Colin Hughes assured the TWU on 24 September that 'Qantas does not require any in-house bid to be documented or presented in a formal fashion, as would be expected of third-party tenders. Rather, we require an in-house bid to cover general concepts involved in the bid. This does not mean that an in-house bid will be at a disadvantage ...' Hughes also wrote, 'We are not setting any hard savings targets for any in-house bid.'

Having specifically asked the TWU not to provide a formal presentation, or to concern itself with any hard savings targets, Qantas used exactly these grounds to reject the TWU bid. Advising Qantas employees on 30 November of the decision to proceed with outsourcing, Andrew David said that 'the TWU national in-house bid was unsuccessful because it didn't outline a plan or any real detail for how costs savings would be practically achieved'.

In his judgment, Justice Lee noted that 'the stated reasons for rejecting the IHB were somewhat curious, particularly [Qantas'] reference to the IHB not being sufficiently detailed when it had told the union that an IHB need not be particularly detailed'. Justice Lee also rejected as 'fanciful' the 'posture' maintained by Paul Jones and Colin Hughes that they were 'essentially agnostic' between the binary choices of outsourcing or the in-house bid right up to Qantas' final decision in late November. Their evidence, his Honour said (as ever, enjoying himself), 'went to great lengths to paint a picture of internal agonising and studious assessment of the alternatives and detachment up until the eleventh hour, but I am unconvinced that this was the case'.

By contrast, his Honour preferred Andrew David's evidence, 'aspects of [which] had the crystal-clear ring of clarity'. The judge might have had in mind the moment when he interrupted David's cross-examination to ask him, 'On 25 August 2020, you must have thought there was very little prospect of any in-house bid process coming close to delivering those benefits [offered by third-party suppliers]. Would that be fair?'

'Yes,' David responded.

Indeed, by early November – at least a fortnight before the TWU even submitted its IHB – Qantas had already selected the preferred external baggage handling companies for each airport and negotiated commercial terms with most of them.

'Put simply,' concluded Justice Lee, the IHB 'was done because it had to be done, but there was never a realistic prospect of it being successful.'

Andrew David was by now boss of Qantas Domestic and International, after Tino La Spina's departure, and Qantas' defence of the outsourcing was built around David being the sole maker of that decision. Much of Qantas' evidence was intended to reinforce that proposition and undermine any suggestion that the decision was made by Joyce or collectively by the GMC – which, by extension, would have implicated Joyce, as GMC's leader.

Qantas' top in-house lawyer, Andrew Finch, spent the best part of three fraught days in and out of the witness box trying to make this case. He started by trying to convince the court that Qantas' GMC was merely a discussion forum for the leaders of its various businesses. 'It's not, as its name might suggest, your Honour, a decision-making forum. It has no decision-making power, no accountability, no responsibility ... and is essentially a gathering ... where our proposals are socialised amongst GMC members ...' Issues might be discussed at its meetings, Finch claimed, but all decisions were made solely by its members individually. 'So GMC is not referred to in our constitution, it's not referred to in any policy or governance documents.' The one exception was the company's risk management policy, 'which charges GMC with the responsibility for reviewing and endorsing the group risk report'.

Qantas' barrister Neil Young tendered this one exception, Qantas' risk management policy, to the court, and asked Finch, for the avoidance of all doubt, 'Is there any other policy or document that confers authority on the [GMC]?'

'No,' came Finch's confident reply.

In a glorious demonstration of the cross-examiner's art, the TWU's barrister Mark Gibian then took Finch through several Qantas documents. On page five of that risk management policy, the GMC was defined as 'the Qantas Group executive decision-making forum for matters impacting the group'.

'You said, I think in very clear terms that it was not a decision-making body,' Gibian reminded his witness. 'You would accept that that is entirely inconsistent with ... the risk management policy to which we've been directed?'

'I would agree that that definition does not accord with how the [GMC] operates or the powers that it has or the authority that it has, yes.'

'Well, it's inconsistent with the way in which you've described it in the answer that you gave to Mr Young; correct?'

'It is also inconsistent with the answer I gave Mr Young, yes.'

Gibian then took Finch to the 'Governance' page of qantas.com, which referred to 'decision-making forums across the group, including the group management committee'.

'So Qantas, in addition to describing it in its own risk management policy, it also publicly describes the [GMC] as a key decision-making forum across the group. Do you see that?' Gibian asked.

'I see that this document does describe ... includes GMC as a key decision-making forum, yes,' Finch replied.

'You say, do you, that the [GMC] is falsely described on [Qantas'] website?'

'It's inaccurately described.'

'And in its own risk management policy ...?'

'Yes, I would say that's inaccurate too. The reference to decision-making, yes.'

The following morning, Gibian took Finch through another Qantas company policy, its contract execution policy, a document sponsored and approved by Finch himself. It defined a 'group management committee member' as 'a member of the Qantas Group executive decision-making forum for matters impacting the group, comprising the CEO, the CEO's direct reports and general counsel'.

'So again, in this mandatory policy required to be complied with by Qantas managers and employees, [they] are required to regard the [GMC] as the Qantas Group executive decision-making forum … correct?' Gibian asked.

'No, employees are not required to regard GMC according to this definition, and this definition will be changing,' Finch replied tartly.

'When you approved this policy, you were satisfied it was accurate and correct …?'

'Yes.'

'Whether the [GMC] was regarded as a decision-making forum was one of the first matters that you dealt with in your [affidavit]. Did you have in your mind that it was important for you to say that, in the context of your evidence in these proceedings?'

'I had in mind that it was important to accurately describe the GMC, so the answer to that is yes.'

'And it was important, you thought, for Qantas' position in this case to describe it not as a decision-making body?'

'Sorry, Mr Gibian, are you asking me, did I tailor my evidence to suit my case?'

At this moment of high drama, Justice Lee intervened, addressing Gibian: 'I'm not suggesting you should, but you have not put to [the witness] that he has fashioned his evidence to suit the perceived forensic exigencies of Qantas' case. I don't understand that has been put.'

'Well, perhaps I will put it more directly then,' the union's silk responded. Gibian now addressed Finch: 'Can I just put it to you: you did describe the [GMC] as not being a decision-making body because of your belief and in order that it would assist Qantas' case in these proceedings?'

'I reject that comprehensively.'

In addition to this miracle of logic, there was, on the face of it, another problem with a powerless GMC. If the only decisions made at Qantas were made by the divisional business managers who reported to Alan Joyce, it followed that no decisions were made collectively, and also, inconceivably, that no decisions were ever made by Joyce himself.

And yet his Honour was content to accept Finch's definition of the GMC's function (or lack thereof). 'There wasn't enough evidence to say that Alan Joyce took the [outsourcing] decision,' Bornstein told me. 'There was certainly evidence available to the judge to say it was a decision of both the GMC and Andrew David, but ultimately he rejected it.' Kaine wonders whether David's concession on the dubious IHB process meant that the judge needed to push no further up the chain. 'It's clear [Lee] wanted David to be the decision-maker and he became more fortified in that after he got that [IHB] concession from David.'

Finch may have successfully executed his gymnastic routine on the question of the GMC's powers, but on another issue he came comprehensively unstuck. Just before the decision on the outsourcing was due to be announced, a question had supposedly arisen at Qantas: whether the signing of contracts with replacement ground handling providers would exceed Andrew David's financial authority. The issue was raised with Finch by Qantas executive manager of industrial relations, Sonia Millen. In cases like this, according to Finch's sworn affidavit to the court, it was 'not uncommon' for Joyce to delegate sufficient financial authority to a subordinate, rather than authorising the expenditure himself.

'Because this process is used regularly within Qantas,' Finch had sworn, 'I usually prepare the request for approval using a "template". On this particular occasion ... following the request I received from Ms Millen ... and working with Mr David and members of his team to ensure the accuracy and completeness of included information, on the afternoon of 18 November 2020, I prepared a request for approval [RFA] to Alan Joyce and accompanying power of attorney. At 8:18pm on 18 November, I sent [them] to Mr David.'

Joyce signed the RFA and power of attorney the following morning.

Gibian commenced his dissection: 'When you say you prepared the [RFA], am I right in understanding that you ... used a template or a previous [RFA] as the base?'

'Yes.'

'So you opened a previous document of some similar type, re-saved it, I assume, as a new document, deleted the text, and then you typed in the text that appears in the [RFA]. Is that right?'

'Yes. Unashamedly plagiarising some text, pasting it in, and then – yes, finessing it into a document. Yes.'

'You say that you worked with Mr David and members of his team?'

'Yes.'

'That is, did you exchange drafts or emails with Mr David about the preparation of this document?'

'I don't recall exchanging emails. I recall having conversations – telephone conversations – with Mr David, and Mr Jones I think. As I cut and pasted the document, put it together, I wanted them to be comfortable that I had accurately described the proposal.'

'Right, and then you completed the drafting of that document, did you, and sent it to … Mr David at 8:11pm?'

'Correct.'

Under questioning, Finch's story continued to evolve. He soon admitted to receiving a phone call that same afternoon of 18 November from a Freehills partner, Rohan Doyle, a call that Millen had warned him to expect. Gibian attacked. 'You were again endeavouring to disguise [in your affidavit] what was going on here, the involvement of an industrial relations and employment partner of Herbert Smith Freehills in preparing this document, correct?'

'Incorrect,' Finch responded.

'And you then spoke to him on the telephone?'

'Not on CB radio?' Justice Lee interjected.

Gibian barely skipped a beat. 'Did you exchange any other form of communication with Mr Doyle on 18 November 2020, other than a single telephone conversation?'

'To the best of my recollection, it was just the single telephone conversation,' Finch replied.

'Did you exchange any emails with Mr Doyle?'

'I don't recall exchanging any emails with Mr Doyle.'

'Did you have any email communications with any person other than Mr Doyle from Herbert Smith Freehills on 18 November 2020?'

'I don't recall having any, no.'

'Now, are you satisfied that you've given us a comprehensive account of the people who you spoke to and the communications you had in relation to the preparation of [these] documents on 18 November?'

'Yes, I believe I am, yes.'

Gibian's trap was set. He now introduced into evidence the Microsoft Word document properties, or metadata, of the RFA document that Finch had claimed – under oath – to have written himself. The metadata showed that it had been created at 6:05pm on 18 November by Brad Popple, a senior associate at Freehills.[13] 'In that context, do you maintain your evidence that you prepared the RFA . . . some time during the afternoon of 18 November?'

'Absolutely, I do. I did.' Finch was sticking to his story, however implausible it now appeared to be.

Finch was then handed a list of all emails, and their times, between Freehills, Qantas' barristers and Qantas executives on 18 November 2020. The contents of the list were excruciating for Finch, given his answers just moments earlier, and Gibian took Finch through them in his ponderous way, fastening upon an email Finch sent to Millen, Doyle and another Freehills lawyer, Jessica Light, at 4:30pm. The subject was 'Fwd: RFA POA – Ground Ops.dox'.

'Do you see that?' Gibian checked.

'I see that, yes.'

'Well, again, do you maintain your evidence that you created that document?'

'I do, yes.'

'Was your evidence that you've then forwarded it to Ms Millen, Ms Light, and Mr Doyle at 4:30pm?'

'Having been prompted by this table, that looks like exactly what I did, yes.'

'You could just see the colour drain from his face,' Kaine recalls of Finch's faltering final morning in the witness box. 'He looked like a corpse. That measured, unflappable demeanour he seeks to project just completely fell apart. He was stumbling over words, he was sweating. It deserved to be televised, it really did.'

One by one, Gibian directed Finch to further emails he had received that evening. 'So you've been party to at least six email communications attaching at least three, and presumably more, Microsoft Word documents, all with the title 'Forward RFA POA – Ground Ops.docx' on the evening of 18 November 2020, prior to sending the document … to Mr David?'

'Yes, so it – so this suggests, yes.'

'They were communications involving persons who you knew to be solicitors at Herbert Smith Freehills, correct?'

Justice Lee intervened. 'I see they weren't only communications with Freehills, they were also communications with counsel.'

'Yes, and involving Mr Follett,' Gibian agreed. Matthew Follett, Qantas' junior barrister in the trial, was at that very moment seated 3 metres from Finch, at Qantas' side of the bar table beside Neil Young. 'Did you know who Mr Follett was at that time?'

'I – I believe I did know who Mr Follett was,' Finch conceded. 'I – I don't know that we had met, but I …'

'That is, you knew he was a barrister who was acting for Qantas?' Gibian asked.

'Yes, I – I believe so.'

'And you knew that Mr Doyle was an industrial [relations] partner at Herbert Smith Freehills?'

'I understood him to be – yes, an industrial relations partner at Freehills.'

'And can I just suggest to you this was a reasonably remarkable event; that is, that you were being communicated with by counsel acting for Qantas in industrial proceedings and [an] industrial relations partner at Freehills in relation to a document that you described as … a template and a common occurrence to approve financial delegations, correct?'[14]

'RFAs are very common.'

'And what you have presented in your affidavit is that the exercise ... was a routine matter, correct?'

'I don't know that I describe it as a routine matter, but preparing RFAs are —'

'Mr Finch,' Justice Lee interjected, 'you were a solicitor at Allen Allen & Hemsley, and someone who received first class honours in law from the University of Sydney?'

'Yes.'

'I may be right or I may be wrong,' his Honour continued, 'but the impression I took upon reading this affidavit is that the evidence that you're putting forward to the court was ... for example, paragraph 14, you "regularly receive and process [RFAs]" ... you give an example of it occurring on a number of other occasions ... I want to be fair to you and I just want your response to this.'

Anyone in the courtroom could have heard a pin drop. Justice Lee held Finch's credibility as a witness – and, indeed, as an officer of the court – in the palm of his hand. Finch's evidence had been truly, categorically awful. It arguably should have ended his viable career as a general counsel of an ASX 100 company. But for whatever reason, this enigmatic judge was inclined to offer Finch, for all intents and purposes a drowning man, a life raft.

'Perhaps I will withdraw that and ask another question,' his Honour deviated suddenly. 'Did you draft this affidavit, or was it something where you gave instructions and it was drafted by somebody else?'

'I think it was the latter, although I obviously had input into it, during the course of —'

'And having had your mind refreshed, would it be fair for me to conclude that this was a very novel course of events that was occurring on 18 November ...?'

'It's unusual for an RFA to go through that process, yes, your Honour.'

'Has it ever happened in your experience before, or since?'

'... By and large, no. They proceed without external advice.'

Gibian closed in for a damaging concession. 'Do you accept that the process that you have described for the preparation of the RFA ... is materially misleading —?'

'I agree that it does not include that detail.'

His Honour interrupted. 'Can you please attend to the question, whether you agree with that proposition or not that's being put to you.'

'The problem answering just yes or no to that, your Honour,' Finch pleaded, 'is I was merely ... attempting to convey the message that I had drafted the RFA. It wasn't – I didn't intend to go into the detail of how it came about. Had I purported to do so ... then I would agree that it doesn't include and therefore misses material information.'

'Yes, all right, thank you.' Justice Lee was apparently satisfied.

But Gibian wanted a final proposition on the record.

'Did you, Mr Finch, understand that the purpose of entering into these RFA and power of attorney documents was to make it look like Mr Joyce and others were not involved in the decision to outsource ground handling operations at Qantas?'

'No, the reason was to give Mr David the power to sign contracts should he choose to do so.'

———

Although some of these legal points were ultimately immaterial to the outcome of the case, the way they were addressed in court is profoundly material to understanding the culture of Qantas management. That culture was of high-handed exceptionalism: of unbelievably aggressive tactics in pursuit of its objectives, of a shared willingness to mislead or even lie, and with little regard for the victims or for community expectations.

This culture had operated beyond the public's line of sight, but TWU v. Qantas placed it all on the public record. Sadly, the trial was never properly covered by the media. That surprised Bornstein. 'There have been big changes during my career – there are now far fewer dedicated industrial relations reporters, so the trial went unloved by the press. It was lengthy, there were parts of it which were very slow moving and it wasn't considered a priority, clearly, by media outlets, but I thought they were missing a huge story.'

'It was complicated and everyone thought we'd lose,' Kaine says, 'and I think those two things together counted against us. It wasn't for want of trying – we were trying to get it out there – but there was still this mythology, even amidst all of this, that Qantas was the bee's knees. No one believed us.'

Qantas capitalised on this lack of public reporting to spin the court's findings right through the two-year appeal process, all the way to September 2023 when the High Court upheld Justice Lee's judgment that Qantas' conduct was unlawful.

Some of the questions unanswered in the trial – particularly in the testimony of Qantas' most senior legal officer, Andrew Finch – were as revealing as the judge's verdict. Neither Finch nor Qantas' counsel offered the court any plausible reason as to why Qantas engaged a phalanx of external solicitors, and even a barrister, to advise on the execution of the company's routine commercial contracts.

No plausible explanation was given as to why specialist *industrial relations* lawyers were advising Qantas on an issue of internal *financial* compliance.

No plausible explanation was given for why the Finch/Free-hills power of attorney instrument was conceived and executed in eighteen hours flat, for contracts that were still several weeks away from finalisation.[15]

No plausible explanation was given for the affidavits of Finch and David characterising this elaborate delegation process as common practice, then Finch and David admitting in cross-examination that the process was extraordinary, if not unprecedented.[16]

No plausible reason was given as to why Alan Joyce didn't, as per usual, sign approval for these contracts himself, instead of signing his authority over to David to approve them. Bear in mind the men's desks were 20 metres apart.

The only plausible reason, as far as I can see, was to white-out Alan Joyce from the sacking of the airline's TWU workforce, whose union Joyce had publicly attacked as 'militant'. It was to outsource the outsourcing decision before it was even made; indeed, to uncouple Joyce, by legal artifice, from his own decision-making power mere hours before Qantas received the in-house bid of TWU workers to save their jobs. And by doing so, to ensure that Joyce could never be put on trial for the decision. What else were highly paid underlings for?

To be clear, Justice Lee did not accept this construction: 'I do not believe I can or should make the jump to conclude ... that efforts were being made to hide the identity of the true decision maker.' But he did pass judgement on the credibility of Qantas' witnesses. He fingered Finch's colleague Paul Jones as a liar. A second Qantas executive, Colin Hughes, his Honour found, gave 'less than compelling' evidence and was '[not] always doing his best to give candid answers'. A third executive, Paul Nicholas, gave 'artificial and unconvincing' evidence. Andrew David's evidence was better, although 'this does not mean that in all respects his evidence was entirely satisfactory': David was 'careful to give evidence' that Joyce had had no input into the outsourcing decision (and had sought none), and had neither met nor spoken with David about the power of attorney.

Somehow, Andrew Finch came in for more lenient treatment. His Honour found that Finch's affidavit was 'incorrect' and 'had the effect of presenting a less than complete impression as to the preparation of the documents ... However, I am not satisfied that this was the result of any conscious attempt of Mr Finch to give false evidence.' Justice Lee chose to blame Freehills for its drafting of the affidavit on Finch's behalf, even though Finch – himself a solicitor – signed and swore the thing. His Honour, it seemed, could not bring himself to make a negative credit finding against a plummy officer of the court with 'a first class honours degree in law from no less a university than the University of Sydney'.

Bornstein says: 'We didn't convince the judge that Finch deliberately misled the court but nevertheless, it was, I think, very damaging to Qantas' case that the affidavit evidence was discredited. All of the holes in their accounts accumulated, and that was very helpful to us.'

When all was said and done, this case was to be decided by Justice Lee answering the following question: Did any prohibited reason under the Fair Work Act form 'a substantial and operative part' of Qantas' reasons for making the outsourcing decision?

Justice Lee agreed that COVID – and more specifically, the operational savings that COVID necessitated – was a major and lawful reason for the outsourcing decision. And ever since, Qantas has clung to this finding as some sort of flimsy exculpation of its (mis)conduct. It most certainly was not. His Honour went on to find that, 'The key concern of making the outsourcing decision at the time that it was made was because of the vanishing window of opportunity.' Justice Lee was 'affirmatively satisfied' that part of Paul Jones' reasons for recommending the outsourcing decision to Andrew David was 'to prevent affected employees disrupting services in 2021 by taking protected industrial action'. It was also part of David's reasons for accepting that recommendation; as his Honour put it, 'Qantas' submissions did not suggest that there was a cigarette paper of difference between the motivations of each [of] these men.'

This was a prohibited reason and thus Qantas' defence failed.

You could be forgiven, however, for believing otherwise – at least based on Qantas' instant public bleating about its 'sound commercial reasons' for the outsourcing.

As Josh Bornstein explains, 'In every outsourcing case that is challenged, from the [1998 Australian] waterfront dispute on, the employer says it had sound commercial reasons. That's not rocket science. I mean, it wouldn't have been a very smart outsourcing decision if there weren't sound commercial reasons for it.

'So Qantas has run around in public relations land saying, "Oh, the judgment's not so much of a problem because the judge accepted that we had sound commercial reasons." Well yes, he did, and then he determined that you contravened the Act because you were also motivated by illicit reasons.'

In fact, the airline's reaction to the Federal Court's ruling was much more extraordinary than Bornstein portrays it, and terrifically revealing of its delusion. Qantas came straight out of the blocks with a thundering press release on 30 July 2021, the day Justice Lee handed down his judgment. The language was so intemperate it sounded less like a corporate announcement than a conspiracy theorist's unhinged rant. 'The TWU has put forward its persecution complex that our decision to save $100 million a year in the middle of a global downturn was really about stopping them from walking off the job at some time in the future.

'The focus of the TWU's case was on a few documents that made reference to industrial action while ignoring the hundreds that don't ... A reference to the risk of industrial action does not automatically mean that it's a reason for the decision.'

This was Qantas at its belligerent best, suggesting that Justice Lee had 'automatically' assigned motive, when in fact he had that very morning laid it out in a painstaking judgment running the length of 120 pages. One really needed to wonder who had the 'complex' here: the workers deprived of their jobs, or the clique of executives with dollar signs in their eyes.

A media teleconference was hastily convened and fronted by QantasLink CEO John Gissing. 'We recognised that we had to move fast to recognise any savings we could,' he said. 'This was about survival ... [Outsourcing] was a right decision, it was a lawful decision and it was a decision we had to make quickly in order to secure those savings as soon as possible.' Then, ascending to Trumpian heights of audacity, Gissing added that 'we believe our executives exhibited the utmost honesty and integrity in the evidence they gave'.

This was alternative universe stuff: to announce, the very day a court ruled that you violated Commonwealth law and your executives gave artificial and even deliberately false evidence, that your actions were lawful and your executives were honest. It also suggested preternatural speed of reading, reflection and response.

There had been no substantive engagement by Qantas with the judgment, parts of which were deeply humiliating to the company. Inside the reality-distortion field swathing the airline's executive floor, nobody seemed to ask, Have we handled ourselves properly here? This was not a group of professionals prepared to reflect on the wisdom of their own conduct in pursuing a course of action contrary to expert advice that it was high risk. Rather, they were deflecting, lashing out, jutting their jaws. Their illegal behaviour was all just someone else's *complex*.

The press conference assembled to defend this position only demonstrated how deluded it was. After Gissing's opening remarks, the first question from the press pack was, 'Why are you doing this press conference rather than Andrew David, who was the sole decision-maker in this matter?' It was a more than fair question, given the premise of Qantas' case was that each GMC member was solely responsible for the decisions of his own business unit, and that the GMC was a mere 'forum' to 'socialise' proposals. How could another GMC member speak for the decision-maker? But Gissing blatantly ignored the question. Inside the Qantas executive force field, dissonant questions didn't even register.

'It was difficult even to be disappointed [by Qantas' response to losing] because it was just fully expected,' Kaine told me. 'Think about what, at that point, they could routinely get away with. They treat[ed] the Australian public with contempt and they just thought they were above the law. There are still [Qantas executives] who think they're above the law.'

That might in part be because they were still being rewarded for it. Justice Lee's judgment identified the perverse incentives for Qantas' illegal behaviour – savings so significant that they outweighed any potential penalty or reputational risk. Qantas knew that by outsourcing its domestic ground handling function it would save *at least* $500 million over the first four years.[17] Qantas also knew that if its decision was found to be illegal, it would be up for maximum penalties of $110 million. The compensation Qantas owed to sacked employees was still to be determined by Justice Lee, but Bornstein estimates that 'if you took a very robust view of compensation, it might be in the two hundred millions'. Qantas was also in the process of racking up more than $15 million in legal expenses.

Therefore, Qantas' law-breaking put it ahead financially from the outset, and the more time that passed, the further ahead it got.

Former Qantas executive Paul Jones was the individual most tarnished by the unlawful outsourcing, so there is some irony in the fact that he was also the most prescient – perhaps with the exception of Ian and Justine Oldmeadow – about its consequences. 'The TWU campaign would be extensive and create challenges for the [Qantas] brand,' he warned the Qantas board in June 2020, 'potentially leading to a British Airways level of negativity with Qantas [being] perceived as the big bad corporate taking advantage of [the] COVID situation and not being on Team Australia.'

The idea that the Spirit of Australia was not on Team Australia would get plenty of re-enforcement over the next few years.

Crossing the Rubicon
Sept 2020–Nov 2022

By 2021, Qantas – and indeed, the entire country – was deep in its new COVID reality. Qantas had told the ASX in December 2020 that it planned to run 80 per cent of its 2019 capacity in the January–March 2021 quarter. But that became impossible as domestic borders opened and then slammed shut. Western Australia shut its doors to Victorians on 31 December, while Victoria closed its border with New South Wales on 1 January. Greater Brisbane entered a snap three-day lockdown on 8 January, so Victoria and Western Australia closed their borders to Queensland. Perth entered a hard five-day lockdown on 31 January, with other states responding in kind. Western Australia reopened on 5 February, but closed its border to Victorians on 12 February. And on it went.

Running a domestic airline network under these conditions was fiendish, though Qantas got better and better operationally at shifting its network and schedule in response to the snap border closures.

There were some tailwinds. Qantas benefited from the uncertainty around Virgin Australia's future under Bain's new ownership. Nearly thirty large Australian companies switched their travel accounts to Qantas from Virgin. Qantas (with Jetstar) commanded a 74 per cent domestic market share in December 2020, domination they'd not enjoyed since the years after Ansett's collapse nearly twenty years previously. Another upside was that every Qantas flight cancelled due to border closures meant more ticket revenue being shifted into flight credits.

The state border dominos acted as a fitful handbrake on domestic travel. Tellingly, Australians were more afraid of getting locked outside their home state than of catching COVID. The approaching end of JobKeeper on 28 March also had a sapping effect on economic confidence, especially in the shattered tourism sector. Qantas and Virgin naturally entertained speculation about further job losses as an implicit threat to the Morrison government.

In response, the government replaced the indiscriminate hose of JobKeeper cash with a targeted tourism industry support package of $1.2 billion. Qantas was, of course, intimately involved in negotiating the package, and under its umbrella would receive $151 million to subsidise the cost of returning its international fleet to service later that year, and another $86 million in an ongoing JobKeeper-like scheme for its 7,500 international crew. Under that scheme, unlike JobKeeper, all of the money went to the employees, and the airline received no benefit.

The headline-grabbing measure, though, was about domestic travel: the government would pay half the cost of 800,000 discount domestic airfares. Qantas soaked up $46 million under this funding stream, whose effect on the tourism economy would be insignificant. Former Qantas chief economist Dr Tony Webber summoned all of his enthusiasm to describe the government-funded airfares as 'obviously better than nothing'. But given that a plane ticket represents, at most, 20 per cent of the total cost of a trip, he surmised, 'People don't go on holidays because their airfare is a little cheaper.'

If anything, the program's greatest contribution to domestic tourism was its publicity impact, which was considerable. Prime Minister Scott Morrison, a former Tourism Australia boss, retained a flair for this variety of stunt.

John Sharp, the deputy chairman of Regional Express (Rex), was clearly raw that Qantas had, in his eyes, managed to benefit so disproportionately from the government's latest aviation support scheme, leaving Rex with scraps: Morrison and his treasurer Josh Frydenberg might have been overcompensating after the criticism of their scandalous handouts to Rex twelve months earlier. By no coincidence, an outlandish skirmish broke out between Qantas and Rex in April 2021.

The spark, seemingly, was a series of relatively unremarkable comments made by Alan Joyce. At an event on 13 January 2021, he had been asked about Rex's entry into capital city routes and responded, 'My personal view is that this market has never sustained three airline groups and it probably won't into the future'; he added that 'you can be guaranteed that Qantas will be one of [the two that survives]'. And then in an interview with the *Australian Financial Review* on 15 April, Joyce extrapolated: '[Virgin and Rex] have the same product, the same aircraft ... they're competing for the middle of the market and their strategies seem to be pretty similar to each other,' he said. 'All I've ever [expressed] is my own personal opinion. The market's history is such that you've never seen three major players survive, you've always seen it rationalise back to two.'

Plainly irate, Sharp responded with an opinion piece in the *AFR* a few days later. 'Rex's patience' had been spent and it was 'now time to set the record straight'. To describe Sharp's screed as histrionic would not be doing it justice. It was actually a wonder the *AFR* even agreed to publish it.[1]

Rex, Sharp roared, was actually the superior business to Qantas, having been far more profitable than Qantas (on a size-adjusted basis) over the thirteen years Joyce had been CEO. 'Qantas continues to burn cash at an alarming rate', and 'its borrowings are a staggering $7 billion', while 'its much vaunted $2 billion in cash holdings are largely encumbered by the banks to secure against the $5 billion of advance sale tickets, most of which is due to be refunded'. Sharp even claimed: 'It could be argued that Qantas is now technically insolvent,' and again emphasised as one of its liabilities 'the refundable tickets worth billions'.

This was tin-foil hat stuff from Sharp. Qantas' cash was not encumbered by the banks at all, and it also owned $2.5 billion of unmortgaged assets – these facts were publicly available. What Sharp was probably trying, but failing, to explain was that most, if not all, of Qantas' $2.6 billion cash balance was revenue received in advance for future flights, and that that cash was currently a liability, not an asset. But this was completely normal: the cash would convert from a liability to an asset once those tickets were flown (or the flight credits expired). And it was also normal that Qantas' cash liabilities exceeded its cash balance; no service business preserved all of its sales in cash until after it delivered the related services, any more than banks are expected to keep 100 per cent of their customer deposits sitting in cash ready to be withdrawn. In practice, Qantas' $5 billion of revenue received in advance was not encumbered in any meaningful way.

Sharp's real beef, which he lacked the clarity to convey, was contained in his references to 'refundable tickets': COVID flight credits. By this method, now twelve months into COVID, Qantas was still clinging onto at least $1.3 billion of refundable money. With any luck, a huge slab of that liability might never be called upon. If the credits expired, the liability would even convert to profit. Sharp was making perfect sense when he said, 'It is now crystal clear that Qantas' best game is played against its customers, leaving hundreds of thousands of mums and dads billions of dollars out of pocket.'

Rex, by contrast, had developed an online refund portal in April 2020, where customers could apply for a cash refund on any existing booking and receive the funds in their bank account within three working days. As Sharp now puts it, 'It wasn't their fault they couldn't take the flight and it technically wasn't our money. The issue for us was handling all of the requests that were overwhelming what is a fairly small call centre already.'

So Sharp was aggrieved that Rex had done the right thing and provided refunds while Qantas got away with confiscating its customers' money and using it as working capital. And to add salt to the wound, Sharp had history with Joyce on this issue.

On 19 April 2020, as a courtesy heads-up, Sharp had sent Joyce a copy of a media release announcing Rex's refund portal, which Rex was proposing to publish imminently. In Sharp's account, Joyce phoned him within two minutes. 'He asked me why we were doing that and how we were going to manage the cashflow implications.

I told him we were worried about the ACCC criticising us for not refunding customers.' According to Sharp, Joyce said that Qantas couldn't afford to refund cancelled bookings and had even removed people from its call centres who usually processed refunds. On that basis, Sharp says he offered to launch Rex's refund portal without fanfare, an offer Joyce accepted gratefully.[2]

'We went out of our way to refund people,' Sharp says. 'When we discussed the refunds internally we decided it's a long journey and at the end of this we wanted loyal customers. Qantas on the other hand said, We'll keep the money because we need it and bad luck to our customers.' And then Sharp perfectly summarises an enduring mystery: 'The disappointing part is that no matter how badly Qantas treats its customers, they still keep flying Qantas. It's extraordinary.'

Nevertheless, the legitimate criticism in Sharp's *AFR* article was completely lost in the melodrama of his overreach. And that's where the matter would have ended, except that Alan Joyce was now irate too. His unbelievably catty response, also published in the *AFR*, was something to behold.

Rex had 'presided over the worst launch of a new jet airline in Australia's aviation history', Joyce fulminated, 'with empty aircraft and announced routes that have never been flown'.

Joyce called Rex's claim to be Australia's most profitable airline (size-adjusted) 'a dubious distinction when you have failed to invest in your fleet and propellers are literally falling off'.

Joyce shifted from taunting to patronising – 'Perhaps if you're used to running a small company, the accounts of a large company can be confusing' – before turning personal: Sharp 'left politics under a cloud and has shown an approach to corporate communications that seems to confuse it with parliamentary privilege'.

'For our part, we are focused on recovering from the COVID-19 crisis and bringing more of our people back to work,' Joyce claimed, while revealing his actual focus was on petty point-scoring.

On the whole, Joyce's dispatch was nasty, undergraduate, self-unaware, and positively radiating self-satisfaction. Stylistically, it bore all the hallmarks of Joyce's PR gofer Andrew McGinnes. Titled

'Struggling Rex poses no credible threat to Qantas' crown', it begged the question of why, if Rex posed no threat, Joyce bothered to submit 700 berserk words about Rex to a national newspaper. Of course, the issue was not whether or not Rex posed a commercial threat to Qantas. It was that Rex posed a *psychological* threat to Alan Joyce.

Here were telltale signs of Joyce's fragility, of his obsessive need to dominate the narrative. He needed the first and the last say. There could only be his version of events. And by trying to impose it, he paradoxically elevated the target of his invective. Qantas was sixty times bigger than Rex.[3] Rex was a speck on Qantas' windscreen, yet Joyce, by his lack of impulse control, had effectively lowered Qantas (or raised Rex) onto a debate platform where the two were equals.

Over a dozen years in the public eye, Joyce had earned the reputation of the meanest street fighter in corporate Australia, punching on with rival airlines, tourism bodies, trade unions, airports, journalists, politicians, and even his predecessor as Qantas CEO. 'People who try to impose their opinions – try to intimidate or get people to back down because maybe they have a weaker or lesser voice in some way – you have to stand up to that,' Joyce said in 2017. But in overreacting to perceived bullies, Joyce could often become the bully himself.

———

In September 2020, early in its search for $1 billion of structural savings, Qantas commenced what it characterised as a review of its national property footprint, led by CFO Vanessa Hudson.

In order to reduce the $40 million it spent each year renting office space, Qantas publicly floated the possibilities of relocating its corporate headquarters from Sydney, and/or Jetstar's office from Melbourne, and/or even its heavy maintenance facility from Brisbane airport.

Hudson spoke of 'opportunities to consolidate some facilities and unlock economies of scale'. The head offices of Qantas and Jetstar could be consolidated, for example. 'Most of our activities and facilities are anchored to the airports we fly to, but anything that can reasonably move without impacting our operations or customers is on the table,' she said. 'We'll also be making the new Western Sydney

Airport part of our thinking, given the opportunity this greenfield project represents.'

Inside Qantas, the property review was assigned the codename Project Rubicon, which was fitting because Qantas had certainly crossed it by attempting this charade.

Firstly, the exercise made no financial sense. The Qantas campus on Bourke Road, Mascot, had been comprehensively overhauled for Qantas between 2011 and 2014, at a cost of $130 million, by the property owner Cromwell Group.[4] Qantas' lease on the site wouldn't expire until 2032. The cost of breaking that lease a decade early would significantly exceed any rental savings achieved by moving elsewhere. What's more, to move Jetstar's office to Sydney (let alone Qantas HQ to Melbourne), the company would need to offer hundreds or thousands of voluntary redundancies to the affected staff, who couldn't be compelled to move interstate. Those payouts would outweigh any rent savings by a factor of ten or twenty. Qantas, remember, was at this stage already deep in the process of spending $1 billion on 9,800 redundancies.

Secondly, these staff were not fungible commodities, like spotty kids flipping burgers. Qantas was a company loaded with niche subject-matter experts – possibly more so than any other Australian company – who were scarce globally. Some of them could be relied upon to move interstate; indeed, there was (and remains) a cohort of employees who would move to Aleppo to keep their jobs at Qantas. But many would not. And an airline can't just find a whole new revenue management or scheduling team in a different Australian city, like they're a drop-in cricket pitch. A significant number of employees would undoubtedly quit before driving 60 kilometres each way to work at Western Sydney airport (there would be no direct train to Sydney city). Hudson may have invoked Julius Caesar crossing the Rubicon, but only the rabble of a Qantas army would follow her over Badgerys Creek.

Thirdly, as Hudson herself intimated, much of the head office workforce interfaced daily with the airline's operations. The Qantas campus was 800 metres from the airline's engineering jet base, itself just four minutes from the Qantas Freight terminal. For pilots and cabin crew, it was a five-minute shuttle bus to Sydney airport, where more than half of all Qantas flights either take off or land, Sydney being the midpoint of the domestic market's golden triangle and the undisputed international gateway to Australia. The arterial road abutting Sydney airport is even called Qantas Drive. The idea that Qantas would drag 3,500 corporate employees from the fence line of Kingsford Smith to the back blocks of Western Sydney to save $5–10 million a year on rent was manifest nonsense.

So if there was no prospect of cost savings, what was the purpose of the property review? It was, in short, a classic Qantas contrivance: an exercise in extorting even more subsidies out of government – state governments in this case. Why would Hudson insult the intelligence of our elected policymakers with such a naked try-on? Because it works.

Literally within an hour of Qantas' announcement, the Victorian, New South Wales and Queensland governments had fallen over themselves to open the bidding in Hudson's sham auction. Victoria had 'a very attractive offer to make', its premier Daniel Andrews said. 'As I understand it, they've got some heavy maintenance jobs. They've got some head office jobs. All of those jobs are essentially up for grabs and we'll be working very hard to make sure that Victoria puts [in] a high-quality bid.' New South Wales Treasurer Dominic Perrottet said the Berejiklian government would offer 'every assistance to Qantas so they can keep as many of their employees as possible in the state. If there is a way in which they can consolidate in Sydney or in Western Sydney, then we are open to those discussions about how we can assist.' Queensland Treasurer Cameron Dick went straight for the heartstrings, saying, 'Queensland is the reason there's a "Q" in Qantas.'

There is also a 'u' in 'sucker'.

Australian Licensed Aircraft Engineers' Association secretary Steve Purvinas saw the play and accused Qantas of using empty threats to extract a 'handout' from the Queensland government. 'That [heavy maintenance] facility [at Brisbane airport] is world class and no one in their right mind would consider moving it,' he said.

And in truth, no one was considering moving it. But only months earlier, Qantas had seen Virgin Australia extract $200 million from the Queensland government (part of which bought the government a small equity stake in the airline) in exchange for keeping the carrier's headquarters in Brisbane.5 That is, in exchange for doing nothing.

Who, then, could blame Joyce and Hudson for seeing dollar signs? Qantas was now nearly four times the size of Bain's slimmed-down Virgin; a proportional state government sweetener would be an even bigger windfall for Qantas than JobKeeper. If a brain-dead state treasurer with a gigantic novelty cheque was out there somewhere, Joyce wouldn't be discharging his duties to Qantas shareholders if he didn't track them down.

This was federation at its worst. Federal Minister for Trade Simon Birmingham described the spectacle as 'a blatant attempt to extract taxpayer dollars from the states and territories'. The unemployment rate at the time was 7.5 per cent. 'I'd have to urge caution from the states. This bidding war won't create one extra job in Australia; it just shuffles jobs around Australia.' He rightly warned of 'a wave of corporate welfare-seeking by big business if we have big companies around the country just auctioning off their head offices to states ... In the end, it's the taxpayers picking up the bill.'

The response from a Qantas spokesman was striking: 'We have to look right across our business for ways to be more efficient. Under those circumstances, it's hard to see why state governments respond-ing positively is a bad thing.' In Qantas World, where every cult member wore self-interest blinkers, the need to be more efficient trumped everything, including the obligation to behave ethically. Comically, even the Qantas spokesman found it hard to tell why anyone wouldn't see it their way.

There was a corporate imperative to rebuking Birmingham, of course. Qantas couldn't have public officials emboldened to call out its egregious economic rents for what they were. That kind of thinking had to be shut down, pronto. And what was so revealing was the way Qantas instinctively dressed up its mercenary conduct in wholesome narratives. Joyce sure as hell didn't see himself as a rent-seeker. He was saving Qantas, and therefore the nation, by his sheer ingenuity.

Qantas executives weren't obtaining an advantage for themselves at the expense of their fellow Australians, not as they saw it; they were ushering the airline through perilous days – and on reduced pay, thank you very much. It wasn't just the Qantas choir wearing angelic white bibs, it was Qantas management too.

Culture in companies tends to be characterised in monolithic terms, but in reality, corporations are run by individuals who transfuse their personal culture into the organisation. Who signs up to their credo? It can be very, very few people. Virtually every public statement from Qantas was coming off the desk of Andrew McGinnes, and the language positively dripped with his nauseating indignation and greatly misplaced sense of superiority. McGinnes was ascendant, but he was just one person. Did the broader population of Qantas head office subscribe to the idea that their jobs were valid bargaining chips for subsidies? That government incentives for Qantas were reason enough to uproot their families and drag them interstate, or merely to the boondocks? Of course not.

The Qantas culture at that time was really just Alan Joyce's culture, adopted expediently by his most ambitious vassals in the C-suite, because only those who signed on got promoted and only those who signed on survived.

In a subplot that underlines the theme, Hudson's property review also included in its purview the fate of Qantas' flight simulators for pilot training, a crucial piece of its infrastructure and indeed its identity as the world's safest airline. The training centre in Sydney had been suspended due to COVID, but also because of Qantas' sense of entitlement to, and brinkmanship over, government handouts. In September 2018, the New South Wales government had announced a deal to acquire land on the fringes of Sydney airport to widen Qantas Drive, as part of the larger Sydney Gateway Project. The acquired land included a portion of Qantas' jet base, which had been a major aircraft maintenance and training facility since the 1950s.

As a result, Qantas' longstanding pilot training centre would need to be demolished by 2022.

Although Qantas owned the very old buildings on the land, it didn't own the land itself: it was merely a tenant of Sydney airport. The government nevertheless agreed to help expedite the planning process for Qantas to build a new centre for its flight simulators on Qantas-owned land directly across Qantas Drive, at King Street, Mascot. This 'state significant' development was quickly approved and construction on the $120 million project commenced in September 2019. When COVID hit the following March, the concrete foundations had been laid and Qantas had already spent around $30 million of the construction budget. In May 2020, Qantas told the New South Wales government it would not complete the centre unless the government contributed to the cost of its completion. The government refused, and so Qantas cancelled the project.

Qantas had only been funding the construction, as Tino La Spina characterised it, 'while we negotiated suitable compensation for having to leave our existing facilities'. But Qantas was never entitled to any compensation. Its lease at the jet base was expiring in June 2020. In Qantas World, however, any inconvenience made the airline (though not its customers) eligible for compensation.

In May 2020, Qantas claimed it would look to permanently transfer its Sydney pilot training capability to Melbourne or Brisbane. This was yet another transparently empty threat. The great preponderance of Qantas pilots – around 45 per cent, or 1,000, of them – were and still are based in Sydney. The cost of sending them interstate for training would be exorbitant, as the airline went on to prove by continuing its bluff. In 2021, eight Qantas flight sims were relocated, at a cost of around $15 million, to Melbourne and Brisbane. Each Sydney pilot spent between one and six weeks training interstate that year, costing Qantas another $10 million. From 2022 to 2024, those pilots continued commuting to Melbourne four times per year for their training, costing the company a bomb in flights and accommodation, accrued travel allowances, and in reduced availability for operating real flights.

In January 2021, all three state governments confirmed they had lodged bids under Qantas' property review. Qantas brought in consulting firm PwC to assess the bids.

On 6 May, Qantas announced the outcome of its property review. Qantas – shock, horror – wouldn't be moving anything anywhere. 'Moving one or both of our headquarters was always a live option and there were times in the process where that seemed to be the most likely outcome,' Joyce claimed, implausibly. In return for doing almost nothing it wouldn't have done anyway, Qantas extracted 'a range of benefits' from New South Wales, Victoria and Queensland, including 'payroll tax relief', 'property rebates' and 'direct incentives'.

A new flight simulator centre would be built in Sydney, as it was always going to be. Sydney would be the launch city for Project Sunrise flights to London and New York, as it was always going to be. Virtually every undertaking announced by Qantas was either recycled, temporary or noncommittal. 'Discussions will now commence', it was revealed, with the Queensland government on basing aircraft in Townsville, which was not a decision. 'Discussions [were] underway' about doing some maintenance work in Cairns, which was not a decision. Jetstar would relocate A320 maintenance from Singapore to Brisbane 'as part of a trial ... with the potential for this to be extended'.

Exactly how much these dubious assurances would cost the Australian public was commercial-in-confidence, but the following month, the *Sydney Morning Herald* published the New South Wales government's leaked draft offer to Qantas of $50 million over four years. The fact that Qantas resolved to keep its headquarters in Sydney for the princely sum of $12.5 million per annum exposed the property review for the pantomime it always was.

Tragically, the new pilot training centre which Qantas had committed to keeping in Sydney would not even be a Qantas facility. On 15 October, the company announced it would sell 14 hectares of surplus land in Mascot to industrial real estate group LOGOS for $802 million, including the King Street site of the incomplete simulator centre, where rusted rebar now protruded aimlessly from the concrete. And in August 2022 Qantas announced that it 'will train pilots at a new purpose-built centre in Sydney', where 'global training provider CAE will maintain the simulators and manage the day-to-day operations of the centre as part of a long-term partnership'.

The language was incredibly tricksy. Why couldn't Qantas admit plainly what it was really doing? It was selling its time-honoured flight simulators to CAE then leasing them back on an hourly basis – and even sharing them with other airlines. This was unlocking 'lazy' capital in what Joyce and his razor gang deemed non-core operations. Qantas had already flogged off inflight catering, and offshored low-hanging lines of heavy maintenance, but now the safest airline in the world was crossing the Rubicon and outsourcing its pilot training.

'It's always better to own and control your own facilities because it limits your risk when things change,' says the Australian and International Pilots Association president, Captain Tony Lucas. 'The parallel I would draw would be with [aircraft] maintenance. Qantas has no heavy maintenance capability for the A380 fleet in Australia so we're beholden to maintenance facilities overseas.' Even by mid-2024, more than thirty months since the relaunch of Qantas International, 'we've still only got six out of ten Qantas A380s flying, because we can't get the other four through those [foreign facilities], which are fully booked.[6]

'When you lose control of your ability to produce things or to perform work that is fundamental to your business, that has downstream risks that I think people don't tend to fully comprehend.

'I don't know the ins and outs of the contract [between Qantas and CAE] but to me, as a pilot who is used to controlling as many risks as I can, it seems an undue increase in risk to outsource a function such as operating simulators, which really should be part of an airline's core functionality.'

Gripes with the proposed facility emerged quickly. There was no room for a pool for mandatory evacuation training on slide-rafts, as there was at the jet base, so training would have to be conducted elsewhere. There was no parking, so Qantas would need to operate a shuttle bus from Mascot, even though the simulators operate around the clock and pilots regularly train in the middle of the night.

As ever, Qantas crew could take it or leave it.

———

On 20 May 2021, Alan Joyce announced good news: Qantas and Jetstar had returned all domestic aircraft to service; all staff, apart from 6,000 international crew, were back at work. Thirty-eight new domestic routes had been announced or already launched – after enduring lockdowns, Australians were desperate to travel, even if only locally. Group domestic capacity was now 95 per cent of pre-COVID levels. From July, Jetstar domestic capacity would be 120 per cent. Qantas Freight was booming and Qantas Loyalty was back to earnings growth. A two-way travel bubble with New Zealand was already in full swing. The only bad news was that the relaunch of Qantas International was being pushed back from October to late December, as a result of the Morrison government's slow-starting national vaccine rollout.[7]

The rebound had come far too late for Qantas to avert a greater than $2 billion loss for the 2021 financial year, but the company was now generating cash and its debt pile was shrinking. 'We have a long way still to go in this recovery, but it does feel like we're slowly starting to turn the corner,' Joyce said.

Qantas was also slashing its commissions to travel agents by 80 per cent, offering voluntary redundancy to several hundred more international cabin crew, and applying a two-year wage freeze to all staff. Of the $1 billion in annual costs Joyce was rending from the company, $600 million would be gone by 30 June. And as the *Financial Review*'s Chanticleer column accurately predicted that day, citing the consensus forecasts of eleven equities analysts who covered Qantas shares, 'the removal of about $1 billion in annual costs will likely see Qantas boost its profitability by 50 per cent compared to [2019] within a relatively short space of time'.

Joyce, Chanticleer marvelled, 'has not wasted the COVID-19 crisis'.

By early July, everything had changed. Greater Sydney had been plunged into a four-month lockdown thanks to the inbound crew of a FedEx freighter infecting a local limousine driver with the Delta strain of COVID-19. Melbourne soon followed, spending three months in its fifth and sixth lockdowns. Short lockdowns also shuttered South Australia and southeast Queensland.

By the third week of July, Qantas' plans to operate at more than 100 per cent of its pre-COVID domestic capacity lay in ashes. Joyce sent an optimistic message to employees about how quickly travel could rebound in the subsequent three months, but the problem was that just 35 per cent of Australians aged over sixteen had received a single dose of a COVID vaccine, and only 14 per cent had received both doses. Qantas and the rest of the travel and hospitality industries had been left holding the bag for the government's botched vaccination program.

On 3 August, Qantas stood down 2,500 domestic staff – a dizzying case of deja vu just in time for the company's financial results for the year to 30 June 2021, the first full reporting period affected by COVID-19. Qantas posted a statutory pre-tax loss of $2.4 billion. For the second consecutive loss-making year, Joyce was awarded his long-term bonus – 325,000 Qantas shares – and for the second consecutive year, he offered and the Qantas board agreed to defer for twelve months the decision whether he'd keep it or not.[8] Excluding that bonus, Joyce was paid $2.6 million in financial year 2021.[9]

'To be candid,' Qantas chairman Richard Goyder said in a statement appended to the company's 2021 annual report, 'it wasn't a foregone conclusion that Qantas would emerge from this pandemic in the shape it has ... Difficult decisions were made that have proven to be the right ones.'

———

The pace of Australia's COVID-19 vaccine take-up increased spectacularly in the late winter and spring of 2021 as the Morrison government secured new supplies of mRNA vaccines from Pfizer and

Moderna, and as the compelling incentive of release from lockdown worked on the citizenry.

By mid-October, Australia had surpassed the United States' vaccination rate. Eighty per cent of New South Wales residents were fully vaccinated, while more than 90 per cent had received their first dose. Victoria hit the 80 per cent level on 29 October and New South Wales and Victoria threw open their borders – including to international flights for Australian citizens and residents – on 1 November. Queensland hit 80 per cent on 9 December and opened its borders on 13 December. Western Australia would not reopen until March 2022.

On 22 October, Qantas brought forward the relaunch of its international division, with Sydney–Singapore flights to commence on 23 November. Six thousand international staff would return to work by early December. Qantas would have two A380s in service by April 2022, another three by July, and the final five back by early 2024.[10] The airline was also seeking to fast-track delivery of the three new 787-9s it had deferred in May 2020.

Releasing a trading update on 16 December, Joyce described the previous six months as 'the worst half ... we have ever seen'. Yet shareholders were far more interested in the outlook: domestic travel would exceed 100 per cent of pre-COVID capacity in the first quarter of calendar 2022, with international travel rising to 60 per cent by June.

But just as the Delta strain destroyed the last set of bullish forecasts, leading into Christmas of 2021 the Omicron variant of COVID-19 – milder, but even more infectious than Delta – was ripping through the community. With mass vaccination achieved, it was inconceivable that lockdowns would return; what was being underestimated was that lockdown's alternative – a different type of restriction – would cause societal disruption too.

Officially, 140,000 people were laid up with COVID that Christmas. Allowing for those who didn't report their illness, the real number was far higher. The regulations required every positive person to isolate for at least seven days. And each of their 'close contacts' – not just members of their households, but anyone they'd spent more than four hours with since being infected – were also forced into seven days' home quarantine.

The exact number of people knocked out of productive circulation at any one time was impossible to ascertain. COVID cases were significantly under-reported, with many preferring not to test, while close contacts were lax in complying with self-isolation requirements. But by April 2022, when the states scrapped self-isolation restrictions for close contacts, more than 5.3 million Australians had dutifully reported their COVID infection to their state government in the preceding four months. Again, the real number would have been far higher.

This affected Qantas in two ways. Firstly, the scale of the disruption of customers' travel was enormous and impossible to mitigate with planning. Many of the cancellations were at the eleventh hour, yet still had to be accommodated. Secondly, frontline Qantas employees were even more susceptible to COVID infection than the average person. Flight and ground crew illness threw the airline's operations into legitimate chaos. This wasn't limited to Qantas. All sectors of the economy were blighted by chronic staff shortages.

As a result, passenger demand collapsed in early 2022 and soon enough, so did Qantas' workable supply of seats.[11] Virgin responded first, on 10 January, slashing its capacity by a quarter, and Qantas followed on 13 January, reducing scheduled flights by a third. A week later, Qantas cut capacity by a further 10 per cent after Western Australian Premier Mark McGowan cancelled the state's 5 February reopening in response to Omicron. Joyce lashed McGowan, saying, 'There's not even a plan to open up. It's starting to look like North Korea.'

As Western Australia remained closed, however, the rest of Australia was opening up again. On 21 February, every other state opened to vaccinated foreign visitors. The same week, Victoria and New South Wales ended their mask mandates and Qantas handed down its half-year result: a pre-tax loss of $622 million but with net debt now down to $5.5 billion – within the company's target range.

The prevailing operating conditions were rocky, but with $2.7 billion in cash (and another $1.6 billion in undrawn facilities available), Qantas had moved past cash conservation and into the recovery phase. With his lower cost base established, Alan Joyce's money-printing machine was primed and ready.

Alongside the airline's half-year loss, the Qantas board announced a recovery and retention plan, to incentivise the continued service of all employees – from frontline staff right up to Joyce and his executive team.

All participants in the plan would be paid this bonus in August 2023, subject to them remaining with the company and the company clearing three performance hurdles. The hurdles were set so low there was no risk of Qantas failing to clear them. Firstly, net debt had to remain below the top end of the board's net debt range, which it already was. Secondly, management had to achieve its target, set in June 2020, to remove $1 billion of annual costs from the business. It had already removed $840 million, with eighteen months left on the clock. Thirdly, Qantas needed to be profitable for the year ending 30 June 2023 – a single dollar of profit would do. Joyce had prevailed upon the Qantas board to dispense to him and his team at-risk remuneration that was scarcely at any risk at all.

On the one hand, the Qantas board was right to deal with attrition risk. The economy was surging, and so were wages because the labour market was incredibly tight. Elsewhere, many talented people had earned terrific money through the pandemic, and in many cases were able to do so while luxuriating at home in their pyjamas. Airline managers – at least those with transferable skills – would have seen this and been crazy not to contemplate greener pastures. By August 2023, no short-term bonuses would have been paid to Qantas executives for three years. In that context, retention was becoming a genuine problem.

There was no less a problem with retaining or rehiring frontline workers. Domestic crew had just survived two emotionally gruelling years of stop-start work. Most international crew had spent those years working alternative jobs, and potentially developed a taste for their alternative pursuits. And now, thanks to Omicron and sundry other forces, aviation was in chaos. How appealing was a Qantas career anymore?

This was also a huge issue for US and European airlines in 2022. After a career hiatus driving a DHL truck, what sane airport ramp agent wanted to resume hauling bags in the snow?

The rewards of Qantas' retention plan were exceedingly top-heavy, as you'd expect of any plan designed by and for the people at the top – a truism of public company remuneration in general, whether in Australia or globally. Regular Qantas employees would receive 1,000 Qantas shares, worth $5,180 on the day of announcement (24 February 2022) but presumably more by their time of vesting. Qantas claimed that its non-executive employees earned, on average, more than $100,000 per year.[12] On that basis, their recovery and retention plan was a bonus equivalent to around 5 per cent of one year's pay. Yet the plan would hand Alan Joyce a share grant thirty times larger. He would receive shares worth 150 per cent of his base salary, or $3.3 million.[13]

What's more, this plan would replace Joyce's short-term bonus for financial year 2022 only. This meant that in August 2023, Joyce would receive his shares under this recovery and retention plan *and* his shares under his short-term bonus plan for financial year 2023. Moreover, these were just Joyce's short-term bonuses. Remember, he had also set aside two lots of long-term bonus shares – 343,500 for 2020, and 325,000 for 2021 – pending his later 'decision' on whether or not to accept them. Of course, what other purpose existed for setting them aside but to trouser them later?

It was a deeply dishonest construct, assuring Qantas employees that, like them, he wasn't getting any bonuses; telling the public he was toiling for a lousy $2 million in those years that Qantas was losing billions, but all along, embalming his bonuses for every one of those years, in readiness to resurrect them all when the coast was clear. In addition to the 668,500 shares he'd already set aside, by August 2023 Joyce would qualify for yet another two tranches of long-term bonus shares (for 2022 and 2023).

The scene was therefore set for Joyce to inherit epic plunder eighteen months hence, potentially eclipsing even his record 2017 haul of $24 million.

In that same 24 February 2022 announcement of results, Qantas adjusted its capacity forecasts down again, by up to 40 per cent, in response to Omicron. Of course by now, Qantas forecasts were being taken with a pinch of salt. The company's predictions of its own operating capacity were about as reliable as Australia's bank economists on the direction of house prices.

What the company did feel certain about was the 'huge pent-up demand' for travel. 'Our frequent flyer surveys show the intent to travel is extremely high, and we're seeing good leisure demand into the fourth quarter,' Joyce said. Easter was shaping as the turning point. Even as the Omicron wave swelled, forward flight bookings were strong and would only get stronger through March. The Morrison government would drop mandatory COVID-19 testing for incoming international passengers in April, though vaccination and masking requirements remained.

Thus began another wave, this one known as 'revenge travel'.

———

Not all employees were being retained, however. Even as the board prescribed healthy doses of bonus shares, Qantas management was not done using COVID as a scalpel to cut staff to the bone. Next in the sights of Alan Joyce and his industrial relations advisers were the long-haul flight attendants, whose enterprise bargaining agreement expired in June 2021.

At that time, Qantas' international division was still in cotton wool. The only long-haul operations were ad hoc repatriation flights chartered by the Australian government, and virtually all of its international crew had been stood down. But Qantas contacted the Flight Attendants' Association of Australia (FAAA) in May 2021 asking to commence negotiations for a new EBA. The union was surprised at the airline's haste, given Qantas still hadn't reached a new agreement with the short-haul flight attendants, whose EBA had expired way back in 2019.

FAAA secretary Teri O'Toole was unnerved by the early meetings between the parties, in which Qantas' negotiating team read directly from a prepared script. 'We'd say, "Hold on, that won't really work. What about this instead?" And they'd just go back and repeat the same words. It was robotic.' Qantas provided a draft proposed agreement to the union on 25 November, less than four months after the parties' first bargaining meeting – 'unheard of' speed, according to O'Toole. 'It was usually eight months or longer.'

Just as Qantas' ground handling workforce was split between the legacy staff employed directly by Qantas and the post-2009 hires employed by subsidiary QGS, the long-haul flight attendants comprised the long-serving crew employed by Qantas and those hired after 2008 by subsidiary Qantas Cabin Crew Australia (QCCA). Qantas' pay deal proposed eradicating all legacy employment terms, shunting everyone onto the inferior conditions of QCCA employees.

'We told them, "This will get voted down,"' O'Toole recalled in 2024. '"It doesn't even matter what we tell [our members], they won't support it."' Which is exactly what happened four weeks later. Put to a ballot before Christmas, 98 per cent of long-haul crew voted down the proposed EBA.

But rather than return to the negotiating table with the union, Qantas upped the ante. On 20 January 2022, the company applied to the Fair Work Commission to terminate the expired EBA. This was an incredibly aggressive move. If successful, the flight attendants would revert to the pay and conditions of the modern award, with none of the special allowances, minimum rest periods or preferential rostering guarantees they'd enjoyed for decades.

The union convinced the Fair Work Commission to send the dispute to conciliation, mediated by former deputy president Peter Sams. 'It was very hostile, it was very awkward, [and] there was no goodwill,' says Steven Reed, a veteran industrial officer at the FAAA. Qantas' negotiators would not compromise on any material point. They refused even to pause the termination application for the conciliation.

The FAAA found itself in an invidious position. Qantas was holding a gun to the heads of its members to sign an EBA they had already roundly rejected, and the leverage of protected strike action was unavailable to them: Qantas' international capacity was still at only 21 per cent of 2019 levels and if necessary the company could crew all of those flights with flight attendants from its bases in Auckland and London. Qantas management 'clearly knew they were in the driver's seat', Reed says. 'They were exploiting a once-in-a-lifetime opportunity to screw over a group of workers.' Another vanishing window of opportunity.

So in February, the FAAA wrote to its long-haul members and advised them to support the proposed agreement at an upcoming second ballot. Better to accept a shoddy offer, it explained, than face the very real risk of the EBA being terminated and crew losing 50 per cent of their income. The agreement was voted up by crew in the first week of March.

The brutality of Qantas' behaviour took the union's breath away. 'It came as a shock to me,' O'Toole confesses. 'I just couldn't believe they were negotiating and behaving like they were after we'd done so much to help and support them.'

This support was material. In order to operate repatriation flights for DFAT throughout COVID, Qantas needed relief from certain provisions of its EBA with cabin crew – specifically to allow rostering of crew at very late notice – which the FAAA granted. 'Without that,' O'Toole says, 'they wouldn't have been able to do a skerrick of recovery flying.'

O'Toole had believed, naively she admits, that 'there was no way in the world [management] would make a termination application' on its cabin crew – the face of the airline. These were Qantas' employees at the absolute frontline, who manned the emergency flights from war zones and COVID hotspots – even from Wuhan itself – and then cheerily submitted themselves to fourteen days' mandatory isolation alongside passengers in Howard Springs. On an all-too-regular basis they ran towards danger. In April 2020, twenty of the twenty-eight crew on a rescue flight from Chile contracted COVID. At that time, it was the biggest COVID workplace cluster of the nascent pandemic.

'Qantas workers are the most loyal group of people I've ever encountered as a union official,' says Emeline Gaske, the assistant national secretary of the Australian Services Union, which represents Qantas' airport customer service staff. 'They don't love management, but they love Qantas, and they love what they do.

'And so many of them have been working there for twenty years, or longer, and often they're married to someone else who works at Qantas. It's part of their identity. And I think Qantas traded on that. They took advantage of their workers' loyalty, knowing that they could get away with treating people poorly and they would likely stay because it was more than just a job to them.'

None of this is to criticise Qantas for trying to renegotiate the very generous legacy conditions of long-haul flight attendants, which were inconsistent with modern standards of labour productivity across the airline industry. Qantas had been trying to diminish them over successive EBAs. The problem was the incredibly dehumanising way Qantas had gone about achieving it this time around.

'I've been doing this since 1988,' Reed says, 'and I have never dealt with a more disreputable group of people in my life as [those] we dealt with during those negotiations. Most of them have gone on to bigger and better things – they've been promoted, received their bonuses, that sort of stuff. But I don't know how they get up and look at themselves in the mirror.'

Qantas' executive in charge of cabin crew at the time, Rachel Yangoyan, was promoted to CEO of QantasLink by Joyce's successor, Vanessa Hudson, in October 2023. In the EBA negotiations, Yangoyan was supported by Qantas' industrial relations department, which was led directly by Sonia Millen and reported to general counsel Andrew Finch – those memorable actors in the case of TWU v. Qantas in 2021.

Millen and Finch, Reed argues, 'undid everything that the previous industrial relations team had done over decades. They saw no value in relationships, in sitting down and discussing things. It was a complete departure from a collaborative working relationship to an adversarial approach.'

The company's behaviour was far removed from the solicitous, entreating tactics employed for decades by Ian Oldmeadow, the company's veteran IR adviser, who had seemingly been sidelined since warning of the huge risks of outsourcing 1,700 ground handling jobs in 2020. And it was way out of whack with the prevailing economic and commercial conditions.

As the country opened up, the physical economy – and Qantas in particular – started to boom. On 24 June 2022, the company announced it was offering $5,000 bonuses to 19,000 staff covered by EBAs, 'as the national carrier shares the benefits of its recovery'. Even this ostensible gift, however, was another attack on its own workers: employees would only receive the $5,000 if they signed up to new EBAs containing a two-year pay freeze followed by meagre 2 per cent annual pay increases. Anyone who exercised their legal right to strike for a better pay deal would become ineligible for the bonus.[14] (Bear in mind that many employees were still waiting to receive the $2,000 bonus Qantas had offered on the same terms in 2018.) Out in the real world, inflation was running at 6.1 per cent, so the real wages of Qantas' frontline workers were falling further and further behind. Indeed, Qantas' airfares were a significant contributor to rampant consumer prices – despite the company's greatly reduced cost base, domestic airfares had risen by 25 per cent and international fares by 44 per cent.[15]

In these circumstances, offering loyal workers – a significant minority of whom had spent the better part of two years stood down on government support – a 1 per cent annual pay rise for four years and a niggardly $5,000 kicker was some kind of bad joke. TWU secretary Michael Kaine teed off: 'This is not a "thank you" payment, it's more like a bribe. The strings attached to this sham payment are just more wage suppression tactics Qantas [staff have] become accustomed to under the 15-year Joyce regime.' The Australian Licensed Aircraft Engineers' Association's Steve Purvinas was even blunter:

'Our members are not that stupid. This trickery by the Qantas CEO must end.'

Luckily for employees, the airline's arbitrary 'wages policy' of 2 per cent increases became untenable virtually upon proclamation: Australia's inflation outbreak became entrenched, the airline's unholy profiteering became apparent, and Qantas workers came under almost intolerable pressure, bearing the brunt of customers' anger at the airline's sustained operational unreliability through 2022. Qantas quickly responded by adjusting the policy to 3 per cent. This, of course, made little practical difference – but it didn't need to. In reality, every pay deal struck after mid-2022 was a case of Qantas *appearing* to comply with its wages policy. The company held pay increases to 3 per cent at the base salary level, but in truth capitulated to increases far greater than that by stuffing additional money in staff allowances and other hollow logs. The unions, understandably, went along with the pretence.

The licensed aircraft engineers threatened industrial action and had a deal by Christmas. While officially their annual pay increases did not exceed 3 per cent, Qantas agreed to remove a cap on the percentage of engineers (12 per cent) who could occupy the highest salary band. This meant that a large number received pay rises, via reclassification, of greater than 30 per cent over six years.

It would have been apparent to Joyce by then that not even six or nine months of higher manpower costs would prevent financial year 2023 from being an unmitigated profit bonanza. As for their impact over later years, well, that would be someone else's problem.

———

None of this meant that Qantas was softening its approach. On 4 May 2022, the Full Court of the Federal Court dismissed Qantas' appeal against Justice Michael Lee's judgment of the previous July. The nation's leading barrister, Bret Walker SC, failed to persuade Justices Mordy Bromberg, Darryl Rangiah and Robert Bromwich of any of Qantas' five grounds for dismissing the finding that it had outsourced its ground handling function for a prohibited reason.[16]

In upholding Justice Lee's finding of illegal conduct, they found that 'Qantas has not made any serious attempt to demonstrate any actual error in his Honour's assessment of the deficiencies in [Andrew] David's evidence ... [and instead are] seeking to trivialise the shortcomings his Honour identified. This falls well short of establishing any appealable error.'

Moreover, Justice Lee's judgment was 'a character, credit and reliability assessment of a kind that, when done properly and thoroughly as in this case, is very difficult for an appeal court to gainsay'. Qantas hadn't landed a blow. Not so much as a dissenting murmur could be discerned from the bench.

The Full Court provided its written judgment to the parties at 10:50am. Being more than 18,000 words in length, it would have taken an hour merely to skim, let alone properly digest or discuss. And indeed, upon reading the judgment, any serious person would conclude that Qantas' position was hopeless. Yet by 11:30am, the company had issued a public statement that 'Qantas will be seeking to appeal the judgment by the Full Federal Court to the High Court'.

Pause to consider the hubris, and what this says about the company's approach to the law. Qantas' case had now been heard by four judges. The persuasive success of its arguments, put by the best lawyers money could buy, stood at zero per cent. Yet Alan Joyce and his chief lawyer Andrew Finch reflected on their cascading wipeout for a matter of minutes before launching boldly into the next and final avenue of appeal. They could not have been properly advised by counsel.[17] The judgment had not given them the smallest hope of success. Their course of action was pre-determined and their position was intransigent: if we lose, we will appeal. We are Qantas, so the courts are wrong until they spit out the answer we want.

Finch had little choice at this juncture but to remain steadfast. Indeed, his reputation internally depended on it. He had led them way too deep into the mire to propose turning back. But Joyce was the boss, not Andrew Finch. It was Joyce saying, Everyone, Andrew's got this! Finch was enabled by his CEO having seemingly lost the ability to be wrong. And their pre-programmed escalation to the High Court did not suggest an environment around Joyce of sober debate.

There was also a potential financial incentive for Joyce to appeal. His final suite of bonuses would be determined against the profitability of the company in the 2023 financial year (which would commence on 1 July 2022, just seven weeks after the Full Court's ruling). The last thing Joyce would have wanted was for the case to return to Justice Lee to determine the quantum of compensation and penalties payable by Qantas, and for that bill – potentially upwards of $300 million – to impair Qantas' 2023 profit. Even ahead of Justice Lee enumerating the damages, Qantas' auditor could force the company to make a provision for them in the 2023 accounts, which would have the same (accounting) effect as actually paying them.

So long as another appeal was under way, however, the legal outcome remained sufficiently uncertain for Qantas to avoid making an accounting provision for it. The High Court could take another year or more to hear and decide the case. That would likely put the verdict in the 2024 or even 2025 financial year, making it another problem – on the growing laundry list of them – that would be someone else's.

But it's at this point that the equation started to change. Using the law as a weapon can work for a while, but it can also draw attention to the law's deficiencies.

The FAAA might have lost the battle for its long-haul flight attendants, but it continued to fight the war, pursuing the matter through the Australian Council of Trade Unions and the new Albanese government, elected in May 2022, not even three months after cabin crew had begrudgingly ratified their new EBA. 'We went everywhere and we lobbied as hard as we could,' O'Toole recalls. 'How can you have a law that allows termination because you're losing the negotiation? This wasn't termination for the right reasons, it was: You'll agree to give up everything or we'll give you worse. You'll go on the award, you'll get 80 cents more per hour than a McDonald's worker to run towards the fire.'

The ACTU and the FAAA certainly had the new government's ear. A month before its Jobs and Skills Summit, convened in September 2022 largely as a piece of political theatre, workplace relations minister Tony Burke blasted companies like Qantas that had resorted to mid-bargaining termination. 'To me, this appears to be more than a loophole, it's a rort – and I'm disgusted that it's even being tried.'

Employer groups and large company bosses, including Alan Joyce, who turned up at the Great Hall of Parliament House to (ironically) negotiate in good faith, were ambushed by Burke's proposals, which contained new restrictions on employers' ability to terminate EBAs. The jobs summit turned out to be the launchpad for radical industrial relations legislation, which would restore trade union powers last seen in Australian law in the 1970s.

Once the first tranche of changes was passed by the Senate and bedded down, Burke launched a second wave, including Same Job, Same Pay legislation which became law in December 2023. The law's mandate was self-explanatory: henceforth, companies could not save money by creating subsidiaries to employ new workers on pay and conditions inferior to those of its existing workers.

This wouldn't affect Qantas' current pay deals but would start to take effect as new EBAs were negotiated. But under this law, Qantas could no longer pay the employees of QCCA (or QGS, if they hadn't all been sacked) less than QAL employees.

Qantas' fifteen years of 'fragmentation' inspired the Same Job, Same Pay laws, ACTU secretary Sally McManus told me. 'Qantas were responsible for bringing a lot of the IR laws on the heads of the rest of corporate Australia. They're part of the reason why the legislation was even called the Closing Loopholes [Bill] and now they'll have to unwind a whole lot of their labour hire arrangements. Qantas was a massive liability for the employer push to oppose improving workers' rights, because [the airline] became a poster child for why those rights were necessary.'

The Business Council of Australia – led by CEO Jennifer Westacott and with Alan Joyce sitting on its board – tried to push back against the changes, but in McManus' characterisation, the magic had worn off. She traced the commencement of his spell back to Joyce's grounding of the fleet in 2011. 'There became this thinking [after the grounding] that he takes the big risks but he gets them right and therefore we've got to continue to back him. I think they applied that logic to every circumstance and that was a bad decision. It just led to overreach. They did not consider the seeds they were sowing and what they would grow into.'

When the former TWU and AWU national secretaries Tony Sheldon and Linda White became senators, Qantas found it had made enemies in the wrong places. Says McManus, 'With other CEOs, usually, there's a moderation around the edges in terms of relationships, or thinking about the consequences of winning a bloody battle. Normally, there will be some sort of consideration as to whether it's the right thing to do on a morality basis, but also [consideration of] whether it's going to cause damage *beyond* that battle. Joyce just didn't do that. He gave not an inch.'

By late 2022, the power balance in industrial relations had plainly shifted away from Qantas. While this change had arrived too late for the airline's long-haul flight attendants, it came just in time for their short-haul colleagues. Qantas's tactics on the domestic EBA were almost identical to the long-haul dispute: proposing a draft agreement that crew would never vote for. 'In retrospect,' O'Toole says, 'it's obvious that Qantas had been setting up to terminate that agreement as well.' When the government's new IR laws dismantled the Fair Work Commission's powers to terminate expired EBAs without the workers' consent, that tactic fell apart.

What had also changed since February was the leverage equation. With Qantas flying at 97 per cent of its pre-COVID domestic capacity in November 2022, any strike action would throw the airline's operations into chaos over the peak summer holidays, when Australian carriers generate a disproportionate amount of their annual revenue. In a protected action ballot that month, 98 per cent of Qantas' short-haul crew voted in favour of taking industrial action against the company.

'We were preparing to go on strike right before Christmas, but we didn't need to because we got a call out of the blue from

Ian Oldmeadow,' O'Toole says. 'He was brought in to save the day, frankly. There's no two ways about it.'

O'Toole and FAAA vice-president Angela McManus rushed off to meet with Oldmeadow and his long-time collaborator John Farrow in an unmarked room at the Sofitel in Sydney's Darling Harbour. 'It was completely different to everything that we'd [recently] experienced,' O'Toole recalls. 'It was three or four meetings and it was a real negotiation.' The parties never met at the same location twice and the meeting rooms were never booked in Qantas' name. But Qantas was paying for lunch, so when the menus came, as an act of defiance the FAAA officers made sure to pick the most expensive thing on the menu. 'I think it was the prawn linguine, but if they'd had lobster, I'd have had lobster every day,' O'Toole jokes.

Justine Oldmeadow joined the final meeting, at the Holiday Inn Mascot – a short walk from both the FAAA's poky secretariat and Qantas' modern headquarters – to draft the clauses of the new agreement. 'We sat down and struck a deal in good faith very, very quickly, and that stopped the industrial action at Christmas.' After a two-year pay freeze, short-haul cabin crew would get a 23 per cent pay rise over four years. Inflation was running at 7.8 per cent.

The union understood that, remarkably, Oldmeadow was negotiating with Joyce's sanction but unbeknownst to Qantas' industrial relations team. 'We believe Sonia [Millen] didn't know about it, that possibly nobody at Qantas [besides Joyce] knew about it. I guess it doesn't matter now.'[18]

Not Match Fit

April–July 2022

Friday 8 April 2022 was the final day of term one in Victoria and New South Wales. In addition to being the start of the Easter school holidays, it was also the weekend of the Formula One Australian Grand Prix in Melbourne. It was the nation's biggest day of air travel in more than two years – the first real test of airline operations resumed at full scale. And it was a catastrophe.

News outlets Australia-wide led their bulletins and home pages that day with stories of chaos at Sydney airport's domestic terminals, where queues of bewildered passengers snaked interminably around the check-in halls and out onto the footpath. The wait to get through security was ninety minutes. When the queues first became a problem the previous evening, Sydney Airport CEO Geoff Culbert had been straight out on the airwaves fronting the issue.

'We're facing a perfect storm at the moment,' Culbert explained. 'Traffic numbers are picking up, travellers are inexperienced after two years of not travelling, and the close contact rules are making it hard to fill shifts and staff the airport. We encourage everyone to get to the airport early and we ask everyone to be patient as the industry gets back on its feet.'

It was Sydney airport's responsibility to manage security screening in its domestic terminals, where the airlines were merely tenants. For decades, the airport had engaged Sydney Night Patrol to conduct screening; in 2018, SNP was swallowed by Certis, a Singaporean multinational, meaning that although Certis employees were

Australian taxpayers and union members, they didn't qualify for JobKeeper because Certis was a foreign-owned company. So in 2020 Certis had laid them all off and in 2022 it was struggling to replace them in a red hot labour market.[1]

Just like Qantas crew, many former airport security agents had found other, better jobs since 2020. Many had been temporary migrants (including foreign students), half a million of whom left Australia during COVID. The huge reduction in that cohort was making it nearly impossible for employers to fill entry level jobs right across the economy. On top of this, the New South Wales government's close contact rules were every day consigning tens of thousands of workers to home quarantine at a moment's notice. Certis didn't have a hope of fully staffing the security lanes.

Enter Alan Joyce, to whom all of the above excuses were readily available. He was also free to refer all enquiries to Sydney airport, but instead he called a press conference and uttered the immortal words: 'I think our customers are not match fit.

'I went through the airport on Wednesday and people forget they need to take out their laptops, they have to take out their aerosols, and the amount of delays that are actually happening because of that,' he marvelled.

This was a stupendous unforced error by Joyce, which he quickly understood. Responding to the immediate backlash, he explained, 'Just to be clear, I'm not "blaming" passengers. Of course it's not their fault. I was asked what the factors were and why the queues are so long at airports. And I explained the multiple reasons.' Joyce had also cited as reasons 'nearly 50 per cent absenteeism' and 'a lot of the security people [being] new [so] they're going to be cautious'. Still, the hellish day of travel for thousands of Qantas and Jetstar customers now included – as a complimentary upgrade – the CEO's judgement on their own culpability.

Culbert had also partly blamed 'inexperienced' travellers, but the savage blowback was reserved for Joyce, whose daft performance had been for the benefit of the TV news cameras. The plain fact was that half of the security lanes in each terminal were closed due to a lack of staff. Rusty customers were simply not a defining factor in the queues, so why say it?

That very afternoon, New South Wales health minister, Brad Hazzard, signed a new public health order exempting all air transport workers from the close contact rules. Victoria did the same four days later.[2] Yet the airport chaos only deepened. By the Easter weekend (14 April), it had spread from Sydney to Melbourne, Adelaide and Brisbane, and the disruption extended well beyond mere queues. Dozens of flights were cancelled, hundreds more were delayed, and Qantas' rate of mishandled bags exploded to more than double the pre-COVID average. Planes were leaving without any bags at all, such was the malfunction of ground handling services. Meanwhile, customers attempting to contact Qantas by phone were left on hold for multiple hours. Sydney airport could not be blamed for any of that.

The Australian government's Bureau of Infrastructure and Transport Research Economics, which releases airline statistics each month, reported that in April 2022, 64 per cent of all airlines' domestic flights arrived on time (versus the long-term average of 82 per cent) and 4 per cent of flights were cancelled (against the long-term average of 2 per cent). Qantas and Jetstar lagged behind the industry, with 59 per cent of their flights arriving on time, while Virgin's rate was 66 per cent, itself hardly flash.[3]

'These are the worst on time performance figures recorded since recording commenced in November 2003,' the bureau said.

They would only get worse.

Qantas customers in 2022 could be excused for feeling gaslit. Flights appeared and disappeared; tickets had been turned into credits and then the credits couldn't be redeemed; the website and app didn't function and the phones went unanswered. At the airports, flights were hours late (or just cancelled), service was abominable and bags were lost. Yet all the while Qantas assured us, usually via public statement rather than personal communication, that all of this was normal, that there was nothing to see here – at least nothing that was Qantas' fault. Were we all going mad?

This chapter explores the reality, with facts and figures about what passengers experienced in those months (which felt like years) and why. It wasn't you, as it turns out, it was them.

The leaders of Qantas' unions were in no doubt about the underlying cause of the airline's inability to deliver a reliable operation. They were 'entirely predictable', said the TWU's Michael Kaine. He told the press that the employees of foreign-owned companies denied JobKeeper had 'left the sector entirely and now don't want to come back to casual, low-paid jobs with bad conditions'. Emeline Gaske of the Australian Services Union, which represented call centre and airport customer service staff, was just as pointed: 'These problems started with Qantas offshoring local jobs and cutting in-airport customer service [in 2021] under the cover of the pandemic.' That put huge extra pressure on call centres and Qantas didn't add any new call centre staff. The ASU was in talks with Qantas, Gaske added, because service staff were 'exhausted and working beyond breaking point'.

Teri O'Toole didn't hold back either: 'Qantas sacked 1,800 ground staff workers, the baggage handlers and the people who drive tugs, and then the catering has been outsourced to dnata, so Qantas has deliberately made these changes and now, to have the CEO say it's the passengers' fault because they're not taking deodorant out of their bags at screening – it's just ludicrous.'

Safe inside their reality-distortion force field, Qantas management maintained full denial mode. Since at least March 2020, Qantas had been assigning 100 per cent of any blame for its own shortcomings to counterparties and/or external forces. Why would it change a PR strategy that had worked so well to date? 'We reject the [unions'] claims that these disruptions are linked to the decision eighteen months ago to outsource our ground handling at airports,' a spokesperson for the airline said. Other airlines in other countries, they said, were having the same problems.

Qantas was speaking in half-truths. While the airline was undoubtedly crippled by acute levels of employee sick leave, illegally firing its ground handling workforce was also having an effect. Qantas had to rely on external providers which simply could not find the workers needed to provide adequate levels of service.

'They were paying ordinary money so they were not attracting people at a time the economy was starting to boom again,' says Captain Tony Lucas, president of the Australian and International Pilots Association. The workers they could find, Lucas says, 'were poorly trained, inexperienced, not well paid and not turning up to work – or legitimately sick with COVID.

'When we had Qantas baggage handlers, we were never short of staff because it was a good job that paid well. Swissport, dnata, Menzies – all of those [companies] that we now contract for those baggage services – they pay like crap. So if it's raining and you're a casual baggage handler, you might just not go to work today because you can't be bothered getting drenched for 25 bucks an hour.'

Virgin's domestic ground handling was still performed in-house: not even the private equity mercenaries who bought Virgin out of insolvency considered it prudent to eliminate that workforce. And Virgin never skipped a beat. Neither did Jetstar, yet its ground handling *had* been outsourced in 2020. The difference was that, compared to Jetstar and Virgin, Qantas had a much higher proportion of passengers with connecting flights and baggage – or, in 2022, *missed* connecting baggage.

Qantas had gained a unit cost advantage, sure, but when it was mishandling 850 bags a day and its customers were in uproar, that was a completely false economy. In April, Virgin mishandled 4.2 per 1,000 bags – consistent with its pre-COVID average. Qantas' mishandled bag rate was 17.4 per 1,000 bags, more than double its own pre-COVID average of 6.3 per 1,000. In every single month up to and including December, Qantas' mishandled bag rate was usually triple – and never less than double – Virgin's and Jetstar's, which peaked at just 5.7 per 1,000 bags.

For similar reasons, Virgin's flight punctuality was persistently superior throughout 2022. Qantas and Jetstar flights were held up not just by the anarchy in loading and unloading bags onto planes, but also in the towing of those planes on and off the airport gates –

mission-critical tasks that had also been outsourced. According to Tony Lucas, in those chaotic months, Qantas pilots were invariably prevented from departing because nobody was available to tow the aircraft. Qantas had in 2020 also reduced the number of cabin crew on a peak 737 flight from five to four, so there was now one flight attendant at the gate scanning boarding passes, two at the front of the aircraft, and just one in economy getting 90 per cent of the passengers seated and the overhead lockers shut. This permanent Jetstar-isation measure had an obvious impact on Qantas' on-time departures.[4]

It was the same story across numerous specialist workforces in Qantas. Many aspects of airline operations are highly manual and so depend on the know-how of trained and experienced labour. Retaining these people was precisely what JobKeeper was designed for, and yet a huge cohort of experienced labour had decided during COVID to leave the aviation industry (or at least Qantas) for good.

Crewing international flights was nearly impossible. Not only did Qantas have to recruit and train hundreds of new pilots and cabin crew, it also had to retrain the existing ones. Qantas had said in April 2021 that 'preparations for the resumption of international flights in late October are continuing, including reactivating aircraft and training employees', yet those preparations and training were patently inadequate. Around 2,500 cabin crew had to be either initialised or refreshed in service and emergency procedures training – the latter needed to be renewed every six months for every flight attendant.

The flight attendants' union had urged Qantas in 2020 to keep up the mandatory training of its stood-down members through the pandemic. 'These people were being paid JobKeeper and then AviationKeeper,' the FAAA's Steven Reed says, 'so we said [to Qantas], "Keep them doing their emergency procedures and keep their skills current." And [Qantas] said, "No, we're not doing that." When they had this mad rush for stand-up, it all turned to shit because nobody was trained.'

As the international ramp-up continued, the pressure on Qantas' crew training capability was immense. In financial year 2023 (starting 1 July 2022), Qantas trained six times the volume of new recruits than in 2018. This caused a shortage of cabin crew safety trainers, whose accreditation with the safety regulator takes twelve months. After the cancellation of the new flight training centre at King Street, Mascot in 2020 and the demolition of the legacy centre on the Qantas jet base in 2022, Qantas was left with no permanent facility in Sydney with a pool for mandatory training on escape slides and life rafts. Crew would now permanently be bussed to Bankstown in Sydney's southwest to train at a Toll facility. At terrific expense, 500 cabin crew were sent to Abu Dhabi in 2022 and 2023 for up to ten days' training at an Etihad facility.

High numbers of brand new recruits were rostered on flights together, leading to poor inflight service levels. As a quick fix, Qantas opened a rehiring round in mid-2022 for former cabin crew who'd taken redundancy in 2020. Around 250 experienced flight attendants – their departures having been counted as a 'structural' reduction to the airline's cost base – rejoined the company. They needed retraining, of course, so they too were jammed into the airline's clogged training pipeline.

The retraining of Qantas pilots was an even greater debacle. The pilots' union had also urged Qantas management in 2020, and again in 2021, to maintain the training of its stood-down long-haul pilots throughout the shutdown of Qantas International. Captain Lucas recalls that Qantas' flight operations department 'was very aware of the risk to [the airline's] ability to restart as a result of pilots not being current, but the decision was made higher up that the airline wasn't going to spend money on that'. Qantas did run a pilot preservation program in 2021, which marginally shortened retraining times in 2022, but it was too little, too late.

Entirely consistent with their pay incentives, the airline's executives were obsessed with cost-cutting over a three-year time horizon, yet when it came to expenditure necessary for the company to function, they couldn't see five feet from their faces. 'They were so concerned about containing costs but actually, it would have been cheaper in the end,' says Lucas, had they 'kept flight crews current by bringing them in [during the shutdown] for a week every two months'.

Qantas pilots run on a seniority system by aircraft type, with the double-decker A380 at the top of the pyramid. Fifty-five (of 105) A380 captains took redundancy or early retirement during COVID. Under the pilots' EBA, Qantas is limited to recruiting new A380 captains from within its pool of existing pilots – mostly captains from the 787 and the A330 fleets. The appointment of one A380 captain can create up to nine internal vacancies (though about five is normal), as everyone shuffles up a position. To fill seats for, say, ten new A380 captains in 2022, ten 787 or A330 captains need to be promoted and trained.[5] To replace them, ten 787 or A330 first officers need to be promoted and trained.[6] To replace *them*, ten second officers need to be promoted and trained, and to replace *them*, ten new second officers would need to be hired off the street. So for each new A380 captain, there was a domino effect of promotion and training. 'All of a sudden,' Lucas says, 'demand on your training system is extreme.'

Not only did Qantas need to replace the departed A380 captains, it also needed fifty new A330 captains, to replace the fifty-five who had taken redundancy or early retirement during COVID.[7] Lucas, an A330 captain himself, calls training something like sixty new A330 captains for 2022 'completely unheard of. That promotional pathway is about thirteen simulator sessions plus [supervised] line flying,' Lucas says. For sixty captains, that's more than 800 sim sessions (or 3,200 sim hours), then hundreds of hours of real flying, plus mandatory rest days. 'Even if you started training your first pilot in June [2021], you wouldn't have been able to get fifty new captains ready by December,' Lucas says. 'Qantas didn't advertise [internally for those positions] until very late August and didn't actually start training those people until November, so of course we were short [in 2022].'

That's before we even get to the training of the first officers to replace the captains, the second officers to replace the first officers, and the new second officers – all of whom needed many hours in the same overrun A330 simulators. Or the issue at the top of the pyramid: training the promoted A330 captains to fly the A380s.

And of course pilots in training are taken off the roster. Lucas says, 'A training course is at least three months, because you do a month of ground school, a month of simulator training and then a month of line training. Those first two months the pilot is not productive, because they're not operating an aeroplane.' Even spaced out over a year, removing 180 pilots from the flying roster of a single aircraft type for two months creates an acute shortage – before taking into account the same problem for the 787 and A380 rosters, and the crushing effect in 2022 of COVID illness on those rosters.

An engineering backlog also had a material effect on Qantas' operations in 2022. The global aviation industry – like many other equipment-heavy industries – was suffering a chronic shortage of spare parts. Just as the pandemic caused an outflow of skilled workers from the airline business, so too had niche manufacturers in the supply chains of Boeing and Airbus switched to making components for other machinery – and they weren't coming back. Parts that once took hours to source suddenly took a week or more.

Leading into 2022, Qantas had allowed the depletion of its parts inventory to critical levels. 'All of those departments that estimate how many parts you need in stock were undermanned themselves and weren't on top of the fact they needed more spare fricken' auxiliary power units or flight control computers and all of the stocks just dwindled,' recalls Steve Purvinas of the Australian Licensed Aircraft Engineers' Association.

All aircraft have a 'minimum equipment list' approved by the Civil Aviation Safety Authority but can continue flying for up to ten days with minor inoperable items, or 'deferred defects'. But a lack of spare parts and a shortage of engineers meant that Qantas aircraft were routinely hitting their ten-day limit with deferred defects and being forced out of service. Then when aircraft were removed from flying to act as back-ups and relieve pressure on the disintegrating flight schedule, those were often mined by engineers for emergency parts and left unserviceable. According to Purvinas, 'You start treating the plane like a Christmas tree and taking off all the baubles but then when you go to use it there are twelve fucken' parts missing and you can't fly it.'

The planes might not have been able to fly, but the chickens were coming home to roost.

—

On 23 June, ahead of the next school holiday period, Qantas assured its customers it would do better. 'Since April, Qantas and Jetstar have recruited more than 1,000 operational team members, including cabin crew, airport customer service, pilots and engineers. Hundreds of additional contact centre staff have helped reduce Qantas' average call wait times to below pre-COVID levels.'

Implicit in this statement was that Joyce had sacked too many people in 2020 and 2021 to satisfactorily resource a fully functioning airline in 2022. 'He really screwed the pooch there,' O'Toole lamented in 2024. But Joyce had been highly incentivised to sack so many staff: of the $1 billion of annual costs he'd promised to rip out of the airline, 60 per cent (or $600 million) were 'manpower' expenses.

Steve Purvinas says the inclusion of engineers in Qantas' boast of 1,000 new recruits was 'deceptive'. 'If they hired any at all, it wouldn't have been more than a dozen, if that. It was nothing near what they made redundant because there was no one to get. The guys all moved onto other industries or retired. There is no spare fucken' tree of engineers that you can pluck from. Four years for your apprenticeship, probably ten years 'til you get a licence – there's no magical fucken' solution.'

Qantas had just over 1,000 licensed aircraft mechanical engineers in June 2020 when it made 339 of them redundant. That left 683. Even by 2024, the number was only back to 705.

The number of airport customer service agents employed by Qantas had also barely risen since the airline laid off 500 – almost a quarter – of them in 2020 and 2021. 'The majority of our workforce is part-time,' Emeline Gaske of the ASU explained in 2024, 'so we were saying to Qantas, "Flex them up" – and [the staff] had room to flex up. But Qantas didn't want to pay for it. Qantas insisted that they had adequate staffing at the airports.' That was certainly not the experience of passengers seeking assistance in airport terminals in that period.

Also deceptive was the company claiming it had 'hundreds of additional contact centre staff'. Qantas employed around a hundred people in its sole Australian call centre, in Hobart, and a hundred people in its Auckland call centre. According to Gaske, 'They might have hired eight or ten additional people in Hobart, but we're not talking about a material change.'

These 'hundreds' were in fact added to the capacity of Qantas' outsourced call centres in Fiji, the Philippines and South Africa. In 2022, those staff were not well trained in Qantas policies or its ticketing systems. Qantas callers were triaged. 'You entered your frequent flyer number and the premium clients got sent to Hobart and everyone else got sent offshore,' Gaske says. 'But those offshore centres had not been set up to do the work they needed to do. Any complex enquiries would get sent back to Hobart.'

Hobart, predictably, was overwhelmed. Meanwhile, on social media and frequent flyer community websites, reports abounded of call dropouts, and offshore agents providing incorrect information and even accidentally cancelling customers' bookings.

Qantas boasted that calls were being answered, on average, faster than before COVID, but what about the average time for customers to achieve a resolution of their issue? That wasn't a metric Qantas contemplated publicly.

Qantas call centres were partly so overwhelmed in 2022 due to the huge number of flight cancellations, with waves of customers contacting the airline to rebook on services convenient to them (often indisposed to the alternative flights Qantas had auto-shunted them onto), and partly due to the widespread dysfunctionality of Qantas' COVID flight credits. The year had begun with Qantas and Jetstar owing their customers $1.4 billion in these credits. By 30 June the balance had fallen to $1.1 billion, and when 2022 ended, the balance of outstanding credits was still $800 million.

Bear in mind, around 80 per cent of credit-holders were entitled to a full refund, not just a new booking.[8] But how many of them knew that? Customers who received credits in March and April 2020 (which was the overwhelming majority of them) received an email in June 2020 – which the ACCC forced Qantas to send – containing 'a reminder that your other options include a refund'. But blink and they would've missed it. Even after that, whenever borders closed and Qantas mass-cancelled flights, it would automatically convert all affected bookings to flight credits and email customers with the oblique, buried aside: 'for other options, including a refund, contact us'. By its cute, even tricky, language and by omission, Qantas had ensured that most credit-holders wrongly believed they had to use their flight credit for a new flight booking.

As for customers who cancelled a non-flexible booking on a flight that Qantas did not subsequently cancel, they *did* have to use their credit for a new booking – their credits were not eligible for refund. They could at least use their credits towards any new flight, or multiple flights, they wished. But in March 2021, when domestic flying had momentarily returned to normal, Qantas toughened the conditions. Henceforth, those customers could only redeem their credits for a single seat of equal or higher value to the original booking. This was known as the 'single use' or 'equal or higher' condition, and it helped Qantas burn through its credits at a higher rate by deflating their value.

The way it worked was that if you had a $300 credit, the credit booking engine showed you only fares higher than $300, even though the regular booking engine might be offering $100 fares on the very same flight. Unsurprisingly, this caused rampant customer anger and confusion, especially because the condition had never been communicated prominently in the process of purchasing the original ticket. The rule also created distortions. If you had a $900 credit from a cancelled Brisbane–Perth flight and you went to use it for a Brisbane–Sydney flight, you'd be offered only seats costing $900 or more, even though you'd just seen $179 seats on that flight on qantas.com. People became irate because they felt they were being royally ripped off – and they were.[9]

The condition applied only intermittently through the pandemic, though as with refund eligibility, Qantas' communications about it were highly confusing, verging on misleading.[10] Even in periods where the condition did not apply, Qantas' flight credit confirmation email informed credit-holders that it did. Well, kind of. The email stated: 'Flight credits can only be used towards a fare of equal or higher value than the original fare you purchased.' It then stated: 'If your original booking was made before 31 December 2020, and you were due to travel on a Qantas flight between 31 January 2020 and 31 March 2021, your flight credit can be used across multiple future bookings provided there is credit remaining.' Plainly, these two sentences contradicted each other. Customers reported receiving similarly confusing or incorrect advice by telephone from offshore call centres. How could Qantas customers possibly have been expected to understand their rights?

Qantas permanently reinstated the 'equal or higher' condition on 1 October 2021 and deemed any credits issued after that date to be regular flight credits, with pre-COVID terms and conditions. It was grotesquely early to be effecting that change, with Melbourne and Sydney both still in lockdown and the Omicron wave yet to rip through the community. By 30 June 2022, Qantas already owed customers $200 million in these 'regular' credits, but that was the last and only time their balance was disclosed.

For the vast majority of credit-holders who were entitled to a refund, actually getting one out of Qantas was a whole other story. To describe the process as an ordeal would not be doing it justice. Undoubtedly, many customers will have extracted a refund without incident, but the sheer cumulative magnitude of the outrage from customers who were forced to go to the most extraordinary lengths to get their money back, and who often still failed, was a latent cultural event. It wallpapered social media and was reported widely by the traditional media. (The ABC's coverage was particularly strong. My personal favourite was its interview with a Newcastle resident who made twenty-six calls, of sixty hours' total duration, to redeem his COVID credits for two flights to Hamilton Island.) Across Australia, Qantas call centre war stories were being swapped around office water coolers, at weekend barbecues and in WhatsApp groups. And while it peaked in 2022, this issue was not fleeting. Securing a refund was gruelling from 2020 right through until 2023, and that created tens of thousands of passionate Qantas detractors across the nation. Qantas totally failed to grasp this.

To get a refund, first you had to apply for one. That meant getting a Qantas representative on the telephone, which in 2022 was practically impossible. Reports abounded of people waiting multiple hours – in some cases more than ten hours – on hold for a Qantas agent. Customers reported being cut off and having to start again at the end of the queue.

Qantas agents, if you could reach one, couldn't actually process your refund. They could only refer it for manual processing, the wait for which was up to sixteen weeks. Many customers had to call back once those weeks had elapsed because their refund still hadn't materialised; their application had been lost, or never existed. Customers reported having to reapply multiple times. From April 2022, you could also initiate the refund process on qantas.com, but first you had to know you could do that. Then, if the refund never turned up, you had to phone Qantas anyway.

Another cohort of customers couldn't even get this far. They knew they had COVID credits but couldn't find the email containing their details among the hundreds of emails Qantas sent them about wine and every other manner of product.[11] Often, the Qantas agent couldn't find the credit in the system without the credit reference number contained in that email. Just as often, that email had been junked, or was never received in the first place. That seemed to be a particularly common occurrence for holders of Qantas Passes, a type of credit hosted externally by global travel payments platform UATP. Qantas transferred about $400 million of its COVID credits into this system, which many other airlines globally used for their COVID credits. Qantas Passes were like burner debit cards for Qantas flights and had greater flexibility than Qantas' own credits – for instance, they could be used across multiple passengers.

To use a Qantas Pass, you needed not only the Qantas Pass number, but also a unique password (different, naturally, to your frequent flyer password) included in the email you may or may not have received from UATP, and which, if you did receive, you probably confused with the earlier email Qantas may or may not have sent you when your credit was originally issued as a normal Qantas COVID credit.

Qantas Passes were redeemed via a UATP booking engine rather than via qantas.com. As I wrote in 2023 in the *AFR*, 'If you have a PhD in Advanced Enigmatology, you may just manage to extract these data and unite them with the booking engine. Completing this on your iPhone is interchangeable with NASA's admission test. If you are older than 65, your chances are zero. If you are busy, you'll never outlast the rigmarole. You can always call the dedicated service centre, if you've got all day and all night. Credit-holders are far more likely to end up with a broken spirit than a flight reservation.

'These systems are visually impossible. Gambling companies have analysts who adapt user interfaces to seduce customers into clicking all the way through transactions. The airline appears to be using similar experts but deploying their acumen in the reverse. The page keeps timing out? That's not a bug, it's a feature!'

This was all so punishing that customers simply gave up. They gave up in untold numbers and quite reasonably found themselves wondering if it was all *designed* to make them give up. Every step of every process was counterintuitive or chaotic. As Qantas rightly pointed out, no airline's systems were designed for the en masse cancellation of $1.6 billion of bookings, but there was also the nagging truth that Qantas was highly incentivised to make its systems unworkable.

These weren't small amounts of money for customers. Forty per cent of Qantas credits had balances of $500 or more.[12] Logic says that if 800,000 people understood they were each entitled to a refund of $500 or more, and retrieving the money was feasible, then those $400 million of credits would have evaporated within days.

Having $1 billion of other people's money left over as interest-free working capital was a tremendous boon but I don't suggest that Qantas' COVID credits fiasco was entirely a case of malintent by the company. Misfortune and ineptitude were also significant factors. About 40 per cent of total Qantas credits were for tickets booked through travel agents and other third parties. Those customers had to endure *their* processes, which were often just as bad. What's also true is that most major airlines globally dealt with their revenue from cancelled pandemic-era flights in this same way or similarly. However,

'Everyone was doing it' has never been a compelling defence. Qantas customers had absolute, not relative, expectations of the national carrier, a point this book will shortly return to.

Qantas would never say as much publicly, but it simply could not countenance repaying $1.6 billion of unflown ticket revenue in March 2020, because it thought it needed that cash to keep itself afloat.

And in 2022, what Qantas needed was *new* cash. The airline didn't want to fill its planes with passengers on prepaid tickets, with people who weren't providing new cashflow – not if it could be helped.

Keeping Qantas customers trapped in Qantas currency enabled Qantas to deflate its liability to them – either totally, by engineering non-redemption, or partly, by creating Central American levels of inflation in the goods the currency could be exchanged for: airfares. (Though Qantas was hardly a lone airline ramping its prices coming out of COVID.)

The credits were just another lever Alan Joyce used to preference his shareholders over his customers. Even shareholders thought so. Pendal's Crispin Murray laments Qantas getting 'caught up in trying to deliver the financial turnaround of all turnarounds and just miss[ing] some bread-and-butter business decisions. The COVID credits, to me, was the obvious one. Why not say that they won't expire? Why argue about them given all the other problems with delays, cancellations, baggage? It felt crazy because it [the credits] was something they could fix in one go, whereas the others were complicated to fix.'

———

Those problems continued to be complicated. Despite having '20 per cent more team members on standby' and 15 per cent more (third-party) baggage handlers ready to cover for COVID illness, Qantas' operations in the July school holidays did not improve compared to Easter; they were decidedly worse. COVID cases were again on the rise, as was the first widespread winter flu since 2019. A woeful 47 per cent of Qantas flights arrived on time in the month of July 2022, the fourth consecutive month of schedule disarray. This trailed Virgin at

53 per cent and Jetstar at 52 per cent. Qantas' rate of mishandled bags had not budged from record highs since April. Flight cancellations were also haywire. In May, the industry's cancellations had risen to 5.6 per cent but Qantas led the pack, cancelling 7.6 per cent of its flights.

By June, total flight cancellations were 6 per cent, again led by Qantas, at 8 per cent – quadruple the long-term average. Qantas' position only began to turn around in July, when Jetstar cancelled 9 per cent of its flights, Virgin cancelled 8 per cent, and Qantas had improved to 6 per cent.

The Australian Competition and Consumer Commission would later sue Qantas for false, misleading or deceptive conduct over its so-called ghost flights in this May to July period, alleging it had continued selling tickets for more than 8,000 flights that it had already decided to cancel. Qantas had failed to promptly tell ticketholders on those flights that their flights had been cancelled. We will return to this case in a later chapter, but the lawsuit was the sole formal repercussion for Qantas' abject failures of its operations in this period. It was implicit in the allegation that Qantas had been more focused on selling tickets for flights than on the viability of operating them. Unambiguously, in light of its severe shortage of healthy and trained staff, Qantas' attempted flying levels moving into mid-2022 were completely unrealistic.

As Tony Lucas recalls, 'We were trying to ramp up capacity but we just didn't have the staff to do it either above the wing, below the wing or in the aeroplanes.'

And why would that be? Qantas had a compelling reason to maximise its flying, irrespective of the chaos its customers were enduring: money. Finally it was gushing through the door – and as a result, the company managed to pay off $1.5 billion – or nearly 30 per cent – of its net debt in those first six months of 2022. International airfares to and from Australia had skyrocketed. 'On average, across all classes including economy, we're seeing the cost of flights sitting about 40 per cent higher than pre-COVID prices,' Flight Centre reported in June.

Left to their own devices, airfares are a product of demand and supply.[13] Demand had risen across the economy, driving rampant consumer price inflation and, in response, interest rate increases by the Reserve Bank; travel demand was particularly pronounced in what was dubbed 'revenge travel'. Having been cooped up for two years, people were desperate to hit the road. Supply of international seats, meanwhile, was returning to Australia sluggishly. Some airlines, particularly the mainland Chinese carriers, hadn't returned at all. Others were flying at nowhere near their pre-COVID levels. Singapore Airlines, the second-largest international carrier to and from Australia, had brought back 85 per cent of its 2019 seats, as had Qatar Airways. But the fourth-largest, Emirates, was at 63 per cent, and the smaller players even lower: Air New Zealand was at 60 per cent, Etihad was at 38 per cent, and Cathay Pacific was at just 11 per cent.

Yet Qantas and Jetstar, as the largest and third-largest international carriers, had the biggest effect on seat availability. Jetstar had returned to 66 per cent of its pre-COVID capacity, and Qantas was at just 49 per cent. This was another source of almighty customer frustration in 2022: Qantas frequent flyer members were sitting on record points balances, but even for those with platinum and gold status, there were no seats available to burn them on.

Qantas simply couldn't add international seats any faster. It lacked the staff, but it also lacked the aircraft. It had sent twelve A380s to the desert in 2020, then fatefully decided to scrap two of them. When Qantas International was relaunched in 2021, the company said it wouldn't have the remaining ten back in service until 2024 (since pushed back to 2026).[14] To make matters worse, it also decided in 2021 to convert two passenger A330s – the aircraft that operates most of Qantas' flights to Asia – into freighters. Qantas, therefore, could not restore its pre-COVID international capacity even had it wanted to.[15]

Capacity was especially limited between Australia and the United States. Virgin Australia had been a significant player on the Pacific but its long-haul operation was jettisoned in insolvency. Qantas was stuck at half of its historical capacity and its joint-venture partner American Airlines had not recommended any flying to Australia. As a result, business class tickets from Sydney to New York were selling for $25,000 – more than double 2019 prices.

Suddenly, Australian travellers were experiencing, simultaneously, the worst service and the highest prices in living memory. It was a foul recipe – worse even than Qantas' inflight catering, which, in the quest for 'structural' savings, had been reduced to a caricature of aeroplane food. Qantas' most valuable passengers were back commuting to North America but each return trip now cost the equivalent of a new car. Once on board, they were offered soup, sandwiches and a chardy worthy of the discount bin. The flight would often be hours late, and when they landed back in Australia their luggage was no certainty to materialise on the carousel.

Qantas management did not appear to comprehend the diabolical risk to their brand of robbing their customers blind, then, as an added bonus, showing them the worst time of their lives. Newspapers had for weeks been publishing searing human stories of Qantas customer woe when, on 17 June, Qantas' chief customer officer Stephanie Tully claimed: 'The customer preference for Qantas has not changed at all. It is recoverable and the brand is in a really strong position.'

That the Qantas brand was simultaneously unchanged and recoverable was a variety of logic typically associated with Sir Humphrey Appleby of *Yes Minister*. Tully would within weeks be rewarded for her penetrating insights with a promotion to CEO of Jetstar. 'What we measure internally is brand trust and brand preference and those two things have been resilient to what happened in April,' she told the *Australian Financial Review*.

Disagreeing completely, Brand Institute CEO Karl Treacher predicted 'there will be substantial short-term and medium-term damage to the [Qantas] brand and that could cost hundreds of millions of dollars in the end'. But Tully perceived none of this risk. 'We don't think there's a long-term impact to what's a global short-term problem,' she said.

'So you don't think you'll get caught off guard again in the coming [July] school holidays?' *AFR* reporter Lucas Baird asked.

Her response: 'We feel really prepared.'

———

Deep in the anarchy of July 2022, Qantas' (and Jetstar's) worst since records were kept, Qantas Domestic and International boss Andrew David sought to calm the baying mob.

David was now acting group CEO. On 22 June, Alan Joyce had taken Qantas' inaugural flight from Perth to Rome, and four weeks later he remained at large on the European continent. It was an ill-judged moment to be taking a holiday, and this would shortly become a matter of public debate. One particularly disaffected customer had, in the very early hours of 12 July, pelted Joyce's mansion on Sydney Harbour with eggs and toilet paper – no doubt unaware that Joyce was overseas and didn't actually live there. Having bought the luxury property for $19 million two months earlier, he was yet to move in.

It was an incursion that very few Australian businesspeople would ever be subjected to. The unidentified vandal had nevertheless captured the febrile mood of the moment. On social media, Joyce's name had become a verb, with hordes of Qantas customers sharing their horror travel stories and complaining bitterly of being 'Joyced'. No wonder he wanted a holiday, and as far away as possible. Old union foes also enthusiastically adopted the term, with Labor senator and former TWU national secretary Tony Sheldon declaring, 'Things have to change ... Qantas' reputation has been Joyced.'

In the face of intense public anger, Andrew David resorted to the method of defence favoured by Qantas' communications boss, Andrew McGinnes: the self-rationalising (and often patronising) apologia in a newspaper. In Sydney's *Daily Telegraph* on 17 July, David began with the fairy story that 'we were 11 weeks from bankruptcy early in the pandemic', before writing, 'There are a number of factors that have led to the problems we are seeing right now', but omitting to mention a single factor (such as sacking too many staff, or not keeping them trained) within Qantas' control. It was the tight labour market. It was COVID and influenza. It was a global phenomenon! These were all legitimate causes, of course, but they were only half the picture.

'As challenging as the recent travel peaks in Australia have been, airlines and airports in Europe, the US and the UK are dealing with far worse impacts,' David claimed.

London's Heathrow was – true to form – an unmitigated basket case, as was Amsterdam's Schiphol, but the assertion that Qantas was outperforming all of its Northern Hemisphere peers was yet another cock-and-bull story out of Mascot. Let's look at the numbers.

The US airlines had clocked up on-time arrivals of 73.5 per cent in June 2022, 14 percentage points better than Qantas and Jetstar. In July, the American carriers managed on-time arrivals of 75 per cent, a shocking 28 percentage points better than Qantas. In Europe, industry-wide on-time arrivals were 62 per cent in both months, the worst on record but still comfortably better than Qantas; individually, however, British Airways, Dutch carrier KLM, and Germany's Lufthansa all performed significantly worse than Qantas in both months.[16]

The US carriers mishandled seven bags per 1,000 in June 2022, compared to Qantas' sixteen bags per 1,000. In July, the US carriers mishandled six bags per 1,000 compared to Qantas' fifteen bags per 1,000.[17] Mishandled baggage rates are not publicly disclosed in Europe, but anecdotally they were very bad.

Qantas' rate of cancellations was also far worse than anything in the United States, where just 3.1 per cent of flights were cancelled in June, and 1.8 per cent in July. Qantas and Jetstar were cancelling flights at double, triple and even quadruple those numbers. The cancellation rate in the Eurocontrol (European Organisation for the Safety of Air Navigation) zone for both months was 7 per cent – not dissimilar to Qantas' and Jetstar's dreadful numbers.

Even if things had been nearly as bad in one overseas region as they were with Qantas, it was a lousy excuse to fall back on. Since when have the minimum standards expected of Qantas been relative?

Since never. How many Melburnians determine their satisfaction with (or trauma from) a trip to Sydney by comparing it to a hypothetical flight they could have taken in France or Japan? None.

The Australian public's strength of feeling about Qantas was in large part the airline's own creation. Since its privatisation in the mid-1990s, Qantas had cashed in on its image as the national carrier. Less than a fortnight before the chaos was unleashed in April 2022, Qantas launched its slick new, goosebump-inducing 'I Still Call Australia Home' commercial. Qantas had been very careful to cultivate the loyalty of the Australian flying public: in this crisis, they failed to understand that loyalty needs to be reciprocal.

Australian travellers have *absolute* expectations of Qantas, and among them are punctuality (of the planes and the bags on them), accessibility (by phone and via humans in the airport terminals) and unsurpassed safety. In a jarringly short space of time, Qantas went from monetising its status as 'the Spirit of Australia' to abrogating the responsibilities that mantle comes with. Until Qantas elected to replace that iconic tagline with its successor, 'Not as bad as Lufthansa', customers would continue to reject the company's pleas of *comparative* adequacy.

Andrew David's *Daily Telegraph* piece was just another signpost to the culture of denialism that had infected the highest-ranking inhabitants of Qantas World. Whether they were soaking governments for subsidies or failing their customers, they were never in the wrong. Some, David complained, were blaming the outsourcing of Qantas' ground handling as a key reason for the chaos. He countered: 'This is not true. We had completed the ground handling changes before Easter 2021 when domestic travel was back to almost 100 per cent, and we didn't have the issues we had at Easter this year.' David was, of course, the sole maker of that illegal decision, and here he still was, making a completely false statement about its unintended consequences.

The numbers don't lie. In April 2021, Qantas' domestic capacity was back to 83 per cent – not 100 per cent – of April 2019 levels. And although it was true that Qantas' ground handling had already been outsourced and Qantas did not suffer the operational problems it did in April 2022, what David left out of his account was that international flying had not returned in April 2021. That was the key difference.

Before COVID, roughly half Qantas' ground handling work hours were directed to servicing Qantas' international flights.[18] In April 2021, only 113,000 international passengers were carried (by all airlines) to or from Australia, which was 3 per cent of pre-COVID numbers – a veritable trickle.[19] So of course with all of their other airline clients barely flying, Qantas' new external ground handling providers had no problem servicing 83 per cent of Qantas' normal domestic capacity plus 3 per cent of its normal international capacity – which, combined, was just 30 per cent of Qantas' normal total capacity.

But by April 2022, the total number of international passengers carried to or from Australia had exploded more than tenfold to 1.2 million. And remember, Qantas now effectively participated in a pool for ground handling with every other airline that flew to Australia (except Virgin Australia). All of these baggage providers had depleted COVID-era workforces when the demand for their services had rocketed by 1,000 per cent versus twelve months earlier, coinciding with the tightest Australian labour market in fifty years and a cresting wave of COVID infection in the community. To use Alan Joyce's words, they were not match fit.

Qantas was saying unbelievable things and foisting ridiculous excuses on the public because, up to this point, it had worked beautifully. Pretty much everyone fell for it, including me. The public mood, however, was beginning to shift, even if nobody at Qantas felt the tremors. The travelling class of Australia was fed up to gagging on the excuses, many of them demonstrably false. Unless Qantas could get real, its trust problem was not going away. Indeed, it could only get worse.

The Best CEO in Australia
July–Sept 2022

Alan Joyce had been in Europe for a month, leaving Andrew David to front an increasingly hostile media every day for a week, when David finally asked Joyce to 'cut short' his trip and return to the helm of the company in what had unmistakably become a crisis.

Re-energised by his Mediterranean sojourn remote from Qantas' anarchy, Joyce got straight to work on 21 July. Every morning, he would scour a briefing pack on the Qantas network's performance the previous day, often finding discrepancies between chart data, then he'd summon the airline's top operations managers to interrogate them over the numbers.[1] Once, frustrated by the information he was receiving, he threatened to call in internal audit.

Joyce quickly determined easy improvements. Identifying tight domestic-to-international connections as the single biggest factor in misplaced bags, Qantas increased minimum connection times from sixty to ninety minutes. It also boosted the number of rostered front-line staff to absorb the 50 per cent spike in sick leave, and the hiring binge continued. And in addition to the domestic capacity reductions announced in May and June, Qantas would now remove even more domestic flights from the schedule, 'particularly at peak times in Melbourne and Sydney', which gave rise to accusations – from those airports, other airlines and the ACCC – of 'slot hoarding'.[2]

Joyce outlined these tweaks in an email to Qantas staff on 10 August addressing the company's 'well-publicised challenges'. He admitted, 'While there are lots of good reasons why, the simple fact is our operational performance hasn't been up to the standard our customers are used to, or that we expect of ourselves.' But though Joyce was conceding internally that standards weren't good enough, Qantas customers were yet to hear any such admission, from him or the company. Qantas customers had not heard nor seen anything at all of Joyce since he went on holiday.

The following week, the *Australian Financial Review*'s Chanticleer column weighed in. Having occupied the masthead's prime, back page real estate for fifty years, under the stewardship of icons like Robert Gottliebsen and Alan Kohler, and latterly that of Tony Boyd, Chanticleer had its pen very much on the pulse of the top end of town.[3] Tony Boyd now called on Joyce to 'think hard about his response to the damage done to the airline's iconic brand', in light of the fact that a procession of CEOs and board directors of major Australian companies were now contacting Boyd to pour shit on the airline.

The column had broad market data: it quoted the latest qualitative research by Roy Morgan, in which Qantas customers said things like, 'I hate how they operate. They take your money, cancel your flight at any time. You have to fight to get your money back,' and 'I don't like their treatment of staff throughout the pandemic.' And it reported that Qantas had slid from fifth to sixteenth in the RepTrak benchmark, 'widely used by the top 60 companies in Australia as an early warning sign of customer service problems', wrote Boyd. Qantas spokesman Andrew McGinnes characteristically dismissed this as a concern, noting that the airline had clawed its way back into the top ranks from fifty-sixth place after its 2011 grounding.

While Qantas was used to tuning out the feedback from its economy class passengers, the real point was that Chanticleer had news from the front end of the plane: in that August week alone, 'two CEOs, who did not want to be named, criticised Joyce for not taking ownership of the problems within the airline's control'. Chanticleer reported gripes with the lack of available frequent flyer redemption seats (which McGinnes also rejected out of hand), and another 'common criticism' was that 'Joyce has not found time to write to Qantas frequent flyer members to share with them his action plan.

Instead, they are bombarded with automated emails about buying wine, insurance and other products.'

It was one thing to be criticised by Aussie battlers in Roy Morgan focus groups, but another entirely for Joyce to sense mutiny among his distinguished peers at the pointy end of corporate Australia. Within forty-eight hours, on 21 August, Joyce had written to those frequent flyers apologising 'for the journeys that didn't meet the standards you expect from us', thanking them for their loyalty and offering them $50 off a return Qantas flight. Ironically, the rush to redeem these $50 discounts caused qantas.com to crash: yes, the apology vouchers for operational issues themselves caused operational issues.

This was the lead-in to Qantas' annual results on 25 August, when Joyce unveiled the airline's third consecutive annual loss, this one down to $1.2 billion. The update to investors revealed the widening gap between the market story and the customer experience.

Qantas had now eliminated $920 million of the $1 billion of structural annual costs Joyce planned to remove by June 2023, so the executives were well on track for their special recovery and retention bonuses (as we've seen, 60 per cent of those eliminated costs were people's wages). Only deep in the fine print could investors learn that Qantas' loss had been softened by a jumbo $870 million in subsidies from the Australian government, just $67 million of which was AviationKeeper (the industry-specific successor to JobKeeper, received by Qantas employees and not the company).[4] This took the total amount of Australian government COVID-19 subsidies received by Qantas in the pandemic to $2.7 billion.

Qantas had abandoned reporting its profit margin on those subsidies, which was a dead set giveaway that its margin had improved out of sight.[5] Of course, the inconsistent disclosures made it maximally difficult to compare apples with apples and understand the true nature of those government payments. A cynical person might assume that this was Qantas' intention.

Also for the third consecutive year, Joyce was awarded his long-term bonus – 371,500 Qantas shares – and yet again, he offered and the Qantas board agreed to wait another twelve months before deciding whether to keep it or not. Added to the 668,500 shares he'd set aside in 2020 and 2021, Joyce had only to say the word in August 2023 to bank more than a million Qantas shares as his performance bonuses for the three years in which Qantas suffered cumulative losses of $6.2 billion. This was Joyce's contractual entitlement, which was an indictment of the Qantas board.[6] Quite aside from that, the manoeuvre Joyce was preparing to bring off was beyond the orthodox boundaries of shame.

Alongside the wage savings and taxpayer subsidies, Joyce announced he would return $400 million to Qantas shareholders via a share buy-back.[7] The company might have posted an annual loss, but it was also flush with cash from advance ticket sales, and it wanted to direct some of it not to employees or back to the government, but to its shareholders. There was nothing balanced about Joyce's holy trinity any longer.

For the uninitiated, a share buy-back is the reverse of an equity raising. In June 2020, Qantas raised $1.4 billion by issuing and selling new shares in itself. That increase in the number of shares naturally diluted the value of the existing shares, making each piece of the Qantas cake smaller. Joyce was now proposing to spend a spare $400 million buying some of those shares back from shareholders and retiring them, making each remaining piece of the cake a bit bigger again.

A buy-back is particularly attractive if a company is buying back and cancelling its shares at a price below what the board considers their true value to be – that is, when the board thinks the company will soon be worth more than the market currently reflects. And it's trebly attractive if the performance metric for your long-term bonus is, as it was in this case, to increase Qantas' 'total shareholder returns' (a calculation of share price appreciation plus the value of dividends and buy-backs) compared to other Australian companies and to Qantas' global airline peers.

It was daring from a narrative standpoint for Qantas to make a conspicuous display of its overflowing cash position on the same day it disclosed the receipt of $870 million in government subsidies in the preceding twelve months, but Joyce plainly did not recognise this juxtaposition as problematic. Indeed, he gave a TV interview that morning to CNBC Asia in which he claimed that, unlike Singapore Airlines, Qantas was still generating losses, in part, 'because we ended up getting very little government support'.

In Australia, that comment came over as particularly tone deaf. Many Australians knew that Qantas was the nation's largest recipient of JobKeeper, a program by this point widely maligned for the profiteering opportunities it provided so many of its recipients.[8] Qantas was not one of those, of course: it was objectively a deserving recipient. But as we've seen, the program was designed to maintain the connection between employers and their employees through the pandemic, whereas Qantas had proceeded to unlawfully terminate 1,700 workers.

Joyce was reinforcing the perception of Qantas' attitude of entitlement to, and lack of gratitude for, its subsidies, a perception that would only metastasise in the minds of customers and which Joyce would do nothing subsequently to salve. There were roughly the same number of individual taxpayers in Australia as there were members of the Qantas frequent flyer program – 14 million. Joyce badly underestimated the relevance of that crossover, the extent to which Qantas customers would link the price-gouging of Qantas and the abysmal experience of flying Qantas with the ungracious receipt by Qantas of their hard-earned taxes.

Joyce's holiday had not restored his antenna for the public mood. The gaffes just kept on coming. While the 'very little government support' remark undoubtedly caused his minders some minor heartburn, it was an interview Joyce gave to *The Weekend Australian* that week which caused widespread bemusement, if not incredulity. Probed about his trip to Italy (and a visit to his elderly mother in Dublin) during Qantas' school holiday disaster, and his unfortunately timed purchase of a $19 million Mosman mansion, Joyce defended his actions petulantly. 'I have an 82-year-old mother who is not very well and I shouldn't have to justify to anybody that I see her. I think it's completely unfair. Why is it relevant what I do in my private life?

I'm not a public figure. People regard the CEO of Qantas as like a politician and it definitely shouldn't be. It's a business figure.'

This was when a siren started wailing in my head.

That final week of August 2022 was the first time I had paid any meaningful attention to the conduct or performance of Qantas since March 2020, way back when Joyce had successfully deprived a flailing Virgin Australia of emergency government support. My day job was to think up, then punch out, five sparkling columns each week for the *Australian Financial Review*. For want of time, their subject matter needed to be fastened upon with haste. Nothing about the chaos at Qantas, or how Qantas justified it, had up to this point jumped out to me as manifestly incongruous.

Qantas was a fiendishly complex company. This worked to the company's advantage in a PR sense because it often required many hours of research – research that I only conducted much later – to learn that its statements were misleading or even plain false. For journalists, it was a hell of a lot easier just to take them at face value. I did exactly that. When Joyce said that August week, 'This is an industry problem – let's not pretend it's a Qantas problem. All airlines are giving bad service at the moment,' I believed him. Penning my first column about the airline in more than two years, I wrote on 29 August, 'Unpopular as this view may be, the causes of Qantas' dysfunction are overwhelmingly global and beyond management's reasonable control.'

On what evidence, exactly, did I base this standpoint? Nothing more, I am embarrassed to concede, than the assertions of the company and a vague sense of pandemonium in the global travel industry. It felt like an easy (and solitary) concession to offer Joyce in a column otherwise devoted to deconstructing, in the most scathing terms, his ridiculous comments in *The Weekend Australian*. I was flabbergasted that Joyce, having been asked a legitimate question about his weeks-long absence through the peak of a crisis at Qantas, had so shamelessly reframed it as a heartless attack on his poor sick mammy.

'Joyce is a skilled misinterpreter,' I wrote. 'Nobody has ever challenged Alan Joyce's right to visit his mother. He is using her as a human shield against legitimate censure for sunning his fanny in Italy while his company is in meltdown. That he cut his vacation short is a tacit admission that the timing was ill-considered.' Joyce should have asked Scott Morrison about the wisdom of taking an overseas holiday in the middle of a crisis. In December 2019, the then prime minister shredded the trust of the Australian public by sneaking off to Hawaii for a poolside vacay during the Black Summer bushfires. The Qantas CEO was now having his own 'I don't hold a hose' moment.

His pretension not to be a public figure was abjectly ludicrous. To begin with, it was a pretension expressed during a scheduled fireside chat with a national newspaper – not the customary Friday morning activity of a deeply private no one. He was also confused. Only the day before, he'd told the press conference held for Qantas' 2022 financial results, 'I think I've had more resignation requests than any other CEO and probably any other public figure out there.' On Thursday he was a public figure. By Friday he was not.

Some sort of argument could be mounted that there are CEOs out there – presumably of small and obscure private companies in industries not meaningfully regulated by governments – who are not public figures. The CEO of Qantas is incontrovertibly not one of them. In any case, it was a distinction without a difference. Joyce ran a company that self-identified as the national carrier. It was also a publicly traded company with 190,000 mum and dad investors. He was a regular and visible participant in the public policy process, advocating positions on everything from marriage equality to company tax cuts. And of course in 2011, Joyce had all but shut down Australia when he grounded the airline. Joyce quacked like a duck and he was a duck.

As a satirical columnist whose metier was dissecting the misguided beliefs of powerful people, I could go months on end without an interview this fertile. What made this one such a standout wasn't just the diamond quality of the delusions billowing from Joyce, but the sheer number of them he'd dropped in one hit. It was nothing short of a confessional implosion.

Next, he'd turned on trade unions. 'When some of the unions' claims are going to put the company in financial distress and cause a lot of people to lose their jobs, I don't think that's fair, and it's my job as CEO to stand up and fight,' he said. This was another fantastically self-unaware statement. When Joyce was appointed CEO of Qantas in 2008, the company had 34,300 employees.[9] By the time COVID arrived in March 2020, he'd reduced it to 29,400.[10] In response to the pandemic, he'd scythed the workforce to just 21,800 (both legally and not) by July 2022, and any Qantas customer could tell you it showed. There had absolutely been fat to cut in the earlier years, and Joyce is not to blame for COVID. It was nonetheless risible for him, the greatest job-slayer in Qantas' history, to say that *unions* caused a lot of Qantas employees to lose their job.

Joyce did not, as he'd suggested, fight unions to save jobs. He fought unions to outsource jobs, to pay 30 per cent less for the same work. And when the airline conducted its largest outsourcing ever – that of 1,700 ground handling casualties in Qantas' 'vanishing window of opportunity' of 2020 – Joyce had permitted himself to be legally deleted from the entire process by an exotic instrument of delegation that nobody at Qantas could recall (under oath) ever having been used before. Alan Joyce, the man who stands up and fights unions, wasn't even there.

After this, I started digging a little deeper into the numbers behind Qantas' bluster.

———

The public pressure on Joyce only intensified in the days that followed his ill-considered interview.

On-time arrivals for August – 62 per cent for Qantas, 60 per cent for Jetstar, and 69 per cent for Virgin – had improved, but for Qantas and Jetstar remained 20 percentage points below pre-COVID levels. Qantas' mishandled baggage rate had recovered to *only* 50 per cent above pre-COVID levels.

Media reporting and social media sharing of flight disruptions had become incessant. The national carrier was suffering death by a thousand fatuous anecdotes, as an array of journalists produced first-person articles about their own imperfect Qantas experiences. In response to one – which portrayed a soggy chicken pie and a twenty-minute security delay as 'the Qantas flight from hell' – Qantas chairman Richard Goyder lamented wearily, 'It's all Qantas at the moment, and it's all Alan.' The *Financial Review* published the results of a reader poll: 47 per cent of respondents wanted Joyce to resign. There was no mistaking the fact that Qantas, more than a decade since its dramatic grounding, had again become the great Australian barbecue stopper.

Come mid-September 2022, with the outpourings of discontent still unremitting, Goyder kicked off a round of media appearances to defend Joyce and the company's actions. For his own credibility, it was a fateful performance. He could have acquitted himself with a firm but dispassionate expression of support for Joyce. Instead, Goyder lavished praise upon him, enthusing bizarrely to the *Sydney Morning Herald* that Joyce was 'the best CEO in Australia by the length of a straight'.

'Being a chief executive is not a popularity contest,' Goyder added, chiding the travelling public. 'Believe it or not, Alan has a heart.'

Alan had a heart! Far from exhibiting an overriding sympathy for Qantas customers, the chairman was betraying, not for the last time, that his primal concern was Alan Joyce's feelings.

Goyder's evidence to support his contention that Alan Joyce was the best CEO in Australia came from the Corporate Confidence Index (CCI), which rated Joyce among the nation's top five CEOs.

The CCI is an opaque phone survey which, on a six-monthly basis, spits out the favourability of Australia's public company CEOs in the eyes of institutional investors. The CEO rankings, however, are only shared with the companies themselves, not with the investors who take the survey. The tremendous secrecy maintained around these results only adds to their occult power. Not one but two BHP chief executives – John Prescott in 1998 and Marius Kloppers in 2013 – were dispatched by the BHP board soon after their poor CCI ratings were strategically leaked to the press. Goyder might as well have said that Joyce was the best CEO in Australia because he'd been granted a knighthood by a secret Masonic order of merit. Or was it the Vatican?

But the CCI had a dirty secret. It was a measure of negligible value because its CEO ratings correlated almost perfectly to the share price of their companies. Prescott's and Kloppers' CCI ratings were only low because BHP's shareholder returns had languished on their watches. The CCI also gave equal weighting to the views of the buy-side (fund managers, some who own the company's shares but many who don't) and the sell-side (the equities research analysts at investment banks who cover the company's shares). While the views of fund managers were valuable, the collective view of sell-side analysts was close to worthless. In 2022 the quality of sell-side research had been on the decline for years, with buy recommendations following stocks all the way up, and sell ratings following stocks all the way down.[11] Most equities analysts would never say anything materially negative about a CEO in case it cost their investment bank that company's mandate to underwrite its next equity raising, or to advise that company on its next major transaction.

The CCI was therefore a case of garbage in, garbage out. Anyway, hadn't Goyder just said that being CEO wasn't a popularity contest?

Flying as they did in the face of customer uproar, these statements were a turning point in Goyder's own credibility, which in the business community had been formidable. He was the blue-chip company director from central casting: a former CEO of Perth conglomerate Wesfarmers turned chairman of Perth oil and gas giant Woodside, and he was also chairman of the Australian Football League (AFL), the southern states' predominant religion. The implication that Goyder thought both current Woodside CEO Meg O'Neill and AFL chief executive Gillon McLachlan inferior to Joyce was just one of many reasons his statement was so poorly conceived.

It also established the perception – one which would end Goyder's chairmanship twelve months later – that Goyder was too infatuated with Joyce to properly manage him. This was consistent with the established view in football circles that Goyder was overawed by McLachlan, who had announced his intention to retire in April 2022 but whose succession process Goyder was slow-pedalling for no apparently good reason. The impression of Goyder's doting was only reinforced by McLachlan's speech at the AFL Commission's luncheon at the 2022 grand final, which was supposed to be McLachlan's farewell but turned out not to be.[12] McLachlan told the audience – which included the prime minister, multiple state premiers, and billionaire media proprietors Lachlan Murdoch and Kerry Stokes – that the Goyders and McLachlans had grown so close that McLachlan's children referred to Goyder as 'Uncle Rich'. As one AFL club president told me disbelievingly, 'If necessary, Richard was supposed to be able to sack Gill, and instead they'd conjoined families.'

Goyder was not afraid to mix business with pleasure. Only three months earlier, he and his wife Janine had travelled with Joyce and a contingent of VIPs on the inaugural flight from Perth to Rome, the flight that marked the commencement of Joyce's long absence from duty. The Goyders even posed for an Instagram selfie with the Joyces and Perth mayor Basil Zempilas. Goyder's predecessor, Leigh Clifford, had travelled on the airline's inaugural Perth–London flight in 2018, but Clifford had also said of his relationship with Joyce that 'you should be friendly but not necessarily friends because sometimes you have to take a differing view'.

As commentator Elizabeth Knight wrote prophetically in the *Sydney Morning Herald* on 9 September, 'In signing up for the role of head of Joyce's fan club, Goyder has put his own reputation on the line. If Joyce is forced out of his job in response to the public outcry … his most vocal supporter won't survive.'

Next, Goyder put his name to an opinion piece in the *Financial Review* on 13 September. While admitting that the airline's performance was 'unacceptable and we know it', Goyder promised that 'we are well on the way to fixing it [and] by next month, we expect to be back to our best.

'If you haven't heard this,' he continued, 'it may be because the data showing the improvement received far less media attention than stories showing how bad things got. In the meantime, the corporate obituary writers have been busy. Their analysis has (mostly) been unencumbered by what's happening at other airlines or that Qantas' performance has turned around.'

This snark sounded absolutely nothing like Richard Goyder and everything like McGinnes and Joyce. It was also delusional. Qantas' performance might have improved since July but it was a very long way from being fixed.

Goyder's article went on to repeat the same self-justifications previously offered by Joyce and Andrew David: that 'companies make deep cuts to survive', and that 'Qantas is little different to airlines worldwide that have struggled' with labour shortages and staff illness. And he refused to recognise the disaster of outsourcing baggage handling, defending it with the same incorrect statistics David had trotted out in July.[13]

The monstrous truth that nobody on the executive floor of Qantas' Mascot headquarters could bear to contemplate was that its outsourcing was not only illegal and unethical, but also partly to blame for Qantas' acute short-term service failures. I'm not suggesting that Goyder comprehended the falsehood he was perpetuating (as Andrews David and McGinnes certainly should have). There is zero way Goyder said to McGinnes, Could you just run me through the evidence behind this highly disputed point of fact I'm putting my name to here? There is nothing to suggest that Goyder ever bothered to verify the accuracy of information he was being spoonfed by Qantas management.

Goyder's defence of the $400 million share buy-back was similarly misguided. Goyder wrote: 'Shareholders gave Qantas $1.4 billion to help the airline restructure and get through the pandemic. This was in mid-2020, when airlines were not exactly looking like a great investment. So, it doesn't seem unreasonable that they should get some of it back.'

This was disingenuous in the extreme. Shareholders hadn't *given* Qantas anything: in June 2020, fund managers purchased $1.36 billion of Qantas shares at $3.65 each, while retail shareholders bought $71 million of Qantas shares at $3.14 each. Alan Joyce didn't launch his equity raising saying, Look, guys, I know Qantas isn't exactly a great investment right now. Rather, he persuaded them that Qantas shares were an attractive prospect because he would use their money to make 6,000 redundancy payments (it ended up being 10,000), slashing overheads so savagely as to bloat the airline's post-COVID profit margin. And twenty-six months later, those shares were trading at $5.34, an increase of 46 and 70 per cent respectively. The capital raising had therefore been a solid or even exceptional investment for all concerned. The need to *repay* these shareholders with a buy-back was an outright contrivance.

Goyder was simply being fed – and reciting – the party line. But interestingly, even some in the investment market disagreed. Gaurav Sodhi, deputy head of research at Intelligent Investor, the subscription-based newsletter for retail investors, deemed the buy-back 'reckless'.

'You've got to distribute an economic surplus with a long-term view and that's what profit is,' he told the *AFR* on 7 September. 'If all you do is take every surplus and give it to shareholders, that'll make shareholders very happy. But you've lots more stakeholders than that and if you want to build a business for a long time and do well for a long time you have to try to keep a lot of different parties happy.

'It's clear customers are angry at them, staff are angry at them, the brand is suffering. Labour is so hard to find and keep right now, I would've thought you'd maybe want to distribute a little bit of your surplus to labour. It seems to me it's excess working capital being returned to shareholders, not excess profitability.'

One small institutional Qantas shareholder, Forager Funds, agreed that the buy-back was inappropriate 'while customers are suffering'. But Qantas' largest and longstanding shareholder, Pendal, vehemently defended Qantas, as ever. Pendal analyst Sondal Bensan, known on the street for his undying love of the stock, spoke in support of the airline's illegal outsourcing of its baggage handlers, and regurgitated the company line that its staffing issues were 'no different' to those faced by other companies.

Pendal, previously known as BT, is a fund manager specialising in Australian shares. Its longstanding position in Qantas was a big conviction holding, with more than 4 per cent of Pendal's flagship Australian shares fund held in Qantas.

Bensan's more dispassionate boss, Crispin Murray, Pendal's chief investment officer, also addressed clients in September, as controversy raged around Qantas. Murray declared the airline's buy-back 'both prudent and appropriate capital management'.

Here we get to the heart of Goyder's CCI defence – that Joyce was a superb leader because institutional investors loved him. But why did institutional investors love Joyce? Because Joyce prioritised their interests over all others. This was natural for Joyce to do because his own interests were closely aligned with theirs. His bonuses, paid mostly in shares, were correlated to the Qantas share price and he was already the largest individual shareholder in the company. From 2017 to 2019, Joyce was a hero for having landed the holy trinity, the perfect balance between the satisfaction of Qantas shareholders, customers and employees. Crispin Murray himself had praised Joyce at the time for this 'very unique' achievement. But by 2022, there was only one god: Joyce's impetus for not just profitability but super-profitability. He was placing shareholders, it seemed, first, second and third.

While institutional investors were collectively the majority owners of Qantas, the problem was that their interests (and indeed the interests of Joyce) could be contrary to the interests of Qantas itself. Institutional investors are focused on index-beating returns for the companies they own. Quite inevitably, this causes them to be monomaniacally fixated on the share prices and capital returns of companies. But enslaving a company to the short-term propellants of its share price is rarely in the long-term interests of that company.

The surest way to boost a company's share price is to boost its profitability, and generally, the way to do that is consistent with the company's enduring health. For instance, companies can remove surplus costs – the kind that won't affect the quality of their products or services. Of course, any well-run company will have done this already. A company can also inflate its short- and even medium-term profits simply by delaying its capital expenditure, which is the regular investment a company requires to maintain its productive capacity.

All this is really doing, however, is degrading the customer experience and superficially inflating present-day profits by stealing from future profits. It is a common trick of private equity owners right before they sell companies.

There was a time-honoured and sure-fire way to do this in the airline game: you just stopped buying planes.

Joyce 1.0

2008–2022

On 2 May 2022, Qantas' malfunctioning operations would have been the furthest thing from Alan Joyce's mind. That day, he was unveiling a trading update, predicting *underlying* earnings – remember those? – of $500 million in the six months ending 30 June. As Joyce had predicted back in 2020 when he asked shareholders for $1.4 billion of equity, Qantas' domestic market share now topped 70 per cent. COVID was over and the company's financial position was formidable.

And that morning, he was also realising a momentous and long-standing ambition. In the cavernous hangar 96 at Sydney airport – the backdrop for all of the company's modern Kodak moments – Qantas formalised its purchase of twelve new planes which would, by late 2025, fly nonstop from Sydney to London and New York.[1] Joyce had been on the verge of placing this historic order in March 2020 when COVID struck. Two miserable years later, Project Sunrise was a step-change – a 'final trophy', as Qantas' largest shareholder had warily described it in 2019 – that Joyce was determined would not elude him.

As news photographers and cameramen jostled for prime images, Joyce sat on a stage beside top Airbus executive Christian Scherer, in the shadow of the A350 Scherer flew in on, and signed the contract for twelve A350-1000ULRs, to be customised for Qantas' groundbreaking range specifications.[2] At the aircraft's list price, it was a US$4.4 billion (AU$6.2 billion) order, though as a large customer, Qantas would have secured a price closer to 60 per cent of that amount.

But Scherer hadn't schlepped all the way from Toulouse just to sell a dozen units. Alongside the A350s, Joyce was also signing a large order for narrow-body planes to begin the renewal of Qantas' dog-tired domestic fleet: twenty A321XLRs to replace the oldest of seventy-five Boeing 737-800s, and twenty A220s to replace QantasLink's fleet of twenty Boeing 717s.[3] Qantas also secured purchase options for a further ninety-four A321s and A220s out to 2034.[4]

Having grandly codenamed this short-haul fleet renewal program 'Project Winton', Qantas was now rolling it together with Jetstar's existing book of 109 firm orders and fifty-six purchase options for aircraft in the A320 family – a total of 299 potential airframes – allowing Qantas to call it 'the largest aircraft order in Australian aviation history'.

This all sounded very impressive to the casual observer but there were important qualifications to consider. Yes, Qantas was ordering up big, but it needed to – because, under Joyce, the airline's fleet had been allowed to age quite radically.

A second and related point is that Joyce was very good at announcing big investments in aircraft, but piss-poor at sticking to them. The A320 was and remains the aircraft that Jetstar uses for all its short-haul flying. Jetstar's *existing* A320 order – the one now being consolidated into the Project Winton order – was placed by Joyce in October 2011. It was originally for thirty-two standard A320s and seventy-eight A320neos (a newer and more efficient model) and it was hailed at the time as – you guessed it – 'the largest single order in Australian aviation history'.[5]

But only eleven planes were ever delivered.[6]

In 2014, Joyce restructured that Airbus order (for ninety-nine remaining planes), adding to its size but deferring the A320neo deliveries to between 2016 and 2022.[7] In 2017, he deferred the introduction of the A320neos at Jetstar until 2019. In 2018, he deferred the Jetstar introduction until 2020, and switched from the A320neo to the A321LR for the first eighteen aircraft.[8] As the pandemic struck in March 2020, Joyce understandably deferred the delivery of those eighteen A321LRs by another eighteen months.

So by May 2022, nearly eleven years after the order was placed, not a single one of those neos had been delivered to Jetstar.[9] Joyce was once again trumpeting the biggest aircraft order in history, while his last one had failed so miserably to live up to the name. Indeed, the Qantas Group had only ever made the biggest *unfulfilled* aircraft order in Australian aviation history.

Sadly, this was the rule, not the exception, in the Joyce era.

Its selection of aeroplanes defines what kind of airline Qantas is. Moreover, understanding Joyce's approach to buying (and not buying) aircraft is central to understanding his career and his mentality. It's a business of eye-watering numbers, so bear with me while we zoom out and consider how the planes we fly around in also work on the Qantas balance sheet.

The first time that Joyce ordered any new aircraft for Qantas was eleven years into his tenure as CEO, when at the Paris Air Show in June 2019 he added ten more planes to his existing 'largest ever' Airbus order and said that maybe not *all* of them would go to Jetstar.

When Joyce became Qantas CEO in 2008, he inherited two large orders of wide-body aircraft from his predecessors James Strong and Geoff Dixon: for twenty A380s from Airbus, and sixty-five 787 Dreamliners from Boeing. Between 2009 and 2019, he deferred and then cancelled eight of those twenty A380s and forty of the 787s. It is difficult to overstate the significance of those decisions: these planes could have increased the Qantas Group's wide-body fleet by as much as 75 per cent compared to its 2019 size (or just allowed for the replacement of old aircraft), most likely defending and potentially even growing Qantas' international market share.[10] Instead, Qantas shrank from 25 per cent of all passengers carried to and from Australia in 2008 to 16 per cent by 2014 (at the time of writing it was 17 per cent). In the same period, Jetstar's international market share grew from 6 per cent to 8 per cent.

More 787s would have delivered Qantas a material step-down in its costs per seat. The new generation Dreamliner burned around 20 per cent less fuel per passenger than the A330 and required far less maintenance.[11] Instead, Joyce elected to shrink Qantas International and grow Jetstar. That is a motif of the Joyce era. On his watch, between 2009 and 2023, Jetstar grew internationally by 65 per cent while Qantas shrank 32 per cent.

It's important to distinguish between the A380 and 787 fleet decisions.

The arguments in favour of Qantas ultimately limiting its A380 fleet to twelve aircraft were strong. The A380 was a piece of equipment so large that its economics only worked for airlines on a few routes with prodigious passenger flows. From Australia – more specifically from Sydney – that's really just London and Los Angeles. As one Qantas executive puts it, 'Passengers love the A380s, but guess what? They really loved the Concorde, too.' The only airline in the world that truly made the A380 work at scale was Emirates, and that was because it operated 123 of them through its Dubai mega-hub.[12]

Joyce's decision to cancel so many 787s, however, was not nearly as unimpeachable. The economics of the Dreamliner were transformational, and having placed one of the earliest large orders with Boeing in 2005, Qantas had secured an enviable competitive edge, with delivery slots ahead of almost all its major international rivals and unbelievably attractive pricing to boot. With so few natural advantages at Qantas' disposal, it was madness to throw hard-fought ones away.

In the end, Qantas took eleven 787-9s between 2017 and 2019, with a final three deferred at the onset of the pandemic until 2023.[13]

While Qantas used those Dreamliners to launch its popular Perth–London flights in 2018, it mostly put them on routes – Tokyo, Johannesburg, Santiago, San Francisco and even some Los Angeles flights – previously operated by much larger Boeing 747-400s, a beloved legacy fleet it phased out between 2015 and 2020.[14] That is, Joyce shrunk Qantas' international division considerably, and therefore chose to surrender market share, by retiring 747s (configured with 364 seats) and replacing them with far smaller 787s (which had 236 seats).

There had been a third option for Qantas. Joyce could have used some or all of those forty cancelled Dreamliners to replace its fleet of twenty-eight A330s, leaving the capacity of the international division largely stable but markedly enhancing its operating economics.[15]

After the A380s and 787-9s, the A330s rounded out Qantas' wide-body fleet and mostly operated Qantas' flights in Asia, along with some flights between the east coast and Perth. They were very similar in size to the 787 but comparatively cost-inefficient, plus the Dreamliner could fly at least 20 per cent further.[16]

In August 2023, sixteen months after Joyce's press conference with Scherer in hangar 96, Qantas decided to replace its A330 fleet with an order for twelve more 787s and twelve more A350s, to be delivered from 2027. The Qantas board could hardly have waited another day to make this long overdue investment. Its A330s were clapped-out already. By 2027, when the first replacements would *begin* arriving, the average age of Qantas' A330 fleet would be twenty-one years. Many of them would be considerably older. Heaven knows how old the last A330s would be when they were finally retired in the 2030s.[17]

Qantas had always been, or at least aspired to be, one of the world's leading premium airlines. The idea that its medium-term strategy was to operate its Asian network with 25-year-old planes was just shocking, and a complete betrayal of the fleet and the standards that Joyce had inherited.[18]

What's more, by 2023, the list price for a 787-9 was US$293 million (AU$450 million).[19] The forty Dreamliners Joyce previously cancelled had been ordered when the list price was around US$150 million per airframe, and with payments due in a period (between 2010 and 2014) when the Australian dollar was at or near parity with the US dollar.

Captain Tony Lucas, head of the pilots' union, compares Joyce's 787 cancellations unfavourably with the 2001 decision by Geoff Dixon, in the weeks following the September 11 attacks, to buy fifteen 737-800s, with options for sixty more, from a distressed American Airlines. These seventy-five aircraft are still flying today as the totality of the dedicated Qantas Domestic fleet.[20]

'Ansett had just collapsed but we were bold and we went for it, still not being sure how the global economy was going to respond,' Lucas remembers. 'There's been no such boldness in COVID, or for [Qantas]

International for years. In 2014, Alan talked about International being in "terminal decline". Now, all evidence is to the contrary but we're short of airframes.'

However misconceived, in hindsight, the cancellation of those 787s was, Joyce and the Qantas board did not make the decision in a vacuum. In the early years of Joyce's tenure as CEO, Qantas' international arm was buffeted by the dual forces of the Global Financial Crisis, which crippled high-yield corporate traffic, and the continued liberalisation of air rights into Australia for Qantas' foreign competitors. Meanwhile, new A380s were rolling in and had to be paid for. It was a huge capital expenditure program Joyce had inherited, and the easy profits to fund it had virtually evaporated. In his last five full years at the helm, Geoff Dixon had delivered pre-tax profits totalling $5.1 billion. In his first five years, Joyce delivered the paltry sum of $366 million of profit.[21] In his sixth year, Qantas posted a $4 billion loss. In business, as in life, timing is everything.[22]

In 2009, Joyce frantically set about slashing costs, shedding 600 senior and middle-management positions and 1,200 frontline staff, launching a three-year, $1.5 billion savings program called QFuture and, of course, deferring or cancelling US$8 billion (at list prices) of spending on aircraft.[23]

But the externalities only worsened. In 2010, John Borghetti, whom Joyce had beaten to the top job at Qantas, became CEO of Virgin Blue and immediately took the carrier upmarket, rebranding as Virgin Australia and going hard after corporate traffic by introducing business class, luxury airport lounges, A330s with lie-flat seats to Perth, and a raft of other premium offerings. In 2011, Air New Zealand took a strategic stake in Virgin Australia, followed in 2012 by Abu Dhabi flag carrier Etihad Airways, and then Singapore Airlines. Alongside Sir Richard Branson's Virgin Group, these strategic foreign shareholders owned 70 per cent of Virgin Australia, held four board seats, and were prepared to absorb large operating losses to fight a bloody and sustained war against Qantas for domestic market share.[24]

As Virgin ratcheted up domestic capacity to capture share, Joyce elected to respond in kind to defend Qantas' 65 per cent market share, an arbitrary shibboleth long referred to by Qantas as its 'line in the sand'. Virgin added 4.5 billion available seat kilometres to the system, so Qantas added 4.3 billion. The Australian market was flooded with seats, airfares plummeted, and the domestic profit pool shrank from more than $700 million in financial 2012 to less than $100 million in the first half of financial 2014. The Qantas Domestic fortress – the company's core profit centre – was not just under siege, but very much on fire.

At the same time, Joyce was complaining in February 2014 that 'Australia has been hit by a giant wave of international airline capacity'. While this lament was true, it was also misleading by omission, because it was equally true that Qantas' international competitors – and Jetstar – were participating in the anabolic growth of travel demand from a very low ebb in 2009, while Qantas was choosing to sit it out. Forty per cent more passengers were carried to and from Australia in 2014 than in 2009, and while Qantas International's seats had remained flat, its competitors had increased their seats by 46 per cent (Jetstar had increased its seats by 58 per cent). Chief among them, of course, was Qantas' partner Emirates, which had become the Australian market's second-largest international carrier, with a 10 per cent share of all traffic. In effect, Joyce had outsourced a significant portion of Qantas International via its 2012 partnership with Emirates, under which Qantas marketed and sold Qantas tickets on Emirates' flights to Europe.

In response to a profit downgrade by Qantas in December 2013, ratings agency Standard & Poor's stripped Qantas of its invest-ment-grade credit rating. In January 2014, a second agency, Moody's, downgraded Qantas debt to junk.[25] Joyce turned immediately to Canberra, begging then Treasurer Joe Hockey for a $2 billion debt guarantee which would effectively restore its investment-grade credit rating over that debt. Qantas had just announced a $235 million half-year loss and an even deeper program of cost cutting – another $2 billion, including 5,000 job losses. Yet the Abbott government was immovable.[26] It was a novel idea at the time, and it would soon enough be novel again, that Qantas would not get its way with the Australian government.

But within months it was apparent that Joyce didn't need the government's help. In August 2014, Qantas reported that eye-watering pre-tax annual loss of $4 billion – a record that still stands today, even after the massive losses of the COVID years. But as Joyce was at pains to emphasise then, it was really only an *underlying* loss of $646 million. Qantas deducted a medley of 'certain other items' from its statutory loss and, presto, the sea of red ink didn't appear nearly so ghastly.[27]

By far the largest 'excluded item' in Qantas' loss was a $2.6 billion write-down of the carrying value of wide-body aircraft on Qantas' balance sheet. The way that company accounting works, when a company impairs the value of its assets, that impairment hits the profit line. 'This is a non-cash charge,' Joyce stipulated, though he'd certainly spent cash buying the planes whose value he was now slashing. 'It will have no impact on the economics of the business.' Joyce was correct to say that this part of the company's annual loss wasn't a trading loss – in the way we punters normally think of a loss being caused by costs exceeding revenue. And Qantas would keep those aircraft in its fleet and use them as per normal.

Qantas proffered a face-saving reason for this write-down: a new, standalone holding structure for Qantas International had triggered a retesting of the book value of its assets. While that might have been technically true, the fact was that the retesting was coming anyway.

Under Joyce, Qantas had now generated no profit over six years.[28] In the company's most recent accounts (for the six months to 31 December 2013), the total equity or net assets of Qantas was stated as $5.7 billion.[29] And yet the market capitalisation of Qantas – that is, the share price multiplied by the total number of Qantas shares on issue – had mostly loitered below $3 billion for the past two years. In circumstances where Qantas shares had traded at a nearly 50 per cent discount to its equity over a sustained period, the company's auditor, KPMG, had to be muttering, Let's get real here, people. The market was telling Qantas in no uncertain terms that its assets simply weren't worth what Qantas was saying they were worth.

Asset write-downs may be 'non-cash' losses but they are nonetheless highly embarrassing. There was no case ever where an airline writing down its planes by $2.6 billion was a sign that things were going well. When the share price is in the toilet (and bear in mind that Qantas shares hadn't been within cooee of $2 for more than three years), incumbent management teams avoid a write-down at all costs because it strongly suggests that they've fucked up. Indeed, big write-downs tend to be terrific catalysts for incumbent management teams to become outgoing management teams.

Their own job security was therefore always the number one impetus for CEOs not taking impairments, but in this unique case, Joyce felt completely secure. He'd been able to paint Qantas' commercial ill-health as not his fault, as out of his control, as solely the product of circumstances Qantas found itself in. This would ultimately turn out to be one of Joyce's great talents – externalising every misfortune, but owning every success. Qantas chairman Leigh Clifford was backing Joyce to the hilt, heedless to the public cries for Joyce's head after six long years of excuses – some persuasive, others feeble. After all, Clifford bulleting Joyce would have strongly suggested that Clifford had fucked up by appointing him in the first place. Ergo the two men's fortunes, their legacies, were almost indivisible.

Once Joyce was certain he could take the write-down and keep his job, it became in his interests to make the write-down as big as possible. It's called 'kitchen-sinking', or taking the trash out, and new CEOs are notorious for it; indeed, at this point, Joyce was behaving like a new CEO. The larger the write-down – the more pain a company took upfront – the greater the benefit to profits in the years following. That's because write-downs reduce a company's ongoing depreciation costs.

When you buy a plane for $100 million with the intention of using it for twenty years, under accounting rules you have to depreciate the carrying value of that plane by $5 million each year. Depreciation is a business expense that hits the profit line just like fuel or wages. Airlines have dozens or even hundreds of planes, and therefore have enormous depreciation bills every year that drag on profitability (just one more reason why airlines are, generally speaking, terrible enterprises to own).[30] But if you could instead write down the value of a plane by $50 million in one hit, then you halve the ongoing annual depreciation cost of operating that plane – without, as Joyce said, altering the operating cash that plane would continue to generate. That's why balance sheet write-downs are also known as 'accelerated depreciation'.

By writing down the Qantas International fleet by $2.6 billion in 2014, Joyce cut the entire company's annual depreciation bill (for aircraft) from $1.2 billion in that year to $840 million the following year. This added $320 million, or 68 per cent, to Qantas' 2015 profit. In turn, the Qantas share price rocketed from $1.40 in August 2014 to almost $4 in August 2015, and Joyce's remuneration from $2 million for 2014 to $12 million for 2015.

Executive remuneration is a terrific system – for executives. In 2014, Joyce's pay outcome couldn't get any lower. His bonus would be zero whether Qantas' loss was $1 billion or $10 billion. But in 2015 and later years, his bonus was correlated to the size of the airline's profit. This system creates a perverse incentive at all public companies for CEOs to make the bad years worse so as to make the good years better.

———

Joyce's $4 billion loss – mostly reported as $2.8 billion by the Australian media – grabbed headlines and established a burning platform for yet more change.[31] But in truth, the worst was already behind Qantas. Fewer than four months later, on 8 December 2014, Qantas issued a trading update forecasting a $325 million profit for the six months to 31 December.[32]

With Qantas stabilised, Joyce was gazing into an entirely different operating environment. The airline's cost base was lower, and shrinking, the domestic capacity war with Virgin was over, and international seat capacity was flat. For as long as clement economic conditions prevailed, Qantas would be able to deliver healthy profits. Over this pre-COVID period (the 5.5 years from July 2014 to December 2019), Joyce racked up pre-tax profits of $6.6 billion and returned $4.3 billion to happy Qantas shareholders in dividends and buy-backs. The share price moved steadfastly from $1.40 in July 2014 to more than $7 in December 2019. Because his bonuses were mostly paid in Qantas shares, many of which had been issued at or towards the lower end of that price range, Joyce earned $70 million for those five years.

Looking back upon this idyllic era, it is apparent that Joyce came to realise there were other ways, beyond front-ending his depreciation expenses, he could materially inflate Qantas' profits. As we saw in the previous chapter, there is no more dependable method of doing this in capital-intensive businesses than by starving them of capital. In the airline game, that means deferring or cancelling spending on aircraft. You can only cancel so many, of course. Sooner or later, either your old planes have to be replaced or your airline has to shrink. But by pushing the capital expenditure into later years, you can increase the profits of earlier years. You steal from tomorrow's profits to pad today's. Private equity has been doing this at scale (before flipping the companies back onto stock markets) since the 1980s. Joyce in the late 2010s was merely adhering to their playbook.

Qantas' longstanding, consistent and very public commitment was to maintain a young fleet of aircraft in line with its top-tier competitors. Qantas' annual report for 2009, the financial year Joyce became CEO, stated that 'the average fleet age is forecast to remain between 8.5 and 8.9 years and is estimated having regard to the existing contractually committed long-term fleet plan'. By 2015, the average age of the Qantas fleet was slightly younger again, at 7.7 years, which was 'below the targeted 8–10 year range'.[33] According to Qantas' 2016 annual report, the average fleet age was 8.6 years, 'within the targeted 8–10 year range'. Further, the report explained: 'The benefits of fleet investment include improved customer satisfaction, environmental outcomes, operational efficiencies and cost reductions.'

Qantas dropped all mention of the age of its fleet, and its targeted eight- to ten-year range, from its 2017 annual report and all subsequent annual reports. The 2017 report instead stated: 'The determination of the optimal fleet age for the Qantas Group balances a number of factors, including the timing of any new technology, the level of capacity growth required in the markets that it serves, the competitive landscape and whether the investment is earnings accretive.'[34] With these weasel words, a solemn and generational commitment was done away with.[35]

As Qantas entered its new and welcome era of profitability, it was in no small part because in 2014 Joyce had engaged in a 'reprioritisation of capital'. He was 'realigning capex [capital expenditure] with financial performance', which was an Orwellian way of saying he had slashed the annual amount that Qantas spent on aircraft from $3 billion when he became CEO in 2008 to just $1 billion in 2015 and 2016, and $1.5 billion in 2017.[36] An incredible figure: in no year from 2013 to 2022 inclusive did Qantas' net capex minus its depreciation exceed $500 million. Under CFO Tino La Spina in 2015, Qantas adopted a rigid financial framework where investments would only be made when they satisfied strict shareholder return metrics.

Disciplined capital allocation is obviously a good thing in a public company but from that moment, shareholder returns dictated everything, and investment in the Qantas business was short-changed at every turn. Qantas was by then generating big free cash flows, paying shareholders dividends and conducting share buy-backs, and yet in both 2017 and 2018, Joyce deferred Jetstar's A320neo order – the one he made in 2011 – yet again. These were also years when Qantas could have been receiving a flood of those cheap Dreamliners. Instead, it took delivery of just five in 2018, three in 2019, and three in the pre-COVID half of 2020.

Joyce preferred to keep old aircraft flying for years longer by replacing their engines and interiors. Between 2014 and 2020, Qantas installed new seats on its A330s and half of its A380s, dispensing with the retro Marc Newson Skybeds in business class. While the seats were improved, the overhead lockers, galleys and other fixtures continued to degenerate, and by 2024 the dunnies were starting to resemble the worst toilet in Scotland from the movie *Trainspotting*.

By this capital-lite version of fleet 'renewal', Qantas reduced its capital expenditure but forewent the lower fuel and maintenance costs of new aircraft – which Qantas used to acknowledge in its annual report and which many of its key international competitors benefited from. Qantas loved marketing its sustainability credentials, but when you willingly fly planes that burn 25 per cent more fuel per passenger than your competitors, those credentials are all too easy to see through.

Some nuance is required here. I am not saying that what Joyce did in this respect was indefensible. Within reason, it was rational to gratify shareholders by decreasing investment and increasing shareholder returns. Shareholders were, after all, the owners of Qantas. The key qualifier is 'within reason'. Qantas could and did subsist on lower levels of investment for a while, but eventually that catches up with a capital-hungry business. By 2022, it had very much caught up with Qantas.

'I'll put my hand up to certain things: as a shareholder, we want to get a better return on capital,' Crispin Murray tells me in 2024. 'You want an airline earning a reasonable rate of return because then it can invest in product. But it's a balancing act between how much capital it spends and how much shareholders get back, because if those fall out of line, you actually end up creating problems with other stakeholders. The perfect situation is where we were in 2018 and 2019, when [all of Qantas' stakeholders] seemed to be happy.'

Leigh Clifford, who retired as Qantas chairman in 2018, says, 'Obviously we were going to look after the shareholders as they were pretty long-suffering. We weren't doing mega buy-backs, they were fairly modest. We were very conscious of having a strong balance sheet for when things go wrong. But it's a very capital-intensive business and when COVID hit, Qantas owned a lot of its new planes outright and the company had a balance sheet capable of surviving.'

It was also true that COVID made this situation worse by wiping out two and a half years of profits and the additional investment those profits would have funded. But the inconvenient truth for Joyce was that Qantas did not have a bulging pipeline of incoming new aircraft when the pandemic descended. Yes, the first eighteen neos would have arrived at Jetstar, as well as three more 787-9s at Qantas. Joyce would have proceeded to order the Project Sunrise A350s in 2020 but they wouldn't have arrived until 2024, and probably later.

Then in August 2021, Qantas came up with an innovative new justification for the unsustainable disinvestment in its fleet. At its full-year results announcement that month, it explained that the reduced aircraft flying hours during the pandemic would net out to around ten months for the 737-800s (Qantas' main domestic aircraft), 1.5 years for the A330s, and three to four years for the A380s, depending on when they finally returned to service. Qantas characterised this reduced flying as 'an opportunity to extend [the] nominal retirement age' of its aircraft 'from [around] 20 years to [around] 24–26 years'. As I joked in the *Financial Review*, 'This brought Qantas into line with its global peers Iran Air and Air Zimbabwe, though Australia is not at this stage subject to international sanctions.' All commercial aeroplanes undergo major heavy maintenance checks every six years, and Qantas planes would henceforth potentially have their fourth checks at twenty-four years, then soldier on a few years longer. In the case of the A380s, three of which still hadn't returned to service by 2024, you could almost accept Qantas' rationale. But for Qantas' other aircraft, it was a piss-take. How do you give a six-year life extension to an aircraft because it's flown ten months fewer?

All of these choices in fleet investment were how Qantas ended up with a passenger fleet whose average age by 2022 was fourteen years, a figure that had nearly doubled in seven years flat.[37] They were how Joyce found himself sitting alongside Airbus' Christian Scherer in hangar 96 ordering replacements, many not arriving until the following decade, for aircraft that were *already* very tired. They were how Qantas found itself so short of long-haul aircraft, with only eleven 787s and five A380s, that its old A330s were operating thirteen-hour flights to India and Los Angeles without proper crew-rest facilities.

Those choices were also how Qantas found itself with a large number of domestic 737-800s in the absolute twilight of their usable lives. One of Joyce's very smart efficiency moves in his early years was to increase the flying hours of aircraft, so these seventy-five planes had been worked harder than almost any other 737 fleet in the world. By 2022 their average age was fifteen years, but fifteen of them were already twenty years' old.[38] Qantas had placed just twenty firm orders for A321XLRs to replace them (increased to twenty-eight orders in 2024). As for replacing the rest of the 737s, there was nothing coming before 2030.

It wasn't only on aircraft that Qantas failed to invest sufficiently. The company's technology spending – particularly on customer-facing improvements, which often reduce staff costs – was inadequate, especially when compared to US carriers, which spend billions every year on technology. Qantas' website was a basket case, crashing constantly on users mid-task. And when Qantas call centres were overwhelmed with hours-long queues in 2022, it was largely because customers couldn't change their flights on qantas.com or on the Qantas app. US carrier Delta had launched same-day flight change functionality in its mobile app in 2021. United Airlines did the same in 2023. Delta introduced baggage tracking to its app in 2016, whereas Qantas and Virgin Australia didn't do this until 2024. In 2019, United launched proprietary ConnectionSaver software, which marginally adjusted its departure times to significantly reduce passengers' missed connections. In 2022, Qantas' analog solution was to increase connection times from sixty to ninety minutes. Strong levels of competition in US aviation drove those customer improvements; Qantas had less incentive to invest in them because its domestic competition was weak and its management team was putting customers behind shareholders in its hierarchy of priorities.

Equally, it was in 2014 that Delta, United and Emirates introduced inflight wi-fi on their international flights (Singapore Airlines did so even earlier). But it wasn't until 2024 that Qantas finally began installing wi-fi on its long-haul aircraft.

Joyce benefited immensely by delaying so much capital expenditure. The avoided spending flowed straight to the company's short-term financial performance and on to its share price and then his pay. The crippling cost of delayed fleet renewal was an unholy inheritance he would leave his successor. In June 2014, Qantas' future capital expenditure commitments were $8.6 billion, more than half of which were only payable in 'later than five years'. In 2019, they were $9.6 billion. When Joyce left Qantas in September 2023, they had ballooned to $21 billion. In 2018, Qantas took delivery of just five new aircraft. In 2019, the year before COVID, it was only three. Yet in 2024, right after Joyce left, Qantas received eleven new planes, with twenty more due to come in 2025, and twenty-four in 2026. Joyce was ejecting himself from the cockpit right before Qantas flew into a capex mountain.

———

This is a complex story because Alan Joyce took a lumbering, former state-owned enterprise and made it far more efficient and competitive against the airlines it competed with globally, but he also made it appear far stronger than it really was by strangling the investment it needed to maintain itself. Both of those things can be true at the same time.

The first half-dozen years under Joyce were painful for Qantas. Some of that pain was arguably self-inflicted. But it would be churlish and historically unreliable to overlook the huge beneficial changes that came out of those dark years.

The Qantas Joyce inherited was a complacent and somewhat arrogant bureaucracy rife with what management guru Sumantra Ghoshal once famously described as 'satisfactory underperformance'.[39] I know this because I worked there at the time. Qantas had higher costs than virtually any of its major international competitors, even the legacy American carriers. Add to this the Global Financial Crisis and the airline was in quicksand.

By incrementally stripping billions out of the company's annual cost base, Joyce significantly improved the economics of Qantas – to the extent that any airline's economics are stable for long. For years it was thankless work. Whatever Joyce removed in costs, still more would evaporate from the revenue line.

Says Crispin Murray, 'If you can bring your cost base in line with – if not lower than – your competitor, then they lose the incentive to adopt a price war strategy to gain share, which should lead to competition based on other factors and prevent the poor returns that had characterised the industry. That was a very reasonable approach and Alan achieved that.'

He also changed the company's culture. I have spoken to many senior Qantas executives from that period who recall a humble CEO who welcomed internal debates where everyone's opinion mattered. Joyce, they say, was collegiate and invited challenge. These would have been easy years in which to display humility. As the losses stacked up, there was no cause for hubris. Joyce was also very young for his position, aged just forty-two when appointed, and was being developed quite artfully as a leader by Qantas chairman Leigh Clifford. Clifford was an executive with thirty-seven years' experience at another iconic, highly unionised and capital-intensive Australian company: mining giant Rio Tinto. Joyce leaned heavily on Clifford's advice and grew in confidence.

For fund manager Pendal, which hunts for companies that will generate better future returns than the investment market realises, this partnership was key. 'Leigh was a very good chairman, and made a gutsy call bringing in Alan,' Murray says. 'And we felt, looking at Alan's background, he'd be someone who'd look at the low returns in the airline industry and think about that differently. They really were a good combination.'

Before 2014, Joyce minimised investment in Qantas out of weakness. From 2015, he was doing so from a position of strength. And as Qantas' fortunes changed, Joyce changed. He received acclamation and naturally enjoyed it. He became a rockstar CEO and started to act like one. The gay marriage plebiscite, in particular, super-charged Joyce's fame. 'It was a good thing that he was involved in that debate and the outcome,' Murray reflects. 'It was one of a number of factors, alongside the importance of Qantas in Australia's psyche, the success of the turnaround and his genuine charisma, which elevated him to a status that I can't recall any other Australian CEO reaching. But I think at some point – and I think it's a slow thing – when you get enough people telling you you're the best, if you're not careful, it can impact how you operate.' This shift, Murray says, 'coincided with Leigh retiring and Richard coming in. I think that was actually quite a big factor here. That dynamic where you have a chair who's happy to sit back, let management run the company, but just has a nose for when the CEO maybe is getting ahead of themselves; that's really important.' Clifford left in 2018 and was replaced as chairman by Richard Goyder, who deferred utterly to Joyce.

On the day Goyder's appointment was announced, influential corporate governance adviser Dean Paatsch expressed scepticism that Goyder was capable of handling the workload, given his existing commitments as chairman of Woodside and the AFL, which made him 'the closest thing Australia has to a secular pope'. Should something go awry at any of these organisations, Goyder could 'very quickly find [his] workload unmanageable', Paatsch said prophetically. 'A scandal at the AFL, a takeover at Woodside, and an air safety incident at Qantas is beyond any one person's capability.'

In effect, Joyce became executive chairman, and Goyder's board were first class passengers. Goyder was very different to Clifford, but Joyce 2.0 was also very different to Joyce the beta testing model.

There are varying accounts as to when exactly Joyce lost his humility and no longer invited challenge, but there is little dispute that this did happen. Some believe the departure in 2017 of Jon Scriven, the company's group executive of people and culture, removed a key moderating force, along with any expertise in employee relations and organisational culture from Joyce's group management committee.[40] Others blame the command-and-control structure, and mindset, that Joyce adopted in the COVID crisis, which he never relinquished.

In the opening weeks of 2020, Joyce told an interviewer, 'I like that challenge, I like people questioning things, I like new ideas.' He even claimed that at every meeting of the eleven-person group management committee, one member was nominated as 'black hat' or chief challenger. This was a practice introduced by Scriven but which multiple insiders assured me had by 2022 fallen into disuse. Indeed, by the time Qantas emerged from the pandemic, the company's arrogance had returned and the only executives left in Joyce's inner sanctum were those who didn't dare challenge him.

Fighting the Facts
Dec 2022–March 2023

By the end of 2022 Qantas was charging its highest nominal prices in history, higher again than in the chaotic winter period when the surging cost of travel first entered the public conscience.[1] Qantas' airfares were by December around 45 per cent higher than pre-COVID for both domestic and international flights.[2] Domestic fares had shot up 24 per cent just since July. Right through the Australian economy, inflation was rampant. Consumer prices increased by 7.8 per cent over calendar 2022, and in response the Reserve Bank had raised interest rates eight times consecutively since May. In the December quarter, the Australian Bureau of Statistics reported that the single largest contributor to inflation was domestic holiday travel. The third-biggest contributor was international holiday travel. Qantas, therefore, was a leading driver of the nation's inflation crisis.

The rise in Qantas airfares correlated directly with the gradual recovery in its operations. In the autumn and winter of that year, Qantas had openly reduced its flights to drive up fares and thus recoup higher fuel costs, but by October Qantas said it was doing so 'to protect the sustained improvement in operational performance'. This worked by taking planes and crew out of the schedule and keeping them on standby as emergency replacements. It had the ACCC on high alert. In December, the competition regulator said it 'would be concerned if the airlines withheld capacity in order to keep airfares high', and would be 'monitoring [them] to ensure they return capacity to the market in a timely manner to bring downward pressure on airfares'.

Qantas' operations had certainly improved but, true to form, the company was pronouncing its clean bill of health prematurely. After chairman Richard Goyder reprimanded the media in September for not reporting Qantas' uptick in reliability, Qantas went on to miss its own 75 per cent on-time departures target for that month by 6 percentage points. By November, Qantas' on-time arrivals were at 67 per cent, finally beating Virgin but still way below the long-term average of 82 per cent. Jetstar was at 61 per cent while its cancellations were stuck at 7 per cent. Qantas' new chief customer officer, Markus Svensson, claimed in December that operational performance was 'now effectively back to pre-pandemic levels', but it just wasn't true.[3]

Joyce went further still, claiming, 'Qantas is now essentially back at pre-COVID levels of service and customers have told me that they have noticed a dramatic improvement.' The improvement in on-time performance from July was indeed dramatic, but it was an objectively false statement that Qantas was back at pre-COVID levels of service. Qantas' domestic on-time performance had not recovered to that extent. The on-time performance of its international flights – which wasn't disclosed publicly – was even worse. Meanwhile, the inflight catering was unrecognisable from the standards of 2019. There were also fewer cabin crew on flights and fewer customer service staff in the terminals. It was irrational for Joyce to be maintaining that he'd slashed nearly $1 billion of costs from the airline but that its service was completely unchanged. Yet he maintained it anyway.

Joyce's remark smacked of confirmation bias, from which we all to varying degrees suffer – of failing to weight-adjust the skewed sample of customers who occupied his world. Supplicants from the highest echelon of public and corporate life shook his hand and gripped his shoulder in the Chairman's Lounge, as firmly as they held onto their coveted membership. And yet these were the same CEOs and public company directors who were bitching to each other, and to journalists, about their hellish Qantas experiences.

Even still, Joyce struck a rare conciliatory tone in a Christmas interview with the *Australian Financial Review*, acknowledging that 'a lot of the criticism we copped [in 2022] was fair enough', and even conceding that the criticism directed personally at him was 'understandable'. It is interesting to wonder how 2023 might have unfolded differently for Qantas had Joyce been able to maintain his access to this fleeting mindset of contrition and qualified self-awareness.

The tone of the incoming year was instead set early by a spate of inflight incidents. Two days before Christmas, a Qantas A380 en route to London was forced to land in the Azerbaijani capital of Baku because of faulty smoke alarms in the cockpit. This was a painful scenario for Qantas because it had no presence in or anywhere near Baku, and Baku's airport was not equipped to handle A380s. Passengers spent more than thirty-six hours marooned before Qantas could extract them with a replacement A380, eventually delivering them to Heathrow on the morning of 25 December. A maximally awkward diversion like this can happen to any airline at any time, but after such a rotten year for Qantas, the Australian media was gagging to report any fresh mishap. The sacrosanct time of year only amplified the matter. The Qantas Grinch had almost stolen Christmas. The airline thus entered 2023 at a low ebb; at least, it seemed low at the time. In hindsight, it was really just the top of descent.

On 18 January, a Qantas Boeing 737 halfway across the Tasman issued a mayday call to air traffic control after one of its two engines failed. It continued to Sydney and landed normally, though was met by emergency services trucks as a precaution – which was not especially rare. The incident raised an absurd level of media attention, with TV networks carrying breathless live coverage of the aircraft landing, as if they were expecting a fireball. By unhappy coincidence, Qantas pilots conducted four more mid-flight diversions in the following week, each of which was treated as major news by the Australian media. In a normal year, Qantas would perform around sixty air returns. That five occurred in one week was just bad luck.

'They've had one real issue and four precautionary returns,' Steve Purvinas said. 'This sequence is not too out of the ordinary.' Andrew David quite rightly told the media, 'I'd be more worried about the airlines that don't turn back than the airlines that do in those situations.'

In high dudgeon, Qantas' PR boss Andrew McGinnes fired off a group letter to the news directors of the major television stations expressing his concern at 'the alarmist and disproportionate coverage that our recent air turn-backs and diversions have received from many media outlets', and asking them 'to please ensure your coverage of all elements of aviation – and of Qantas – is proportional'. McGinnes was absolutely correct that the media coverage had been inordinate. Periodically, this happened to Qantas. Every few years, the media generated a false sense of an upsurge in inflight incidents which in actual fact was only an upsurge in the reporting of them. It usually occurred after a major safety event and then petered out.[4] In this latest outbreak, the Australian media was simply feeding the demand of its audiences, which possessed voracious appetites for stories of Qantas calamity due to their own direct and recent scars from it.

Three days after McGinnes' letter, the *Sydney Morning Herald* published an op-ed by Joyce. While his piece addressed the over-reaction to Qantas' series of mid-flight air returns, it also sought to explain to the travelling public why Qantas airfares were so high. 'In order to make our operations more reliable, we had to reduce our flights to give us more buffer,' Joyce wrote. 'Less supply and lots of demand meant fares went up. Higher fares also reflect inflation in general and higher fuel prices in particular, which are up 65 per cent in the past six months compared with pre-COVID. Naturally, that flows through to how much you pay for a flight. There's not much we can do about the cost of things such as fuel, but the fact our operations have stabilised means we can steadily put capacity back in. Domestically, we're almost back to 100 per cent of pre-COVID flying levels. Internationally, we'll be about 80 per cent by the middle of the year and we've recently seen most of our competitors announce a major ramp up in their capacity – so you can expect to see fares trend down.'[5]

Joyce's thesis was debatable in a number of ways. Firstly, jet fuel prices (in US dollars) had actually peaked at a 30-year high in June 2022 and had been falling ever since.[6] By February 2023 the price of avgas had fallen 33 per cent (albeit still at historic highs) yet airfares had not fallen at all. Secondly, while Qantas' fuel costs were elevated by historical standards, the airline had significantly reduced all of its other costs – especially its staff costs. The company's non-fuel unit costs had risen just 8 per cent since 2019 (despite inflation over that period being 12.5 per cent) while its unit revenues were up 46 per cent.[7] Consequently, Qantas was now generating super-profits. For the six months to 31 December 2022, it made a profit of $1.435 billion, more than the airline had ever made in a full twelve-month period.

Thirdly and finally, by attempting to portray airfares as being wholly determined by external forces – i.e., by demand and supply – Joyce was obscuring his own agency in the setting of Qantas' ticket prices. As we've seen, Joyce had made the choice to withdraw significant supply of seats from the market, and as a result was able to make the choice to increase his airfares by a terrific magnitude. Weeks earlier, with Qantas customers complaining to the press about economy seats at business class prices between Melbourne and Sydney, Rex's John Sharp observed that Qantas had 'mastered the art of explaining the problems [behind sky-high pricing] as being beyond their control ... but they're actually not'.

Remember, only twelve months earlier Joyce had said, 'We have told the ACCC that ... we are going to be flying for cash [flow over profit].' He'd also said, 'We just need to generate cash so, for us, 2022 is not about making money.' Back in October 2020, he'd said 'That is the right business decision for probably a number of years. I think the next few years are going to be very good for consumers.' Alas, it was not to be.

Just as it was previously Joyce's strategy, and within his discretion, to drop prices and operate profitless flights to stimulate demand for travel, it became Joyce's strategy to withdraw seats from a red-hot market – his justification for doing so having morphed from fuel costs to reliability – and ratchet up prices to maximise profit. This was only one of many options available to him, another of which was to accept slightly lower profits and keep airfares within the realm of sanity. Joyce was even admitting that he would reduce his prices the second his international competitors forced him to. He was effectively saying, Fares are coming down; until then, bend over.

I'm not suggesting that Qantas should not have restored itself to profitability as soon as practicable, but the notion that Qantas was powerless over its prices was absurd.

———

Nine days later, on 14 February 2023, the *Australian Financial Review*'s editor-in-chief, Michael Stutchbury, was summoned to Qantas headquarters in Mascot by Andrew McGinnes for an audience with Alan Joyce to discuss my latest column about the airline.[8] Dragging an editor out to the airport was an extremely Qantas thing to do. The CEOs and chairmen of companies ten or twenty times bigger than Qantas would routinely call upon Stutchbury at the *AFR* newsroom in North Sydney.

'So I go in there, and there's McGinnes, and there's Alan, and we just go into a room and have a chat for an hour or so,' Stutchbury recounts. 'It was a pleasant enough chat.' Stutchbury – or Stutch as he's widely known – is maddeningly unflappable. He would describe being dangled by his ankles over a sheer cliff face as a pleasant chat, and he would actually mean it. 'I just let them vent, really. What was I going to say? I let them make the case, but it is what it is. I said, "If there are any factual errors, I'm more than happy to address those. It's my job to sort those out."'

But Joyce and McGinnes didn't identify any factual errors. 'I certainly can't recall any, and if there'd been a serious one, we would have acted upon it, or at least got into a further stage [of review] on it.' Instead, McGinnes conveyed an allegation to Stutchbury that my coverage of Qantas was driven by personal animosity, describing both my wife and me as 'disgruntled' former employees. McGinnes, in Joyce's presence, requested that I henceforth be required to disclose my employment history at the end of every column I wrote about Qantas.

It had been more than thirteen years since I'd left Qantas, and as Stutch says, 'There was no secret about that.' In the intervening years, I'd written many glowing things about Qantas and about Joyce, and at various times had turned my guns on their rivals. Qantas had never raised my alleged lack of objectivity then. My wife had left Qantas three years previously, before COVID, when she was offered a more senior role at another airline. To suggest that I'd lain in wait for years to exact revenge on Alan Joyce for some unspecified slight against my household was just plain mad. It was grossly unprofessional and it was desperate. But in the decade I'd spent writing about the grandest delusions of corporate Australia, I'd seen this behaviour so many times. This is what the worst executives do: they grasp for any reason external to themselves to explain away the criticism they deserve. They cannot contemplate the truth of the criticism, so they must try to discredit it, and when that fails, their next step will always be trying to discredit the person expressing it.

I did not learn about this request for me to disclose my non-existent conflict of interest to *AFR* readers until some weeks later, in April 2023. Which is to say, it did not play any part in what happened next.

———

Qantas handed down its record-smashing half-year profit on 23 February 2023. The yawning gap between the prices its customers were being charged and the quality of service they were receiving had already been firmly established in the minds of the public. But there was another glaring dichotomy, and that was the amount of financial support the Australian taxpayer had provided to Qantas compared to the company's long-term contribution to public coffers. The first to recognise this resentment bubbling through the national zeitgeist was cult satirical news service *The Betoota Advocate*. 'Alan Joyce Laughs When Asked Whether a Billion Dollar Profit Means Qantas Will Pay Tax This Year,' its headline blared that same day, accompanied by a cropped image of Joyce's $30,000 porcelain grin. The story began: '"Don't be stupid, Qantas doesn't pay tax," laughed the man who raked in a $23.9 million pay packet in 2019. "That's how basic economics works you morons."'[9]

The *Betoota* article continued: 'When asked whether the government would see any return on the [$2.7 billion it] gave the private company with no strings attached, Joyce started laughing again. "Stop," he giggled. "You are cracking me up."' This mocking rendition of Qantas' half-year results conference that morning struck a chord with me (and undoubtedly many others), and I decided to take up my pen to elaborate on the theme. My article was entitled 'Alan Joyce has Canberra all figured out'.

Qantas would not pay any Australian company tax on its $1.4 billion first-half profit because it had nearly $1 billion of tax credits in the bank from its $6.2 billion of losses over the 2020, 2021 and 2022 financial years. As a result, the company told investors that day, it wouldn't need to pay company tax until 2025.

This was the second time in Qantas' Joyce era, I explained, where the airline had enjoyed a run of tax-free years owing to its previous losses. Qantas' huge $4 billion loss in 2014 had left it with $1 billion of tax credits, which it took until 2018 to exhaust.[10] It then paid $411 million in company tax in 2019 and 2020. Then COVID hit and Qantas' losses began again.

From the 2010 financial year (the first full year that Joyce was CEO) until the present day, I wrote, Qantas 'paid Australian income tax of just $288 million'. In a column of only 850 words, I didn't bother explaining that I'd arrived at that number by deducting from the $411 million figure the tax refunds Qantas had received in 2010 and 2011, which amounted to $131 million, then adding back $8 million of tax paid between 2012 and 2015, which I suspected but couldn't prove were actually foreign taxes.[11] That is, $288 million was the maximum Qantas could have paid in Australian company tax during Joyce's tenure but it was more likely $280 million. If anything, I was being generous.

I deemed it 'instructive to compare Joyce's entire contribution to Commonwealth consolidated revenue of $288 million with the $2.7 billion of government money he mainlined during the pandemic', including 'a relief package, a readiness scheme, subsidies and waivers, a juicy freight assistance mechanism and even an aviation-specific JobKeeper after the regular JobKeeper ended.[12]

'Qantas didn't and won't repay any of those subsidies, nor is it obliged to. Instead, Joyce is returning $900 million to shareholders in buy-backs in this financial year. More fool the Morrison government.'

Shortly after my piece was published, a member of McGinnes' PR team called and asked me where I got the figure of $2.7 billion for total COVID subsidies received by Qantas. Incredulous, I informed him that $2.7 billion was the sum of the subsidies listed in note 24 of the company's 2020, 2021 and 2022 annual reports.

Two days later, in response to my article, Qantas submitted an opinion piece to the *Financial Review* in the name of CFO Vanessa Hudson. As ever, in the interests of open debate, Stutchbury was only too happy to publish it. Having read it in advance, I could barely contain my excitement. Qantas was committing a monumental unforced error.

My piece, Hudson began, 'makes some big mistakes' by 'getting important numbers wrong, and not by a little'. My article, she continued, 'claims Qantas has paid only $288 million in company tax since 2010. The actual figure is $411 million.' Hudson, the airline's chief numbers person, had completely missed the tax refunds Qantas received in 2010 and 2011.

Whether the correct number was $280 million, $288 million or $411 million was almost beside the point.[13] Even the highest of these amounts still represented a meagre amount of tax over a decade and a half. As I'd made clear in my article, that was because in net terms, even excluding the COVID years, Qantas had generated meagre profits under Joyce. It was surreal that Hudson, Joyce and Andrew McGinnes thought they'd made an argument in their favour. We paid $411 million tax in fifteen years, not $288 million, so there!

But this wasn't even the most misconceived part of Hudson's rebuttal. '[Aston's] article says our company tax payments are the sum total of our contribution to the government's consolidated revenue, but that's not right either,' Hudson continued. 'We collect and pay multiple taxes from our activities, from [goods and services tax] and [fringe benefits tax] to ticket taxes and fuel excise.' This line of reasoning was not credible. GST and ticket taxes were paid by Qantas customers, not by Qantas. The airline just collected those taxes and remitted them to the government on its customers' behalf. They unequivocally did not represent Qantas' contribution to government coffers in the way that income tax on its profits did.[14] By this twisted logic, Qantas should have trumpeted the personal income tax it withheld from its employees' pay cheques each fortnight. It would've been no more ludicrous.

Hudson then moved on to 'the circa $2 billion of funding Qantas received from the government'. Again, the point of her treatise was to accuse me of citing incorrect numbers, yet she was smoothly misstating Qantas' COVID subsidies by $700 million in a tract about numerical accuracy, and after I'd provided her PR minder with a pointer to the correct amount in her own audited accounts.

Hudson's greatest sensitivity, however, was reserved for the company's JobKeeper haul: 'While JobKeeper was a wage subsidy for most employers, for Qantas it was largely welfare for people who had no work do to,' Hudson explained. 'Half of it went straight to staff, rather than offsetting non-existent wages, when the airline was in deep hibernation ... [Aston] calls it a fault in the system that a now-profitable Qantas isn't paying these elements back. That argument again: Qantas should pay back the money it passed on from the government to its people, because it had no work for its people, because the government shut the border.' This was a deranged explanation: that JobKeeper wasn't a wage subsidy for Qantas in the way it was for other employers because Qantas gave half of it to out-of-work staff. Er, what was the other half?

A strawman argument is a variety of logical fallacy whereby an arguer takes their opponent's argument, repackages it to be weaker, then defeats that version of the argument rather than their opponent's actual position. It is a common high school debating technique and was the unmistakable watermark of Andrew McGinnes.[15] My piece never said that Qantas should have to repay the half of JobKeeper it passed on to staff. My piece never went so far as to say that Qantas should repay any JobKeeper at all. I had merely lamented the Morrison government giving billions to Qantas on a non-recourse basis and Qantas management then prioritising the interests of Qantas shareholders over the interests of Qantas customers (who, as taxpayers, had ultimately provided those non-recourse billions). I had dared to explain the full extent of the public's financial support of Qantas. There was a prevailing lack of clarity over how much of the $2.7 billion was profit margin and how much represented Qantas' service delivery costs. But that wasn't the public's fault, nor was it mine. The confusion was caused by Qantas initially disclosing the profit margin on its subsidies, then shifting to disclosing the profit margin on its subsidies excluding JobKeeper, then ceasing to disclose any margin at all and attacking anyone who talked about it.[16]

Hudson concluded her counterattack by claiming, 'These are not the first errors of fact or judgement in the many [of Aston's] articles ... focused on Qantas in the past six months, but it's the first time we've moved to correct them publicly. Even satire should have its limits.' She was accusing me of previous – but unidentified – instances of inaccuracy, an especially cheap shot because they were impossible to disprove, or alternatively, to rectify.

This accusation of unidentified inaccuracies misfired, and not just because Hudson's piece had demonstrable inaccuracies of its own. It also converted me from a casual critic to an incensed and highly motivated one.

I was far from the sole messenger in Qantas' sights. In November 2022, consumer advocacy group CHOICE had given the airline top spot in its annual Shonky Awards for 'a disappointing trail of delayed flights, lost baggage, excessive call waiting times and customer difficulties in using travel credits'. All of these problems had been acknowledged at one time or another by Qantas, and yet its response was to attack: 'These awards are clearly out of date and the data CHOICE is using is itself a bit shonky,' a Qantas spokesperson said. 'We had several months of poor performance earlier in the year, but it's improved significantly since August and we're back to our pre-COVID level of service.'[17] This was an *annual* award Qantas was attacking for not limiting its data to Qantas' favourite months. What other large Australian company carried on like this?

In February 2023, research firm Roy Morgan released its latest 'net trust' rankings of Australian brands, a widely respected measure because it shows net brand trust (which is brand trust adjusted for brand distrust). In the second half of 2022, Qantas had collapsed from the sixth most trusted Australian brand to the fortieth. Roy Morgan CEO Michele Levine described it as the most 'dramatic fall from grace' of any company 'without a singular crisis', which was caused by the airline's operational issues but also by 'a leadership team that was seemingly out of touch' and which had treated Qantas staff poorly.

'CEO performance and pay is not often cited as a reason for distrusting a company in Australia,' Levine later told me, and yet in November 2022, a top-three reason offered by Roy Morgan respondents for distrusting Qantas was its 'overpaid CEO' (the other two reasons were its poor service and recent record as a poor employer). January 2023 was the final month that Qantas maintained (narrowly) a net trust rating, falling quickly and deeply into net distrust after that.

'Australians have now clearly had enough and Qantas' historical reservoir of goodwill has breached its banks,' Levine said to the *Financial Review* on 10 February. 'It makes Qantas a fragile brand.'

None of this was news to Qantas' top executives. Markus Svensson received a confidential briefing pack from corporate reputation firm RepTrak and shared it with Joyce and the entire Qantas group management committee on 24 November 2022. In that briefing, RepTrak told Qantas that it was 'undergoing a significant reputational crisis' and that its benchmark score had fallen below Virgin Australia's for the first time since 2013. Among the key drivers of public perceptions that RepTrak measured, the biggest fall for Qantas was in the category of leadership, with its rating on whether the company had 'a strong and appealing leader' falling by 10 percentage points in three months. 'What may be surprising is the extent of the decline especially on drivers such as leadership, which [has] been such a strength for the company over the past decade,' RepTrak reported. 'Perceptions of Qantas' CEO is also a key driver of its reputation and work will be needed to rebuild trust, admiration and respect towards the leadership team.'

Qantas' leadership team did not share this RepTrak report with the Qantas board.

And damningly for Qantas' preferred narrative that its failures were aviation-industry-wide, Air New Zealand topped the RepTrak benchmark – and not just the airlines. The Kiwi carrier beat other top-five brands JB Hi-Fi, Woolworths, Samsung and Toyota to be the most respected company in Australia.

RepTrak had offered Qantas solutions to dig itself out of its crisis. 'To improve reputation, focus on having a strong and appealing leader ... being fair in business, behaving ethically ... [and] demonstrating concern for wellbeing of employees.' Fast-forward three months and Qantas was intent on pursuing its own solutions.

——

Seared perhaps by the blowback to Qantas' epic half-year profit, Alan Joyce once more seized the narrative.

On 3 March 2023, the day after he'd been named as Sydney Theatre Company's new chairman, Joyce convened a press conference at Melbourne airport with key trade union leaders and federal Minister for Skills and Training, Brendan O'Connor, to announce that Qantas would hire 8,500 new employees over the next ten years. He also unveiled the Qantas Group Engineering Academy, which would train up to 300 new engineers each year for Qantas, Jetstar, and other aviation and defence companies. Qantas needed to recruit 200 new engineers a year, which Joyce acknowledged well exceeded the current talent pool. 'A fully licenced aviation engineer typically takes a minimum of five years of practical and classroom training,' he said. What he didn't acknowledge was that he'd made 30 per cent of Qantas' licensed engineers redundant in the pandemic and had been unable to replace them, a shortfall which had contributed to Qantas' operational problems.

It was a grandiose announcement – 8,500 jobs! No politician ever declined such a priceless photo opportunity. But how could you not be cynical? Qantas would train and hire precisely the minimum number of people it needed to super-profitably deliver the product it overcharged for. It wasn't a community service. Joyce had cut the number of Qantas Group employees from 34,300 in 2008 to 29,800 when COVID struck, and to 20,600 by 2021.[18] The number had since bounced to 23,500. He had spent $1 billion on 9,800 redundancies to cut $600 million of 'permanent' salary costs, for which his reward would soon be a $4.5 million recovery and retention bonus. Now, in his final year, Joyce was promising to hire them all back, and more! The Qantas workforce would be restored to 32,000 in a hiring binge he would never see the bill for – just like the bill for the incoming armada of replacement Qantas planes.

It was the emptiest of pledges. In one of the most volatile and punishing industries on earth, how could any airline confidently predict the size of its workforce a decade in the future? Rather like being eleven weeks from bankruptcy, 8,500 new jobs emanated a false sense of exactitude when really, the number might as well have been scribbled on the back of a pie bag. Suddenly, in a press release not lodged with the stock exchange, Qantas was foreshadowing a 25 per cent leap in its size and its costs when it had been assuring investors that its unit economics would only get better from here on. It wasn't technically impossible, but it implied the airline would be able to massively increase its seat capacity at the same time as maintaining or even widening its profit margins. But where would the demand for these extra seats come from, and how could Qantas know what its competitors would do with their capacity and their prices? When this sort of forecast was being made without a detailed business case and strategy alongside it, you could be forgiven for assuming that the proper processes of a large public company had broken down, substituted with the personal PR agenda of the CEO.[19]

This was a vanity exercise, designed to expunge Alan Joyce's public image as a job slayer. 'The problem was that Alan began responding to everything like a politician,' one of Joyce's top lieutenants later conceded to me privately – an ironic attitude for someone who claimed not to be a public figure. The 8,500 jobs were what's known in Australian politics as an 'announceable': a proclamation whose soundbite was the full extent of its substance (and purpose). RepTrak had advised Qantas to 'focus on having a strong and appealing leader', but instead of install-ing someone who fit that description, Qantas was attempting to make the shoe fit Joyce, with his fifteen years of bunions.

This attempt to restore Alan Joyce's brand was laughable. I wrote in the *Financial Review*: 'You can't have both hands in both pockets of every travelling Australian and then catch up with them after the event and say, "Hey, did you know I'm a ripper bloke? I'm for skills, I'm for training, I support the arts, please love me. I was a rapacious businessman who fucked over everyone, but geez I'm a good person. Look at the sunlight glint on my Order of Australia pin."'

Three weeks later, drawing the raffle at the annual Chief Executive Women dinner, Joyce described Vanessa Hudson as 'the best CFO in the country'. As I explained to readers of my column, what made Hudson the best in Joyce's eyes, after her botched defence of Qantas' taxes and subsidies in the *AFR* earlier that month, was 'her willingness to be thrown on grenades with his name on them. Not so much to protect the company's reputation, but to protect *his* reputation, the restoration of which seems to be the company's driving preoccupation.'

Joyce had drawn the raffle because Qantas had donated the prize: a $1,000 flight credit. I took the chance to pick at this thread. As a result of the columns I'd written about Qantas, I'd been contacted by umpteen disaffected Qantas customers and heard a litany of different complaints. The source of the deepest anger was Qantas' flight credits system. Qantas and Jetstar customers still held $800 million of diffi-cult-to-redeem COVID flight credits. With one customer, I'd even stepped through the redemption process to see how it worked, or more accurately, how it didn't work. Anyone who had ever tried to use a Qantas COVID flight credit, I wrote, 'will appreciate the madden-ing folly of this bargain. If I'm exaggerating, why do two-fifths of these credits remain unclaimed?' Any unused credits would expire on 31 December 2023, at which point the airline could bank the remain-ing balance as bonus profit.

I concluded: 'This is fees for no service, scarcely different to National Australia Bank or AMP charging dead people, except Qantas customers aren't dead, they just feel dead on the inside.'

Alan Joyce could explain away a lot of things – flight cancellations, baggage chaos, record airfares – as beyond his control, and heaven knows his explanations had been exotic. But how could he explain away this? Without quite realising it at the time, I had stumbled upon Joyce's Achilles heel.

———

Two days later, I penned another column – this one about Alan Joyce's pay, that uncommon drag on the Qantas brand. Financial 2023 was three-quarters complete but the Australian media hadn't yet twigged to the scale of Joyce's impending plunder. There was his base salary of $2.2 million, his short-term bonus of between $2.2 million and $4.3 million, his special COVID recovery and retention bonus of $4.5 million, and his long-term bonus of $8.8 million.[20] That was a total haul for 2023 of between $17.6 million and $19.8 million.

But just in case everyone had forgotten – and Joyce surely hoped they had – there were also three deferred long-term bonuses from 2020, 2021 and 2022, years in which Qantas suffered losses of $6.2 billion. The deferral was a cynical construct, of course. The decision had never been in question: he would take every last dollar. Those bonuses, preserved in carbonite like Han Solo, were worth another $6.8 million. 'In Alan Joyce's industrial instrument,' I wrote, 'the Better Off Overall Test is that everyone else makes him better off overall. He makes a killing in the good years. He sets aside his [long-term incentives] in the terrible years but then takes them later anyway. What a method.'

Joyce, then, was looking at a remuneration outcome for 2023 of between $24.4 million and $26.5 million – better even than the $23.9 million he earned in 2017. That would take his total earnings as Qantas CEO to the cusp of $130 million. This averaged out at $9 million per year, which was much more than the pay earned by the CEOs of Australia's big four banks – and they were ten or even fifteen times larger than Qantas.

It was an eye-watering amount of money. Defenders of executive largesse would say it was only as eye-watering as Qantas' corresponding profit. But what blew my mind was Joyce plainly preparing to defrost his carbonite bonuses from the loss-making years, when Qantas workers had been either subject to a pay freeze or stood down on a government wage subsidy.[21] That $6.8 million kicker was awarded not for Qantas' absolute shareholder returns in those years, but for its returns as compared to international peers. That is, because other airlines fared even worse, Joyce made bank. The Qantas board was operating by the principles of financial *and* moral relativism.

The calibration of Joyce's incentives was all wrong. For ripping $1 billion of annual costs out of the business, Joyce would receive $4.5 million. Yet for the severe service disruption and brand damage caused by sacking too many people, Joyce would not be penalised.[22] Indeed, that would also be rewarded, to the extent that it had increased short-term profit. 'To trash the brand on the way out the door – that is an absolutely calculated bargain by management to maximise their money,' I wrote. 'After the lean years they are filling their boots. It's a cyclical business and this is their time!'

To be clear, Joyce's perverse incentives were not Joyce's fault. It was the responsibility of the Qantas board to set rational reward targets for the CEO and his team. Its miscarriage in that regard would ultimately become conspicuous, but not yet. In March 2023, the Qantas board was preoccupied with more immediate concerns.

At that month's board meeting, the directors spent some time discussing my recent spate of columns. Joyce was outraged: in his mind, these were unjustifiable personal attacks and they had to be stopped. Revealingly, the board didn't reflect on – nor did it direct Joyce to reflect on – the substance of these columns. Nor did anyone grasp that I was only saying (albeit in impertinent fashion) what multiple respected brand research firms were also saying about Joyce: that he'd become the company's biggest liability. Instead, Joyce's view prevailed; the board resolved that Joyce would lodge another complaint in person with my editor-in-chief, and that as a show of the entire board's support, Goyder would accompany him. Qantas was invoking *lèse-majesté*, whereby any insult to the dignity of its ruler was a crime.

March and April of 2023 were a time of high tension at the airline's Mascot headquarters. I'd lived through the company's last change of leadership in 2008, from Geoff Dixon to Joyce, and had some sense of how surreal things could be. Now, according to those around him, Joyce arrived at the office impossibly early and spent significant amounts of time consuming the media coverage of Qantas, reading every article, standing at his desk and watching every TV clip. 'It's problematic for your PR team when he's read and watched everything by 6am,' one executive commented to me. Often, an informal caucus on the executive floor would discuss the negative coverage. The self-narrative of moral hero was not Joyce's alone: these people felt like they'd been to war together. The CEO's outrage was mostly shared. A few executives, such as Andrew David and QantasLink boss John Gissing, gently implored Joyce to let my criticism go, to no avail.

Joyce was incensed and wanted to fight every word, but there were no histrionics. His style was calm and analytical even under acute stress – an enviable leadership quality during the widespread panic of early COVID. Yet he was clearly in psychological turmoil. Joyce was intellectually brilliant and breathtakingly numerate but seemed to lack the emotional capacity to process criticism; even the Qantas executives who praised Joyce's leadership to me conceded he lacked emotional intelligence. As Joyce saw it, he was the man who saved Qantas, an Australian business legend. His future was on the most prestigious corporate boards, a sought-after speaker and expert, an MBA case study, a carded member of the innermost inner sanctum of elite society.[23] He was on his victory lap, seeking to raise up his name, not have it dragged through the mud.

At the same time, the board's deliberations identifying Joyce's successor were well under way, with presentations to the board scheduled for mid-April. Goyder would later claim the board 'looked globally' and 'listed close to forty potential candidates to take over,' but only two were invited to make their pitch: Vanessa Hudson and Olivia Wirth, the CEO of Qantas Loyalty.

But in fact Goyder had come to prefer Hudson as Joyce's successor far earlier than this. Hudson had proved her mettle by executing emergency debt and equity raisings in the pandemic. She was a 28-year veteran of the airline, having worked everywhere from catering to sales to inflight product; she had run US operations then been chief customer officer. Better yet, Joyce was strongly backing Hudson's candidacy, and when had Goyder ever disagreed with Joyce?

Simon the Likeable
30 March–15 May 2023

Alan Joyce, Richard Goyder and Michael Stutchbury met for break-fast at the Fullerton Hotel in the old GPO building on Sydney's Martin Place on 30 March 2023 to discuss my articles. At least, this time, Stutch didn't have to schlep out to Mascot.

McGinnes had set up this meeting and when doing so, according to Stutchbury, had delivered the implied threat of 'commercial implications', presumably arising from noncompliance with whatever direction Goyder and Joyce intended to deliver.

'I'm sitting across from Goyder and we're chatting away,' Stutchbury says, 'and then he says to the waiter, "Is there a quieter place we can go?" And I think, Uh oh!' After taking a new table in a deserted corner of the restaurant, Goyder launched into his pitch, decrying my 'abusive, personalised attacks that were unfair on Alan', in Stutch's recollection.[1] 'Goyder did most of the talking, because he was there to use the authority and prestige of the [chairmanship] to make that case, and I dutifully listened.'

Stutchbury had been quietly absorbing this pressure and aggro on my behalf for nearly twelve years. Nine times out of ten, I wouldn't even know about a meeting like this. There were literally dozens of them. Stutch's implacability, as so many journalists know, was not a given; many editors fold under the weight of powerful forces, and there was none so powerful in corporate Australia as Qantas, with all of the leverage and inducements at its disposal.

'I said, as I always say, that I was happy to listen and to keep an open dialogue, but I didn't make any promises about changing anything. I told them I'm not ever saying Joe won't say nasty things about you anymore. The fallback is always that if they've got any serious error of fact to raise, I will definitely act on that. But they couldn't give me one, two, three things that were wrong here that I could action.'

For Joyce – so long a master of all he surveyed – to be powerless to shut down criticism in the nation's business publication of record must have been beyond frustrating.[2] I was not in the least bit surprised to discover that he had complained to my boss – but I was astonished that Richard Goyder had done so. Throughout the entire period that I'd been writing about Qantas in earnest, beginning in August 2022, I was in regular contact with the Qantas chairman. Starting in his days as CEO of Wesfarmers, we'd crossed paths often and maintained an amicable and (I believed) candid relationship. In March 2018, soon after Goyder retired from Wesfarmers, I had written a column critical of his final bonus award and the financial returns of the conglomerate under his leadership. In advance of its publication, and even afterwards, he engaged with all of my criticisms and was incredibly gracious. I quickly became a fan.

I'd called Goyder in September 2022 to warn him I was going to write about his statement that Joyce was the best CEO in Australia 'by the length of a straight'. In November, we'd met for lunch in Melbourne to discuss my concerns about Qantas: not for the first time, I expressed my incredulity at Qantas' patronising and aggressive attitude towards the media, which was unlike anything I'd seen in more than a decade of writing about and dealing with large Australian companies. I talked to Goyder again in the hours after Hudson's bungled op-ed on Qantas taxes was published in March. In the two months before he sat down with Stutchbury to register his complaint, I'd spoken to Goyder on half a dozen separate occasions and not once had he complained to me directly, not even in the mildest of terms.

Goyder was of course free to make whatever complaint he liked to my editor, although it would have been advisable to have an error of fact to complain about. The revelation was that Goyder was so conflict-avoidant he'd been trying to mollify Alan Joyce about me, and me about Alan Joyce at the same time. I was stunned at my own naivety for believing I had this terrific rapport with Goyder, who was taking my adverse feedback ever so seriously. No: I was being *managed* by Richard Goyder, who was everything to everyone.

In the midst of these internecine dramas, Qantas threw its biggest party in nearly a decade. The airline had turned a hundred in November 2020 but its long-planned program of centenary events had been washed out by the pandemic. The day after their breakfast meeting with Stutchbury, on 31 March, Joyce and Goyder hosted 1,000 VIP guests at a belated hundredth birthday gala dinner in hangar 96 at Sydney airport (where else?). In the shadow of a looming A380, Kylie Minogue sang, Neil Perry served up king prawn cocktails, and Prime Minister Anthony Albanese and Alan Joyce back-slapped in their tuxedos for the cameras.

The prime minister delivered a soaring speech. 'There is probably no other Australian company whose logo stirs the emotions quite like the sight of the flying kangaroo on a Boeing 737,' he said, 'and there are very few organisations that project Australia's character and qualities to the world in the way Qantas does.'

Prime ministers and other dignitaries had been delivering a similar spiel for over a generation – ready-made oratory that sounded inspirational and was, broadly speaking, endorsed by the Australian public. In the previous twelve months, however, that sentiment had shifted dramatically. While Albanese didn't specify the Australian qualities that Qantas projected to the world, he plainly did not intend to evoke greed and callous indifference. A core political skill is reading the public mood: how had he missed this shift? Perhaps because it had been twelve months since he'd taken a commercial flight. He'd been flying on the prime-ministerial jet since May the previous year and would have been a relative stranger to the airport chaos of 2022.[3] He certainly would not have waited eleven hours on the phone to redeem a COVID flight credit or to track down a lost bag.

And there was another reason, too. The PM continued to remind the gathering that he'd been the minister responsible for aviation for many years, 'And every day in that job, I knew if there was a crisis anywhere in the world, whether it was a natural disaster or a violent uprising, I could pick up the phone and Qantas would swing into action, getting Australians to safety. The last few years have reminded us all how important that is.' But in the ultimate crisis, Qantas had shuttered its international network for eighteen months, leaving more than 100,000 Australians to broker a way home on foreign airlines. It may have been necessary for Qantas' survival, but it hardly amounted to swinging into action and getting Australians to safety.

Albanese had the right speech for the audience in the hangar on a happy occasion, but the wrong speech for those rolling TV cameras that took it out into punter land. This didn't matter yet, but it soon would.

———

Two weeks after Stutchbury's breakfast meeting, I travelled to Adelaide for the AFL's inaugural Gather Round. On the evening of Wednesday 12 April the AFL Commission hosted a lavish dinner at Penfolds' Magill Estate for South Australian Premier Peter Malinauskas, AFL commissioners, club presidents and CEOs, the bosses of the game's broadcasters and corporate sponsors, and various other hangers-on (like me). Before guests were seated, I was chatting with Collingwood president Jeff Browne when Goyder approached.

'I hear you've complained about me,' I said straight up.

Taken aback, Goyder assured me, 'Oh don't worry, everything's fine.'

'Well, it's obviously not fine,' I responded, but suggested we have that conversation at a more appropriate time. Later, we arranged to catch up after the AFL's official luncheon on the Friday.

At the conclusion of that lunch, Goyder came over to where I was sitting beside Andrew Dillon, who Goyder was at that point attempting to overlook for the position of AFL CEO. Goyder and I talked as we walked back to our hotel, where we continued talking for another thirty minutes. The dynamic was civil but tense. I told him I was mystified that he had gone over my head, something that in fact made it more likely I'd continue to write about Qantas, to demonstrate that such a pressure tactic never, ever worked. I also vented my exasperation at Goyder's unwillingness, in the face of overwhelming evidence, to recognise Qantas' fragility and its Joyce problem. I warned him that Qantas was on track to be the next Rio Tinto, the mining giant whose reputation had imploded in 2020 after it detonated the Juukan Gorge caves, which contained sacred Indigenous artefacts, over the protests of their traditional owners. Oblivious to the mounting outcry, Rio Tinto's board steadfastly backed the CEO, Jean-Sébastien Jacques, clearly believing its share-holders would never revolt while the company was printing so much money.[4] They revolted. Jacques was sacked, the chairman had to resign, and so did another Rio director, Michael L'Estrange, who by chance was also a member of the Qantas board.[5]

Funnily enough, the following month, May 2023, I was given the opportunity to make the same comparison in a talk to Rio Tinto's top 200 managers at an internal conference in Brisbane. I had been one of Rio Tinto's primary antagonists, and the fact that Jacques' successor, Jakob Stausholm, invited me to speak was an indication of his admirable preparedness to look unflinchingly at the company's failings. A much more important step had been appointing former Sex Discrimination Commissioner Elizabeth Broderick to run a no-holds-barred culture review, which uncovered systemic bullying, sexual harassment and racism across the organisation. At Stausholm's town hall, I raised the uncanny parallels between Rio in 2020 and Qantas in 2023 – including the record profits; their incredibly aggressive playbooks in external relations; dominant, criticism-averse CEOs making outlandish public statements; and boards of directors with their heads in the sand. But while there were parallels, there was also a key distinction. There had been a single, decisive catalyst for the public outrage that consumed Rio Tinto, liquidated its leadership and disfigured its brand. Qantas had experienced a steady accumulation of slights but no catalyst for major action – at least not yet.

Forty-eight hours after my talk with Goyder in Adelaide, the column I foreshadowed with him was published in the *Financial Review*, revealing that Joyce and Goyder had lodged a formal complaint against me because they were 'aggrieved that my criticism of Joyce has become personal'. My response was: 'It is not personal, of course. I am unconcerned whether Joyce is short or tall, gay or straight, Irish or Australian, here or there. I've never criticised his DNA, only what he says and does in the course of his work.

'Joyce confuses personal criticism with individualised criticism, and my criticism is individualised because he is the individual whose ego totally dominates the Qantas organisation. His executives are in the bunker with a mad king in his last days and for any person who presents a truth he doesn't like, the consequences are real.'

As one Joyce lieutenant recounted to me, 'The notion that a conversation between an editor and a chairman winds up in the paper – for you to report that, everyone [at Qantas] thought, Fuck, Joe's going to write whatever he wants to write and the *AFR* has no control over him. We interpreted it as a pathological hatred of Alan and of Qantas, and that you were now coming for Alan every other day.'

I was writing not out of hatred, but disbelief at Joyce's behaviour and the board's sluggishness in protecting the company. I had concluded my column by urging the directors to focus 'on getting him out the door before he does the company any further reputational damage'.

———

As we saw in an earlier chapter, Goyder had a history of dragging his heels when appointing new CEOs. The AFL community had gone from restive to mutinous over the absurd length of time the AFL Commission was taking to appoint a successor to Gillon McLachlan, who had announced his retirement back in April 2022.[6] More than twelve months later, McLachlan was still there and the clubs – which for better or worse were the shareholders of the AFL – had no idea what would happen next.

To make matters worse, the league's all-important position of general manager of football had been unoccupied for six months, and there were two vacancies on the commission which Goyder, unconcerned by the club's pleas, hadn't got around to filling. Since 2021, when former premiership player Jason Ball stood down, there had been nobody serving on the commission who had played AFL or managed an AFL club. *The Age*'s respected footy journalist Caroline Wilson said on Nine's *Footy Classified* that she'd 'never seen so much dissatisfaction and unrest among the clubs'. Their nickname for Goyder was 'Over to you, Gil' – apocryphally his opening words at any meeting of the commission. The equivalence with the situation at Qantas was not lost on anybody.

Goyder's supporters credited him with a deliberate and methodical decision-making style. However, in addition to Qantas and the AFL, Goyder was also chairman of oil and gas giant Woodside Energy, where in 2021 the investment community had roundly criticised him for overseeing an incredibly messy CEO transition when Peter Coleman retired after a decade in the job. Peculiarly, Goyder named Meg O'Neill acting CEO in April that year before confirming in August she had won the role permanently. But O'Neill had been a key executive since Goyder became chairman in 2018: he'd had literally years to size her up. Where was his succession planning? 'They say the extrovert sits in the front row and knows nothing while the introvert sits in the back row and knows everything,' one Woodside insider explained to me. 'Meg is a classic introvert, and that just wasn't resonating with Richard at the time. He didn't think she had executive presence to hold a room, which was important to him, and I think he was judging that off an Alan or a Gillon.'

Appointing O'Neill initially on an interim basis made it appear – accurately – that he lacked full confidence in her. Says the Woodside insider: 'We all watched the AFL [succession] play out and it was so similar – Richard just couldn't bring himself to make a decision. These are big organisations with competent boards and tier 1 search firms working for them. There's no reason this needs to happen.' One factor was that Goyder was simply too busy. Indeed, privately he was indicating he'd soon step down from Woodside to focus on Qantas and the AFL.

But the AFL succession wasn't taking so long because Goyder was methodical; it was because Goyder was inert and because, frankly, he didn't want McLachlan to leave. 'Richard doesn't action advice,' one senior AFL figure lamented to me. 'He seeks advice, but then he just sits on it. That's his pattern. People have said to him on multiple occasions, "Richard, if you don't want to get in these situations where people are bashing you up, you've got to take charge and make decisions and then people won't." He'll agree, even say, "You're 100 per cent right," but then he still doesn't do anything.'

This same figure likens Goyder to Simon the Likeable, a character from 1960s sitcom *Get Smart*, 'a man so unassuming, so modest, so sweet and warm that you take one look at him, and you like him'. But Goyder's likeability was starting to curdle. At the Gather Round dinner at Magill Estate, Goyder chose to make light of the situation. He began his remarks with a joke about the similarities between McLachlan and Malinauskas – tall, handsome, and both had played Aussie rules at Adelaide private schools – and then quipped, 'Peter, come speak to me about a job we're looking to fill afterwards.' The gag went down like a cup of cold sick with the club presidents and CEOs in the room, but not nearly as badly as did Goyder's follow-up: that there would be a new AFL CEO in place 'by 2028'. Shared looks of disbelief rippled up and down the long tables.

Goyder was on a hiding to nothing speaking at these events. He was invariably up against McLachlan, a gifted raconteur, plus an MC (usually McLachlan's brother Hamish) and political leaders who charm crowds for a living. It was hopeless for Goyder to try to crack funnies because he wasn't very funny. His AFL job should have been so easy; he only had to bring the gravitas. Instead, he looked like he was trying (and failing) to imitate McLachlan.

The mood wasn't helped by a rumour which had swept through the hall like a Mexican wave. The commission had finally decided – so it went – and McLachlan would be succeeded by a rank outsider in Western Bulldogs president Kylie Watson-Wheeler. The hares were set running by her abrupt change of plans (which were fact, not rumour): she'd been advertised as the guest speaker at a football dinner in Melbourne on the same night and had originally sent her apologies to the AFL's Adelaide soiree. At the last minute, she changed her RSVP and turned up with her husband, Mark Wheeler, a talent manager at under-eighteens club the Sandringham Dragons.

AFL and club officials alike were in disbelief. Andrew Dillon had spent the last twenty-three years at AFL House. Another contender, Travis Auld, had been there nine years and spent seventeen years before that at AFL clubs Essendon and the Gold Coast Suns. Another, Kylie Rogers, had been the AFL's chief commercial officer for six years.[7] If the commission preferred an external candidate, Brendon Gale had been CEO of Richmond for fourteen years and taken the Tigers to three premierships. He had run the AFL Players' Association for five years before that. McLachlan himself had spent fourteen years working under his predecessor, Andrew Demetriou, before finally succeeding him. While Watson-Wheeler served on a club board, she had never actually worked in sports administration. She was, though, the managing director of US entertainment giant Disney in Australia, and for a sport that saw itself as a giant of entertainment, that sounded great.

This misconception prevails in Australia – alarmingly, even in ostensibly sophisticated circles – that the local heads of foreign companies like Facebook or Netflix or Uber are somehow equivalent to the CEOs of local companies like Telstra or Coles. In fact, the former positions are closer to a state sales or territory manager of Telstra or Coles, and that's arguably being generous. This misconception has led to some mid- and low-ranking executives at foreign multinationals landing some stunning promotions. Michelle Guthrie, a Singapore-based managing director at Google (which employs literally hundreds of managing directors), was appointed the one and only managing director of the Australian Broadcasting Corporation in 2016. She was sacked in 2018 (and the following year, the ABC and Guthrie settled an unfair dismissal claim). Google's managing director for Australia, Maile Carnegie, was hired as ANZ Banking Group's chief digital officer in 2016, and in 2022 was promoted to lead ANZ's entire retail banking operation. By 2022, the bank's customer-facing technology was the subject of widespread ridicule. In 2018, Carnegie's successor at Google, Jason Pellegrino, became CEO of ASX-listed real estate company Domain. Under Pellegrino, Domain spun its wheels, falling catastrophically behind its main rival, REA Group.

Being the local managing director of Disney might have sounded grand but it didn't make Watson-Wheeler a senior Disney executive. She didn't sit at the top table with Bob Iger. Disney Australia was principally a regional sales office – a shopfront for funnelling streaming revenue back to headquarters, with a dash of cinema distribution, merchandise, and live event sales to boot.

The other misconception that seemed to reign was that anybody could run the AFL, a $1 billion business, and this was a credit to McLachlan and his management team. They made it look easy when it was anything but. As I wrote in the *AFR* in 2022, 'It is an elaborate mission of cajoling warlords and orchestrating utterly seamless live and broadcast stadia events on a practically daily basis. It's a U2 world tour every year in five states simultaneously, a meticulous operation that necessitates an exceptionally high attention to detail.'

Nobody – at least nobody I spoke to – bore any personal animosity towards Watson-Wheeler, but her experience didn't come close to the other candidates in the field. Incredibly, that didn't dissuade Goyder from attempting to install her. McLachlan was dismayed, and according to multiple insiders with direct knowledge of the situation, he threatened to reverse his retirement in order to head off the appointment.[8] 'Gillon was saying, "This is craziness," one official recalls. 'It was very serious and if not for the intervention of a few people I think it would've happened.'

Goyder pushed Watson-Wheeler's candidacy as far as he could at the commission table. The majority of his fellow commissioners were immovable. They favoured Dillon, so Goyder ultimately read the room and quietly fell into line. One by one, cracks were appearing in his longstanding image as a corporate leader of discerning judgement.

———

And then, as if they were somehow connected, Goyder resolved both successions almost at once.

On 1 May 2023, the AFL announced Dillon's appointment as CEO, to take effect right after McLachlan's (second) farewell grand final in September. After fronting the media in Melbourne with Dillon, Goyder flew to Sydney to chair that afternoon's Qantas board meeting, where Vanessa Hudson was selected as Alan Joyce's successor. That decision was announced the following morning, and soon thereafter Hudson, Joyce and Goyder took the stage at a packed press conference in Mascot where the news cameras clicked and flashed.

This was a big deal. When Joyce retired and Hudson took over at the airline's annual general meeting in November, she would be only the twelfth CEO of Qantas in 104 years, and the fourth since its privatisation in 1995. Since then, by comparison, there had been eight prime ministers and seven captains of the Australian men's cricket team. Despite the national significance of the moment, though, Hudson's unveiling had a surreal quality, as the apex Qantas delegation and the journalists engaged in two completely unrelated conversations.

'Our net debt [three years ago] was $5.8 billion and at our recent half-year results it [was] $2.4 billion,' Goyder crowed, adding that the company had started to buy back shares. Joyce said, 'I'm very happy that Qantas is coming out of this financially stronger than it went into it, with a better balance sheet, record profitability, and it's well positioned for the future.' Tellingly, all of their measures of Qantas' health were financial; all of them the priorities of shareholders, not customers or staff. Debt was low and cash was leaping into the till, which was the beginning and end of all relevant considerations. Everything was all good!

The press gaggle had descended from an alternative universe – the one occupied by their audiences, the travelling public. A journalist at the *Sydney Morning Herald* asked: 'Qantas' reputation has slipped since the onset of COVID-19 [so] how, Vanessa, will you work to restore that reputation and consumer confidence?'

The ABC asked: 'Qantas has suffered a bit of reputational damage after the last few years ... What was your pitch to say you're the right person to actually turn that reputation around and restore Qantas to the prestige it once was as a brand?'

And *The Guardian* asked Hudson: 'People have touched on the kind of reputational damage that's occurred and I think throughout this time there's been quite a combative relationship with unions and some of the workers at Qantas – do you plan to do things differently?'

With Joyce sitting beside her congratulating himself, Hudson could scarcely say, Yes, everyone hates us and we need to do far better. Indeed, there was nothing to suggest she even believed that was the case. She was Joyce's continuity candidate. It had got her this far, which was all the way. The closest Hudson came to offering anything resembling a relevant answer to those questions was saying, 'Last year, we were very upfront ... that the customer experience was not where we wanted it and we've invested an enormous amount of money – $200 million this year – in getting the performance back to where it needs to be. And it is back where we were pre-COVID.'

This was false when Joyce and Markus Svensson said it in December 2022, and it was still false.

Internally, Qantas measured 'the customer experience' via its net promoter score (NPS), an internal research metric which correlated almost perfectly with its domestic on-time performance. But Qantas' NPS was not back to where it was pre-COVID. It wasn't even close.[9] And while its on-time performance had improved considerably from its dysfunctional lows in mid-2022 (and was now consistently better than Virgin's), that had also not recovered to pre-COVID levels.[10]

There were plenty of other ways the customer experience, as any Qantas customer would define it, remained deficient. International on-time arrivals in April 2023 were 64 per cent. Domestic cancellations in April 2023 were still 70 per cent higher than the long-term average. Finding a frequent flyer points seat on a Qantas flight was as likely as spotting a Tasmanian tiger. The inflight catering stood as a homage to wartime rations, the predominant aircraft were even deeper into their senescence, and key airport lounges were literally threadbare. Yet Hudson was defining all of these as past problems. This seriously underestimated Qantas customers, many of whom were even angrier at being told they were imagining the continued poor service than they were at the poor service itself. Hudson's 'top priority', I wrote in the *AFR*, was 'pushing customers to their outer limit [while] telling them what a marvellous experience they've had!'

Joyce was unsurprisingly in legacy mode, and Goyder warned of the interminable victory lap to come: 'There'll be plenty of time to talk about Alan's achievements as the year unfolds.' Joyce framed his pandemic service as he wanted it immortalised: 'When it came to Qantas' 100 years in 2020, I think my intent was to look at that year as the appropriate time to go, but I never got there … As Richard said, if it hadn't been for COVID I would've retired a few years ago, but I agreed to stay here for this length of time to help the company get through a terrible crisis.'[11]

Joyce was brazenly rewriting history, the sole purpose of which was to raise him up as Qantas' saviour. In May 2019 – comfortably pre-COVID – *The Australian*, the *Australian Financial Review* and the *Sydney Morning Herald* had all reported that Joyce had agreed to extend his tenure for 'at least' three more years.[12] Thirteen months later, when Joyce agreed as a condition of Qantas' June 2020 equity raising to stay as CEO until at least 2023, the *Financial Review* reported it as 'the second contract extension Mr Joyce has received in just over a year, with the previous one coming amid an executive reshuffle in May last year'.

Joyce's comment was untrue and yet he seemed to believe it deeply. The contrary evidence didn't even seem to register with him. These were self-deceptions necessary to sustain his narrative of exceptionalism, a narrative that was psychologically non-negotiable. This also helped explain why Joyce internalised the airline's every success and externalised each of its failures. Of having survived COVID (along with virtually all the world's major airlines), and of Qantas' record profitability in 2023, he took full ownership. But for lost bags, schedule chaos and woeful customer service he blamed global factors. And his trajectory was clear: 'I'm really excited about future opportunities,' he said. 'Me [*sic*] and my husband are staying here in Sydney, we're looking forward to doing a lot more in the community here, as we have over the years.'

Underlining the surreal tenor of Hudson's naming ceremony as Qantas CEO, Goyder signed off with an almighty gaffe. 'While I say it's never easy, the board firmly feels Olivia is the right person to take Qantas forward,' he said, name-checking the unsuccessful CEO candidate Olivia Wirth, before bouncing off the stage.

———

Appointing a new CEO wasn't the only bold action Qantas was taking at that time. In the following days, it became apparent to executives at Nine Entertainment Co., publisher of the *Australian Financial Review*, that something was amiss.

In July 2022, Qantas had struck a commercial deal with Nine, News Corp and the ABC to provide its passengers with free access to the *AFR*, *The Australian* and ABC News content in Qantas lounges and on domestic flights via its wi-fi network.[13] But word was now filtering back to Nine from bemused travellers that the *AFR*'s content had abruptly vanished. Inside the Chairman's Lounge, physical copies of the *AFR* had always been displayed prominently and provided as a courtesy to members. Suddenly, we were hearing from senior businesspeople and politicians that the paper had disappeared. Chairman's Lounge members were told it was no longer available. Soon after, Qantas advised Nine that it had terminated its deal with the *AFR*. No explanation was offered, but none was needed.

The *Sydney Morning Herald*, also owned by Nine, reported Qantas' *AFR* boycott on 7 May, including a statement from Nine's managing director of publishing, James Chessell: 'It's disappointing Qantas management has decided to deprive its customers of the country's best business and finance journalism because it can't countenance robust criticism. We've been here before with Qantas and, as always, our editorial independence won't be affected by commercial pressure.

The vast majority of people I speak to think Joe's Qantas coverage is tough but fair.'

'We've been here before' was a subtle reference to a 2014 dispute between Qantas and the *Sydney Morning Herald* and *The Age* over the newspapers' coverage of Joyce's management.[14] Joyce viewed the work of business journalists Adele Ferguson and Matt O'Sullivan as unduly amenable to the worldview of Qantas' trade unions.[15] Not only that, but after Joyce had posted a run of anaemic financial results then begged the Abbott government for a $2 billion debt guarantee and subsequently unveiled Qantas' record $4 billion loss, Ferguson all but called for Joyce's resignation on the front page of the *Sydney Morning Herald*.

The pressure was direct. As Ferguson's colleague, Matt O'Sullivan, recounted to me, 'I remember going out for a coffee with Andrew McGinnes and him telling me that he'd give me one last go, or words to that effect. I took it to mean that if I didn't toe the line, my job reporting on Qantas would get harder.' Joyce had also phoned Fairfax Media chief executive Greg Hywood to complain about the reporting. Hywood told me, 'I explained to Alan that when you have bad results, you get bad stories and when you have good results, you get good stories, and that's just the way it goes.' Hywood had spent twenty-five years as a Fairfax journalist and editor, including as editor-in-chief variously of the *Financial Review*, the *Sydney Morning Herald* and *The Age*. He could speak from experience: at the time, Fairfax management was generating acres of critical headlines over its collapsing revenues and massive cost-cutting. But that didn't soften his message to Joyce. 'I wasn't particularly sympathetic. I said to him, "You can't really complain about this, you've just got to hunker down and see it through."'

Several weeks later, Hywood learned from his subordinates that Qantas was terminating its $2 million advertising spend with the *Sydney Morning Herald* and *The Age* and removing complimentary copies of the papers from domestic boarding gates and onboard flights. He called Joyce for an explanation and Joyce told him there was no point running Qantas ads in newspapers that carried negative stories about it. 'I asked him, "Alan, do you believe in the freedom of the press?" He said, "Of course I do." So I said, "Well, the thing about the press is that it asks questions of institutions and people in power that they can't or won't ask of themselves and by doing so, keeps the community cohesive and civil and prevents it from breaking down. Government and the commercial world must understand that it's to everybody's benefit, including theirs, that this system is sustained, and it's sustained by advertising. If every advertiser pulled their ads because there were negative stories, the system would simply fall apart. So what you're doing is jeopardising the underlying principles of the freedom of the press."' Unsurprisingly, Joyce didn't see it that way.

In response to Qantas' advertising boycott, Fairfax shifted its $2 million corporate travel account from Qantas to Virgin Australia. In turn, Virgin significantly increased its advertising in Fairfax's newspapers. While Qantas wanted to continue advertising in the *AFR* to reach its business customers, Hywood turned Qantas away and handed Joyce's arch-rival, Virgin's John Borghetti, advertising exclusivity across all Fairfax mastheads.

'In the context of Qantas' revenues or our revenues it wasn't enormous, but I decided to make the point that we weren't submitting to threats,' Hywood says. 'This was an early hint, I suppose, of [Joyce's] glass jaw and his sensitivity to criticism. To me, what he did was take issues that were difficult for him personally and transpose them into decisions that affected Qantas. He might've had an explanation to justify that, but I certainly didn't think it was justified.'

Nevertheless, Joyce did hunker down and see it through, and by 2017 he was being celebrated by the *AFR* as its businessperson of the year. This was much to Hywood's annoyance, but did highlight the independence of Fairfax's editorial line from its commercial management. Stutchbury, an unapologetically pro-business editor, remained supportive of Joyce's leadership: 'The *Herald* said he should be sacked in 2014 but we were on his side and we editorialised favourably,' he says. 'He got the costs down and cleaned Qantas up. It was a very protected industry in the old days and he had all sorts of legacy stuff to fix. That took a lot of guts.'

By 2023, however, Joyce had lost even this staunch support. 'It may be harsh, but by the end of it, he deserved the criticism for taking his eye off the interests of customers, which should've been his core interest,' Stutchbury explains. 'And he was making a hell of a lot of money out of it, as you do, but you've got to be prepared to take criticism if you don't live up to standards.'

The *Sydney Morning Herald*'s May 2023 piece revealing Qantas' new *AFR* boycott was quickly followed by a similar report in the *AFR* itself. Andrew McGinnes was straight on the phone to James Chessell, miffed that Chessell had publicly condemned Qantas and intimating that it was all a misunderstanding; that the *AFR* had been banished by a rogue, overenthusiastic Qantas junior burger misinterpreting instructions or acting beyond their authority. McGinnes' intended meaning was unmistakable: this was not a decision sanctioned by Alan Joyce. In actuality, it was very much Joyce's decision. Multiple Qantas executives familiar with the internal machinations confirmed to me that Joyce directed Markus Svensson to implement the boycott, undeterred by McGinnes' advice that it was a bad idea.[16]

But how it had happened was really of no concern to Nine. Chessell comprehended from the get-go that Qantas had kicked a sensational own goal, and that every particle of the resulting furore would be 100 per cent, money-can't-buy PR for the *Financial Review*. McGinnes plainly understood this too, and his immediate concern was how to fix it. As Chessell recounted to me, 'Qantas then realised [to save face] they needed a little bit of time until it was quote-unquote fixed, but there was an almost instant understanding that the *AFR* would be reinstated.' But as a senior Qantas executive concedes, 'This was the moment Alan lost his way. He poured petrol on the fire.'

It was indeed the great crossing-over point for the Qantas–*AFR* feud. It was no longer a financial debate for a narrow audience about share buy-backs, fleet investment and company tax. It was now a story intriguing to non-*AFR* readers: Qantas was engaging in retribution and censorship, and the nation's most famous CEO was throwing his toys out of the cot (again). It also crystallised everything that had for many months been showing up in the consumer research, and drew attention to the Chairman's Lounge, a secret society that symbolised the elite for whom the airline seemed to be run.

Inevitably, the boycott exposed Qantas to ridicule, with passenger provocateurs leaving copies of the *Financial Review* strewn around Qantas Clubs. As one Chairman's Lounge member recalls, 'The staff kept a couple of copies for us hidden behind the front desk like they were porno magazines. I was half surprised they didn't hand it over in a brown paper bag.' More coverage sprang up across the media, including a segment on ABC's *Media Watch*. But the most seismic aftershock came when Michael Miller, executive chairman of Nine's blood rival News Corp, waded into the dispute to attack Qantas publicly. 'This is pretty pointed,' Miller said. Qantas' position, he claimed, was: '"We don't like what you're saying so therefore we won't have a commercial relationship." As someone who people attempt to intimidate when they don't like coverage, I take exception to the pressure put on journalists and the media to stifle free speech. I don't have a view on what Joe Aston says, but I'll defend his right to say it.'

To say that Miller's intervention surprised the *AFR* and Nine, albeit pleasantly, would be a material understatement. Joyce and his lieutenants were equally astounded, having assumed they could count on the backing of News Corp against its sworn media enemy. 'It is amazing, isn't it, how Qantas brings everyone together?' marvelled *Media Watch*'s stand-in host John Barron.

Despite the hullaballoo, Stutchbury says, Joyce's boycott 'didn't matter much' and 'created no significant sense of pressure'. Much more important was that the *AFR* 'had punctured the thing and catalysed a collective venting of the whole travelling class of Australia who were mightily browned off about it all'.

Greg Hywood says, 'Qantas is essentially a national asset, and markets itself as one, even though it's a private company. There are broader responsibilities it has to meet. [Joyce] was clearing tens of millions of dollars in remuneration. You get paid the money and you pay the price and that price is public scrutiny, most of which, if you do controversial things, is negative. You just have to cop it on the chin.'

Joyce's powerlessness to resist retaliation was incredibly telling. By his own description, he was a compartmental thinker. 'The trick to dealing with these tough times is to compartmentalise life,' he had said six weeks after Qantas' sensational grounding in 2011. 'I am able to go home and switch off. I suppose that's my background in mathematics and physics. I have always been able to compartmentalise my life very easily.' This orientation is common in many high-functioning and highly numerate people. Their cognitive processes are cerebral as opposed to emotional, and literally formulaic, like a software program. The same systemising method also applies to defining themselves. Joyce could switch his normal workday stresses on and off. He could ground an airline then go out to dinner. He could sack 10,000 people and sleep soundly. But presented with a threat to his ego, he malfunctioned. He was an intellectual and motivational powerhouse and yet he had a very limited emotional range. That could be seen in his responses to criticism, but also in his lack of natural empathy for angry customers. And once he decided he was right, that's where he stayed. 'He was single-minded to the point of failure,' says Labor senator Tony Sheldon. 'If anyone had a different view, they were wrong. And that led to a culture of absolutism.'

Joyce had invested everything in his identity as Qantas CEO. With that under attack, he was compelled to react, to do anything that would put his narrative – his formula – back together. It was literally a compulsion. He was particularly sensitive because he was at such a delicate juncture in his life. While his Qantas identity was everything, it was borrowed, and it was evaporating. The countdown was on. He was seeking a smooth transition from Mr Qantas to Mr Generic Business Legend and Mr Community. The most important thing to Joyce now was what other people thought of him. Approval was priceless. That was the long-term bonus he was chasing.

But he was seeking this moral elevation right as his balloon was losing air. I was denying him what he needed most. I was a virus in his software.

Alan's Enchanted Spectacles
19 May–26 July 2023

On 19 May 2023, Joyce assembled the news cameras to record the turning of the first sod at the site of the new, outsourced pilot training centre near Sydney airport. 'This flight training centre is going to train 4,500 Qantas and Jetstar pilots every year and it's going to be open from early 2024 – that's a very fast process,' Joyce told a media pack straining to hear him over the freeway traffic and aircraft noise.[1] 'We have one brand new aircraft arriving every three weeks and we will need 8,500 new people over the next decade.'

There was nothing new here. The outing was an elaborate distraction from the only real Qantas news of the day, which Joyce and Andrew McGinnes knew would cause uproar among Qantas pilots and cabin crew. That morning, the airline announced an increase to its international flights, made possible by the arrival, finally, of three Dreamliners deferred in 2020 plus a new deal to lease two A330s from European carrier Finnair for five years. The stinger was buried in the fine print. For the first two and a half years, this deal would be what's known in the aviation industry as a 'wet-lease', meaning that Qantas would lease not only the planes from Finnair, but also Finnair pilots and flight attendants to crew them.[2] From October 2023, customers travelling on any Qantas flight between Sydney and Bangkok, and on certain Sydney–Singapore flights, would find themselves onboard Finnair planes with Finnair staff.

The closure of Russian airspace since the invasion of Ukraine had forced Finnair to cancel almost half its Asian capacity, leaving it with surplus aircraft and crew.[3] No doubt this afforded Qantas excellent negotiating leverage but it was a galling development, to put it mildly, for Qantas crew. Only six months earlier, Qantas had retired two A330s from its passenger fleet and converted them to freighters. 'The decision to wet-lease illustrates the failures of the fleet planning processes of the last five years,' president of the pilots' union Captain Tony Lucas said that day. As Lucas explains in 2024, 'If you're running an airline properly you don't outsource your flying to another airline. [Qantas management] made poor fleet decisions. They didn't order enough aeroplanes of the right size at the right time.'

It was a stark reminder that Joyce and the Qantas board had created a significant capability gap by failing to renew its A330 fleet. Eleven of its twenty-six A330s had been in the fleet for nineteen years or longer and Qantas still hadn't ordered any replacement for them. Even once Qantas did get around to ordering replacements, the first of them would take years to arrive.[4]

It was one thing to outsource catering or ground handling, but Joyce was increasingly outsourcing the flying itself. On a far larger scale than the Finnair A330s, Qantas was already wet-leasing sixteen Embraer aircraft (since increased to twenty-six) from Alliance Airlines to operate QantasLink flights on routes like Adelaide–Hobart, Canberra–Darwin, Darwin–Singapore and Brisbane–Wellington.[5]

Qantas' attempted distraction from the Finnair bombshell was 'pretty unsuccessful', Lucas says. 'It was Qantas Media 101 but that sort of thing doesn't distract pilots. We had our communications out within an hour of the announcement, but even before that my phone was lighting up with messages from pilots incandescent with anger. And I got their anger. If [Qantas had] come out and said, We don't have our fleet plans right and so we have to do this, we would've had far more respect for them.'

Joyce, however, would not take a single step backwards. Challenged at his press conference about the wisdom, in retrospect, of handing two passenger A330s to Qantas Freight, he insisted, 'Those aircraft were domestic aircraft that were perfect for converting into freighters.' But there was no such thing in practice as a domestic A330 – at least not the way Qantas used them.[6] They were just A330s, and they flew wherever you pointed them. In the final month that those two 'domestic' Qantas A330s flew as passenger aircraft, they operated services to Auckland, Bali, Jakarta and Singapore.

To journalists at Joyce's press conference, and their audiences, this was detail beyond their level of interest or comprehension. To experts, however, like the pilots who routinely operated these planes, Joyce sounded unhinged. 'You see him on the news,' Lucas says, 'and you think, That's bullshit! But you know that nobody there knows the subject matter well enough to pull him up on it.'

Joyce's blizzard of misinformation at that press conference continued. 'What the Finnair pilots are going to be doing is flying services from Singapore back into Australia to allow the Qantas pilots to fly more flying [*sic*] into Japan. That's the way it actually works. This doesn't lose a single Australian job, it creates Australian jobs. These aircraft ... are positive for the creation of jobs and anyone who says anything else is just completely wrong.'[7]

This was crazy talk, up there with 'I'm not a public figure'. He was deep inside what I called in the *AFR* Joyce's 'house of cognitive distortion. In this magical palace, put on your enchanted spectacles and you, too, can inhabit a universe where anyone who says anything else is completely wrong.' But while ridicule is good fun, the CEO of an airline repeatedly saying mad, untrue things – that was a serious issue. Something very odd was going on here, and the pattern was unmistakable.

When Joyce's self-narrative was under attack, he compulsively leapt to protect it, even at the expense of the situational narrative. That is, he was reverse-engineering his account of situations to keep his view of himself intact. It went like this: 'I am a virtuous job creator, ergo, it can only be true that hiring foreign pilots is positive for Australian jobs. I always make the right decisions, therefore, those discarded A330s cannot be the kind of A330s we desperately need now. I am the saviour of Qantas, so Qantas must have been weeks from bankruptcy. I make enormous self-sacrifices; accordingly, I shelved my (non-existent) retirement plans in 2020 to get Qantas through a terrible crisis.'

This thought process displays what evolutionary psychologist Robert Trivers describes in his book *Deceit and Self-Deception* as 'the hallmark of self-deception': 'the unconscious running of selfish and deceitful ploys, the creation of a public persona as an altruist ... as well as false historical narratives of past behaviour that hide true intention and causality'.[8] These biases also manifest in groups, especially after surviving a collective existential experience. That was Qantas World, a form of unusually potent in-group delusion.

A second factor, I believe, behind Joyce's aberrant behaviour was the profound effects that his social and professional power had likely wreaked on him. In 2022, Dean Paatsch, co-founder of corporate governance firm Ownership Matters, introduced me to the work of another American psychologist, Dacher Keltner, whose lab research over twenty years supported the contention that power has a debilitating cognitive effect on powerful people, often causing them to exhibit the symptoms of traumatic brain injury. Over time, power makes them more impulsive, less risk-aware, and less adept at seeing things from other people's point of view. People of high status also become less attuned to social reciprocity, which subliminally prompts us to laugh when others laugh or tense when others tense. The powerful, Keltner says, 'stop simulating the experience of others,' creating an 'empathy deficit'.

In *The Power Paradox: How We Gain and Lose Influence* Keltner writes: 'When it comes to the injustices that we ourselves perpetrate, our power makes us quite adept at rationalising such acts so that we can preserve the belief that we are moral, ethical agents. Our power blinds us to our own unethical actions.'[9]

Furthermore, powerful people produce narratives of exceptionalism about themselves because their high status requires moral justification. 'The human mind justifies inequalities of wealth and power,' Keltner writes, 'with stories about the unique and extraordinary qualities of those at the top.'

Power is said to *progressively* affect the powerful. Any natural perceptual deficits inherent in Joyce's hyper-numerate, rigid cognitive orientation were likely amplified by fourteen and a half years as Qantas CEO – one of the most powerful offices in the land.

None of this, I should clarify, is to say that Joyce is a uniquely bad or ill-intentioned person. But the upshot was that Joyce often sounded crazy when under challenge and was unable to perceive how crazy he sounded.

———

Qantas released a trading update to the stock exchange on 23 May, forecasting a profit for the 2023 financial year – ending five weeks later – of more than $2.4 billion, which would exceed the company's previous record annual profit by more than $1 billion. The $400 million share buy-back that Qantas had announced in February, and which was 78 per cent complete, was now increased to $500 million. Total seat capacity was back to 90 per cent of pre-COVID levels and rising. Heading into the 2024 financial year, airfares remained elevated and forward bookings extremely strong. The message to investors was clear: the good times were only just beginning.

A week later, Qantas held its first strategy day for financial analysts and institutional investors since 2019. The presentations by the airline's management team could scarcely have been more bullish. Shareholders were promised a panoply of delights as the company reintroduced plump earnings margin targets across all of its flying segments, missing since 2019. Qantas Domestic would henceforth aim to produce an earnings before interest and tax (EBIT) margin of 18 per cent; pre-COVID, it was 12 per cent. Qantas International would aim for an 8 per cent margin, compared to 5 per cent pre-COVID. Again, Qantas' message was unmistakable: these succulent margins were not the anomaly of a post-COVID minute where insatiable travel demand had coalesced perfectly with strangled supply and a starved cost base. According to Joyce and Hudson, this was the new normal. The targets were for financial year 2024 and beyond, and 'we're going to maintain that going forward', Hudson said. She had uncoupled Qantas from the economic cycle. Qantas was now permanently super-profitable, and only getting more so. 'Not only has our cash flow structurally lifted,' she said, 'it's going to continue to grow from here.' Once fully operational in 2028, she claimed, Project Sunrise would add $400 million to annual earnings.

Qantas executive Andrew David (of illegal outsourcing fame) humbly volunteered 'to reflect and provide you with some personal thoughts on the international market'. He continued, 'I think every one of us in this room is aware that international airline profitability has been up and down in the past for a variety of factors. One of those [was] an oversupply of capacity.' But not anymore. 'I've never seen such favourable international conditions,' he vouched. He even showed a graph depicting projected worldwide airline demand and supply out to 2030, explaining that 'demand outstrips supply for the immediate future and through to the end of the decade'.

David was, apparently, a qualified soothsayer. On the quiet, he'd been taking night classes at South Sydney TAFE and attained his Certificate IV in Psychic Studies.

I joke because, frankly, this was a joke. Armed with some finger-in-the-air assumptions about 2030 from IATA, the International Air Transport Association in Montreal, an airline operations guy in Australia was divining the future of the global market – a market hopelessly exposed to black swan events.[10] No caveats or probabilities, just a few personal reflections! Of course, not a single investor in the room asked him to drill further into his prophecy.[11] Not one of them said, Andrew, what's this really got to do with Australian inbound and outbound traffic? This wasn't economics, it was stock marketing. David might as well have handed around 'Stronger for longer' bumper stickers.

Pointedly, Hudson used this event to signal her solidarity with Joyce's strategy for Qantas. She was at pains to show the investment community that there was not a cigarette paper of difference between the two of them, or indeed between Joyce and the entire ongoing leadership group. 'The strategy that you've seen today is a strategy that has evolved not just over the last month. It has evolved over years and it is collectively owned by the management team across all levels ... The one thing I think it's really important not to miss today is the fact that we've done an investor day as a part of our transition period and it is very symbolic because it demonstrates that we are committed to the strategy, it demonstrates there's a continuity to the strategy and that that is enduring … It's the right way forward and we believe that deeply.' Long-suffering Qantas customers and staff, it seemed, could only expect more of the same.

It was a day of rampant, almost profligate optimism, a Landmark sales conference crossbred with a Hillsong service. The operating environment would remain magnificent. The company's cost base was transformed. The battalion of new planes on order would revolutionise its economics. There was no consideration that its penny-pinching had ruined customer satisfaction and trust. There was no recognition that Qantas hadn't placed firm orders for nearly enough planes, or that the cost of the belated fleet renewal program – $15 billion or more – would devour cash flows as far as the eye could see. Qantas analysts at Australia's major broking desks had been summoned to catch the Spirit of Australia, to wave and clap (and slap an upgrade on the stock), while Joyce called it down from the sky.

Less than forty-eight hours later, the most astounding thing happened: Alan Joyce sold 83 per cent of his shares in the airline, cashing in $17 million. A CEO selling shares wasn't in and of itself remarkable.[12] What was remarkable was a CEO selling virtually all of his shares five months before his retirement and without a convincing explanation.[13] *That* was rare, given the litany of questions it raised for shareholders, the first of which was 'What does he know that we don't?' Jaws crashed to the floor across the investment market and corporate Australia.

The explanation offered by the company – privately to journalists, although never formally to the stock exchange – was that Joyce required the proceeds of the share sale to fund the purchase of a residential property. Since 2008 Joyce and his partner Shane Lloyd had lived in their half-floor apartment in the Harry Seidler-designed Cove building in Sydney's CBD, and only recently the other apartment on their floor had become available for sale. In 2022, the couple had purchased their grand harbourside home in Mosman – the one decorated with eggs and toilet paper in the dark of night – for $19 million. Joyce and Lloyd had now decided to flip that house, buy their adjoining apartment for $9.25 million and consolidate it with their own.

The couple were DINKs in a rarified wealth echelon. They were entirely bankable. As Qantas CEO, Joyce had been paid more than $40 million in cash alone.[14] It was difficult to believe he couldn't raise 20 per cent of the apartment purchase price from existing liquidity or against his other properties, and even if he couldn't, there was no plausible reason his financial institution wouldn't have extended a bridging loan for a matter of weeks.[15] A mere eight weeks later, Joyce and Lloyd had exchanged on the Mosman house for $21 million. Twenty per cent of the apartment purchase price, incidentally, was just $1.85 million, but Joyce sold $17 million worth of shares. So what was the other $15 million for?[16]

Like any of his peers at ASX-listed companies, Joyce was required by his board to maintain a minimum shareholding, a requirement designed to guarantee the ongoing alignment of management's financial interests with shareholders'. Under Qantas' rules, Joyce had to own shares equivalent to 1.5 times his base salary, or $3.3 million. His share sale reduced him to the absolute threshold of his minimum. Should Qantas shares fall any lower than $6.75, the price he secured on 1 June, Joyce would breach that minimum. By 30 June, when the Qantas share price closed at $6.20, Joyce had fallen below his minimum shareholding requirement.

Joyce's obligation to own a minimum number of shares would end the day he retired in November. He could sell every last one of his shares and nobody would bat an eyelid.[17] Joyce also had a deluge of new shares vesting before then. In late August, he would receive his COVID recovery and retention bonus of 698,000 shares, his 2023 long-term bonus of 1,349,000 shares, and his deferred bonuses for 2020, 2021 and 2022 of 1,040,500 shares, collectively worth $21 million.[18] Joyce could have waited until those shares vested and nobody would've begrudged him selling a big lick of stock while continuing to honour the board's minimum shareholding policy. What, then, was the mad rush?

There were yet more complicating factors. Qantas, of course, was in the middle of a share buy-back. The airline's treasury team was in the market every day purchasing its own shares in order to cancel them, an activity which undeniably acted as a cantilever for the Qantas share price. On 1 June, the same day Joyce sold 2.5 million Qantas shares, Qantas spent $12.6 million buying back 1.85 million shares. On that day, Joyce was likely the largest seller of Qantas shares in the market, while Qantas was likely the largest buyer of them. There is no sinister effect arising from that juxtaposition, but in public markets it's considered a really bad look.[19] Qantas completed its buy-back on 20 June.

Only later did it become public knowledge that when Joyce sold these shares, Qantas was under investigation by the ACCC over its ghost flights – the 8,000 services between May and July 2022 that it had cancelled but continued to sell tickets on for a period of weeks. Qantas received its second compulsory information notice, which required it to hand over relevant documents to the regulator, on 26 April 2023. On 29 May, just seventy-two hours before Joyce's share sale, Qantas provided the ACCC with a 410-page spreadsheet particularising the 10,000 flights the regulator was targeting.[20]

Bear in mind, Joyce couldn't just phone ANZ Private Bank and bark a sell order down the line as the thought came to him. Before dealing in Qantas shares, Joyce needed the written approval of his chairman. So Joyce sought Goyder's permission to dump four-fifths of his shares five months from his retirement party, forty-eight hours after a roadshow where he'd been speaking in tongues about the company's outlook, on the same day the company was buying back its own shares, and with a live ACCC investigation bubbling along in the background, and Goyder's answer was, 'No problem, Alan!' Goyder had no plausible reason to say yes, and yet that's what he did.

Major shareholders were quick to raise their concerns with the company about the transaction, including Qantas' biggest shareholder, Pendal. Says Pendal's Crispin Murray, 'The share sale was just not a good idea. You can debate whether any sale should have been allowed but the quantum of it was problematic. That's where the chairman should have said, The optics of this are poor and I can't allow you to do this.'

'I've spoken to Alan briefly and I said that the share sale looked pretty bad,' Goyder's predecessor Leigh Clifford tells me in 2024. 'I told him whilst I didn't know the circumstances, I would've been reluctant to agree to it.'

This was a startling development and potentially a red flag for investors. Joyce considered himself a businessman of steadfast capital discipline and financial acumen. Why should it be any different when it came to his own investment portfolio? Joyce would never sell his Qantas shares at $6.75 if he believed that price was significantly below their value. Joyce the skilful transactor, the value guy, would only sell if the price was very good. That was the other logical discrepancy in this transaction – the discrepancy between Joyce's selling and his messaging at the investor day two days earlier that Qantas' salad days were only just beginning.

Investors were – other than the Qantas board – Joyce's final bastion of support.[21] He had already lost the trust of Qantas staff, customers and the wider public. The respect of the investment community was incredibly important to him, which would suggest that he only sold the shares because he was blind to how it would be perceived in those circles. Again, here was behaviour reinforcing the notion that Joyce couldn't see himself, or, more exactly, couldn't see how others saw him.

Goyder and Joyce self-evidently should have comprehended the optics of Joyce's share transaction occurring during a live ACCC probe. They can be excused, however, for never having dreamed that the ACCC would proceed with Federal Court action, as it did three months later. To Joyce, the ACCC was just another pesky regulator to hobble and condescend to.

The week following Joyce's share sale, the ACCC issued its final quarterly report on the domestic aviation market, instigated by Treasurer Josh Frydenberg in June 2020 to monitor airfares and profits after Virgin entered administration.

The head of the ACCC's Airline Competition Taskforce had in September 2022 sought Qantas' views on the merits of extending the reporting regime beyond June 2023. Unsurprisingly, Qantas argued against it. This was a view Qantas also put to the federal departments of treasury and transport. On 23 November 2022, Joyce met separately with Prime Minister Anthony Albanese and transport minister Catherine King in Canberra.[22] When Qantas' lobbying of the government ballooned into a major political issue in August and September of 2023, Albanese, King and Joyce repeatedly evaded questions in parliament and from the media about the contents of their private conversations. Helpfully, King's department had prepared a briefing note in advance of her meeting with Joyce.[23] It said: 'Qantas officers have indicated to Treasury officials they are interested in learning whether it is likely that ACCC monitoring will continue beyond June 2023.' It seemed unlikely that Joyce did not lobby King to allow the ACCC's quarterly monitoring powers to expire, which is precisely what King did, even though the ACCC had formally sought an extension of those powers and Qantas was the sole party opposed to it.[24] Little wonder, then, if Joyce thought he had the ACCC's measure.

It was an egregious capitulation by King, given the finding of the ACCC's final report that 'a lack of effective competition, which has characterised the industry for decades, has resulted in higher airfares and poorer service for consumers'. Qantas and Virgin enjoyed 94 per cent market share between them, and ACCC chair Gina Cass-Gottlieb described domestic aviation as 'one of the most concentrated industries in Australia, barring only natural monopolies such as electricity grids and rail networks. Without a real threat of losing passengers to other airlines, the [two] airline groups have had less incentive to offer attractive airfares, develop more direct routes, operate more reliable services and invest in systems to provide high levels of customer service.' The regulator also reported that a frightful 10 per cent of all Melbourne–Sydney flights were cancelled in April 2023. 'After showing signs of improvement earlier in the year, it is disappointing for consumers that the airlines' service reliability has declined again and remains worse than long-term trends.'

Things were so bad that Cass-Gottlieb called on the Albanese government to urgently establish an ombudsman to police the airline sector and a regime to force airlines to compensate passengers for certain delays and cancellations. Signing off, the ACCC included this ominous observation: 'Our monitoring role has significantly expanded the ACCC's knowledge of the airline industry, and we have developed a deep understanding of airline practices that may contravene [consumer law].'

Joyce's response to all this was utterly dismissive. 'I'm baffled by some of the commentary because the domestic market has never had as many competitors as it has today,' he said from Istanbul, where he was attending IATA's annual general meeting. It was convenient for Joyce to point to the launch of low-cost carrier Bonza and the expansion of Rex, but as Canberra Airport CEO Stephen Byron told *The Australian*, that was 'like thinking that a servo selling eggs and milk is providing price competition to Coles and Woolworths'.

'The biggest indicator of the lack of competition between the two airlines that control 95.1 per cent of the market,' Byron argued, 'are the sky-high airfares, record profits, the extraordinary cancellations and the problems with booking fares using airline credits.'

Down the video link from Turkey, Joyce was moved to make yet another blindingly untrue statement. 'The reason why we're making a record profit is we've taken a huge amount of efficiency into the organisation,' he said. 'A billion dollars of costs have come out; we think that's a step-change. The way we're getting to those record profits is through those structural changes in the business, not through the higher airfares, because we are forecasting that airfares are going to normalise, certainly as capacity comes back to 100 per cent.'

Qantas was not making record profit through higher airfares! Next, Joyce would claim the sun rises in the west, or the Axis powers won World War II. The record half-year profit Joyce had unveiled in February was due to a 46 per cent increase in revenue per seat versus pre-COVID. Costs per seat, excluding fuel, had not changed by any such magnitude. Joyce's $1 billion of savings in costs was a factor in increased profitability, of course, but it represented a reduction in

Qantas' ex-fuel cost base of significantly less than 10 per cent. His statement also came a matter of days after Qantas had told its investor day audience all about its 'structural uplift' in domestic revenue per seat kilometre, and that international yields were 'moderating but are expected to stabilise at 150 per cent of FY19'. Here, again, Joyce was distorting reality in compulsive defence of his self-narrative: I am not anti-competitive, I am not a price-gouger, therefore my super-profits are the result of cost savings. This was how the world appeared through Alan's enchanted spectacles.

The following week, I was eating breakfast with my wife at Hotel Costes in Paris. We were luxuriating in our glorious remoteness from Australia and its affairs when, across the courtyard, my eyes met Richard Goyder's. The Qantas chairman was dining with fellow AFL commissioner (and former Wesfarmers director) Paul Bassat and their wives. This would not be a one-off encounter. An exotic medley of Australian business leaders, celebrities and the idle rich, it soon turned out, had colonised the hotel for the lavish society wedding of Franco-Aussie chef Guillaume Brahimi and designer Tamie Ingham (of the chicken and horseracing family).

Despite my tense exchange with Goyder in Adelaide two months earlier, and the explosion of hostilities between Qantas and the *AFR*, my most pungent criticisms had been reserved for Alan Joyce. The blows to Goyder had been glancing at best. Still, he was a complete alien to this sort of disrespect. Chairing Qantas and the AFL was a ticket to stratospheric social status, including society weddings. In Goyder's native Perth, a one-newspaper town where fealty to local media baron Kerry Stokes was an accepted impost on everyone in public life, Goyder was a protected species. He even chaired Stokes' pet charity, the Perth Telethon.

Each time we stumbled into them that weekend, the Goyders were unimpeachably nice. I oscillated between guilt for inadvertently haunting this lovely couple's holiday and bemusement that, while Qantas was in reputational freefall, its chairman was in Europe at a celebrity wedding with Karl Stefanovic and the cool kids. The final time we spoke, I joked, 'I can't for the life of me get a copy of the

Financial Times in this hotel. Did they write something nasty about Qantas?' Goyder returned my gaze blankly.

———

At the annual Skytrax World Airline Awards in June, also held in Paris, Qantas' ranking plummeted from fifth to seventeenth, its lowest ever place.[25] For some peculiar reason, the 'global factors' affecting quality and reliability seemed to be affecting Qantas much more acutely than its global peers.

The Skytrax Awards were determined by the votes of travellers, whose dissatisfaction with Qantas was only growing louder. The *AFR*'s letters page was flooded. A Brisbane reader's account, on 13 June, of his business class flight to Europe was a classic of the genre – a tirade the late, fearsome writer A.A. Gill would've been proud of. In Singapore on the return leg, he was 'lumped into an ancient, rattling A330' with faulty USB charging ports and an inflight entertainment system bereft of entertainment. 'The food served was probably the most atrocious meal I've ever seen anywhere, let alone on a plane', with coffee that 'can only be described as putrid dish-water'. In conclusion: 'This could not be Business Class on any other airline.' In fact there were still many airlines worse than Qantas, but the undeniable truth was that Qantas had vacated its place among the best.

Also in June, the *AFR* reported what could have been an even greater danger to Qantas' business: the Albanese government was considering allowing Qatar Airways to double its flights into Australia's four major cities, from thirty-five to seventy per week.[26] The Qatari government had in fact initiated the process in August 2022; Qatar Airways CEO Akbar Al Baker put the inspiration in a nutshell on Sky News in October that year, pointing out that Qantas had cut its international flights by 50 per cent and 'more than doubled the price of airfares to the Australian people [for] the benefit of shareholders'.

Qatar Airways – which Skytrax ranked second in the world, behind Singapore Airlines – was one of only four airlines to maintain continuous commercial flights to Australia through the pandemic, picking up the considerable slack left by Qantas shutting its international operation. Qatar flew 220,000 Australians home during COVID but also repatriated 15,000 vulnerable Australians at the request of Australian embassies and consulates and even their local MPs. Qatar had also evacuated Australian embassy staff and military personnel from Kabul before the city fell to the Taliban in 2021. The airline felt confident this heavy lifting would be rewarded by Canberra.

Its case was also being pushed hard by Virgin Australia, which had struck an alliance with Qatar in 2022 to sell tickets on each other's flights and offer reciprocal frequent flyer benefits. Virgin's private equity owner, Bain Capital, was looking to refloat the company on the ASX and was rumoured to be talking to Qatar Airways about taking a cornerstone equity stake.[27] Qantas was anxious about Qatar's deep pockets, and the brutal experience of competing with Virgin the last time it was owned by foreign airlines.

But Qantas was also practised at nobbling Qatar. In 2018, Qatar had applied to increase its weekly flights into major cities from twenty-one to twenty-eight, so it could launch a daily Brisbane service. Qantas lobbied transport minister Michael McCormack to include a 'fair competition' clause in the deal, something the United Arab Emirates, for instance, had never been asked to sign by Canberra.[28] Qantas was even quoting research by US carriers alleging that Qatar was heavily government subsidised, but omitted to mention that the research was actually into the state subsidisation of Qatar *and* Emirates (and Etihad). As one Qantas insider justified it to me, Emirates was 'the most commercial of the least commercial airlines in the world', whereas Qatar was simply 'the least commercial of the least commercial'. It also didn't hurt Qantas that McCormack's new chief of staff, Damian Callachor, had been hired straight out of Qantas' in-house lobbying team. Wrangling over the competition clause held up the deal for eighteen months, and then COVID arrived. It wasn't until January 2022 that the Morrison government granted Qatar those extra seven flights per week. Qatar launched its Brisbane service, but it immediately wanted more.

In October 2022, Virgin Australia had made a formal submission to the Department of Infrastructure and Transport in support of Qatar's new application to further increase its flight allocation. As part of the process, in the first week of January 2023 the department then sent a decision brief and a proposed negotiating mandate to transport minister Catherine King; King met with Virgin CEO Jayne Hrdlicka and discussed the matter on 23 January. According to Hrdlicka's later evidence to a Senate inquiry, King told Hrdlicka that Alan Joyce was unhappy that the department was recommending negotiations with Qatar and that he'd asked to speak to King. 'Nonetheless,' Hrdlicka said, 'I was left with a very clear impression that a decision to proceed was very compelling and imminent. Based on this conversation, I felt comfortable that Qatar would be granted additional air rights.' Indeed, Hrdlicka was 'so sufficiently comfortable that I did not raise Qatar with the prime minister when I hosted him at the Australian Open [final] in January as part of my responsibilities as chair of Tennis Australia.' Her comfort would be short-lived.

Qantas, like Virgin, had provided a formal submission to King's department in October, but opposing Qatar's application. Behind the scenes, the Qantas influence machine had jolted into action. According to one Joyce lieutenant, 'We were told the department was going to give Qatar a big increase in traffic rights. That was bad news given how they behave commercially. We had a view and we were entitled to put that view. We said, "How are we hearing about this at the end of the process?"' King, this Qantas executive told me, 'felt blindsided by her department'.

Qatar's application (and Qantas' still-phoney war with the ACCC) was in the ether when Alan Joyce met with King – and separately with Prime Minister Albanese – at Parliament House on 23 November 2022. Albanese attended and delivered his stirring speech at Qantas' gala dinner on 31 March 2023 and Joyce also met with King at Parliament House on 10 May.[29] Albanese would later deny he ever discussed Qatar's air rights with Joyce, while Joyce and King refused to say one way or the other.

Nevertheless, by April, Hrdlicka was worried that Qatar's bid seemed to have stalled. When she spoke to King again on 1 May it 'was a very different conversation from my conversation with the minister in January'. King now indicated that the government had reservations about Qatar's application in light of 'the Doha Airport incident of 2020'. Hrdlicka was completely taken aback.

The Doha airport incident was a grisly story with lingering consequences. On 2 October 2020, a newborn baby girl was found inside a plastic bag in a bathroom rubbish bin at Doha's Hamad International Airport. Police – employed by Qatar's Ministry of Interior – conducted an urgent search for the child's parent/s, including onboard ten aircraft at nearby gates. One of these was a Qatar Airways flight bound for Sydney. Officers ordered numerous female passengers, among them thirteen Australians, off the flight and into ambulances, where they were subjected to abdominal examinations to ascertain whether they'd freshly given birth.

The barbaric and incompetent episode shocked the public and made global headlines. Prime Minister Scott Morrison described the incident as 'appalling' and 'unacceptable', while the Minister for Foreign Affairs, Marise Payne, demanded an explanation from her Qatari counterpart. Qatar's Prime Minister Sheikh Khalid bin Khalifa Al Thani expressed his 'sincerest apology for what some female travellers went through', while his deputy described the incident as 'a violation of Qatar's laws and values'. The police officer in charge was sacked, charged and convicted, and received a suspended jail sentence, while the child's mother – who had been on another flight entirely and was identified only as being of 'Asian nationality' – was charged with attempted murder and her extradition sought. In November 2021, having received a confidential report from the government of Qatar, Morrison declared himself satisfied, noting that 'there was an investigation, there has been a conviction, and there's been a significant change to airport processes in Qatar'. Diplomatically, the case was closed.

Quite understandably, five of the women put through this ordeal in Doha didn't see it that way, and in 2022 they sued both the airline and Qatar's Civil Aviation Authority in the Federal Court of Australia.[30] Initially, the Qatari respondents sought to have the suit thrown out, arguing they were entitled to sovereign immunity. Qatar Airways dropped that defence after Minister King's office quietly communicated her unhappiness with it, and submitted itself to the court's jurisdiction in February 2023, arguing instead that it had no ability to refuse the directions of Qatari police.[31] Handing down its judgment in April 2024, the Federal Court agreed. The judge found that 'the proposition that Qatar Airways was able to exert any relevant control over the officers conducting the police operation or the nurse in the ambulance can fairly be characterised as fanciful, trifling, implausible, improbable, tenuous or one that is contradicted by all the available documents'.

A sordid tale, to be sure, but a bizarre input for determining flight routes and frequencies. As Hrdlicka later told the Senate, 'I was now concerned the air rights may not be granted. As the weeks passed, that concern only grew.' When Hrdlicka spoke on the phone with Albanese on 13 July, the prime minister also expressed concern about the Doha incident. By then, though, it was all too late: on 10 July, King had written to the women suing Qatar Airways, informing them that 'the Australian government is not considering additional bilateral air rights with Qatar'.

Qatar Airways only learned of its rejection when the *AFR*'s aviation reporter, Ayesha de Kretser, broke the news on 18 July.[32] Senior tourism industry figures erupted in outrage. Flight Centre co-founder Graham 'Skroo' Turner described it as 'the most ridiculous decision I've ever seen. The cost of airfares is a huge problem for travellers,' he told the *Sydney Morning Herald*, noting that Qantas '[does] not have the capacity for additional services and yet we're rejecting Qatar's extra capacity'. Turner added that it would be 'totally illogical' to block Qatar's application on the basis of the 2020 Doha incident. 'If the conduct of a country's police force is the reason they were rejected we wouldn't let half the world's carriers fly to Australia.'

James Goodwin, head of the umbrella group for the country's airports, also told the *SMH* that King's decision was 'a bad outcome for tourism and sends a bad signal to international carriers wanting to fly into and out of Australia'. The federal opposition marvelled that Qatar's application had had the support of not only the airports and travel agents, but also the New South Wales and Victorian governments, and even King's cabinet colleague, trade minister Don Farrell.

Problematically for the Albanese government, this protection of Qantas in the international market converged with a growing sense that it was protecting Qantas in the domestic market too.

Hot on the heels of Gina Cass-Gottlieb's scathing verdict of extreme market concentration in the domestic aviation sector, the ACCC revealed that for the second consecutive year it had received more complaints about Qantas than any other company. And in the same week as King's Qatar decision, former Productivity Commission chair Peter Harris lashed out at Australia's aviation policy settings. Harris had designed Sydney airport's slot system in the 1990s, then in 2021 had authored an independent government review calling for a major overhaul to counter 'slot hoarding' – the practice whereby Qantas and Virgin scheduled peak-hour Sydney flights they never intended to operate (to prevent Rex and Bonza getting those valuable take-off and landing slots) and then cancelled them at the last minute. 'I'm pretty sure that the Sydney–Melbourne corridor is the second or maybe third largest utilised aviation corridor in the world … To say it can only support two airlines seems to me to be the height of absurdity,' Harris told a parliamentary hearing on 25 July.

Sydney Airport CEO Geoff Culbert also argued for more competition. He stated publicly that the recovery in domestic air travel had stalled because 'steep airfares and high cancellation rates on popular domestic routes are suppressing demand', concluding that if Qantas and Virgin 'have decided to fly less, then they should relinquish slots to [other] carriers who want to … provide more choice for customers'.[33]

The seeds of a seductive political idea had been sown: the system was rigged, and Australia had an airline competition problem. Mostly, Australia just had a Qantas problem. The idea found fertile ground in a public already decidedly sick of Qantas and its CEO, but it might never have flourished so robustly had King not made the most extraordinary hash of explaining herself. On 26 July, she told the *Sydney Morning Herald* that the Doha incident was not a reason for her blocking Qatar's additional flights.[34] She said, 'I want more capacity for people to be able to enjoy travel, but equally I want to be able to decarbonise the transport sector.' This was a seriously dubious rationale – the first of many King would proffer – given Qatar operated one of the youngest and most fuel-efficient fleets in the global airline industry, far superior to the emissions profile of Qantas International.

But the idea that the system was rigged for Qantas really blossomed into the political conversation the following week when I revealed in my *AFR* column Rear Window that Alan Joyce had bestowed membership of Qantas' elite Chairman's Lounge on the most unexpected individual: the prime minister's 22-year-old son.

A Very Valued Benefit

2–27 Aug 2023

The Qantas Chairman's Lounge is not one particular lounge, but a network of them in every mainland state capital and in Canberra. These vast, hidden, hushed spaces allow members to relax, graze, work and network in privacy and luxury before their domestic flights. Behind the black sliding doors simply marked 'Private', the chosen elite can order from the à la carte restaurant menu, partake of bottomless premium wines and spirits, recline on designer armchairs and read the daily newspapers (except, in 2023, the *AFR*). When a member's flight commences boarding, a lounge attendant personally comes and informs them.

This offering was established in the 1980s by Australian Airlines, before its 1993 merger with Qantas, and was a facsimile of Ansett's exclusive Managers Lounge.[1] It was (and remains) a globally unique offering. While the US and some European carriers have invitation-only tiers in their frequent flyer programs that come with worthy perks, none of them operate dedicated lounges for those customers.[2] Members of the Chairman's Lounge receive those same perks, like complimentary upgrades to business class (subject to availability), or to first class on international flights, and a dedicated VIP service line, the value of which increased exponentially during and immediately after the pandemic. Chairman's Lounge members did not wait hours on hold trying unsuccessfully to redeem a COVID credit or track down a lost bag. And post-pandemic, should their child be stranded by a missed connection at a foreign airport, they are one phone call away from a salvage operation unavailable to mere mortals.

And who are these members? They are the board directors, CEOs and senior executives of Australia's major companies – or any company which spent sufficient millions each year travelling Qantas. They are virtually every member of federal parliament, and state government ministers; they are the secretaries and deputy secretaries of all Commonwealth (and many state) departments, and senior military officers. They are the chairs and CEOs of government agencies, including Qantas' regulators: the corporate cop, ASIC; the competition cop, the ACCC; and even the safety regulator, the Civil Aviation Safety Authority. All judges of the Federal Court and the High Court are Chairman's Lounge members, as are newspaper editors, certain commentators and breakfast television hosts, and an assortment of B-list celebrities. And in most cases, their spouses are also members. In 2023, there were around 5,000 consecrated primary members of the Chairman's Lounge – 9,000 if you count their approved spouses.

The Chairman's Lounge is a speakeasy for Australia's ruling class, yet it is so much more than that. Possessing its membership means passing the mystical velvet rope of high social status – something Western consumer culture conditions us all to strive for. It is confirmation that you've made it, entitling you quite literally to breathe different air to regular people. Of course, it is a classic chimera, because if you'd really made it, you'd be at the ExecuJet terminal boarding your own Global Express. Most Chairman's Lounge members are only there in return for spending a tremendous amount of other people's money.

This system has been terrific for Qantas because while Australia's leading corporate and government figures would never shell out their own money on a five-star ego massage, they are more than happy to squander shareholders' or taxpayers' funds on the very same. Countless Australian companies elect to spend 25 per cent more on a travel deal with Qantas – instead of requiring staff to take the cheapest available flight – solely because their boards and top executives prefer the lounge memberships to the savings. The Australian government's travel policy of the 'lowest practical fare' is openly flouted by MPs and public servants, with Qantas receiving more than 80 per cent of Common-wealth spending on domestic flights. Outrageously, in financial 2023 Virgin Australia received only 11 cents out of every dollar spent on domestic travel by MPs and their staff, despite Virgin offering the lowest practical fare at least 90 per cent of the time.³ Such was the power of the Chairman's Lounge, the Shangri-la of corporate patronage.

It was also the power of Qantas' loyalty program and public officials' hunger for status credits. Achieving lifetime Qantas gold or platinum status courtesy of the taxpayer was a holy grail pursued by many, as a soft cushion for post-political life. Kevin Rudd's finance minister, Lindsay Tanner, ended the accrual of frequent flyer points on all government travel in 2010, saving $40 million per year, but he fatefully allowed politicians and public servants to continue accumulating status points.

Qantas well understood the enormous clout derived from operating what Joyce himself described as 'probably the most exclusive club in the country'.⁴ The Chairman's Lounge enabled Joyce to render the pointy end of modern Australia in his own image. He alone decided who was in and who was out – and inevitably, this bred fear of, and kowtowing to, Qantas among this ruling class. When it comes to Chairman's Lounge membership, current, aspiring or former members do not behave rationally. Highly intelligent and otherwise high-functioning individuals completely lose their senses. Those who eventually received Qantas' merciless form letter of annihilation – 'I trust you understand that we are not able to extend your membership beyond its current expiry' – often fell into a kind of madness.

'Let's just say it's a very valued benefit,' former Qantas chairman Leigh Clifford concedes drily. 'Some of the calls you get, and some of the pleadings, are unbelievable. People forget that it's a commercial decision. I had one guy ring me up and say, "I'm going to take this further!" I'm not sure who he was going to take it to after me.'

The receipt of benefits by company executives is a matter for those companies and their shareholders, but benefits provided to politicians are a matter of public interest. Sadly, the Chairman's Lounge is where Qantas' skilful influence peddling meets the spectacular entitlement culture of the nation's parliamentary caste. A large part of the resulting problem is the opacity of these benefits, due to the scandalously loose disclosure regime governing them. All MPs are required to declare any gifts, sponsored travel or hospitality (including to their spouse or dependent children) worth more than $300. Yet there are no practical consequences of failing to do so. Despite the $300 reporting threshold, MPs performatively declare every worthless souvenir handed to them by interest groups: books, bottles of wine, a box of chocolates, a pair of thongs. It is an affectation of pedantic transparency, behind which many quietly enjoy the far grander perquisites of office.

Flight upgrades are specifically required to be disclosed and while some MPs disclose them, others disclose none.[5] 'Like the American alliance and the offshore processing of asylum seekers,' I wrote in the *AFR*, 'undeclared airline freebies are a bipartisan article of faith.' Anthony Albanese regularly reported flight upgrades for himself, though did so only once for his family. In July 2009, when he was transport minister in the Rudd government but travelling in a private capacity, he received an upgrade to business class from Qantas on Sydney–Los Angeles return flights. In April 2010, he and his son received a 'ticket upgrade' on Sydney–Rome return flights from Emirates. No classes of travel were specified, making it impossible to know the precise monetary value of this gift, but it would've been in the vicinity of $10,000. Again, in July 2011, and still transport minister, Albanese 'accepted upgrades from Emirates travelling unofficially to and from Europe'. On a personal trip to Hawaii on 29 December 2012, he was upgraded to business class by Qantas from Honolulu to Sydney. And in March 2013, Albanese travelled with Joyce on Qantas' inaugural flight to Dubai, as its partnership with Emirates commenced in earnest.[6]

The upgrades continued after Labor returned to opposition, when Albanese became shadow transport minister. In September and October 2013, Albanese received free upgrades from economy to business on ten different 'privately funded flights' within Australia on Qantas and Virgin. He was then upgraded by Qantas on 'personally funded flights' from Sydney to London on 30 November and from

Rome to Sydney, presumably on Emirates, on 5 December. Again, Albanese did not disclose which class of travel he was upgraded to or from. It would be a safe presumption that he paid for an economy ticket in the full knowledge he would never have to set foot in that unholy cabin. The price difference between a return first class Sydney–London ticket and an economy ticket was more than $10,000 – or 4 per cent of a shadow minister's (then) pre-tax annual salary. Even the fare difference between business and first was around $5,000 (as was the differential between economy and business).

In October 2016, Qantas again upgraded Albanese's 'personally funded' flights both ways between Sydney and London but again, he did not identify what class he was upgraded to or from.⁷ And in October 2019, by which time Albanese was opposition leader, Qantas again upgraded him on a flight to Honolulu. According to Qantas insiders, Albanese would liaise with Joyce directly about his personal travel. While other Qantas executives could authorise 'space available' upgrades in flight bookings, meaning an upgrade would occur only if there was an empty business or first class seat after check-in had closed, only Joyce could issue 'confirmed' or guaranteed upgrades, the kind that Albanese was treated to.⁸

None of this made Albanese Robinson Crusoe in the parliament – far from it – but neither did that make it right. In all of these cases, Albanese was either transport minister or shadow transport minister, so he was accepting gifts worth tens of thousands of dollars from one of the largest and most important stakeholders in his area of policy responsibility, creating at the *very least* a perceived conflict of interest regarding the independence of his decision-making. Yet nobody batted an eyelid. That was the most disturbing part – that it was utterly common practice in Australian politics. It was a slice of fortune that fuelled Qantas' hubris: the new prime minister was an 'asset' the airline had been developing for fifteen years; a transport minister who'd been upgraded to the top job.

MPs are also required to declare 'membership of any organisation where a conflict of interest with a member's public duties could foreseeably arise or be seen to arise'. Most MPs declare their

Chairman's Lounge and Virgin Beyond memberships, but many do not – and again, there are no repercussions. Albanese first disclosed his Chairman's Lounge and Virgin club memberships in 2019, more than twenty years after his election to parliament. He never disclosed the Chairman's Lounge membership of his then wife Carmel Tebbutt – the widely respected former deputy premier of New South Wales. In October 2022, he did disclose the membership of his subsequent partner Jodie Haydon.[9] And according to multiple senior Qantas sources, who requested not to be named, soon after Albanese became prime minister in 2022, he asked Joyce to make his son Nathan a member too. What was Joyce supposed to say?

Minutes after I'd put the fact of Nathan Albanese's Chairman's Lounge membership to the Prime Minister's Office for comment, Anthony Albanese called *AFR* editor-in-chief Michael Stutchbury. As Stutchbury recalls, the PM 'made the case that politicians' families should be off limits, but he came away knowing we weren't going to kill the story, so he was pretty unhappy about that. I think he's still unhappy about that.' Stutch had already sense-checked my story with other senior heads in the *AFR* newsroom, concluding, 'No one was necessarily saying it was a terrible thing, but there was a public interest in knowing that.'

It was Alan Joyce, not Albanese, who responded to my story, which was still hot off the press when Joyce was door-stopped by a huddle of reporters at a tourism industry event in Brisbane on 3 August. 'I don't deny it and at the same time [I] don't confirm it,' he said, as his PR minder huffed at the journos to change the subject. 'I've been good mates with Albo for some time,' he added defiantly.

Chairman's Lounge membership, Joyce insisted, 'is not a gift, it's a commercial arrangement that we do. Some of the politicians are … our largest flyers and we facilitate access to our lounges if you're in BHP, if you're in Rio. The government has a big contract with us – it's absolutely no different.'

Joyce was yet again presenting an account of the situation that was hopelessly compromised by logical shortcomings, the first quite obviously being that Albo's son was not a member of the government, nor was he an MP's spouse. The second was that BHP and Rio Tinto did not regulate Qantas. They couldn't deny traffic rights to Qantas' competitors, defund the ACCC's airline monitoring powers on Qantas' behalf, or shower Qantas with taxpayer subsidies.

Thirdly, the exact number of Chairman's Lounge memberships that a mining company or bank might receive was determined by how much it spent on travel, and those companies decided which of its executives or directors got them.[10] In contrast, Qantas gave Chairman's Lounge privileges to literally hundreds of Commonwealth officials, and Alan Joyce decided which ones. Yes, the government spent many multiples of what even the airline's largest corporate clients spent, but the number of Chairman's Lounge memberships given to government figures was not formulaically linked to that spend. How could it have been, when the government's travel policy was *supposed* to be based not on any guaranteed minimum paid to Qantas, but on every government traveller taking the cheapest flight of the day? Here was the entire point: the Chairman's Lounge was an inducement – and a very successful one – for government travellers to defy policy and misspend public money.

'This is just a nonsense that Qantas has this unbelievable influence that can dictate anything with the government,' Joyce railed. 'I don't know how that mindset has got there because it's just not right.' This was almost a replay of his Finnair press conference ten weeks earlier, where 'anyone who says anything else [was] completely wrong'. Joyce could not see that the mindset he was denouncing was that of the overwhelming majority, and indeed, one of his own creation. As proof of Albanese's non-capture, Joyce said the then transport minister 'had a go at me when we grounded the airline in [October] 2011'. Albanese was so angry he didn't even ask Joyce for a free upgrade that Christmas – though he was straight back on the Qantas-Emirates gravy train the very next year.

Virgin's Jayne Hrdlicka addressed the same tourism event in Brisbane that day and subtly lent the Qatar issue fresh oxygen, complaining, 'Australia should be [a hot destination] given the exchange rate. Australia should be great value for international inbound, but it's not. Airfares are so high because there isn't enough capacity and there's a huge amount of demand.' Days later, Qantas' former chief economist Tony Webber outlined the foregone economic benefits of Qatar's additional flights in the *Financial Review*. Based on twenty-one flights per week, the international visitors on those extra inbound services would have spent $500 million each year in Australia, 'generating thousands of local jobs', while the flights would also have forced down all airlines' fares on those routes, benefiting the 1.7 million Australians who fly to Europe each year.[11]

And who would these flights have made worse off? According to Dr Webber: Qantas, which wanted to 'drip-feed capacity back into the market and allow continued pent-up demand to drive up yields' (which, in airline speak, are just airfares adjusted for distance). Qantas' international yields, he explained, were 64 per cent higher in the six months to December 2022 than they were in 2019. The next most adversely affected by Qatar's flights would have been 'the other Middle East carriers, notably Emirates and Etihad'.[12] Webber concluded that, given Qantas' partnership with Emirates, 'the negative impact that additional Qatar capacity may have [had] will not have gone unnoticed by Qantas management'.

The deal between Qantas and Emirates, in operation since 2012, was far deeper than the nascent alliance between Virgin Australia and Qatar, which merely sold seats on each other's flights and offered reciprocal frequent flyer benefits.[13] Qantas and Emirates did those things too, but they effectively operated as a single company, even jointly setting their airfares and flight schedules. The ACCC granted authorisation for this cartel conduct in 2013, 2018 and, incredibly, again in August 2023, despite the two carriers commanding a 52 per cent market share between Australia and the United Kingdom (the next largest was Singapore Airlines on 16 per cent), and a 37 per cent market share between Australia and Europe (trailed by Qatar on 22 per cent). As I wrote at the time, 'Could you imagine ANZ and NAB being allowed to merge their branches or Coles and Aldi getting a green light to combine their distribution centres? Never.' Irrespective of its lessening of competition for the travelling public,

Anthony Albanese was an unabashed fan of the Qantas–Emirates tie-up. In May 2023, he told a Labor Party fundraiser in Brisbane that it was one of his proudest achievements as transport minister in the Rudd and Gillard governments.

On the other hand, Albanese was no fan of Qatar's Akbar Al Baker, who had dared in 2012 to complain publicly about Sydney airport's curfew. This wasn't anything that even the airport itself wasn't saying, but it wasn't politically smart. As Sydney Airport chairman Max Moore-Wilton lamented, Albanese had 'a massive conflict of interest' as both the transport minister and the local member for the suburbs under the airport's western flight path. 'Really he is the minister for no noise over Marrickville,' Moore-Wilton said. Albanese bitched the following year that 'Qatar Airways made its position clear in the pages of the *Daily Telegraph*, which was the first I had heard of it,' and even wrote to Qatar's Civil Aviation Authority encouraging Qatar to fly to destinations other than Sydney. Albanese never forgot what he perceived as Al Baker's disrespect.

Tony Webber was pinpointing what very few people had perceived: that in the battle with Qatar, Qantas was just a front, behind which loomed Emirates, the fourth-largest airline on earth.[14] Sir Rod Eddington, a former CEO of Cathay Pacific, Ansett and British Airways, and who also served on the Qantas board, agrees: 'Emirates was the major winner in keeping Qatar at bay. I don't know the minutiae of the Qantas–Emirates joint service agreement but I have no doubt that Qantas is an economic beneficiary of Emirates' success on the kangaroo route and it was very clear that for Emirates, more capacity for Qatar would have been a problem.'

Launched in 1994, nine years after Emirates, Qatar Airways had spent the pre-COVID decade growing explosively on Emirates' doorstep. Compounding the aggravation, Qatar had for years exploited the United Arab Emirates' open skies policy to operate nearly twenty daily short-haul flights between Dubai and Doha, effectively stealing Emirates passengers for its own network. That ended in 2017, when the UAE – along with Bahrain, Egypt and Saudi Arabia – severed all diplomatic ties with the state of Qatar over its support for Iran's regime.

All flights between the two countries were suspended and relations only fully normalised in 2023. The animus towards Qatar Airways' Al Baker from his Emirates counterpart Sir Tim Clark only intensified when Al Baker poached Clark's heir apparent, Thierry Antinori, to be Qatar's second-in-command in 2019. Clark was furious – though he had poached Antinori from archrival Lufthansa in 2011.

There was also rich history between Al Baker and Alan Joyce. At the launch of Qatar's second Australian route – to Perth – in July 2012, Al Baker said publicly that he was in negotiations with Qantas for a codeshare partnership. Later that day, Joyce called Al Baker to call off the talks: Qantas was doing its deal with Emirates instead. Still, the two CEOs maintained cordial relations and continued to discuss a potential future partnership, especially after Qatar joined the oneworld alliance in 2013. 'I of course started to push him more,' Al Baker says. 'Otherwise what is the purpose of joining oneworld if you're not going to work with your alliance partner and you're working instead with an airline that is not [an alliance member]?' Al Baker says Joyce repeatedly told him he would consider a deal once the second five-year term on Qantas' Emirates agreement ended.

In 2018, the two men were on a conference panel in Sydney when Al Baker made the unseemly remark that 'of course [Qatar Airways] has to be led by a man, because it is a very challenging position', causing an immediate furore and sparking an apology. Al Baker was nothing if not unreconstructed, having complained in 2017, 'You are always being served by grandmothers on American carriers . . . the average age of my cabin crew is only twenty-six years.'

In October 2021, the world's aviation chieftains gathered in Boston for IATA's annual meeting. Al Baker and Joyce met for dinner. According to Al Baker's version of events, 'We were walking towards the venue and he opened the subject with me. He said, "Look, we still have two years on our contract with Emirates, but once it is over, then we would be very interested to work with Qatar."' Al Baker responded that 'since we had waited so long, I had no problem to wait a little longer'. Forty-eight hours later, Qantas and Emirates announced another five-year extension of their partnership, until

2028. As Al Baker sees it, he was misled. 'It made my team feel that we were dealing with a dishonest person, to put it very mildly. I never came across somebody that had such a double standard as this man.'

The bad blood between Qatar and Qantas placed enormous strain on oneworld, a formal grouping of international airlines that offered their customers reciprocal loyalty points, lounge access and seamless international connections.[15] Qatar's influence in the alliance was becoming outsized, due not just to its own growth but also its large shareholdings in other oneworld airlines: British Airways, Iberia and Cathay Pacific.[16] Al Baker had threatened to pull Qatar out of oneworld in 2018 over Qantas' lobbying against its bid for a daily Brisbane flight. Joyce almost dared Al Baker to do it: 'If Qatar feel they do better outside of oneworld, that is up to them.'

In May 2021, Al Baker had succeeded Joyce as oneworld's chairman.[17] The oneworld CEO since 2018 was Rob Gurney, a former executive at Qantas and Emirates. There was no love lost between Gurney and Al Baker's deputy, Thierry Antinori, stemming from their days together at Emirates, and Qatar saw Gurney as a Joyce proxy. 'Akbar just rode Rob like you wouldn't believe,' one alliance insider tells me. Gurney ultimately resigned in May 2023 without a successor in place.[18] But before then things became so hostile that in 2022, Qatar moved to have Qantas kicked out of the alliance.

Back in Mascot, Joyce and Markus Svensson were treating expulsion as a real prospect. 'We were seriously discussing our alternatives to oneworld,' a colleague recalls. Joyce worked the phones to his fellow member CEOs across the globe. Robert Isom, the CEO of oneworld's largest and most powerful member, American Airlines, ultimately played peacemaker, managing to lower the temperature and narrowly averting a disastrous splintering of the alliance.

Senior Qantas executives now concede privately that Qantas was acting at Emirates' behest in lobbying against Qatar's bid for additional flights to Australia. It was an audacious proxy mission in circumstances where the lack of available seats had sent international airfares skyrocketing and Emirates itself was only operating half the flights it was allowed to Australia.[19] One Joyce lieutenant says Clark was 'exercised' by the news that Qatar was on track to double its traffic rights, having spent twenty years building Emirates' Australian rights (most of which, ironically, was opposed by Qantas before the two climbed into bed together; it was also ironic because Emirates had doubled its rights in one hit – from forty-two to eighty-four per week – in 2007). Another told me, 'It probably made more sense for [Qantas] to be in business with Qatar than Emirates but Alan's allegiance to Tim Clark was just so strong. That's the story that everyone missed: we did all that bidding on his behalf, and we sustained all the damage.' Qantas would become a victim of its own vaunted lobbying prowess.

'It was a mistake by the Australian government to deny Qatar Airways,' says Rod Eddington, who is nevertheless a long-time friend and supporter of Albanese.[20] 'They continued flying here through COVID when pretty much everybody else had pulled the pin ... I have no idea what went on in Canberra, but Qantas are masters at getting the outcomes they want – particularly on the traffic rights front.'

Nobody knows that better than Eddington, who competed against Qantas for his first twenty years in the airline game. Eddington was Cathay Pacific's commercial director in the 1980s, when it was restricted to a meagre four flights a week to the east coast of Australia: this meant each flight had to stop in both Melbourne and Sydney. Cathay's product and service were so superior to Qantas' – and the market was so starved of capacity – that Cathay's 747s were booked solid. 'We made a fortune flying to Australia and when we finally got the right to a fifth weekly flight, I may have even opened a bottle of champagne. That's how good Qantas was at keeping us out.'

Singapore Airlines was a much greater threat to Qantas than Cathay was, and more successful at winning traffic rights. Eddington recalls: 'They were formidable competitors to Qantas into Asia and beyond and Qantas CEOs spent their lives in Canberra trying to stop Singapore getting any more capacity.' In the late 1990s, when Eddington was executive chairman of Ansett, Emirates was limited to four flights per week – all into Melbourne because 'Qantas had kept them out of Sydney; Sydney was the motherlode. Emirates then was Qantas' new public enemy number one.'[21]

In 2000, Eddington became CEO of British Airways, and saw Qantas up close: BA owned 25 per cent of Qantas and Eddington briefly served on the Qantas board. 'For as long as I've been around, they've been bloody good operators up in Canberra. Indeed, it's difficult to think who might be better.'

———

On 9 August 2023, Alan Joyce and Vanessa Hudson descended upon Canberra. Their presence in Parliament House was conspicuous from the outset: Joyce's Apple Watch set off the metal detector at the security checkpoint and his rescreening briefly held up traffic. The irony – that perhaps he wasn't a 'match fit' traveller – wasn't lost on anybody.

The outgoing and incoming Qantas CEOs met privately with Catherine King in her office at 11:30am.[22] And shortly before 3pm, King was obliged by the opposition in question time to expound upon her Qatar decision. 'We only sign up to agreements that benefit our national interest, in all its broad complexity,' she told the House, as Albanese sat beside her at the despatch box nodding and smiling. The prime minister would face no questions in the House about soliciting an extra Chairman's Lounge membership from Alan Joyce. Which opposition MP would dare cast the first stone? Who among them had never asked Qantas for a 'small favour'?

'That includes ensuring that we have an aviation sector through the recovery that employs Australian workers,' King continued. 'We will always consider the need to ensure that there are long-term well-paid secure jobs for Australians in the aviation sector.'

Suddenly, Joyce's bold promise in March of 8,500 new jobs by 2033 made perfect sense: it had been shameless bait. Yet this confected jobs justification for denying Qatar was almost as implausible as King's previous decarbonisation excuse. And moreover, there was an easy counter: what of the thousands of Australian jobs that would spring from thirty-five new international flights per week bringing an extra 150,000 tourists to Australia annually?

In reality, Joyce continued to wage war on secure Australian jobs in the aviation sector. Qantas had just launched a new route to New York via Auckland, and all the flight attendants on those flights would be

Kiwis. Cheaper New Zealand-based cabin crew were also operating certain Qantas international flights out of Australia (Brisbane–Los Angeles, Melbourne–Delhi), and its trans-Tasman flights were crewed by Kiwi flight attendants *and* pilots. Qantas' London flights were operated by London-based cabin crew, and its flights to Bangkok and Singapore were now on Finnair A330s, with Finnair pilots and flight attendants provided by Asian labour hire firms. No lesser Labor ally (and authority on jobs) than ACTU secretary Sally McManus demolished King's latest position: 'There needs to be a high level of scrutiny put on Qantas' claims about Australian jobs because Qantas has been the biggest shedder of Australian jobs of late,' she told ABC radio on 11 August.

On the evening of their Canberra visit, Joyce and Hudson hosted dinner for Albanese's entire cabinet. Qantas had hired the members' dining room at Parliament House – and even flown in its celebrity chef, Neil Perry – for the occasion. But news of the intimate soiree had circulated parliamentary offices the previous week and been reported by *The Australian*, giving an insurgency time to rally. 'There's no way I was going to let that mongrel have his day in the sun,' recalls Joyce's old foe at the TWU, now Labor senator Tony Sheldon. 'It was critical to show everyone in the parliament, those workers who'd been sacked, all the customers ripped off, that there were a whole bunch of us who were going to hold him to account.' All members of the Labor caucus were invited to a 5pm briefing hosted by Sheldon; his successor at the TWU, Michael Kaine; and ACTU president Michele O'Neil. (To avoid any chance encounter with their antagonists in the public corridors, Qantas executives were spirited directly to the dining room from the car park via the service lift.) 'For those who are also attending the Alan Joyce dinner,' the invitation read, 'the briefing provides an opportunity to hear both sides of the Qantas story.' More than twenty members and senators attended – including, notably, cabinet ministers Tony Burke and Bill Shorten – and they were the first to hear the news that Sheldon, with the support of Nationals senator Matt Canavan, had succeeded in compelling Joyce to appear before a public Senate inquiry on 28 August.[23]

Tony Sheldon had been warring with Joyce for fifteen years – and, frankly, losing. Now he had pulled off quite a feat: it had been nine long years since Joyce had faced a parliamentary hearing. Sheldon had a score to settle with the Qantas boss on behalf of those 1,700 TWU members sacked illegally. The stage was set for an explosive public showdown between the two archrivals.

Further, it was now glaringly apparent that Albanese, when it came to Qantas and his friend Alan Joyce, had diverged not just from popular sentiment, but from his own tribe – and this was especially unusual since Albanese purported to be as tribal as they came. Five days after the Qantas dinner, on 14 August, the prime minister paraded his unaccountable Qantas blind spot in hangar 96 (again), joining Joyce to launch the airline's formal support for an Indigenous Voice to Parliament.

Albanese's proposal to write into the Australian constitution a representative body – or Voice – for the country's First Nations people would be put to a national vote in October. Qantas was hardly alone in backing the Voice – so had fourteen of Australia's top twenty public companies, including all of the big four banks, Telstra, and both Coles and Woolworths. In addition to providing free flights to the 'Yes' campaign, Qantas was unveiling three planes emblazoned with the campaign's 'Yes23' logo. (In the *AFR*, I couldn't resist the quip, '"Yes23" is Albo's answer to the dual questions: would you like a secret Chairman's Lounge membership for your son and how old is he?')

In hangar 96, out came the prime minister's customary, tin-eared rhapsody to the most complained about company in Australia: 'I say to Qantas, not just because I'm a former transport minister, but there is no company in Australia that immediately says Australia like this brand of Qantas. Qantas has a long history of doing its bit to carry the nation, to lift all of us a little bit higher.'

Not just because I'm a former transport minister – it was a revealing protestation.

The Voice was dear to Albanese's heart. He had pledged to hold this referendum in his election-night victory speech the previous year. Yet here he was, powerfully aligning its prospects with one of

Australia's most toxic corporate brands, and with the nation's most reviled business leader. Polling conducted at the time by Freshwater Strategy showed Albanese's net favourability rating at +2, Peter Dutton's on -8, and Joyce almost in his own category on -33. The prime minister's political antenna was still on the blink – his thraldom to Joyce had knocked it out of action. According to leading pollster and strategist Kos Samaras of Redbridge, Albanese 'along with many people in Canberra' did not understand that sentiment towards big business among the voting public was 'at the lowest it's ever been'. And it affected the result: '[Corporate Australia's] social licence [to operate] was in the bin and at the absolute forefront of that problem was Qantas,' he told me. 'You would not put the Qantas brand next to anything you were trying to sell politically. That was one of the worst strategic decisions made.'

An inkling of the misstep might have explained Albanese's desire to avoid scrutiny: although this was a media event, Albanese and Joyce were swept from the hangar by their minders without taking a single question from the media – a fact that didn't escape the press pack or their newsrooms. He had a lot to run from: four weeks since the Qatar decision, and nearly two weeks since news of his whole-of-family account with the Chairman's Lounge, he had managed to avoid a single question about either.

The very next day, Catherine King elevated the Qatar issue to high farce, offering her third discrete public explanation for the decision.[24] 'Our major airline Qantas has just purchased brand-new planes – that's at a significant cost,' she told Cairns radio. 'They're bigger planes, they're quieter planes, they're better for the environment.' This was her worst reason yet, and it was a high bar. Every airline in the world bought aeroplanes. And Qantas was a week away from handing down the biggest profit in its history – mostly because the shortage of seats had enabled it to charge international airfares 52 per cent higher than before COVID.

King's inability to provide a rational explanation – or even just stick to a single irrational explanation – was creating a serious headache for the government. 'She's a funny unit,' one of her colleagues told me, 'and she totally exists in the cabinet because of Albo's support.' Certainly in the *AFR* newsroom, and the Canberra Press Gallery, heads were shaking in disbelief.

None of this was helping Qantas either – and the airline scarcely had spare reputational bark to lose. Roy Morgan's latest net trust rankings were announced on 17 August and the numbers were even worse than the previous toe-curling batch, released in February: Qantas was now Australia's thirteenth most distrusted brand. The previous year it had been Australia's sixth most *trusted* brand: an unprecedented fall of 181 rankings.[25] Roy Morgan CEO Michele Levine had no doubt about the root cause of Qantas' collapse: 'There was moral blindness everywhere,' she told a client webinar, 'but the biggest example was Alan Joyce refusing to pay back any of the $2 billion in corporate welfare despite the company surging back to billion-dollar profitability.'[26]

On 21 August, the prime minister finally addressed the thorny issue of his son's membership of the Qantas Chairman's Lounge. He was forced to do so by a new revelation in my column: that in 2021, when he was opposition leader, Albanese had secured an internship for his son at accounting firm PwC. Albanese could never have known that by 2023, PwC would be dominating the headlines week in, week out, in a scandal that would ultimately cost it a CEO and most of its management team, 200 partners and its entire government consulting arm. After the *AFR*'s Neil Chenoweth and Edmund Tadros revealed that PwC had been designing tax avoidance schemes to circumvent new anti-avoidance laws it had been helping the government design, the firm was brutally dismembered by two parliamentary inquiries which drew out ever more damaging evidence. The PwC tax leaks scandal, as it became known, was the story of the year, and in the winter of 2023 it briefly afforded Qantas some welcome relief from the media's focus.[27]

Before he was sacked for his (relatively extraneous) role in the affair, Sean Gregory had been PwC's government relations boss in Canberra, and it was Gregory who Albanese approached seeking an internship for his son. The firm didn't have an internship program, but bespoke opportunities could always be arranged for an important enough stakeholder. In June 2021, Nathan Albanese completed a two-week, unpaid internship under PwC's chief economist. Albanese thanked PwC's CEO Tom Seymour at a function some months later.

The morning my column was published, Nine's managing director of publishing, James Chessell, received an emotional phone call from Albanese, who had given up on appealing to the mercies of Michael Stutchbury.[28] 'He wasn't shouting or ranting but he was upset,' Chessell recalls. 'He said it was really hard for his son, who was getting a lot of unwanted attention, and that he [Albanese] was fair game but not his family.'

'The fact that his son had been named in these stories had more to do with the prime minister's own decisions than anything the *AFR* had done, but he was completely uninterested in that point of view. I told him it was a reasonable story and that was it. We were so far apart on the issue there was no point doing anything else.'

The Australian media had long reported on the perquisites of the adult children of prime ministers. A 2014 investigation by *The Guardian* revealed that Frances Abbott, daughter of then PM Tony Abbott, received a scholarship to attend a college whose chairman was a Liberal Party donor. Nevertheless, hours after his conversation with Chessell, Albanese complained to reporters, 'My son is not a public figure. He's a young person trying to make his way in the world.' Of course, nobody had ever suggested Albanese's son was a public figure, nor that he'd done a thing wrong. The issue was his father *not* letting him make his way in the world, using the highest office in the land to solicit secret favours on his behalf from corporations doing hundreds of millions of dollars of business each year with the Albanese government.

Yet Albanese and his inner circle fumed. His chief of staff Tim Gartrell was 'personally very angry', according to a colleague. 'Lots of us have relationships with Nathan; he's regularly around the office. People were upset on his behalf.'

The prime minister insisted, 'I completely comply with all the requirements of the [parliament's] register [of member' interests].' He could only have been relying on a dubious technicality to maintain that Nathan's Chairman's Lounge membership did not require public disclosure: that he was not a dependent child. Yet in May 2022, Albanese (then still opposition leader) had said, 'We're close, we live together.' Albanese was an expert in complying with the letter but not the spirit of the rules governing MPs. Between 2008 and 2020, he charged taxpayers nearly $20,000 for flights to, and accommodation in, Melbourne for official business which just so happened to coincide with five AFL grand finals and five Australian Open tennis finals.[29] Similarly, post-COVID, he travelled to Melbourne and attended each and every AFL grand final and Australian Open final in 2022, 2023 and 2024. He certainly wasn't the only MP doing this – former foreign minister Julie Bishop was notorious for it, too – but he was one of the best. That was the grand irony of Albanese's working class origin story (and of his election on an integrity platform). For all his talk of growing up in public housing, his appetite for sponsored VIP hospitality and travel was insatiable. Entitlement to largesse was a lifelong practice – he'd been elected in 1996, so had barely opened his own wallet in nearly thirty years. He promised in his election victory speech to 'change the way politics operates in this country', but Albanese was no drainer of the Canberra swamp; he was its ultimate creature. And nothing reinforced that growing perception more than his abiding compact with Alan Joyce.

———

Alan Joyce fronted his final financial results announcement on 24 August and unveiled the Moby Dick of profits – colossal, and ultimately fatal for its protagonist; a once unthinkable $2.5 billion for financial year 2023, a full $1 billion more than Qantas' previous record profit in 2016.[30] 'Our financial position is the strongest it's ever been,' Joyce boasted, flanked by Vanessa Hudson. 'We've taken more than $1 billion in costs out and there's been a structural change to our earnings to deliver a new level of profitability going forward.'[31]

The opening question, from the *Sydney Morning Herald*, set the accusatory tone of proceedings: 'You mentioned Qantas' financial position is the strongest it's ever been. Why did you choose to sell the majority of your shares in the company two months ago?'[32] Joyce initially stammered in response, then recovered to insist, 'I more than meet the minimum level that the CEO is expected to hold.' But this was false. Joyce's minimum shareholding requirement was $3.3 million of Qantas shares, and his remaining shares were worth only $3 million.[33]

The media's questions didn't grow any less sceptical. 'I'm curious how do you justify the high cancellations on routes out of Sydney?' asked *The Guardian*. 'How much of your profit is because of unredeemed flight credits?' wondered the ABC. 'Can I just ask you ... whether you're satisfied with the quality of the airline right now?' queried Sky News.

'Qantas isn't returning to full international capacity until the second half of 2024,' queried the *AFR*. 'How is it possible to justify pushing against more flights into Australia with Qatar Airways in this context?' Qatar's requested flights, came Joyce's retort, 'could actually distort the market' and 'there shouldn't be rights granted where there's huge amounts of capacity [being] put back in'. Of course, it was Joyce distorting the market – along with his partner Emirates – by *not* putting enough capacity back in.

'Is this as good as it gets in terms of the profit performance for Qantas?' asked *The Australian*. This question captured the recent scepticism in certain quarters of the investment market. On 6 August, Morningstar analyst Angus Hewitt had said, 'There is a lot of pent-up demand at the moment and that's really driving tremendous profitability. We think this is about as good as it gets for airlines.' The same week, rabble-rousing stockbroker Angus Aitken told his clients that 'we cannot see how this period for Qantas is not as good as it gets'.[34]

Hudson stepped in to respond. 'I think the really simple answer to that question is it's not as good as it gets,' she said. 'We are going to see with capacity coming back that our cost position is going to materially improve. And so, therefore, the future earnings potential of our business is going to continue to grow.'[35] To frame this obscene profit as the new low-water mark was dauntless to say the least. Plain common sense suggested that Hudson was fashioning a rod for her own back.

Qantas ended the press conference after thirty-seven minutes (the first thirteen of which Joyce spent reciting a prepared statement), with a queue of reporters still waiting to ask questions. But there was plenty more scrutiny of Joyce to come. He would sit that day for a 32-minute interrogation by Sarah Ferguson for the ABC's flagship *7.30* program.

'How much money did Qantas receive from the taxpayer during COVID?' she asked him, forcing him to concede the figure was $2.7 billion. (Hudson, in her furious *AFR* op-ed in March, had maintained it was 'circa $2 billion'.) 'Was there ever any consideration of repaying any of that money with the very large profits that you are reporting today?' Ferguson pressed.

'I think companies like us will be paying that back because as we are making money, we'll be paying corporation tax again,' Joyce responded. 'We are paying other taxes like ticket taxes, excise duties —'

'That's not paying money back,' Ferguson scoffed, 'that's paying the money you have to pay according to [the tax system].'

'But I would say it's because the company survived ...'

Ferguson framed 'the overall question about today' as 'whether Qantas under Alan Joyce runs on a philosophy of profit first, no matter the cost to customers'.

'Well, that clearly isn't true because over my term – fifteen years as the CEO of Qantas and five years as CEO of Jetstar – we've spent over $20 billion dollars on new aircraft ...'

'If you keep profits up and you keep the share price high you personally get a multi-million-dollar bonus every year. Doesn't that personal profit motive tend to distort your decision-making?'

'When the company does badly I don't get paid,' Joyce countered, falsely. 'The three years of COVID as an example, no bonuses were paid, so there is a correlation between what happens with the performance of the company and what management is paid.' But the very next day, Joyce would finally receive nearly $11 million of Qantas shares under his various incentive schemes. More than $6 million of those were his frozen long-term bonuses for 2020, 2021 and 2022 – the three COVID years over which Qantas lost $6.2 billion. Back then, he knew it would have looked appalling to take those bonuses, so he chose (with the complicity of the Qantas board) to set them aside to take later. Now it looked appalling *and* tricky, but that just wasn't how Joyce saw himself. So he told himself, and Ferguson, a different story. But he was running out of road for his delusions. No CEO of a public company can get away with making such demonstrably false claims on national TV – and certainly not three days before they are due before a public Senate inquiry.

'Australians care about Qantas because you've taught Australians that Qantas means something more than just a business to them – [that's been] a fundamental part of your advertising for a very long time,' Ferguson pointed out. 'Thirty per cent of Australians have family overseas and Qantas markets itself as an airline that delivers family reunions. Can you really justify those high prices when people were searching to ... make those family reunions happen?' Joyce could absolutely justify it, and proceeded to do so at length.

Ferguson was skilfully drawing Joyce out, exposing the full extent of his magical thinking. Next, she turned to the 1,700 illegal sackings. 'Do you regret anything about that decision?'

'The decision from that judge was that Qantas made a decision for the appropriate commercial reasons in his mind but couldn't rule out whether subconsciously there was an illegal reason for this to happen,' Joyce asserted. 'That's subject to a High Court opinion and I believe that we will win that case.' Joyce had no basis for his confidence. He was also mischaracterising the liability judgment of Justice Lee: far from entertaining the idea that Qantas' illegal reason was subconscious, his Honour found that Qantas executive Paul Jones was positively motivated by an illegal purpose and that the motives of Andrew David, the ultimate decision-maker, were exactly the same.[36] Justice Lee rejected David's evidence that he'd been motivated solely by commercial reasons.

As Ferguson scrupulously made her way through the infringements on Qantas' social licence, the sheer number of them made for devasting television. Finally, she turned to arguably the worst of them all. 'Another source of discontent is the way Qantas handled $1.8 billion dollars of flight credits during the pandemic. Did you make it so difficult in the hope that people would eventually just give up and yield the credits?'

'Well, that's again not true because over a billion dollars has been —'

'Do you understand the damage that was done to people's relationship with Qantas?'

Joyce may have been punch-drunk from Ferguson's working-over, but his response to this question set off a chain of events that rendered his position untenable. 'We didn't get it right and we needed to fix it, and the important thing is we did fix it ... We've only got $370 million of credits left. We're really encouraging people ... we'd rather have those credits at zero by the end of the year.'[37]

Qantas had begun 2023 still owing $800 million in COVID flight credits to its customers. This balance, which included Jetstar, had been disclosed at the company's February half-year results. Undoubtedly in response to the enormous volume of negative media reports about the credits, plaintiff law firm Echo Law began advertising on social media on 4 June for credit-holders to join a potential class action against Qantas. On 26 June, Qantas announced a renewed push for customers to use their COVID credits 'towards booking a trip before the deadline of 31 December'.[38] What the announcement didn't say was that after 31 December, all remaining credits would expire and their balances permanently confiscated by the airline, adding hundreds of millions of dollars to its 2024 profit. Qantas' new push did include a carrot – bookings using credits would earn double frequent flyer points.[39] And a new Find My Credit online portal was launched, the issue of Qantas credits being lost in the ether having long plagued the redemption process.

Also in this announcement, Qantas revealed an updated balance of 'around $400 million in COVID credits now remaining for Qantas customers in Australia'. At the end of its long press release, a footnote disclosed that the $400 million 'represents COVID-era credits for Australian Qantas customers yet to be redeemed'. While slightly ambiguous, this seemed to confirm that the figure excluded Qantas customers outside Australia. On another exclusion it was unambiguous: 'Does not include Jetstar.' It is safe to say that virtually nobody digested this fine print, and certainly none of the news coverage explained these exclusions, enabling a false belief to take hold: that Qantas' outstanding COVID credits had fallen from $800 to $400 million.

Two months later, on 24 August, when Joyce told Sarah Ferguson, 'We've only got $370 million of credits left,' he offered no qualification that he was spruiking an incomplete figure. There was no footnote to his statement. Joyce and Vanessa Hudson had also done something highly suspect that day: they had omitted from their financial results the slide disclosing the full balance of COVID credits. That slide had been included in every full- and half-year investor pack since 2021, yet now, four months before Qantas was going to confiscate that money from its customers, all reference to it had vanished.

The previous week, on 18 August, Echo Law had filed its class action in the Federal Court, alleging Qantas had breached its contracts with customers by failing to provide cash refunds instead of flight credits, and had contravened consumer law by misleading customers as to their refund rights. 'We completely reject these claims,' came Qantas' default response. The airline even claimed, 'We've always been very clear to customers that if Qantas cancelled the flight, they are entitled to a refund.' This was false. The ACCC had in June 2020 forced Qantas to inform its customers of their refund rights; and even then, the ACCC lamented, Qantas' communications had remained unclear.

Armed with all of this, I prepared my next column for the *AFR*, explaining that Joyce was misleading the public and that 'the total balance of credits is probably greater than $500 million'. I asked Qantas for the balance of *all* credits – including Jetstar and overseas customers – but Qantas flatly refused to provide it. When those credits expired in 126 days, I wrote, 'Qantas is going to legally steal approximately half a billion dollars from its customers.' This was quite the allegation to be making against a public company in a national newspaper, and I felt its full weight as I clicked the 'publish' button in the *AFR*'s production system.

This column appeared in the edition of Monday 28 August, the same day Joyce was due to face the Senate inquiry. Tony Sheldon now had all the ammunition he needed.

Grand Theft Aero

28 Aug–5 Sept 2023

The Senate Select Committee on the Cost of Living held its public hearing at Victorian Parliament House in Melbourne. Alan Joyce was seated at a long oak table facing seven senators, flanked by his PR chief Andrew McGinnes and Jetstar CEO Stephanie Tully. The committee's chair, Liberal frontbencher Jane Hume, declared the hearing open at 3:27pm and Joyce launched into an interminable opening statement. 'How long is this going to go? This is now close to ten minutes!' Tony Sheldon interjected.

Joyce concluded his remarks soon after, and questions commenced. From the outset, Joyce was naked in his determination to stonewall. Asked if he'd discussed Nathan Albanese's Chairman's Lounge access with the prime minister, he said, 'I will not be making any comment on that confirming or denying it.'[1]

Asked if he'd discussed Qatar's air rights with Anthony Albanese or Catherine King, he said, 'Any conversations I have with the prime minister or a minister I never divulge. I've kept that for all seven prime ministers and I have no intention of changing my approach.'

Senator Hume asked, 'Had Qatar been granted those additional routes, the cost of airfares to consumers would have gone down – is that true?'

Joyce responded, 'The cost of airfares is coming down.'[2]

'But would they have gone down further if Qatar had the additional routes?'

'I would say the cost of airfares is coming down. You would not have known the counterfactual fully.'

'Are you telling this committee that airfares would not have come down?'

'I say that Qatar can still add a lot of capacity to this market. They can add bigger aircraft to the cities that they've been granted. They can add aircraft and services to cities like Adelaide, like Darwin and like Cairns if they want to. There's nothing stopping them doing that.'

Joyce was a fatigue negotiator. He could talk around anything. *Let me address your question by reframing it* was his tactic. *Forget this, you've got to understand that.* Unluckily for him, the committee members were highly attuned to his bulldozing and not in the mood for it.

'You deferred your 2020, 2021 and 2022 long-term bonus shares,' began the Nationals' Senate leader, Bridget McKenzie. 'Are you going to do that [again] this month, or have you chosen to accept these shares?'

'I have chosen to accept these shares because the company is now back in profit.'

McKenzie had clearly watched Joyce's 7.30 interview. 'How can you say that when the company does badly you don't get bonuses?' she asked. 'In actual fact, you've just been able to defer the bonus until it's able to be realised.'

'That's not true, because what happens on the bonuses is linked to a number of different components. During COVID our short-term cash bonuses were not paid to anybody in the senior management team —'

'Sorry, Mr Joyce, you actually set aside your [long-term] bonuses so you can take them later. Qantas can make a $6.3 billion loss and you can collect $6 million in bonuses at some later date.'

'I think you're misunderstanding the different categories of the —'

'I'm not misunderstanding. It's a very cosy arrangement that you've set up for yourself.'

Watching the live webcast at home in my study, I was literally slack-jawed. McKenzie was indeed not misunderstanding anything.

The CEO of Qantas really was denying the undeniable truth like a stark raving lunatic. His malfunctioning subconscious mind was telling him: I self-sacrificed through COVID like thousands of Qantas staff, therefore that $6 million of bonuses couldn't have been for those loss-making years.

McKenzie now swiftly pivoted. 'How many flight credits is the Qantas Group holding on behalf of Australian customers, and why should Qantas keep their money if it's not claimed by 31 December?'

Joyce asked Stephanie Tully to answer. She said, 'We're sitting on about $360 million of Australian customers' credits.' The evidence was only getting more absurd: the CEO of Jetstar was excluding Jetstar's credits from her answer. McKenzie pressed her again for the balance of 'all Qantas customers not just Australian customers', and Tully claimed, 'We've got a small amount from offshore [and] some Jetstar credit' but 'the absolute majority of that credit is $360 million'.

When Tony Sheldon's turn came, the atmosphere was electric. 'I want to start with the extraordinary revelation in the *Financial Review* this morning that you've been misleading the Australian public about outstanding flight credits, Mr Joyce. Last Thursday you said that there were $370 million, and we've just had that repeated by Ms Tully. That is money that you've taken from customers in exchange for nothing. What you didn't say is that you've excluded Jetstar and overseas customers from the total. The *Financial Review* says that, when asked, you refused to provide the full total. I'm going to insist that you provide the full total. Just tell me what is the total sum value of flight credits remaining across the whole Qantas Group.'

Andrew McGinnes responded for Joyce. 'Senator, we're happy to take that question on notice, simply because we don't have those figures in front of us. There's been no lack of transparency though, can I say —'

'Mr McGinnes can't answer the question,' Sheldon said to Joyce. 'Can you answer the question?'

'Mr McGinnes is answering the question.'

Sheldon's outrage was on a steep ascent. 'You are the senior CEO of this operation. You have made a series of comments regarding the

$370 million. Does the $370 million include Jetstar credits and credits for overseas?'

'We have always been very clear that they are Qantas Australian-based credits, because that's what the media was asking us about.' This was a ludicrous suggestion – that the media had asked for a selective sample of remaining credits; it was almost as ludicrous as Joyce's spin doctor claiming to be transparent while refusing to give up the real balance.

'You have put an arbitrary deadline of December this year when people will lose that money and the money will stay in the pockets of Qantas and Jetstar, and you're seriously telling the Australian public that you don't know how many tens of millions of dollars are involved above that $370 million?'

'What we are saying is that, since March 2020, $3 billion of refunds have been granted,' went Joyce's inapplicable answer.

'Ms Tully,' said Sheldon, 'you're in charge of Jetstar. What is the value above the $370 million that is credits for the Jetstar operations? Is it more than $100 million?'

'Jetstar's is around $100 million,' she conceded. The temperature in the committee room rose five degrees as the devastating admission landed. Tully rushed to add, as if in mitigation, 'About 50 per cent of that credit is held by people and it's less than $100, so you can imagine the context of contacting those customers to use that amount.'

Here was another breathtaking statement from Jetstar's own Marie Antoinette, that communicating with people owed less than $100 was beneath her. There was also a resounding logical incoherence here: at this hearing and in his 7.30 interview, Joyce expressed pride at having ushered in the 'democratisation of air travel' as the father of Jetstar's '380 million airfares for under $100'. So $100 mattered when it was a data point for how Alan Joyce had transformed Australian life for working people, but when $99 was owed to a customer, it wasn't even worth following up, let alone disclosing. Joyce might have democratised airfares but he sure as hell wasn't going to democratise refunds. What Tully had also unwittingly admitted was that $50 million of Jetstar's remaining credits were owed to a *minimum* of 500,000 Australians. This was going to be a mass theft event.

Sheldon pressed on. 'On the question of overseas credits, is it more than $100 million?'

'It's less than $100 million,' Joyce said.

'Is it more than $50 million? I'm not asking for an exact figure.'

'We'd be reticent to play warmer-colder on this,' McGinnes chimed in. 'We're happy to take it on notice.'

'I'm not asking you what you're happy to do! I'm asking you: is it more than $50 million?'

'I'm honestly not sure,' said McGinnes. 'To be clear: we've been very transparent,' he repeated nonsensically.

'You have not been transparent!' Sheldon thundered.

McGinnes was nothing if not loyal. He had followed Joyce deep into his enchanted unreality. Safe inside Qantas World, this wasn't a calamitous reputational injury befalling them, it was just an honest misunderstanding. The airline was running full-page newspaper ads and emailing customers urging them to redeem their credits, McGinnes explained. Ninety eight per cent of refunds were being processed within seven days, Joyce said, while call answering time was just seven minutes.

The ads in the newspapers were a signal to politicians and the media that great effort was being made, not evidence of any real effort itself. A more effective effort would have been deploying extra agents to call credit-holders – starting with the 15 per cent owed more than $1,000 – to confirm their valid credit card details and then remit them their money. That didn't happen of course, because it would've worked. Neither did any of the regular emails to these customers have the subject line: 'Qantas owes you $1,357 – click here for an immediate refund.' Qantas was focused on *being seen* trying to reunite customers with their money while subtly making it difficult for that to occur. The obvious question was: if getting a refund was now as easy as Joyce claimed, why had the balance of Australian-based, Qantas-only credits fallen by just $30 million in the two months since Qantas made it so easy? As one Qantas executive later said to me, 'By the time we were advertising in 2023, people were just too traumatised [from their earlier attempts] to try again.'

Sheldon took one last pass at his fatally wounded opponent. 'Has the board made any comment about the fact that the credibility of Qantas has collapsed under your leadership?'

'But that's not true, Senator. All of the market research that we're doing —'

'The board has raised no issues about the fact that the company is at its lowest ebb in the eyes of the Australian public?'

'But Senator, you're making a whole series of points that are just incorrect. And your basis —'

'Mr Joyce, yes or no, has the board raised with you the company being the most discredited company in Australia?'

'Because the board do not see it the way you're raising it, because the facts that you are raising are wrong.'

It was notable that Joyce considered himself authorised to speak for the Qantas board. But he was correct. The Qantas board had not seriously dealt with the company's collapsing public credibility because it did not accept it as fact. The Qantas board's failure in managing Joyce and protecting the Qantas brand was abject, and that failure would emerge as the essential plot line in the final chapter of this story.

———

The following morning, the front page of Sydney's *Daily Telegraph* sported a smiling Joyce being grilled over more than $500 million of COVID credits. The headline screamed: 'JUST GIVE IT BACK.' On this issue, even Albanese had to part company with his old mate Joyce, telling a Perth radio station, 'When people have made bookings in good faith, then they need to either have that money returned or they need to be able to use those [for] future flights.'

The dam had broken and nobody was holding back. Opposition leader Peter Dutton slammed the government for providing 'no coherent reason' for its Qatar decision, adding, 'Anthony Albanese hasn't found a red carpet that he's not willing to trot down with Alan Joyce.' Virgin's Jayne Hrdlicka said, 'There's no understandable reason

why [Qatar was] denied those rights,' and called for the government
to reconsider. Future Fund chairman Peter Costello described it as
'hard to fathom', while ANZ Banking Group CEO Shayne Elliott
said he was 'quite disturbed ... particularly when any of you who fly
know that all the planes are full and they're really, really expensive.
I thought that we believed in the market economy and competition.'

Senator Jane Hume and Flight Centre co-founder Graham Turner
both publicly accused Catherine King of overruling her department after it had recommended approving Qatar's flights. Bridget
McKenzie accused the government of 'running a protection racket'
for Qantas. Former trade minister Andrew Robb described Qantas
as 'bullies' who 'want to protect themselves from competition at any
cost'. Canberra Airport CEO Stephen Byron labelled slot hoarding
at Sydney airport 'a national disgrace' and a 'plan and a deliberate
policy of Qantas', while Rex's John Sharp marvelled that Qantas had
ensured the Harris review into the slot system 'sat gathering dust on
someone's shelf for the last two and a half years'.

Former Treasury secretary Ken Henry said, were it him, Qantas'
refusal to repay a dollar of its $2.7 billion of subsidies would weigh on
his conscience. Incoming ASIC commissioner Alan Kirkland drew a
'clear link between the competition issues that are allowing Qantas
to continue to charge high prices and the way in which they've been
able to treat customers', and added, 'Qantas portrays and prices itself
like a premium airline but frequently the service it provides doesn't
live up to that positioning.' Kirkland concluded, 'If the government
did act on recommendations from the ACCC and other bodies to
actually provide more competition, then not only would you see lower
prices, but you'd also get better service because [Qantas] would be
forced to compete on the basis of that.'

And once again, the government's curious bungling only heightened the sense of something improper about its protection of Qantas.
On 23 August, Treasurer Jim Chalmers had launched a major review
of competition policy, to be led jointly by economists Danielle Wood
(subsequently appointed to chair the Productivity Commission) and
former ACCC chairman Rod Sims. But on 29 August, the morning

after Joyce's appearance at the Senate inquiry, Assistant Minister for Competition Andrew Leigh said the aviation industry would be excluded from that review. 'We are simply being pragmatic ... in not looking to overlap with existing government processes. The issue of airline competition,' he said, 'will be explored in the aviation green paper' (over)due to be handed down by Catherine King. Wood and Sims then said they hadn't been told aviation was excluded from their review, and soon after, Chalmers contradicted Leigh and confirmed that aviation was indeed included. By then, Sims had already teed off, saying the Albanese government's approach to airline competition 'dates back to the old tariff mindset'. As for the Qatar decision: 'We haven't had a really good explanation and that's unfortunate. When you are taking actions that have the effect – because there's no doubt they do – of decreasing competition and maintaining higher airfares, you need really clear explanations.'

Assistant Treasurer Stephen Jones, meanwhile, had his own ambiguous explanation for the Qatar decision: Qantas' record $2.5 billion profit was 'a good news story', and if the government pushed airfares too low 'we will design our markets in a way which will make it unsustainable for the existing Australian-based carriers'. Within minutes his comments were leading news websites. In Perth the same day, Catherine King held her own doorstop, and said, 'I wouldn't have used the same words that Stephen did.'

'When you say you wouldn't have used those words,' one journalist pressed King, 'has [Jones] got the wrong end of the stick? Do you disagree with what he said?'

'No, no, I think that you should read his full transcript – his transcript in full,' she insisted. But Jones' office didn't email the transcript to journalists (as it routinely did for all of the minister's interviews) and didn't publish the transcript online for several days. Either way, it was farcical of King to rebuke her colleague for his choice of words. She'd already provided three different reasons of her own for rejecting Qatar's application, each of which made far less sense than his.[3]

Albanese scarcely diminished the perception that he was in cahoots with Alan Joyce when he began parroting Joyce's talking points on Qatar. The morning after Joyce told the Senate that Qatar could add flights to Adelaide, the prime minister held a doorstop in Adelaide and said, 'Qatar can fly into Adelaide, as many planes as they like; they can fly in bigger planes that bring in more people.' But Qatar already operated two flights every day to Adelaide, a huge amount of capacity for a city that size. Emirates had ended its single daily flight to Adelaide when COVID hit and still hadn't returned, and Qantas itself hadn't operated international flights from Adelaide since Joyce axed them in 2013.

South Australia's Premier Peter Malinauskas was soon enough casting shade at Albanese. 'Qatar was flying in and out of Adelaide when others weren't,' he said. 'That really mattered to the South Australian economy when others went missing, so we're grateful to Qatar for that ... I think sometimes we've seen evidence of Qantas wanting to enjoy the status of being the national flag carrier. If they want to uphold that, I think they should be looking closely at Adelaide.'

Qantas, and the Qatar decision, had become the dominant national media story of the day. What the federal government needed was something bigger to come along and change the subject. But when something bigger did come along, the subject stayed the same. At 9am on 31 August, less than seventy-two hours since Joyce's disastrous Senate appearance, the ACCC dropped an atomic bomb: it was suing Qantas in the Federal Court for deceptive and misleading conduct.

The competition watchdog alleged that between May and July 2022 – a period when Qantas' operations were in total disarray – Qantas had continued to sell tickets on more than 8,000 flights for weeks after it had actually cancelled them. Existing ticketholders on 10,000 cancelled flights weren't informed of the cancellations for an average of eighteen days afterwards. 'We allege that Qantas made many of these cancellations for reasons that were within its control, such as network optimisation including in response to shifts in consumer demand, route withdrawals or retention of take-off and landing slots at certain airports,' said ACCC chair Gina Cass-Gottlieb. The following morning, Cass-Gottlieb told Radio National she would be seeking a $250 million penalty from Qantas – double the record fine paid by Volkswagen in 2019 for misleading customers over vehicle emissions.

As a young revenue manager at Irish carrier Aer Lingus in the early 1990s, Joyce had – with the help of his younger brother Anthony, an actuary – designed the mathematical model for overbooking flights on the basis that a percentage of passengers never turn up. 'That's how he made a name for himself at the start of his career, and he's ended it the same way,' I wrote in the *AFR*. 'He's optimised revenue to the point where it's now the planes that don't show up for the flights. It's a logical extension.'

Joyce might have clipped the ACCC's wings by having its airline monitoring powers defunded in June. He might have largely flouted the ACCC's demand in 2020 to clearly communicate to his customers their right to refunds instead of COVID credits, but the regulator was having the last laugh. And Cass-Gottlieb wasn't finished laying waste to Joyce's farewell tour. 'Qantas has suggested that [its] COVID credits will expire at the end of December 2023,' the regulator added in its statement. 'The ACCC has written to Qantas strongly objecting to this proposed position and will continue to monitor the situation to ensure Qantas continues to make available refunds to consumers.' It also advised that 'affected consumers may be able to seek remedies against Qantas' as part of Echo Law's class action.

Within fifteen minutes of the ACCC's announcement, Qantas was briefing journalists that it had cancelled the looming expiry date on its COVID credits. Just like that, half a billion dollars of free profit had slipped through the airline's fingers.[4] Just after 1pm that day, Qantas released a video message from Joyce. 'These credits and vouchers will never expire,' he assured the public. 'We're doing this because we've listened.' In truth, Joyce and Hudson were doing this because they'd finally been forced to. Cass-Gottlieb had informed Qantas months earlier of her objection to the expiry of its COVID credits yet only after she served the airline with Federal Court proceedings did it back down.

'We know the credit system was not as smooth as it should have been,' Joyce continued in his broadcast from the Mascot bunker.

'And while we've improved it recently, and extended the expiry date several times, people lost faith in the process.' But people had not simply lost faith in the process, they had lost faith in Qantas and in its leadership.

That afternoon, Qantas advised the Senate committee and the media that its total outstanding balance of COVID credits – including Jetstar and foreign customers – was $570 million, a lazy $200 million more than the number Joyce had been using publicly, and $50 million higher than even its admissions in the Senate hearing.[5]

The furore ratcheted up another several notches. 'CON AIR' screamed the next morning's *Daily Telegraph*. 'The Lying Kangaroo' roared Melbourne's *Herald Sun*. There was now a gigantic snowball rolling downhill in Alan Joyce's direction, and sprinting away from the impact radius were Anthony Albanese and his senior ministers. Jim Chalmers called the ACCC's allegations 'deeply concerning', while the PM was at pains to remind everyone, 'Something I called for in recent days was [for] Qantas ... to not have those credits expire.' But distance between them couldn't suddenly be manufactured. The Qatar decision, the Voice launch, the Chairman's Lounge affair, defunding the ACCC's airline monitoring, its steadfast inaction on slot hoarding: the perception firmly prevailed that the government was in Joyce's pocket.

'Your government couldn't have been more loved up with Qantas,' came *Today* host Karl Stefanovic's ear-lashing of Deputy Prime Minister Richard Marles. 'It's toxic and you all hitched your wagon to it.' In the *AFR* newsroom and among the many other senior businesspeople I spoke to at the time, there was a real sense of wonder at the ferocity and scale of the tempest *finally* engulfing Qantas. Like Mike in *The Sun Also Rises*, Joyce had fallen into disrepute gradually, then suddenly. ACTU secretary Sally McManus agrees. 'The most interesting thing to me is, when he fell, how quickly he fell. It was so spectacular and so absolute.' McManus says the Qantas board 'never appreciated the accumulative effect of the poison dripping away' over years. 'It does just get to a point where that's it, and then it's completely fucked.' Or as I put it in my column: 'So many Australians are enjoying Joyce's implosion, marvelling as he slices up the Qantas brand, watching the man in the enchanted spectacles burn down his own house.'

Just before 3pm that day, Friday 1 September, Qantas advised the stock exchange that one week earlier, it had granted Joyce more than 1.7 million Qantas shares worth nearly $11 million, including the $6.5 million of COVID-era bonuses Joyce told Senator Bridget McKenzie she was misunderstanding the existence of.[6] Again, the timing could hardly have been worse. The Australian Council of Superannuation Investors (ACSI) – which represented the industry super funds that collectively owned around 20 per cent of Qantas – issued an ominous statement soon after: 'ACSI will be watching the Qantas board very closely to see how the ACCC proceedings and the significant damage to reputation the airline has sustained over the last 12 months, in particular, impact the awarding of [Joyce's] bonuses in 2023.' The Qantas board had not yet granted Joyce his 2023 bonuses, which comprised a short-term bonus of up to $4.3 million and a long-term bonus of up to 1.3 million shares worth $8.4 million.[7] As one investor told the *AFR*, 'For the size of the company and compared to other Australian companies, it would seem that he has been paid excessively.'

In response to ACSI's warning shot, Richard Goyder said, 'We take these matters extremely seriously and will work through them without knee-jerk reactions.' At that stage, none of the week's ignominy had altered Goyder's conviction that Joyce deserved to complete his victory lap and retire as planned in November. But on the weekend, some semblance of reality set in; Goyder broached an early departure with Joyce and by the Sunday, Joyce had come around to his fate.

It wasn't until 8:30pm on the Monday that the Qantas board met (by teleconference). And while the directors must have understood that Joyce's resignation was possible, it was only once the meeting began that it became apparent it had been called for that express purpose. Of course, this jarred with Goyder's statement before the weekend that the board was 'fully engaged'. The chairman joined the call from Perth; former Cathay Pacific CEO Tony Tyler joined from his home in the south of France; Maxine Brenner was also overseas. The meeting was convened so hurriedly that former American Airlines CEO Doug Parker, who'd only joined the Qantas board in May, was fast asleep in the United States. Parker was ropeable when he woke to discover that Joyce, a long-time industry peer, had fallen on his sword without the genuine consultation of the full board.

Joyce came off the board hook-up into a snap meeting of the group management committee to break the news. It was late, so most of the group dialled in, but QantasLink boss John Gissing, Loyalty CEO Olivia Wirth, and PR boss Andrew McGinnes had stayed back with Joyce. When the meeting ended, they were joined by Joyce's executive assistant of twenty years, Jenny Borden, while Andrew David returned to the office for the impromptu wake. The Qantas wine cellar was raided – one would hope for something superior to the vinegar Qantas had been serving its customers. A quiet shock prevailed, although as one attendee recalls, 'Alan was stoic, kind of unshakable.'

And that was it. After fifteen years as one of the nation's most prominent and powerful people, it was a desperately ordinary goodbye. No prime ministers or corporate titans, no lionising speeches, no standing ovations; it was all far removed from the exalting soirees initially planned for the lead-up to his November retirement. After twelve months of defiance and warfare with his critics, Joyce bowed out not with a bang but a whimper. When his husband arrived to drive him home, the man with the enchanted spectacles stepped over the threshold of Qantas World never to return. Joyce, the great compartmentaliser, would've slept like a baby.

Soon after 8am the next morning, Qantas announced that Joyce 'had advised the board he will bring forward his retirement' to that day. The decision was presented as Joyce's alone. Quitting early, Goyder said, 'goes against every one of his instincts', adding, 'Alan has always had the best interests of Qantas front and centre, and today shows that.' The Australian public were hurling metaphorical brick-bats at Joyce, but to the very end, Goyder had nothing but bouquets.

Joyce did not return to Qantas headquarters that day. That evening, he headed to Sydney airport to catch Emirates' last flight to Dubai and onwards to Dublin. He was captured by a *Daily Telegraph* photographer rolling his suitcases through the departures hall, an image that was emblazoned across the next day's edition. 'Australians all let us REJOYCE' went the headline – the same pun I'd deployed on the front page of Qantas' staff newspaper when Joyce started the job all those years ago.

The popular joke that day in TV news bulletins and newspaper columns was: finally, Qantas had managed an early departure. But the gag was flawed. Joyce's grand miscalculation was to leave four years too late.

———

Back in May 2021, Alan Joyce had sat down for a fireside chat with veteran broadcaster Kerry O'Brien at Griffith University. 'What would you want said about you when you're gone from this mortal coil?' O'Brien asked. 'What would you most want to be remembered for by this nation?'

'I hope people would see me as a good custodian,' Joyce responded. Furthermore, he wanted Australians to say of him: '"He did the right thing about our brand, he did the right thing by its people, he did the right thing by its customers, and he left it in a better position than he found it."'

Had Joyce retired in 2019, sated by eleven years in the job (and the $97 million he was paid for it), his legacy would have by and large matched his description. But implicit in everything he said in 2023 was Joyce's belief that he still qualified to be remembered this way. By his thinking, it was only by virtue of his courageous decisions that Qantas had survived COVID, and that made those decisions the right thing for staff and customers. It was impossible to know the counter-factual: would Qantas have survived COVID in Joyce's absence? But, I ask, why would it not have? To use Virgin Australia's 2020 collapse as a data point ignores the reality that, due to long-term financial mismanagement, Virgin was basically insolvent before COVID blew it over.

None of the world's leading airlines failed to survive COVID. Yet by 2023, Qantas routinely portrayed its survival of the pandemic as a uniquely Joycean feat, while defining 100 per cent of its operational failures as symptoms of an industry-wide phenomenon. None of that is to trivialise the extraordinary injuries COVID inflicted on Qantas, or Qantas' decisive efforts to achieve hibernation then manage through oscillating lockdowns. But rather than swallowing Joyce's post hoc rationalisations offered in 2022 and 2023, I have relied in this book on what he actually said and did in 2020 and 2021.

Joyce was abundantly clear in March 2020: Qantas didn't need or want a financial lifeline from the government – with the exception of JobKeeper. He was just as clear in June 2020 when he raised $1.4 billion of new equity from shareholders. He needed that money not for short-term survival, but for the upfront costs (mostly redundancy payments) of a merciless cost-cutting program to fatten Qantas' profit margins for when the pandemic was over. The extent of that cost-cutting was not in the best interests of the Qantas brand, its customers or staff – either those jettisoned or those still on the frontline absorbing customers' wrath.

This was only confirmed by one of Vanessa Hudson's earliest decisions as the new CEO: restoring $230 million of spending on 'customer improvements'.

Qantas was privatised in 1995 as a hulking, highly protected government enterprise and every CEO – James Strong, Geoff Dixon and then Joyce – made it incrementally more efficient. But where, if ever, was that process supposed to end? When Qantas became Jetstar, just with higher prices?

Joyce had certainly tried to do the right thing by shareholders – and he was a large one himself. Qantas' financial position, he said at his final press conference, was the strongest it had ever been. By the yardstick of 2023 profitability and debt, that was true, but it failed to account for the deferred spending Qantas could defer no longer:

the massive bill for new planes he was leaving Vanessa Hudson. And indeed, Joyce's disinvestment in fleet and technology – which was an intentional pre-COVID strategy that was only compounded by COVID – had a similar effect on the brand and customers as his excessive cost-cutting.

As a result of the nosedive Joyce left Qantas in, despite its record profit, Qantas shares slumped to $4.74 the month after his resignation, a wipe-out of 30 per cent since June, when Joyce had cashed out his shares. The airline's biggest investor, Crispin Murray, sees it this way: 'In order to go out on a high, it felt like Alan was caught in a mindset of needing to move from losing a lot of money to record profits in a very short space of time,' he told me. 'But if the company had made $200-300 million less and done the right thing by its customers, the [share price] probably would have been significantly higher. So by trying to maximise profits in that year, they ended up hurting shareholders as well as their other stakeholders. That's the irony.'[8]

What also eluded Joyce was his desired status as a good custodian in the eyes of others. That much was obvious in the intensity of public ill-feeling towards him. As Roy Morgan's Michele Levine told Sky News the week Joyce resigned, 'So much of the venom and anger is towards Alan Joyce [personally]. He is actually seen to be, by the public, almost like the devil incarnate.' Some of the criticism of Joyce was over-the-top, but he had otherwise brought legitimate scorn upon himself. He'd been there for fifteen years and had colonised the company's brand. Who else were mistreated customers supposed to direct their anger at? The devil needs a face and a name.

Joyce had also insulted the intelligence of customers (as had Hudson in her early public forays as CEO designate), first by claiming that Qantas' appalling operational performance and outrageous airfares were entirely outside its control, and then by claiming that the customer experience was back to pre-COVID levels when customers knew firsthand it wasn't. 'Whenever I sat down with a group of regular customers I was always struck by how much they knew about the different pieces of the aviation jigsaw,' says airline industry doyen Sir Rod Eddington. He told me: 'They spend a lot of time in airports and a lot of time on aeroplanes and they've got their wits about them. You can't treat them like mugs.'

The animus towards Joyce also arose from the airline's double-edged status as 'the national carrier'. Qantas occupied a singular place in the Australian psyche and that was not an accident – it was the commercial objective of the company. Its emotive, nationalistic advertising cultivated a deep love of the airline among the populace and Qantas had shamelessly monetised that love – in the very same way that Qantas management had exploited frontline employees' love of the company. It was perfectly understandable, then, that Qantas' betrayal should incite an emotionally outsized response.

This was also the basis for the public anger towards Qantas over its \$2.7 billion of COVID subsidies from the Australian government. This was not an unreasonable level of government support for a business shut down overnight by government mandate, and by global standards it was very much on the low side. The Trump and then Biden administrations had pumped US\$80 billion into the US airline industry (US\$19 billion were loans that have been repaid, while US\$60 billion was payroll support even more generous than JobKeeper). European governments injected €20 billion into their flag carriers, but secured large equity stakes in return.[9]

The public backlash against Qantas' subsidies was a result of not the subsidies themselves, but the company's conduct while in receipt of them: outsourcing staff illegally while banking JobKeeper, tricking customers into COVID credits and making refunds impossible, followed by the incredible profiteering. Had Qantas conducted itself like the national carrier and behaved ethically between 2020 and 2022, it is unlikely there would have been any real public pressure for its subsidies to be repaid.

Joyce's custodianship of the hallowed Qantas brand was also tarnished by the perception that he wielded undue influence over public officials, right up to the prime minister. He raised the grooming and capturing of strategically important people to high art, demonstrated superbly by the regular upgrades to Anthony Albanese's personal travel for the entire period that he was transport and then shadow transport minister. Then Joyce got unlucky. He wasn't doing anything his predecessors and competitors hadn't always done, but the combination of Albanese's grasping, entitled behaviour and his government's farcical inability to explain its protection of Qantas, set off a feeding frenzy from which Joyce couldn't recover.

When Joyce, the eleventh managing director of Qantas, resigned in September 2023, it was exactly one hundred years since Hudson Fysh was appointed its second managing director. Fysh served in the role for thirty-three years, then spent a further twelve as chairman – and perhaps Joyce was inspired by his longevity. In 1948, Fysh wrote a long letter to his executives laying out his ideals 'on ethics and other things'. For seventy years, that letter had been a touchstone for the company, and when Qantas' marketing department led a review of the airline's 'purpose' in April 2023, Qantas' (and Jetstar's) top hundred executives attended a presentation littered with quotes from Fysh's ideals. One in particular was described as 'the group CEO's guiding principal [*sic*]', and went: 'Minds should always be open, and business has no place for the pig-headed individual who will die upholding an idea which his reason should tell him is wrong.' The irony of assigning such a standard to Joyce was not lost on some of those in that meeting.

Indeed, reading the presentation now, the use of Fysh's values seems almost sarcastic: 'It may be maintained that duty towards our shareholders comes before our duty to the public. I maintain that duty to the public comes first, in that if we are unable to provide [a] "worthy service" it is doubtful if we should be in business.' His words serve as a succinct condemnation of how his beloved airline had gone on to conduct itself.

One of Fysh's ideals was compromise, which 'consists of both sides taking less than they wished for the good of both'. Joyce, as we have seen, was uncompromising.

'Fair charges should always be adhered to,' Fysh insisted. 'This not only exemplified fairness to clients but is actually the best business in the long run.' Joyce imposed maximum charges.

Fysh maintained that 'in all our dealings, integrity should be taken first and the spirit of an agreement taken before the letter. For instance, the forcing of an advantage to which the company had the legal right,' he said, 'would be unthinkable.' With flight credits, Joyce could not only think it but do it.[10]

'Always keep out of court whenever this is possible with honour and fair dealing,' Fysh pronounced. 'Companies or people having frequent court actions are usually not of the best repute, and it is bad publicity anyhow.' Under Joyce, Qantas launched appeals before it could even digest the judgments it was appealing against.

The 'initiative and enterprise' of Qantas, Fysh argued, 'should spring from competition' and ensure that 'we keep our end up with the international operators whose routes we will parallel'. Joyce's initiative and enterprise were dedicated to stymieing competition.

'Without realisation of the basic principle of "service" to other members of the community we are a failure,' Fysh believed. This was indeed Joyce's ultimate failure: the idea of service to the travelling public was subjugated to the interests of investors.

Finally, Fysh held that 'real character is often only brought out under the stress of great pressure'. From the moment that COVID enveloped Qantas through to his resignation in a storm of opprobrium and legal action three and a half years later, we saw great pressure compact Joyce's character, leaving only his diamond ego.

The world has changed almost beyond recognition since World War II. It would be jejune and unfair to judge Joyce today solely in terms of Fysh's hail-fellow-well-met principles. Yet this is a company whose heritage is central to its identity. The strength of the Qantas brand, says Sally McManus, was 'like a shield for his bad behaviour and for years you just couldn't touch him no matter what he did. But the brand wasn't something he built up – it had been there for a hundred years.'

A hundred years of good faith cast down in fewer than four years of vainglory. Even by Joyce's own scorecard, as he'd rendered it for Kerry O'Brien, this was scarcely the work of a good custodian. How long would it take for Qantas to set things right?

Captain, You Must Listen!

1 Sept–3 Nov 2023

As Joyce stumbled around in the kill pen, having been hit between the eyes by Gina Cass-Gottlieb's stun gun, the Qatar imbroglio was consuming the Albanese government. No lesser figure than the Labor Party's federal president Wayne Swan called for Albanese to conduct 'an appropriate review' of its Qatar decision, 'given all these revelations' about Qantas. Queensland's acting premier, Steven Miles, said if additional Qatar flights were a decision for the state government, 'they would be approved.'[1] Western Australia's Premier Roger Cook went further, belittling Qantas as 'our so-called national carrier' and arguing that Qatar 'should have been backed when it came to their request for extra routes'. With South Australia's Peter Malinauskas also in Qatar's corner, Albanese was now at odds with the Labor leaders of three states.

In the Senate, the Coalition and the crossbench joined forces to establish an inquiry into the Qatar decision (which the government, with the Greens' support, narrowly failed to block). Flight Centre, meanwhile, launched a national advertising campaign calling on the government to overturn the Qatar decision, while polling conducted by RedBridge showed that 59 per cent of Labor voters wanted the same thing.

Yet Albanese remained a picture of defiance, shouting into a clamorous question time that Qatar 'can fly as many flights as they like into Adelaide, into the Gold Coast, into Avalon, into Hobart and into Canberra'.[2] Virgin's Jayne Hrdlicka responded archly that airlines 'need to add seats where the demand exists; it's a bit of an obfuscation to say "fly into cities where there is no demand".' Indeed, Qantas didn't operate international flights from any of those airports. 'How can they ask us to fly to a destination – like Darwin or Cairns – where there are only 20 passengers to Europe?' a confounded Akbar Al Baker wondered to me.

The prime minister even reproduced his line that Qatar could upgrade its existing flights to double-decker A380s 'and fly more people in here'. Qatar's daily Sydney service was already operated by an A380. Of course, A380s were four-engine aircraft, consuming much more fuel per passenger than Qatar's mainstay A350s and 777s, and one of Catherine King's grounds for blocking Qatar was allegedly 'decarbonisation'. As Al Baker muses, 'There was no consistency in what they were saying.'

Australia, Albanese persisted, had 'the most competitive aviation market in the world, bar none'; he added, 'I see the former [transport] minister shaking his head to agree.' And Michael McCormack was indeed sitting on the opposition frontbench nodding gormlessly.

But even that assertion fell apart upon cursory inspection. 'I don't know how you can make that claim,' said former Qantas chief economist Tony Webber, pointing instead to the ultra-competitive EU, US and even Chinese markets, and to academic research in 2017 and 2023 which found the Australasian aviation market to be the world's *least* competitive. Australia had 'open skies' agreements with just nine other countries. Canada had twenty-three.

The prime minister would have been right had he said that Australia had the most liberalised domestic aviation market in the world. Foreign capital was permitted to invest in Australian airlines, or even establish new airlines to operate domestic flights, but that still didn't make it competitive – when two players had an iron grip on 95 per cent of the traffic, what serious investor would bother? In the US, by comparison (obviously with more than ten times the population), no airline had a greater market share than 18 per cent. Yet this was all irrelevant, even if it was somehow what Albanese meant: the matter at hand was the access regime for international flights.

Albanese's next statement was just as unconvincing: he said he had never been lobbied by Alan Joyce over Qatar's flights (something Joyce had refused to confirm or deny). 'I had one extensive conversation with someone about Qatar [and] it was not someone from Qantas,' he said. Nobody believed him.

Alan Joyce had resigned on Tuesday 5 September, and even on Wednesday the Qatar issue continued to dominate parliamentary proceedings, and the media. 'In twenty-five years,' one aviation old-timer said to me, 'I have never seen page one after page one on a bilateral air rights agreement.' That afternoon, Albanese jetted out to Jakarta for the ASEAN summit, leaving hapless Catherine King to defend the government's position in question time. Four times she was asked whether she had spoken to Joyce about Qatar, and four times she refused to answer.

In Jakarta, meanwhile, Albanese held a press conference with foreign minister Penny Wong, just after Sky News revealed that Wong had called Qatar's prime minister forty-eight hours earlier. Asked about her sudden interest in Qatar–Australia relations, Wong said, 'I initiated the call to discuss a range of bilateral matters. One of those, obviously, [was] the Hamad airport incident. That's something I spoke about in opposition. Obviously, it was a very distressing event for the women concerned.' She added that 'the bilateral air services agreement was not discussed in the call'.

Wong's was yet another baffling contribution to the government's Qatar tangle. Why was she raising the airport incident with the State of Qatar nearly two years after the Australian government told Qatar the case was closed? If the matter was so important to Wong, why was she first raising it sixteen months after being sworn in as foreign minister? And why did she *not* raise with her Qatari counterpart the one issue – air rights – it might have made sense for them to discuss?

The chaos extended into the Thursday, when King released the government's long-awaited aviation green paper, a draft statement of policy priorities in her portfolio. King had promised that her green paper would 'go to issues of competition and international aviation agreements'. Instead, the document turned out to be absurdly vague.

The ACCC had been virtually begging King to implement the recommendations of the Harris review into slot reform at Sydney airport, which had been sitting on King's desk since the previous election, yet the green paper said only that the government would 'have more announcements to make about these reforms in due course'.[3] The co-chair of the government's own competition review, Rod Sims, lamented, 'I think the green paper is extremely thin on competition, it just does not seem to be much about competition, which is unfortunate.'

In the absence of any clear competition policy for the aviation industry, the *AFR*'s Michael Stutchbury wonders, 'Against what framework were we supposed to judge the minister when she comes out with this crazy list of different [reasons for blocking Qatar]?' While Qantas was 'perfectly entitled to put their view, they were seeking to restrict competition. That's not good for their customers or anybody else's and it was definitely a total failure of policy when you've got excess demand for air travel causing higher prices. It was no different to import protection, and that fed straight into *Financial Review* orthodoxy of the past fifty years and made us confident as a masthead to prosecute the story.'

Out on the airwaves, selling her anaemic policy statement, King demonstrated her singular facility for making a bad situation worse every time she opened her mouth. When the ABC's *AM* presenter, Sabra Lane, asked her about the Hamad airport incident's influence on the Qatar decision, she replied, 'Well, it wasn't a factor in the decision, but it certainly provides context to the decision, and I can't pretend that that didn't happen and that I didn't know about it.' The sophistry was truly something, and ensured that the issue then dominated that day's question time too. 'She just keeps changing her story and I don't know what's fact and what's fiction,' marvelled Peter Dutton.

The following Monday in parliament, Albanese refused to say whether he'd directed King to make the Qatar decision. King admitted she 'consulted relevant colleagues' but wouldn't say which ones, and again refused to say directly whether or not she had discussed the issue with Qantas. On and on it went ...

———

With Joyce gone under the (Air)bus, Richard Goyder shifted his focus immediately to saving himself. 'If there is stuff from a board or governance point of review that requires doing, I'll do it,' he told *The Age*. 'If I need to live in Sydney for a period that is fine,' he offered desperately from his Perth base. 'I will get to work on these things, and we'll do what we need to do,' he told the *AFR*. 'And I think my role in that is pretty important.' He added, 'I think it's a time for humility, and I think you'll see plenty of that as well.' Goyder was reaching into his shaving cabinet for the bottle of humility cologne he'd been saving for just such an occasion. A couple of splashes would make everything right! But where was his humility twelve months earlier when his response to the public's anger was to insist defiantly that Joyce was 'the best CEO in Australia by the length of a straight'?

The Qantas chairman was now promising to 'get to work', which only begged the question of what he had been doing before. It was eerily reminiscent of Tony Abbott promising in 2015 that 'good government starts today' – eighteen months after he'd been elected prime minister. Goyder even claimed that 'the Qantas board has been appropriately challenging and certainly had strong governance'. Nobody outside of the Qantas board room believed this, and, indeed, even the board itself would soon raise the white flag on its governance conduct. But not yet.

If only Goyder had stood up and said, Yes, this catastrophe occurred on my watch and I ignored all the warnings; I'm falling on my sword. Doing so would have put a floor under his professional reputation. But Goyder couldn't face that. He promised humility, not humiliation. And so his unravelling continued.

For Qantas' largest shareholder, Pendal, Goyder's refusal to put his hand up 'shaped our perception of what needed to happen'. Crispin Murray is another who sees parallels with Rio Tinto's Juukan Gorge crisis. In both cases, he pointed out, 'If the chairman had come out right away and said, "This is unacceptable, we're going to make major changes to ensure this is never repeated," you actually can redeem yourself. But hedging your bets, it looks like you're thinking, "What's the least we have to do to get through this?" – that mindset tells you that there needs to be change. But in these situations, the more pressure applied, the more defensive people can become, and that's unfortunate.'

How was Richard Goyder the only person in Australia who saw Richard Goyder as part of the solution, not part of the problem? In politics, backbenchers return to their electorates from Canberra and find out pretty quickly what real people think. One of Goyder's problems was that he spent zero time with real people. He was chairman of Woodside – so basically a sheikh in Western Australia. He was literally the chairman of the Chairman's Lounge, the pope of Australia's power clique, accustomed to floating above the rest of us in a world of unbelievable deference.[4] None of this was supposed to happen to people like him. He had spent his entire professional life not preparing for this moment.

Meantime, the remnants of Qantas' shell-shocked management team was staggering around the Mascot campus like liberated survivors of Ceausescu's Romania. Awaiting Vanessa Hudson on Alan Joyce's old desk, I wrote in the *AFR* on 5 September, was the world's largest, overflowing sick bag. 'The parmesan waft of Joyce will haunt the Qantas headquarters. It will long linger in the nose of every customer sitting in every soiled seat on every senescent 737.' Goyder was 'running up and down the aisles spraying his scent of humility'. The imagery was absurd, but so was the company's response to the crisis it had brought upon itself. Hudson had snidely suggested in March that 'even satire should have its limits', but Qantas – and Goyder in particular – was proving that satire was boundless.

The investment community was giving Goyder no reason to believe his minimisation strategy would suffice. 'The early departure of the Qantas CEO this week has not erased the issues that concern us, and we are interested in the terms of his exit,' came a further statement, on 7 September, from ACSI, which was also 'keen to hear the board's plan to repair the reputational damage done to the airline in recent times'. Proxy adviser ISS, which advised large investors on how to vote at AGMs, said that 'the board has to make it clearer what action it's going to take, if any, and who is accountable for all of this'.

Joyce's 2023 remuneration of up to $26 million was not only unacceptable to investors; out in the general community, it was toxic.[5] Federal minister Bill Shorten captured that sentiment by describing Joyce's package as 'so over the top, it's sort of breathtaking'.

Goyder gave another interview on 9 September, telling *The Age* that it was 'complete bullshit' he was a hands-off chairman or in thrall to Joyce and the AFL's Gillon McLachlan. The previous weekend, he'd sat down and handwritten two lists: one of everything going well at Qantas and another of everything going badly. 'I was trying not to kid myself,' he said. It was an incredibly revealing admission. Goyder had been urged many months before to think deeply about Qantas' problems, including by me. Why was he only doing it now?

———

The next bombshell landed on 13 September, a week after Joyce's resignation, when the High Court of Australia handed down its decision in TWU v. Qantas. In a unanimous 7–0 ruling, the court upheld both the primary decision of Federal Court Justice Michael Lee and the judgment of the Full Court of the Federal Court in the first appeal.[6] It was now final and inescapable: Qantas had broken the law.

Joyce's exceeding confidence that Qantas would win this appeal, expressed two weeks earlier on national television, had been his final misjudgement – perhaps his final self-narrative distortion: the High Court will enact my truth that Qantas always did the right thing.

Three years of legal truculence had been fully endorsed by the Qantas board, an endorsement likely based on nothing more rigorous than Joyce's (and Andrew Finch's) say-so. Beyond the financial penalties to be paid and the compensation now owed to 1,700 workers, the company's moral self-injury was stunning. Again, Bill Shorten cut through the outcry by asking of the Qantas board, 'Is there nothing they would ever resign over?'

The Senate inquiry into the Qatar decision, meanwhile, had called Goyder to appear before it two weeks' hence. And Catherine King was stonewalling. Invoking her immunity powers, she blocked the inquiry from seeing her department's advice on Qatar's application for more flights, a move that strongly suggested the advice was inconsistent with her ultimate decision. Moreover, having asked the inquiry for additional time to respond to its request for that advice, King then responded on a Thursday evening after parliament had risen and just as she was commencing two weeks' annual leave. She was running from scrutiny, and given her powers of explanation, who could blame her?

King's department also blocked the release of relevant correspondence between itself and Qantas, on the extraordinary basis that it would not only cause Qantas 'embarrassment, exposure to ridicule or public criticism', but would, were the information made public, 'have the capacity to prejudice or undermine the department's relations with other countries'. The mind boggled: what could the correspondence possibly reveal that might lead to *even more* embarrassment for Qantas, or difficulties for Australia with Qatar?

The inquiry kicked off on 19 September, with aviation economist Tony Webber giving evidence that Qatar's extra flights would have reduced airfares from Australia to Europe (across all airlines) by between 7 and 10 per cent. Sydney airport's Geoff Culbert complained that Qatar was using all its allocation of flights into Australia, while Emirates and Etihad were using only eighty-four of their 168 weekly flights. 'That's just inefficient, and it leaves ... less choice for consumers and ultimately higher prices.' Canberra airport's Stephen Byron told the inquiry, 'Qantas will not change unless they're brought to heel,' citing QantasLink's cancellation rate on the Sydney–Canberra route in August: a shocking 15 per cent.

The next day, 20 September, Qantas released its eagerly anticipated 2023 annual report, revealing the board's decision on Joyce's epic haul of cash and shares. His short-term bonus was reduced by 20 per cent to $2.2 million, 'in recognition of the customer and brand impact of cumulative events'. That $2.2 million was withheld pending the outcome of the ACCC's lawsuit. The same cut and lock were applied to all of Joyce's group management committee, including Vanessa Hudson.

As for Joyce's $8.4 million long-term bonus (also in a holding lock), Goyder claimed that it would be clawed back 'should the board determine that necessary', but he conceded this would only be in the event of 'significant misconduct' (meaning accounting fraud or a proven breach of Joyce's legal obligations). Reputational damage – however significant – didn't meet the hurdle, and clearly, the board had failed to ensure that the discretion which the circumstances demanded was written into the company's executive pay contracts.

The 20 per cent cut for Joyce equated to $546,840, or just 2.5 per cent of his total pay outcome for the year. It wasn't even close to enough for investors. 'It is a surprise to read that Alan Joyce is eligible for an annual bonus of over $2 million given the issues the company is facing, including poor customer outcomes,' ACSI said. 'The ACCC investigation might impact that bonus, but the issues are broader than just that investigation.' This was ACSI's fourth public statement in under three weeks. Its CEO Louise Davidson was now being incredibly pointed: 'The [annual] report is interesting for what it doesn't say. There is no discussion of board accountability for ongoing customer issues, the recent High Court decision and the ACCC investigation. That is what investors would like to understand.' She was spelling it out: Qantas' big shareholders wanted board scalps.

Even still, Goyder was not picking up what they were putting down. 'In terms of decisions made at the time and appropriate governance oversight, I think compared to almost any airline in the world Qantas has done a pretty good job,' he told ABC Radio on 21 September. 'I'd certainly reject the notion that [this] is a rolling crisis.' Satire was supposed to have its limits, but Goyder was now doing his best impression of Leslie Nielsen in *The Naked Gun* shouting, 'Nothing to see here, please disperse!' as the plumes of smoke and flames billowed from the wreckage behind him.

Goyder even claimed that all of Qantas' major shareholders remained 'very supportive' of him. 'The latest read I've got is that [they] want me to continue to do the role.' Curiously, not a single one of them would express this support publicly, despite a battalion of journalists asking them on a daily basis to do so.

In reality, Qantas' largest shareholders wanted Goyder gone because every time he opened his mouth and paraded his strange non-cognisance of Qantas' failures, he was illustrating just how Joyce had got away with everything he did. Goyder was immune to their fury at the share sale: 'Alan hadn't sold many shares in his entire time as CEO and Alan met every requirement to sell shares.' Goyder rationalised the illegal outsourcing with Qantas management's stock phrase: 'The courts actually held that we had sound commercial reasons for making that decision.' Eleven out of eleven judges had ruled that Qantas acted illegally and the chairman was still arguing the toss. Goyder even justified Qantas' botched 2022 reopening as 'us wanting to get [our] people back to work [and get] our customers to places they hadn't been able to get to'. That's right, Qantas had simply been too altruistic, too community-minded.

Twenty-four hours later, Vanessa Hudson had clearly come to the conclusion that salvation lay in the opposite direction and was broadcasting a prostrate apology to Qantas customers: 'I know that we have let you down in many ways and for that I am sorry.' More than two weeks into the job, she'd been slow to the realisation, but still faster than her chairman. 'We haven't delivered the way we should have, and we've often been hard to deal with ... We understand we need to earn your trust back not with what we say, but what we do and how we behave.' Hudson came across as completely overwhelmed by the reputational tornado she'd been inaugurated into. And in her defence, who wouldn't be? Hers had all the hallmarks of a hostage video. She was Vanessa the unimpressor.

This was more prime material for the annals of satire. The CEO was pleading, bug-eyed, for forgiveness while the chairman maintained the delusion that Qantas' problems were being blown out of proportion (having previously maintained the delusion that Qantas didn't have any problems at all).

On 25 September, Hudson unveiled a milestone trading update. The airline would now pour $230 million into customer improvements in the 2024 financial year, $150 million of which had been 'previously budgeted'. This spending would be funded from profits. Fuel costs and foreign exchange impacts had also increased by $250 million in the six months to December, and Qantas would absorb those costs rather than (as it had done since early 2022) raise fares to cover them.

Qantas had little choice, having burned through its last particle of customer goodwill. It now released more seats for redemption with frequent flyer points, increased compensation for passengers when flights were cancelled or delayed, upped its spending on inflight catering, and initiated 'a review of longstanding fare and customer credit policies for fairness' – an implicit acknowledgement that its policies had been unfair for a long time.

Hudson's heroic claim that Qantas' 2023 profit was 'not as good as it gets' had lasted an entire month. Across the board, major stock-brokers downgraded their price targets for Qantas shares, which had fallen 17 per cent since the August profit announcement and 24 per cent since Joyce sold his shares.

The new customer investment also made a farce of the $1 billion of 'permanent' (non-fuel) annual costs Joyce and Hudson had supposedly taken out of the business in the three years to 30 June 2023. Like Joyce, Hudson had received a special bonus for this accomplishment: hers was $1.6 million. Yet for the financial year that began the very next day, on 1 July, Hudson had already budgeted to put $150 million of costs back in.

If Goyder's position was already terminal, on that same day, Qantas' own pilots administered the killer blow. Their union, AIPA, issued an unprecedented statement noting that Goyder had 'overseen one of the most damaging periods in Qantas' history', including 'the illegal sacking of 1,700 workers which the chairman continues to try and justify as a "sound commercial decision"', and 'objection-able behaviour relating to COVID credits'. Their call to action was unambiguous: 'Mr Goyder's position as chairman is now untenable, and he should resign.' These were the professionals whose judgement Qantas trusted to keep its customers alive. As one influential corpo-rate adviser said to me that day, 'That's it, Richard's dead.'

AIPA's president, Captain Tony Lucas, felt despair that day. 'I was watching the company that I love get absolutely smashed from pillar to post,' he recounts to me. 'My preference was not to come out and criticise the airline that I work for – that wasn't a decision taken lightly. But it got to the stage where we couldn't not say something.'

Lucas draws an analogy with the 'raise' process, for speaking up on the flight deck when potential safety threats arise, which Qantas pilots have drilled into them in training. First, a pilot relays information to their co-pilot. If the co-pilot doesn't respond, the pilot escalates to verbally indicating concern. Third, the pilot moves to suggesting alternative options. Finally, if the threat remains unresolved, the pilot must escalate to emergency language and say, 'Captain, you must listen!' Lucas is thankful he's 'never had a crew member have to say that to me, but it's designed to cut through everything, and all of us felt we'd reached the "Captain, you must listen" moment. For so long we'd been saying to management, "This is not the direction you want to go in."'

Being chairman certainly elevated Goyder's culpability, but he was also just one member of the Qantas board. His fellow directors had so far escaped any meaningful scrutiny of their own roles in enabling – or at the very least failing to avert – Qantas' crushing brand damage. Each year at the annual general meeting, one-third of the board faced re-election and this was the formal opportunity for shareholders to exact, in the choice euphemism of ACSI, 'board accountability'. The 2023 AGM was six weeks away and counting. Goyder had been re-elected in 2022, so would not be up again in 2023. The airline's official notice of meeting, published on 22 September, revealed which directors were in the immediate firing line.

Retired bureaucrat Heather Smith and former American Airlines boss Doug Parker were brand-new additions to the board, and nobody would hold them culpable. Another former bureaucrat, Michael L'Estrange, was slinking off the board at the AGM, sparing himself richly deserved ignominy. Of all the directors, L'Estrange should have seen Qantas' disaster unfolding with clarity, given his personal ownership – as author of the shameful L'Estrange report – of the Rio Tinto board's appalling minimisation of the Juukan Gorge disaster in 2020, which resulted in Australian shareholders blasting the CEO, the chairman and him out.

Jacqueline Hey was chairman of the Qantas board's remuneration committee, so Joyce's obscene compensation, and its precedence of financial targets over customer satisfaction, lay squarely at her feet. But she was not up for re-election either. Neither was Maxine Brenner. Both women had been on the Qantas board for a decade.

One director who was up for re-election was Belinda Hutchinson. She too should have been positively allergic to an all-powerful CEO dominating a board on which she sat. In 1997, she had joined the board of QBE Insurance, in the same month that company stalwart Frank O'Halloran was named its new CEO. Hutchinson became chairman in 2010, and O'Halloran was *still* CEO. In fact, by then at QBE, he was God. His strategy was to buy everything in sight – the company made more than 125 acquisitions on his watch and integrated virtually none of them. When he retired in 2012 – like Joyce, after fifteen years at the top – just as the performance of many acquisitions began to sour, Hutchinson invited him to rejoin the board six months later as a non-executive director. She defended the move as consistent with good corporate governance, which of course it wasn't.[7] Sense prevailed and O'Halloran didn't rejoin, but by the following year QBE's finances had deteriorated so dramatically that Hutchinson had to resign herself. The company took a decade to recover. Now there was little evidence to suggest that Qantas shareholders had benefited from this salutary lesson.

Up for re-election alongside Hutchinson was Todd Sampson, the former advertising executive and star of TV shows *Body Hack*, *Redesign My Brain* and *The Gruen Transfer*. Sampson was appointed to the Qantas board in 2015, to widespread bemusement in corporate circles. The Toddster certainly didn't get the call-up for his auditing prowess; he was there for his marketing expertise – to be the left-field thinker, the director who says, Listen here, you myopic, pinstriped comptrollers: what about the *brand implications* of this rapacious decision? What was the point of him otherwise? And now Sampson had presided over arguably the greatest collapse in brand equity in the modern history of Australian business. For shareholders, he was ready-made roadkill.

According to several Qantas executives who regularly participated in board meetings, the directors repeatedly pushed Joyce on the
airline's pricing and customer service shortcomings in 2022 and 2023.
'They were saying there was a problem long before Alan admitted it,'
says one. Board members travelled frequently and so experienced the
issues firsthand. One debate ensued over the $5,000 price of business
class seats between Melbourne and Perth – Goyder's twin cities. In
another session, Brenner and Hey pointed out the mismatch between
Qantas' customer research as presented in the board papers and
what they were seeing themselves and hearing from their networks.
Brenner's questions, in particular, annoyed Joyce. And as chairman of
Bendigo Bank, Australia's most trusted bank, Hey well understood
brand tracking metrics.

The problem, therefore, was not a blanket unpreparedness to challenge Joyce – at least not at a surface level. The problem was the
directors' weak acceptance of his magical explanations, and their
unwillingness to create a genuine conflict situation at the boardroom
table when one was needed.

Such reticence did not make the Qantas board unique at all.
There are precious few public company directors willing to pierce
the cordiality of board proceedings with inexpedient truth. For most,
the unspoken personal objective is continued membership of the
professional directors' club, the closest thing Australia offers to life
peerage. And the Qantas board was its highest prize.

The elite status and soft perquisites of Qantas board membership
were widely recognised, but its financial value was not. Qantas directors who partook even moderately of their travel entitlements were
easily the highest paid directors in Australia – comfortably more so
than the directors of BHP and the Commonwealth Bank, companies twenty times larger than Qantas.[8] This fact was always hidden
in Qantas' financial statements because Qantas heavily discounted
the reported value of those travel benefits. This was permitted under
the Corporations Act and Australian accounting standards, whose
rules on remuneration reporting are incredibly loose.

Every Qantas director, their spouse, and every one of their children aged under twenty-six is entitled to three long-haul return trips and nine short-haul trips anywhere on the Qantas network *every year* (the chairman and his family get four long-haul and twelve short-haul trips each). These tickets are all complimentary, confirmed seats in the highest class of travel on the aeroplane. The rest of the Qantas work-force – even most executives – are only entitled to expired inventory at cost: that is, discounted travel in the seats that were left unsold after a flight had closed.

But that's not all. Directors are also entitled to free flights *after* they leave the board, as are their eligible family members – one long-haul and three short-haul trips each, per year, for every year of board service (for the chairman and their family, it is two long-haul and six short-haul). Qantas shareholders would therefore be shouting Maxine Brenner and her family free flights until the end of 2034 – twenty-one years after she joined the board. The Goyders' freebies would expire in 2031.[9] This Qantas board and its CEO were monomaniacally focused on modernising the company and phasing out legacy pay and conditions, except for themselves.

On the (imperfect) assumption that the 2024 price of a Sydney–London first class return ticket is $18,000 and a Sydney–Melbourne business class return ticket is $1,500, the market value of the maximum annual travel entitlement (and associated fringe benefits tax) of a Qantas director with a partner and two children under eligible age is more than $500,000. The chairman's is higher again.

But Qantas' annual remuneration report did the maths differently. The tickets themselves were assigned a nominal value only slightly higher than the cost of the taxes and charges (which would be $700 on the London flight and $220 on the Melbourne flight). Qantas then paid fringe benefits tax on 75 per cent of the retail fare (which was the fare offered to corporate customers, even though Qantas directors were individuals, not corporates). Together, this meant that Qantas reported its directors' non-cash remuneration at just 38 per cent of its full value.[10]

For instance, in financial 2023, Maxine Brenner's travel benefits were reported as $161,000. In reality, the retail price of those flights plus the full-freight FBT was around $400,000. Add that to her $210,000 base pay and Qantas was really paying her more than $600,000 (and that was before accounting for the value of her post-employment flights). CBA directors earned less than $300,000. Even Macquarie Group directors – known for their high pay – only got $400,000.

Goyder's travel benefits in 2023 were reported as $117,000, but in reality were $308,000, in effect taking his pay as chairman north of $1 million – well in excess of CBA chairman Paul O'Malley's $850,000. Belinda Hutchinson's travel benefits were valued at $78,000, which was really $205,000, taking her real pay as a Qantas director to $461,000. Of course, not all board members used their full entitlements.[11] In 2023, Todd Sampson's benefits were put at $34,000 (really $89,000) while Michael L'Estrange's were just $7,000.

Even aside from the outrageous accounting fudge, the idea that the adult children of a Qantas board member should fly first class to London and back three times every year for free was hilariously out of line with community expectations. Qantas justified it as standard practice in the global aviation industry, which was exactly the justification it invoked for all of its dubious practices, including its COVID credits and its broader treatment of customers in 2022.

Returning to Charlie Munger's principle of 'show me the incentive and I'll show you the outcome', a disguised, extra $300,000 of remuneration per year created the incentive for Qantas directors to endure in office, and inversely, a disincentive to rock Alan Joyce's boat. Quite aside from the ethics of the relevant individuals, that was the plain behavioural psychology at play in the arrangement.

———

On 27 September 2023, Goyder and Hudson flew to Canberra to front the Senate inquiry into the Qatar decision, with general counsel Andrew Finch in tow. Those hoping for a repeat of Joyce's blockbuster implosion before the cost-of-living inquiry four weeks earlier would be sorely disappointed.

Qantas well understood that it had been called before the Qatar inquiry to explain its lobbying of the Albanese government on the matter. All of that lobbying occurred on Joyce's watch, but Joyce had declined the committee's summons to give evidence by video-link from Dublin. While the committee could compel witnesses in Australia to appear, their powers did not extend to witnesses overseas. Inquiry chair Bridget McKenzie raised the dramatic prospect of throwing Joyce in jail, but it was all theatre; Joyce could safely wait offshore until the inquiry closed.

Whereas Joyce had turned up to the inquiry the previous month with Andrew McGinnes, Qantas' government relations boss, McGinnes' absence now was striking. 'Is there a reason why Mr McGinnes isn't here today?' asked Liberal Senate leader Simon Birmingham.

'He's on holidays,' Andrew Finch replied. 'He's in Tasmania, I believe.'

'Or whoever, then, is acting in his position for the government affairs team?'

'There is no-one acting for Mr McGinnes.'

Qantas' chief lobbyist just happened to be on holidays on the day the Australian Parliament had questions only he (and Alan Joyce) knew the answers to. The idea that McGinnes couldn't have rescheduled his holiday or appeared by Zoom from Tasmania was implausible. His truancy meant that no Qantas witness had direct knowledge of the relevant communications between the airline and the government, especially not Joyce's communications with Anthony Albanese and Catherine King. It was clearly a tactic by Qantas to avoid the truth of its conduct emerging – and this not even a week after Vanessa Hudson said that Qantas should be judged 'not [on] what we say but what we do and how we behave'.

The senators were incredulous. 'How many are in the government relations team?' asked McKenzie.

'Six or seven,' was Hudson's answer.

'And none of them can fill Mr McGinnes' shoes while he's on holidays?'

'The matters that we thought were going to be discussed today were sufficient to be covered by myself, Mr Finch and the chairman.'

'Ms Hudson, as the new CEO, you haven't been in contact with ministers in relation to this issue. The guy in charge of that relationship is on holidays, and old mate is overseas. It beggars belief that a company of your sophistication and muscle has come here today with precisely the wrong group of people to answer senators' questions about the relationship between Qantas and this government.' McKenzie ordered Hudson to respond to 'a swag of questions on notice' and warned, 'I hope that Qantas would show this committee the respect that it needs to and makes sure those questions are answered.'

Qantas' middle finger to the Senate inquiry would be quickly forgotten. What was burned into the memories of the political class was the extraordinary performance of Andrew Finch. His chairman had promised humility but Finch clearly didn't get the memo. His mortification under cross-examination in the Federal Court in 2021 plainly had no deflating effect on him. Asked to share Qantas' government submission on Qatar with the senators for their confidential viewing – and even then, redacted of any commercial-in-confidence material – Finch responded, 'Does the provision of it in confidence ensure its retention of confidence, chair?'

'Yes it does,' McKenzie responded patiently.

'Was that not the Deloitte CEO's expectation when they provided salary information?' came Finch's retort. The previous week, a Senate inquiry into the big four accounting firms had published pay data that those firms wanted to remain confidential. Its chair, senator Deb O'Neill, noted that 'the Senate has the power, if necessary, to compel witnesses and information' and 'the purview to decide which information it does and does not receive on a confidential basis. No company is empowered to dictate the terms on which information is received and utilised by the Parliament.'

'Be very careful what you are asserting, Mr Finch,' McKenzie warned.

'Sure, so I'm just checking that if we were to release the document to you in confidence we can be certain that it won't be released publicly.'

'No, absolutely not,' McKenzie said. 'That's actually how "in confidence" works. This might be your first time, Mr Finch —'

'Sorry, we can be certain or we can't be certain? I said, "can we be certain", and you said —'

'Mr Finch, we can play *LA Law* all you like. The Senate committee process has significant powers to compel and significant responsibilities to ensure we uphold the integrity of the system, so if we say in confidence, we mean in confidence.'

'Thank you,' Finch said. 'I think you answered my question negatively.' In Finch's mind, apparently, the parliament's reasonable request to produce information was a negotiation. But what bargaining power did he think he had? Goyder and Hudson just sat there. As Senator Tony Sheldon puts it, 'If I was the chair of the board and my senior adviser had pulled that stunt, he wouldn't be my senior adviser for much longer.'

Finch's tour de force was not yet over. 'Chair, it's 6:30pm. The last flight to Sydney leaves in about 35 minutes. We have been here since three o'clock.'

Australia has a cottage industry in ex-government staffers whose role is solely to coach company executives for these parliamentary hearings. The first thing inculcated into witnesses is that they're on the MPs' turf and are governed by their rules. 'You can't just walk out like it's a play you don't like,' says one regular consultant. The other universal rule: never, ever be a smartarse; it worked once for Kerry Packer and then literally never again.

'I guess you're delayed, Mr Finch, at the discretion of the committee,' McKenzie said.

'I beg your pardon?'

'We've still got questions, and we will be pursuing them until we're finished.'

As Simon Birmingham put it to me later, 'There's often one moment when hours of disciplined effort by those around you is undone, where you lose the room in an instant. [Finch] worrying about the time of the last flight was that moment.'

'I've never seen anyone express the arrogance that Finch expressed on that day,' says Tony Sheldon. 'To say, "You're all wasting my time, I've got better things to do, I'm catching my flight" showed so little respect to the Australian public.'

The committee excused Goyder, Hudson and Finch at 6:40pm. Theirs was a long drive back to Sydney.

——

Perhaps unsurprisingly, Bridget McKenzie's hope that Qantas would show the parliament respect and properly answer the inquiry's questions on notice was dashed. On 6 October, Qantas provided its responses in writing, a considerable number of which were outright non-answers.[12]

ACT senator David Pocock had asked, 'How many free upgrades has Qantas given over the last 12 months [and] how many of these upgrades were to politicians or public servants?' Qantas responded: 'For privacy reasons, we are unable to disclose personal information regarding flights taken by individuals ... It is up to members and senators to update their register of interests as appropriate.' But Pocock's question didn't ask Qantas to identify anyone. He'd asked for two numbers, not anyone's name. Whose privacy could that possibly breach?

'How many Australian public servants have access to the Chairman's Lounge?' Pocock also asked. Qantas admitted that membership was offered to the secretaries and deputy secretaries of all departments, the chairs and CEOs of Commonwealth agencies, and 'senior members of the military', but didn't reveal how many – which again was the actual question.

Next, Pocock had asked how many staff in Catherine King's department were Chairman's Lounge members. The answer: 'Qantas does not divulge membership details of any of its lounges, so this question is best directed to the department.'

Pocock also asked if any personal staff of federal ministers were Chairman's Lounge members, and was told: 'This question is best asked of the ministerial offices themselves as Qantas does not divulge membership details of any of its lounges.'

These obfuscations were ludicrous, and again made a mockery of Vanessa Hudson's supposed new beginning. The entire premise of questions about upgrades and Chairman's Lounge memberships was that they were, in effect, bribes. Qantas was insisting on protecting the privacy of individuals it may have unduly influenced. Yet even more telling was its refusal to disclose even the scale of its influence, in an aggregate number of upgrades. The airline was desperately trying to thwart the revelation that upgrades were being provided to public officials on an industrial scale while the government handed Qantas 80 cents in every dollar it spent on domestic travel (in contravention of its own 'cheapest fare' policy).

It was unusual for a parliamentary inquiry to tolerate the flat refusal of witnesses to answer its questions on notice. The Qatar inquiry overlapped, for instance, with the Senate's inquiry into the integrity of consulting services. When that inquiry received inadequate evidence from PwC and its rivals, the senators dragged those witnesses back to explain themselves a second – and in some cases even a third – time. It was a tripartisan assault from Labor, the Liberals and the Greens. But when Bridget McKenzie pushed for her inquiry to be extended (including to hear evidence from Alan Joyce), Labor, the Greens and the crossbench – including David Pocock! – voted to shut it down. Of course, unlike the PwC scandal, the Qatar affair was party-political and Labor needed it killed.

The Qatar matter was never satisfactorily explained, and short of forcibly injecting Joyce and Albanese with truth serum, it never will be. The federal transport department had supported granting the additional flights; it told the inquiry it sent a negotiating mandate to King in January 2023, which was the next step towards approval. The Department of Foreign Affairs and Trade also supported the flights, as did the powerful trade minister, Don Farrell. King herself was supportive until suddenly she wasn't. According to a senior Albanese confidant, 'Alan getting to Albo was the only thing that made sense.'

Albanese lost a painful amount of political skin on this issue and refused every opportunity to back down or even compromise. There is only one plausible explanation for that refusal: it was personal.

Says his confidant, 'He's a relationship guy and Alan cultivated him for a long time, even in opposition. Albo's a loyal, loyal guy.'

Qatar's Akbar Al Baker, who retired as CEO without warning in October 2023 after twenty-seven years at the helm of the Gulf carrier, is in no doubt as to what happened: 'It was Alan Joyce blocking us by his relationship with the prime minister.' Al Baker accepts the Australian government's desire to 'look after the national carrier' but insists that 'the national carrier was not delivering'.

'In COVID, we were your national carrier,' he argues. 'We lost over US$150 million flying to Australia, operating this long route with only fifteen passengers on board for nearly two years. We never told anybody to wait for weeks or months to get your refund, or that we won't give you a refund. We showed our commitment was not to swindle people, not to sell tickets on cancelled flights – in my country you'd go to jail for this.'

Ironically, while the Greens and crossbenchers had blocked the extension of the Qatar inquiry, they were the ones publicly throwing their Chairman's Lounge memberships on the pyre. Seventy per cent of respondents to a *Sydney Morning Herald* poll opposed federal MPs being Chairman's Lounge members, coinciding with Teal MP Monique Ryan handing hers back. David Pocock soon followed, describing it as 'an example of what's wrong with Australian politics when it comes to lobbying; the use of soft power and little benefits here and there that over time add up'.[13] Then came Greens senator Barbara Pocock (no relation to David). 'Perception is important,' she said. 'You don't have to be taking a cash kickback or be in consultation with Alan Joyce to have a perception of conflict.' She was joined in Chairman's exile by her lower house colleagues, Brisbane MPs Stephen Bates and Elizabeth Watson-Brown (who also quit Virgin's equivalent club, Beyond).

Not a single major party MP was moved to follow their lead.

———

Goyder spent the week following his inquiry appearance in back-to-back meetings with Qantas' major shareholders, alongside his board colleague Jacqueline Hey and the airline's head of investor relations, Filip Kidon. Goyder had claimed in the Senate inquiry that he'd spoken to, and received expressions of support from, 'about 14' of Qantas' top twenty shareholders. Now he faced those shareholders again and found their support had evaporated – or, more likely, had been misconstrued in the first place. But by Friday 6 October, Goyder comprehended the message: he needed to go, and on the way out deliver a wider cleanout of the board. Otherwise shareholders would vent their anger at the AGM on 3 November.

Crispin Murray had several conversations with Goyder in this period. 'We felt let down as investors and we believed there had to be observable accountability for what happened,' he says. 'It wasn't even just about Qantas by that stage, it was about the precedent. Like with Rio [Tinto], there was a bigger thing at play, which is the message it sends to other companies, [and that] ultimately goes to the integrity of the market.'

On 9 and 10 October, Goyder negotiated the coming board blood-bath. Jacqueline Hey and Maxine Brenner would retire by February 2024, while Goyder would go prior to the AGM in October 2024. Goyder had a crucial job to do before then: find his successor. Choosing wisely would help atone for the damage of his own dismal tenure. The board also resolved to conduct an independent review of 'key governance matters over the past 12 months', and committed to sharing its findings by June. Announcing the group hara-kiri on Wednesday 11 October, the day before I walked out of the *AFR* newsroom for the final time, Goyder conceded, 'As a board, we acknowledge the significant reputational and customer service issues facing the group and recognise that accountability is required to restore trust. The recovery has not been easy, and mistakes were made.'

'Mistakes were made' was a phrase popularised in the Nixon era as a device to evade personal responsibility for mistakes. American political scientist William Schneider described it as 'the past exonerative tense', and it was also the subject of a terrific book by two eminent social psychologists called *Mistakes Were Made (But Not by Me)*. The singular, first-person pronoun was deployed by Goyder only in self-justification: 'I have always sought to act in the best interest of Qantas.' He might have sought, but he had failed. It takes a lot to accept that the problem is you, and Goyder just couldn't get there. Collective, deidentified responsibility was the most he would cop to. His denialism was understandable on a human level: he didn't want his failure to be true. Who among us would easily give up the chairmanship of Qantas, the honour of a lifetime?

Goyder was going, but the lead-in to Qantas' AGM was still ugly. All five proxy advisers – Glass Lewis, ISS, Ownership Matters, ACSI, and the Australian Shareholders' Association – recommended voting against Qantas' remuneration report. Ownership Matters' reasoning was: 'there has not been an appropriate reduction' to Joyce's bonuses. As we've seen, the Qantas board had deferred its decision on bonuses 'as it awaits further information' on the airline's illegal outsourcing of ground handling and the ACCC's ghost flights lawsuit. Ownership Matters noted in its report to Qantas investors: 'It is not clear what further information the board requires in order to respond to the unanimous High Court decision, which has exposed the airline not only to reputational damage but financial penalties and compensation … to the former employees.'

Ownership Matters and ACSI also recommended voting against the re-election of Todd Sampson, with Ownership Matters saying he had 'heightened responsibility [for] the collapse in Qantas' reputation and public standing … given he has been a director for more than eight years and his background in advertising, marketing and brand management'.

Some two weeks prior to Qantas' AGM, Telstra had held its own, on 17 October, at which new director Maxine Brenner received a 17 per cent vote against her election. It was a protest against her performance as a Qantas director.[14] On 26 October, Australia's sovereign wealth fund, the Future Fund, announced that it would vote its Qantas shares against Todd Sampson's re-election at the AGM the following week.

At the Qantas AGM on 3 November, 83 per cent of shares were voted against the remuneration report – the second-highest in

Australian corporate history, after only National Australia Bank's 88 per cent strike in 2018. 'The board has the discretion to reduce awards for executives – including the former CEO Alan Joyce,' ACSI's Louise Davidson said immediately after the meeting. 'Today's vote is a clear signal that the board should apply that discretion judiciously.'

Todd Sampson told the AGM he had 'reflected a lot' on his decision to stand again. 'I've spent a career helping other clients in similar brand situations. This is why my experience will be most valuable.' But when Qantas had really needed Sampson's help, in 2022 when its brand crisis began, what help had he provided? As Tony Sheldon told me, 'I don't watch *The Gruen Transfer* anymore because I can't stand that hypocrite.'

Thirty-four per cent of shares were cast against Sampson's re-election, including the 5 per cent owned by Pendal. It was a humiliating protest vote, but Sampson had survived.

In parliamentary democracy, legitimacy is winning 50.1 per cent of the vote, but corporate governance is not politics. Ninety-five per cent of the AGM votes were cast before the meeting, so Sampson turned up that day knowing that many of Qantas' largest shareholders wanted him gone. The honourable option – to resign – was available, and he declined to take it. But Sampson was the useful idiot on the ballot paper and on the stage – absorbing anger that would otherwise be directed elsewhere. Shareholders and the media were so stunned by Sampson's chutzpah that Belinda Hutchinson's re-election passed with nary a murmur.

The 2023 AGM was always going to be hostile, given the airline's live controversies and also its large cohort of retail shareholders. But Goyder only made it worse. Responding to a shareholder who questioned the morality of the board's recent decisions, Goyder harumphed, 'I have absolutely zero concern about the ethics of the people who sit alongside me on the Qantas board,' then ordered the shareholder's microphone be turned off – an appalling tactic that Goyder had deployed previously at Woodside AGMs. And when the meeting closed, the directors walked straight back to their green room instead of mingling with the shareholders in attendance, which at public company AGMs is standard practice. The shareholders had been promised humility but treated to stupendous arrogance.

'It's disappointing that the board didn't come out and engage further with retail shareholders,' Australian Shareholders' Association CEO Rachel Waterhouse lamented. These were exactly the kind of regular people Goyder could have benefited from some rare contact with. Had he spent any time with retail shareholders six or twelve months earlier, he might have got an inkling as to what was happening in the real world – in the world outside the Chairman's Lounge.

Feel the Difference?

Oct 2023–Oct 2024

Qantas' brand was now beyond freefall. It could scarcely fall any further, and the research Vanessa Hudson was receiving proved it. In June 2022, Qantas had dropped from fifth in the RepTrak benchmark of sixty brands to sixteenth. It then fell to twenty-sixth in September of that year, at which point RepTrak declared the Qantas brand to be in crisis. In retrospect, that was nothing. By October 2023, Qantas was fifty-eighth – ahead of only the hated Reserve Bank, and News Corp Australia rooted permanently to bottom place.

Hudson wanted to be judged on her actions, but in her early weeks few of them instilled any confidence that she was taking a materially different approach to her predecessor. Not even four weeks after saying it would absorb higher fuel costs instead of passing them onto customers, Qantas decided to raise airfares from 27 October – by 3.5 per cent on Qantas tickets, and 3 per cent on Jetstar's. (Qantas subsequently increased fares twice more in February and March 2024.) Hudson saw off her highly regarded leadership rival Olivia Wirth, whose resignation was announced on 16 October (she was quickly appointed executive chairman of retailer Myer), yet kept Andrew Finch and Andrew McGinnes around.[1] And on 30 October, Qantas filed its initial defence to the ACCC's lawsuit in the Federal Court. The airline argued that the regulator's action was defective because it misunderstood the service Qantas was providing. 'The ACCC's claim wrongly proceeds on the basis that the "service" that Qantas rele- vantly supplies ... is a "particular flight." To the contrary, the "service"

Qantas relevantly offers is a bundle of contractual rights, which are consistent with Qantas' promise to do its best to get consumers where they want to be on time.'

This was a technical legal argument, of course, but at this juncture, even those needed to withstand scrutiny outside the courtroom, and unsurprisingly this abstruse 'bundle of rights' defence was pilloried. Finch – under the watchful eye of his zombie chairman and hesitant new CEO – seemed determined to widen the gap even further between customers' reasonable expectations and Qantas' own surreal aloofness. ACCC chair Gina Cass-Gottlieb was unfazed, pointing out that her lawsuit was not about Qantas' contractual right to cancel flights, but about its conduct 'after it had cancelled the flights': failing to inform customers their flights had been cancelled in many cases 'impeded consumers' ability to obtain alternative flights at the time that they chose and needed to fly and also [forced them] to pay more for alternative flights'.

Hudson had also pledged in September to try to reach a settlement to compensate its 1,700 illegally sacked employees 'as reasonably and quickly as possible'. Justice Michael Lee appointed retired Federal Court chief justice James Allsop as mediator between Qantas and the TWU and insisted that Hudson personally attend the first day of mediation on 13 November. As it happened, there was no second day because Qantas would not return to the table. By December, the TWU was accusing Qantas of paying lip service to the mediation process, and not even responding to the union's communications. Roughly half of the sacked employees had drawn on their superannuation to survive, TWU secretary Michael Kaine complained, while Qantas had just posted a record $2.5 billion profit. Virgin Australia, meanwhile, announced it would hire more unionised staff and in-source the baggage handling for its flights from international terminals in Brisbane, Melbourne and Sydney, which had previously been performed by contractor Swissport.

Then on 16 November, in another devastating repudiation of Qantas' treatment of employees, the New South Wales District Court found the airline guilty of illegally standing down a Qantas Ground

Services health and safety delegate, Theo Seremetidis, in February 2020, after he raised concerns about cleaners working on planes that had just landed from China. Adding insult to injury, months later, while he was still stood down, Seremetidis was then one of the 1,700 workers Qantas outsourced illegally. Judge David Russell described the company's conduct as 'quite shameful'. Further, he noted, 'Even when [Seremetidis] was stood down and under investigation, [Qantas] attempted to manufacture additional reasons for its actions.' He also found Qantas had 'deliberately ignored' multiple provisions of the Work Health and Safety Act. Qantas agreed to pay Seremetidis a paltry $21,000 in compensation, while the court also imposed a $250,000 fine. In a statement responding to the judgment, Qantas again pushed the boundaries of satire by claiming that 'safety has always been our number one priority and we continue to encourage our employees to report all safety related matters'.

Unhelpfully for Hudson, the Albanese government continued to draw the public's attention back to its inexplicable Qatar decision. Catherine King provided yet another ludicrous addendum to her explanations, telling a conference on 14 November that she 'very clearly did not take the commercial interests of either Qantas or Virgin into consideration when I was making that decision', which contradicted the (third) reason she'd offered up in August: that Qantas 'has just purchased brand new planes ... at a significant cost'.

Offering a whole new reason for the decision, King said she'd really taken into account the nation's ability to repatriate Australians from war zones – citing the recent evacuations 'out of both Israel and out of Gaza'. But DFAT could and did commission repatriation services from any major airline. Only four weeks previously, immediately after Hamas' 7 October attack, Qantas, Qatar Airways and the Royal Australian Air Force all evacuated Australians from Israel.[2] Yet Anthony Albanese repeatedly thanked only Qantas 'for the support it provided'. None of this had anything to do with the government granting peace-time air rights, however. King's new reason was even less logical than her previous reasons, though who could possibly keep track?

King also claimed she'd been asked for 'an unprecedented amount of access by Qatar Airways', which wanted to increase its major airport frequencies from thirty-five to seventy per week. But in 2007 Emirates had been granted a larger increase, from forty-two to eighty-four. And in 2015, the UAE's frequencies (for use by Emirates and Etihad) were increased again, to 168. The strange obfuscations kept mounting.

The travel industry remained deeply unimpressed. On 15 November at Flight Centre's AGM, founder Skroo Turner labelled King 'the minister for higher airfares'. King responded a week before Christmas by granting twenty-one services per week to the government of Turkey, for use by Turkish Airlines.³ This was a public relations coup for the Albanese government, as the Australian media widely disseminated the false impression that these rights particularly mattered, or were in some way equivalent to Qatar's, or indeed Emirates'.

Turkish Airlines would launch one-stop flights, via Singapore, between Melbourne and Istanbul. For any Melburnian whose final destination was Singapore or Turkey, it was an agreeable new offering and would lower prices on those routes. But for anyone travelling to London, Paris or elsewhere in Europe (which was 95 per cent of traffic), flying Turkish would be two stops from Melbourne – a deal-breaking inconvenience for premium passengers. Moreover, Turkish would start with a grand total of three flights per week. Qatar wanted to operate twenty-eight more flights per week. Unlike the Qatar rights, Qantas did not oppose the Turkish rights, which reveals exactly how much of a threat Turkish represented to the Qantas-Emirates stranglehold: none.

—

Each year, Australia's ruling class slithered into hibernation in the days before Christmas, and despite performative signals of work in early January, barely stirred until the Australia Day weekend. The opening power event of the year was the Australian Open tennis finals, where Virgin Australia CEO Jayne Hrdlicka reigned supreme. Her other role, president of Tennis Australia, saw her hosting the top dignitaries and celebrities in the prime baseline seats. In the twelve years that I went for the *AFR*, Anthony Albanese was the only prime minister to attend. It was terrible retail politics to be flying to Melbourne at taxpayer expense and taking free tickets in the front row of a televised grand slam, but Albanese didn't seem to understand or care. Hosting Albanese in January 2023, Hrdlicka had been so confident that Qatar's air rights would be approved that she didn't even raise the issue with him. In January 2024, after Qatar's rejection had paralysed the government through the winter and spring of the previous year, Albanese still accepted Hrdlicka's invitation. She didn't dare raise Qatar with him, and he was hardly going to bring it up.

Albanese had at least by now comprehended that aligning himself with big business, let alone Australia's most hated business, was dumb politics. Days earlier he had kicked off the political year with the traditional speech at the National Press Club, where he announced that he'd instructed the ACCC to conduct a twelve-month inquiry into price-gouging by supermarket giants Coles and Woolworths. As political strategist Kos Samaras puts it, 'He went from mid-year hugging Alan Joyce to the end of the year realising he needed to put them in stocks and throw tomatoes at them.'

Emirates president Sir Tim Clark also flew in from Dubai for the Australian Open (which Emirates sponsored), and even hosted Vanessa Hudson in the front row at both the men's and women's finals. In a round of press interviews, Clark denied Emirates was involved in blocking Qatar. 'Access to Australia is in the hands of the federal government, it has nothing to do with us whatsoever,' he told the *AFR*. He expressed sympathy for Alan Joyce – 'I'm not sure he deserved what he got' – and said, 'I remember the days of Geoff Dixon and his predecessors and how difficult it was to get access to Australia because Qantas was so predeterminant in their thinking – it was basically "keep everybody out".' Really, Joyce had continued the tradition; the only thing to have changed was that Emirates became his ally and Qatar the rising threat.

Earlier that January of 2024, company director John Mullen and his wife Jacqui had invited my wife and me around for dinner. I had known and respected Mullen for years; in my *AFR* days, we would catch up for the occasional lunch at Darlinghurst institution, Beppi's. John had stepped down as Telstra chairman in October 2023, though he still maintained a full dance card as chairman of logistics giant Brambles, and as the new chairman of Penfolds maker, Treasury Wine Estates. At dinner, conversation inevitably turned to Qantas and the book I had just started writing. I told John that if he wasn't already so busy, he'd be a terrific candidate to succeed Goyder at Qantas. There was a split-second of unease in his expression and his answer was equivocal, which I remarked upon to my wife on our drive home then promptly forgot about.

Then on 21 February, Qantas announced that Mullen would succeed Richard Goyder as the airline's chairman. He was to formally assume the role on an unspecified date before the next AGM, and would 'reduce his [other] professional commitments over time'. His former Telstra board colleague, the unflinching Nora Scheinkestel, would also join the Qantas board (but unlike Mullen, immediately) and replace Jacqueline Hey as chair of the all-important remuneration committee.

To his immense credit, Goyder had indeed chosen wisely. Mullen was the perfect Qantas chairman for its troubled times. He had industry expertise, with twenty-five years as an executive in the global transport industry. He also had the character for the task; Mullen was forthright and tended to go against the grain rather than drift in the direction of the herd – the kind of thinker that had been in short supply in the Qantas boardroom. Back in 2016, he had been one of very few business leaders to speak against the Turnbull government's company tax cuts, saying, 'the last thing we need now is to divert more money into corporate coffers' and that the government was 'doing a very crap job of understanding what the ordinary person wants out of life'.

As TWU secretary, Tony Sheldon had faced off with Mullen in his various roles. 'I've always found him honest, competent, a listener, and he'll never lead you down a garden path. See, that's the thing: you can make money and have ethics at the same time. You can make money and share the benefits of making money, and motivate people in the service industry to go above and beyond. That's what Joyce killed.'

Twenty years before, when Mullen was running the Asia Pacific business of global courier giant DHL Express, he had flown to Sydney specifically for a meeting at Qantas headquarters with then chief executive Geoff Dixon. After sitting outside Dixon's office for an hour, Mullen was told by Dixon's secretary that the CEO was too busy to honour their meeting that day. 'I've just flown the whole way from bloody Hong Kong for this!' Mullen remembers griping in disbelief. 'At least he could have stuck his head out the door and said, John, there's a crisis, I'm so sorry.'

A safe assumption: nobody at Qantas would keep Mullen waiting, let alone cancel on him, again.

On the afternoon of 21 February, the very day his appointment was announced, the new chairman elect received an email from the Qantas Chairman's Lounge. It was the infamous form letter of annihilation: 'Dear Mr Mullen,' it began, before informing him that his membership was attached to his former position at Telstra, not to him personally. 'I trust you understand that we are not able to extend your membership beyond its current expiry,' the letter concluded regretfully. The nation's pre-eminent citizens lay awake at night dreading this moment, but Mullen could afford to laugh. 'I sent it to Vanessa and Richard and said, "I was only announced six hours ago. What a nice welcome!"'

Not only was Mullen's membership reinstated posthaste, but soon *he* would be the final arbiter of who was in and who was out of the Chairman's Lounge. With such unbridled power, could he hold onto the common touch?

———

After mediation between the parties had got nowhere, TWU v. Qantas returned to the Federal Court in March 2024 for Justice Michael Lee to determine the quantum of compensation owed to the 1,700 former Qantas employees. The highly technical hearings spanned ten days. For tactical reasons that needn't concern us,

Qantas took the rare step of waiving legal professional privilege over a particular internal document: the transcripts of two meetings on 1 June 2020 between key Qantas executives; its industrial relations lawyers from Freehills; and Qantas' external IR advisers, Ian and Justine Oldmeadow. The meetings' purpose had been to war-game the outsourcing proposal.

Whether or not this high-stakes reveal would succeed in diminishing the airline's compensation liability remained to be seen; as this book went to print, Justice Lee was yet to hand down his judgment. But the waiver unquestionably achieved one end: the contents of the document infuriated the judge. They put him right inside the room Qantas had been so careful to keep him out of, showing that from the outset, as his Honour complained in the hearings, '[Qantas'] lawyers were involved in road-testing the [purported] reasons [for the outsourcing decision] from the start, and all through the prism of: "We're going to structure this in a way which is best designed to withstand a challenge in the Federal Court of Australia." That's what happened.'

In and of itself, there was nothing strictly improper about that.[4] But it was completely irreconcilable with the picture of organic and iterative decision-making painted by the sworn evidence of the key Qantas witnesses, which Justice Lee now referred to as 'a fantasy'. In the 2021 trial, his Honour fumed, Qantas had decided that 'we will [rely] on these affidavits which bear no relationship to reality and assume the judge came down in the last shower'.

'What seems to me to be fairly clearly established [by the meeting transcripts] is what I suspected but was not in a position to find in [the original] judgment: that there was just a huge degree of artificiality about how this all came about,' Justice Lee declaimed. 'What does cause me concern is that then evidence [was] presented to the court which [did] not frankly disclose that reality.' His Honour even reserved an honourable mention for Andrew Finch's pièce de résistance: the power of attorney to delegate Alan Joyce's authority to Andrew David, which the affidavits pretended was a perfectly routine practice at Qantas.

In his original judgment, Justice Lee had expressed 'a sense of disquiet that I do not fully understand the true extent and nature of the dealings' between Ian Oldmeadow and the relevant Qantas executives, 'and, in particular, what precisely was said by Mr Oldmeadow and to whom about the risks and rewards of outsourcing'. The document over which Qantas now waived privilege answered all of his Honour's questions.

'I reckon you're playing with yourself,' Oldmeadow had told Freehills partner Rohan Doyle. Doyle's advice to the Qantas executives was that their stated reasons for the outsourcing 'were lawful ones ... subject to the decision makers being able to convince the court and be believed in the witness box'. Freehills was also agreeing with Qantas' airports team that various risks arising from the outsourcing were 'moderate'. Oldmeadow continued: 'GMC [group management committee] has been told we're 100 per cent sound on legal reasons but when I press you on the reasons we're in a world of fucking hurt, mate ... So you understand, I have a view that we should be working to get out of ground handling, but the reasons you have been given [by Qantas] may not stand up if the union has a good crack, and they will have a good crack.'

'We're disagreeing with the moderate assessment,' added Justine Oldmeadow. 'Our recommendation is to change to high. [This] could also risk in its own right our relationship with government and [increase] the possibility of legislative change. JobKeeper is to keep jobs, but Qantas can take JobKeeper and then make people redundant?'

'If we are going to sack everyone to give the work to Swissport, to put the risks as "moderate" is undercooking it,' her husband agreed. 'Why does Qantas have this [outsourcing] imperative? We have no competition. Hello?!'

In June 2020, of course, Virgin Australia was in administration.

'Every business has an imperative to save cost and maximise shareholder value,' Doyle quibbled. 'It's a valid objective – in fact, on one view, one you *have* to pursue.'

'Look, just as a hint for the future,' Ian Oldmeadow said, 'I would have rung [us] and got some input.'

'Yes, but that's why it's a draft – so we can have this discussion.'

'But you don't want to change it!'

'I haven't said that at all. We agree it's an aggressive timeline.'

'But the problem is the [GMC] will read "moderate" as "achievable". These things are all "high" risks. "Media campaign" is not "moderate". [The TWU] has airport rallies on this Wednesday on Same Job, Same Pay. I don't know if you guys had a look at Michael Kaine's behaviour since he became general secretary? He's running campaigns and using social media. He's a lawyer and he likes litigation. We need to map these issues out for Alan. It's going to be a very bloody fight. As I said, I support the objective, but I'm very nervous about this. [We have] agreement on where to go, the question is how. Revolution is higher risk than evolution.'

Qantas ignored its longstanding IR expert, opting to wage revolution. Oldmeadow may have taken some comfort that events proved him completely right.

———

On 6 May 2024, Qantas reached a settlement with the ACCC over its 'ghost flights' lawsuit. The airline agreed to admit to breaching consumer law and misleading consumers, pay $20 million in compensation to 86,000 affected customers, and a $100 million penalty to the regulator. Qantas also confessed that its failure to promptly inform ticketholders of their cancelled flights occurred over a period of more than two years – not just the three months in 2022 that were the original scope of the ACCC's case.

By any measure, ACCC chair Gina Cass-Gottlieb had played a blinder. Having publicly signalled her ambit claim for a $250 million punishment, she had the airline feeling victorious about paying a near-record $120 million, and even the financial commentariat calling it a 'win' for Qantas. In announcing the settlement, she described Qantas' conduct as 'egregious and unacceptable' but acknowledged its cooperation 'in admitting that the conduct occurred for a longer period and seeking to resolve this early and for the benefit of consumers'.

Facing the media that morning, Hudson was apologetic but still at pains to minimise Qantas' wrongdoing as merely 'delays in communications', and she insisted that 'we absolutely have maintained and continue [to maintain] that we did not take fees for no service'. It was true that as part of the settlement, the ACCC had agreed to drop its allegation that Qantas wrongly accepted payment from customers who bought tickets on flights that Qantas had already decided to cancel. Hudson was also right that, in practice, the ghost flights were a technology failure, with Qantas' ticketing system Amadeus unable to automatically process mass cancellations. Jetstar and Virgin – which used different software – had no such issues. The heart of the wrongdoing was this: Qantas had made the fateful choice to manually reaccommodate nearly 100,000 customers on new flights and only then tell them that it had done so, instead of informing them as soon as their flights were cancelled and before their alternative flights had been allocated. For many customers, particularly domestic flyers, the inconvenience was small, but for tens of thousands the last-minute changes were disruptive, stressful and in some cases expensive. It is also worth remembering that the mass flight cancellations in 2022 were only necessary in the first place because, with both eyes firmly on the money, Qantas sold tickets on far more flights than it was in any position to viably operate.

Bear in mind that the ACCC's investigation into the ghost flights evolved out of its original investigation into Qantas' infernal COVID credits. From an ethical standpoint, the administration of those credits was easily the worse of the two schemes. Yet the regulator took the unsentimental view that its legal position was stronger on the ghost flights. It was therefore a strange irony that Qantas was being punished and humiliated for the lesser misconduct. Of course, the class action on the credits remains on foot; anything is still possible.

One thing hadn't changed in the transition from Joyce to Hudson: the company's magical accounting. Hudson assured investors that the ACCC settlement liability would not be counted in Qantas' 'underlying' profit.

At the airline's half-year profit result in February 2024, Hudson revealed that the balance of COVID credits had fallen to $468 million.[5] At its full-year result in August 2024, the balance had fallen further to $375 million.

In October 2024, Hudson ushered in meaningful change by abolishing one of Qantas' most loathed and unfair policies: that when passengers cancelled their flight, they had to – unless they had purchased a flexible ticket – use the resulting credit on an 'equal or higher fare' (the 'single use' condition). This rule particularly infuriated those customers who'd been caught in the COVID credit double-cross. Henceforth, all Qantas flight credit-holders could opt for the lowest available fare, and use them across multiple flights. The decision would not be cheap for Qantas. The incremental revenue from railroading credit-holders into higher fare classes had been worth many millions of dollars each year.[6] 'I'm sure my revenue management team – if you asked them – would be very angry,' Hudson jokes to me when we speak on Qantas' results day in August 2024. 'But it's the right thing to do and I think that you win loyalty and over time you earn that [revenue] back.'

But what Hudson and her revenue management boffins gave with one hand, they took away with the other. Also in October 2024, they jacked the airline's booking and change fee from $99 to $119. For a customer with a $300 flight credit, for instance, the booking fee automatically stole 40 per cent of their credit balance. And this was a fee imposed on customers even when they *self-administered* their bookings on qantas.com (as most of them did).

In April 2024, Qantas also unveiled a major overhaul of its frequent flyer program – changes conceived by the recently departed Olivia Wirth – with a new redemption tier and a major increase in seat availability (which had already improved as Qantas' international capacity climbed back to 84 per cent of pre-COVID levels). Offering more seats for fewer points would in the short-term cost Qantas $120 million a year but in the long-term make its loyalty program even stronger.

Hudson was starting to rebalance the pursuit of profit with the fair treatment of customers – which, as Sir Hudson Fysh had said, 'is actually the best business in the long run'. By 30 June, Qantas had crawled from fifty-eighth spot in the quarterly RepTrak survey to fifty-sixth – a lowly position it briefly held in 2011 right after the grounding. It had now climbed over Optus and the Australian Taxation Office, but still lagged behind former in-crisis brands AMP and Rio Tinto. Virgin Australia sat at twentieth. It would be a long road back. This time, the Qantas board would be watching, with RepTrak results now being formally reported to it.

Also in August 2024, two years since railroading its long-haul flight attendants into a pay deal that 98 per cent of them had already voted to reject, Qantas revised its enterprise bargaining agreements with its short- and long-haul flight attendants, handing this one work group an extra $90 million a year. Qantas claimed that its cabin crew would now be earning triple the rates of cabin crew at some of its Asian and Gulf rivals, and that it would have to raise fares or find other cost savings to recover the money (the third option they didn't mention: surrender more profit).[7] It was unclear how much of the wages increase was discretionary and how much was necessary to comply with the Albanese government's new Same Job, Same Pay laws, but inevitably other Qantas unions would now demand their own sugar hits. Keeping labour costs controlled was a game of expectations. One of Alan Joyce's great feats for the delicate economics of the airline was keeping these costs below inflation (while driving higher productivity) for more than a decade. By 2022, even he could suppress wages no longer. And it was a thin wire between cost discipline and opening the floodgates.

Hudson was discovering that rebalancing the interests of customers and employees wasn't free; it was a trade-off. Her first full-year profit, for financial 2024, was $1.9 billion, 24 per cent lower than the previous year's $2.5 billion – the result that she'd claimed was 'not as good as it gets'.[8]

The lower profit wasn't just a cost issue, of course. Airfares had moderated considerably (as they were always going to), costing Qantas $860 million. Investors were unconcerned – Qantas shares closed at $6.37 – preferring a moderately less profitable airline than a super-profitable airline reputationally on fire.

Hudson had by now found her feet. There were no more hostage videos: she exuded far greater confidence in her public appearances. Internally, she was setting a very different tone, making a point of mingling with junior and frontline staff at headquarters and launching an internal mantra – 'Feel the Difference' – evoking distance from the Joyce era.

Meanwhile at Virgin Australia, CEO Jayne Hrdlicka had announced her resignation in February 2024. By September, her replacement still hadn't been named, though it was strongly rumoured to be Virgin's chief customer officer Paul Jones, the former Qantas executive whose credibility was incinerated by Justice Lee's judgment in TWU v. Qantas. How convincing did Hudson even really need to be?

Of course, scepticism of Hudson's bona fides as a change agent was perfectly reasonable. She had, after all, been Joyce's first officer throughout the entire COVID period, and succeeded him in her thirtieth year as an employee of the company. As CEO designate, she had promised the 'continuity of [Joyce's] strategy', which she insisted was 'collectively owned by the management team across all levels'. That was what she'd said, but as CEO in her own right, and for better or worse, she was clearly remaking that strategy.

Hudson was also slow to move on Joyce's attack dogs. PR chief Andrew McGinnes' departure was announced in January 2024, and Andrew Finch's in August. Finch was not due to leave until late October, more than twelve months after the High Court ruling and his insolent Senate inquiry performance. The illegally sacked Qantas baggage handlers had still not received a dollar of compensation, yet Hudson allowed Finch to earn another year's fat salary and bonuses. Taking a year to do the right thing is the same as doing the wrong thing.

Shareholders also remained unconvinced by Hudson's pick for chief financial officer, Rob Marcolina, who had no specialist background in finance. Since 2012, he'd run the airline's strategy team, before which he'd spent his entire career as a management consultant. In 2019, Joyce had added responsibility for people and culture to Marcolina's remit – a specialist field he also had no experience in, and which had previously been a dedicated GMC-level role. There was some irony in Marcolina being Qantas' HR boss given that his bonus had been zeroed out in 2017 for misconduct. Marcolina was chairman of Basketball Australia and in 2016 had interfered inappropriately in a commercial negotiation between the sporting body and Qantas staff; as a result, he resigned his role at Basketball Australia. He was also replaced as Qantas' representative on the board of ASX-listed travel company Helloworld. That skeleton notwithstanding, nobody thought poorly of Marcolina in a cultural sense – unlike some of his departing colleagues – but he had finite time to gain the market's confidence, and Hudson was under no illusion about that.

All these gripes aside, Hudson undoubtedly brought a normal – even low – dosage of ego to the helm of the airline, and this enabled its culture of fear to dissipate and the tone of its business dealings to shift.

Qantas even began to re-engage with me, answering dozens of my questions, including those whose answers were unflattering. Was there an advantage to be gained in furnishing me with information that tended to verify my thesis on Joyce? Arguably, but Qantas also provided answers that were highly unflattering of Hudson. That, to me, was a sign of real cultural change. Under Joyce and McGinnes, Qantas' reflex was to either attack its critics – who could forget Hudson's timeless op-ed on Qantas' taxes? – or to flatly ignore them. In August 2023 I had asked, 'What was the true and full outstanding balance of COVID credits?' We're not telling you, the company responded. It was extraordinary. Now, chairman-in-waiting John Mullen was also helping set a vastly different tone, observing in a media interview in June 2024, 'None of us likes being pilloried in the press from time to time, but the press is usually right if we're honest.'

At the time he said this, the press wasn't doing much pillorying of Qantas. The airline had launched a new route – daily flights from Perth to Paris – and Hudson took the press pack on a seductive, pre-Olympics junket in the City of Light. The media reports were customarily obliging and *Media Watch* made its usual hay with the fawning breakfast television coverage. These kind of freebies had always been, and would always be, the company's special sauce in soft media influence – the Chairman's Lounge in another form. They inevitably meant that journalists covering Qantas – just like politicians – always forgave the airline's sins faster than its customers did: only the previous month, Qantas had sunk from seventeenth to twenty-fourth in the passenger-voted Skytrax World Airline Awards, once again its lowest ever ranking.

A press delegation also followed Hudson to Dubai in June for the International Air Transport Association's annual meeting – the global airline industry's power networking event of the year. There, Qatar Airways' new CEO, Badr Mohammed Al Meer, expressed optimism that 'in the next few months we will get some positive news from Australia and we're looking forward to expanding and growing more in the Australian market'.

If he was talking about securing more international flights into Australia, his optimism was misplaced. There was no suggestion that Albanese or King had shifted their stance. But Al Meer might just as easily have been referring to Qatar taking a large ownership stake in Virgin Australia, which had been widely speculated. Such a transaction would have to be approved by the Foreign Investment Review Board and the federal treasurer. If King had invented half a dozen absurd reasons why a few more Qatar flights were contrary to the national interest, what would the government say about Qatar being a major shareholder of Australia's second airline?

This potential political firestorm looms at the time of going to print. The politics are even more fraught because in the space of three months in 2024, Australia's two domestic minnows, Bonza and Rex, both sank into administration. Both airlines had made huge strategic errors. Bonza was flying low-fare, low-traffic routes with aircraft that were too big. Rex was trying to operate capital city trunk routes without enough jets to offer viable frequencies for business travellers. Rex was also a governance basket case. Those mistakes were welcome cover for Anthony Albanese. 'There are a range of issues relating to Rex,' he told the media on 1 August. 'A regional airline made decisions to invest in routes that they hadn't previously gone on ... Sydney to Melbourne is not a regional route.'

But two things can be true at the same time. Yes, Rex's decisions were poor. But the domestic aviation industry was, according to the ACCC, 'one of the most concentrated industries in Australia', and time and again, small airlines were crushed under the Godzilla of the market.

Qantas and Jetstar had combined to shift their balance of domestic capacity enormously since the onset of COVID. In 2021, Jetstar transferred a swag of A320s out of its Japanese and Singapore subsidiaries and into its Australian operation. By 2024, Jetstar was operating 38 per cent more domestic seats between capital cities than in 2019. This shift allowed Qantas to move its 737s and 717s onto larger regional routes and free up more Dash 8 Q-400 turboprops to start flying smaller regional routes (the source of Rex's profits) where, naturally, airfares tumbled. Between 2019 and 2024, Qantas reduced its capital city seats by 27 per cent and increased its regional seats by 45 per cent.

Just in the first half of 2024, Jetstar increased its domestic seats by 13 per cent, adding more seats than the total number of 737 seats Rex operated. On some of Rex's key capital city routes, Jetstar added even more: 24 per cent on both Melbourne–Sydney and Adelaide–Sydney. Naturally, again, airfares on those routes tumbled. So quite aside from its own epic missteps, Rex was tactically swamped from both ends. That was the might of Qantas and Jetstar, being deployed as two weapons in the one arsenal.

Qantas was unassailable with the highest-paying customers, thanks to the Chairman's Lounge and its loyalty status tiers. Jetstar mopped up all the cheapest traffic and turned a decent buck on it, undercutting Virgin Australia, which was stuck in the middle, getting 32 per cent of the passengers but less than 20 per cent of the profit.

The Rex and Bonza collapses revived the public debate about the structure of the domestic airline industry, and finally forced Catherine King to act on the slot system at Sydney airport. Asked by reporters (en route to Paris) if the domestic market was big enough for more than three airlines, Vanessa Hudson said that 'history proves not', citing Australia's small population compared to the US market. But the problem was not whether the country could support three or more airlines, Canberra airport's Stephen Byron told me, 'it was that two of them were owned by the same company'.

That wasn't something Qantas should apologise for. It had dug out then defended its position by the sheer ingenuity of Geoff Dixon creating the two-brand strategy – something airline groups all over the world had sought to emulate, with limited success. The iron grip of one player over 63 per cent of the traffic but 80 per cent of the profit was the product of multiple complex factors. One of them was Virgin's own strategic errors. Another was the industry's high barriers to entry. Another was successive federal governments being captured by Qantas and failing to create policy that fostered competition. That policy should have included a fundamental aspect of functioning capitalist economies: that when players become too dominant, they trigger anti-trust action. Qantas acted with impunity because the forced divestment of Jetstar has never even been a plausible threat. Indeed, when shadow transport minister Bridget McKenzie floated this as merely worthy of consideration in September 2024, she was leapt upon by the Albanese government and within hours weakly abandoned by Liberal and National leaders Peter Dutton and David Littleproud.

A huge advantage Qantas wielded over Virgin was its international network. Given that Virgin relied on partners like Qatar to compete with Qantas internationally, it was grossly unfair of the Albanese government to hamstring Virgin by blocking Qatar's fair access to Australia compared to its Gulf peers. If Canberra is going to unfairly advantage Australia's dominant airline, the ACCC should withdraw its authorisation for the Qantas–Emirates partnership. As it was, re-authorising it in 2023 was an inexplicable decision by the competition regulator.

It was marvellous for Qantas that Virgin was owned by private equity, the kind of investor that always minimises capital investment, because it reduced pressure on Qantas to invest itself. That's what the ACCC meant when it said: 'without a real threat of losing passengers to other airlines, the [two] airline groups have had less incentive to … invest in systems to provide high levels of customer service'. It's the reason why Qantas was in 2024 seriously considering yet another refurbishment of its ageing 737-800 fleet, rather than activating enough orders for replacement aircraft.

The final piece of Qantas' market dominance was its loyalty program. The 62 per cent of the Australian population who were members were more likely to know the points balance of their frequent flyer account than their superannuation balance. As one federal minister marvelled to me, 'my constituents understand the frequent flyer redemption system far better than preferential voting'. This was the dirty secret that Qantas would never admit to, but which was nevertheless true: no matter how poorly its customers were treated, a large majority would always come back for more punishment – the giveaway sign of an effective monopoly.

————

As 2024 progressed, the Qantas board continued its fraught wrestle with both the independent review of the company's governance and, relatedly, what to do about the 2023 bonuses – still floating in limbo – of Alan Joyce and his top executives. Tom Saar, retired partner at consulting firm McKinsey, was preparing the governance report, interviewing directors and executives individually to glean their confidential input. But Saar did not consult Joyce or the other former GMC members.

At the same time, Colin Carter – corporate *éminence grise* and, like Goyder, a former AFL commissioner and Wesfarmers director – was advising the board on how much of those bonuses should be paid and how much should be cancelled. Carter was supported by law firm King & Wood Mallesons (led by partner Stephen Minns). He interviewed all the 2023 GMC members, including Joyce on 12 June, and others who had subsequently left the company.

Anticipation had been burning in the market for weeks when on 8 August, Qantas announced the outcome of both processes. Saar's findings, compiled into a Qantas board report, were damning. For the avoidance of doubt, Saar catalogued the events that led to Qantas' collapse in public trust: late flights, lost bags, call centre wait times, the lack of support for frontline staff, the handling of COVID credits, post-COVID airfares, the ACCC lawsuit, the 1,700 illegal redundancies, Qantas' two Senate inquiry appearances, the Qatar air rights application, the record 2023 profit, Joyce's share sale, and even 'the removal of the *AFR* from Qantas lounges'. (On that last, Mullen says, 'It's hard to understand, because everyone [internally] tells me it was a terrible decision. So I asked, "Well why did it happen?!" A petty thing like that ... was just totally out of touch with reality.')

Saar then 'distilled ... the root cause dynamic that underpinned' this catalogue of shame: a focus on financial performance before stakeholders and non-financial risks; the 'top-down' leadership style of a 'dominant and trusted CEO' leading to 'insufficient listening and low speak up'; and the board giving 'too much deference to a long-tenured CEO who had endured and overcome multiple past operational and financial crises'. Qantas' external communications, meanwhile, were 'adversarial' and 'at times combative', and 'poor relationships with some external stakeholders exacerbated problems for Qantas'. I was tempted to send Saar an invoice for a cut of his undoubtedly hefty fee, given that his findings read like an AI-generated summary of my thirty-plus columns the previous year. And, as a top executive at AFL House joked to me, 'Change the names and you'd be talking about us.' Everyone's name, that is, but Goyder's.

As for Qantas' culture, Saar found that Joyce's 'command and control' leadership style 'impacted empowerment and a willingness to challenge or "speak up" on issues or decisions of concern except in relation to safety matters'. This exception was no doubt news to former health and safety delegate Theo Seremetidis, stood aside illegally for daring to raise entirely warranted safety concerns in 2020.

But the Qantas board, Saar found, implausibly, 'had limited visibility or appreciation of the manifestation of this cultural characteristic'. It was audacious of the Qantas directors to bleat to Saar that they didn't know Joyce was dictatorial. I had written the following words on the back page of the *AFR* on 16 April 2023: 'His executives are in the bunker with a mad king in his last days and for any person who presents a truth he doesn't like, the consequences are real. Joyce's lieutenants mete out the same justice to their underlings. Goyder has been warned about this culture on multiple occasions and has declined to act.' That was a month after the board had discussed my criticism of Joyce and sent Goyder to lodge a second official complaint with the newspaper. It wasn't that the Qantas board didn't know, it was that they didn't *want* to know.

Humiliatingly for Goyder, the report recommended, and the board adopted, 'tightened protocols for the approval of share trading by the CEO'. So much for Goyder's excuse in September 2023 that 'Alan met every requirement to sell shares'. Hereafter, both the Qantas chairman and the board's audit committee chair would need to approve any share sale, but any sale that pushed the CEO below their minimum shareholding requirement would require the approval of the full board. While adding a second and third layer of transaction approval was not a bad thing, it was a modesty screen being constructed around what had been a human failure. There was nothing wrong with the process. There was something wrong with Goyder's judgement, which is actually all shareholders paid him for.

While in places unsparing, the report was also replete with this bent of euphemism and de-identification. 'The board was collegiate in their approach,' Saar found. This was code for: the board was conflict-avoidant. 'The mode of engagement between the board and management did not always facilitate robust challenge on some issues,' went another key finding. This was the directors, with Saar as accomplice, devolving their personal dereliction to a mode, or a style. On the contrary, the lack of challenge to Joyce was simply caused by Qantas directors choosing not to challenge him. It was bog-standard professional laxity.

Another change recommended and adopted by the review was that formal board consultation and approval would be required for Qantas' 'involvement in significant stakeholder and community issues'. Pointedly, this was a reaction to Qantas' support of the 'Yes' campaign in the Indigenous Voice referendum. Mullen's view on that was unambiguous: he told a media lunch in June 2024 that there were 'quite a few lessons to be learned' and that 'whether you agree with it or you don't agree with it, the way that corporate Australia went about supporting it I think has been detrimental to the image of corporate Australia among many, many people'.

Tony Sheldon speaks for many with his cynical take on the progressive political stances struck by Qantas: 'I equate it to the mafia going into Little Italy and putting on the fete and, you know, supplying all the kids with fairy floss.'

There had been a blurring of the line between where Qantas' activism ended and its celebrity CEO's began. In 2011, Qantas became a sponsor of the Prostate Cancer Foundation, even painting a Movember moustache on an aircraft, not long after Joyce himself had been treated for prostate cancer. And in 2017, Joyce was the public face of the successful plebiscite campaign for marriage equality.

The Qantas board did approve the airline's support of the Voice in 2023, but implicit in the language of the Saar report was that board members felt it was presented to them by Joyce as a fait accompli. This, of course, was a ridiculous construction. The extent to which Joyce used the board as a rubber stamp was not Joyce's fault, it was the board's for letting him. Joyce was entitled to assume he was being properly supervised. In the absence of any negative feedback – indeed, with his chairman publicly exalting him as the best CEO in Australia – how could he be expected to believe otherwise?

Saar's negative findings about Joyce's leadership style at the end of his tenure were entirely merited, but they were reached in a process that by its design maximised Joyce's culpability and minimised everybody else's. Saar invited only the *surviving* senior executives (plus former and current board members) into a room and asked them for anonymised feedback. The plain incentive of those survivors was to save themselves, to convey a sense of their own powerlessness in the debacle, not to say, I, too, was guilty of perpetuating a toxic culture and did nothing to protect the people below me. Ask yourself this: what would you have said? It is hardly surprising, then, that Saar 'learned' that all of Joyce's underlings – and even his superiors! – were too afraid to speak up. Whatever happened to the standard you walk past being the standard you accept?

The findings of the Saar report informed the Qantas board's decision on the 2023 bonuses. And that decision in respect of Joyce was unprecedented in corporate Australia: he would lose 100 per cent of his long-term bonus, whose hurdles he had already met.[9] The shares forfeited were worth $8.4 million. The board also reduced the short-term 2023 bonuses of all GMC members by 33 per cent. That cost Joyce another $900,000, taking his total reduction to $9.3 million. Nobody needed to cry for him: he still earned a sickening $15 million in 2023, including that $6.5 million of bonuses for the three prior years, when Qantas lost more than $6 billion.

Still, no other Qantas executive was docked a single share from their long-term bonus. Hudson's silence in the 'low speak up' culture had taken her all the way. Now she was docked just $420,000, taking home more than $6 million for 2023. As the sole decision-maker in the illegal sacking of 1,700 Qantas employees, Andrew David was docked just $367,000 and so was paid $5.7 million for 2023. What kind of message did that send? Despite the explicit findings in Saar's report of hostile external communications and poor relationships that damaged the company, head of PR Andrew McGinnes kept 100 per cent of his long-term bonus and 67 per cent of his short-term bonus. As did Andrew Finch.

Fronting the announcement on the bonuses, Mullen said he had no wish 'to throw Alan under the bus ... but he's captain of the ship, and unfortunately that's what comes with the territory'. (Had he thrown in mention of Joyce derailing Qantas, Mullen would have covered every mode of transport except aviation with his mixed metaphor.)

Qantas knew that, due to the lack of board discretion in its executive pay contracts, its legal position on Joyce's bonuses was far from impregnable – that if Joyce sued the company, he had half a chance of getting his $9 million back. The board had made a calculation: it was worth the risk. Shareholders would not cop the board doing nothing, and neither would the public.

That day, Goyder met Joyce for a coffee in Sydney's CBD to commiserate, or placate him. It was a tragic image: once two of Australia's most powerful people, who operated like an enmeshed family; Joyce destroyed by his hyper-aggression, Goyder by his weakness; Joyce undone by self-blindness, Goyder by blind admiration for Joyce.

Days later, Joyce was photographed by the *Daily Mail* walking his dog near his Palm Beach residence on Sydney's northern beaches. 'The face of a man who just lost his $9 MILLION bonus,' the headline screamed; 'Shattered ex-Qantas boss spotted looking glum on a park bench after receiving devastating news.'

Goyder, meanwhile, haunted Qantas until 16 September. His slowness to move on – and let the company move on – was a source of muffled frustration internally. He still had his remaining roles at the AFL and Woodside. Indeed, Goyder told Woodside shareholders in April, 'I have never been more energised and excited at the prospect of serving as chair.' But twelve months earlier, he'd been preparing to quit the thankless Woodside role, with all of its dissentious climate politics, to better enjoy his Qantas ride.

Even in the life of a chairman, beggars can't be choosers.

———

Just after the Qantas board announced the Saar review and its decision on Joyce's bonuses, I sat down for that lunch in Sydney with John Mullen. He had spent the previous several months in a revolving door of meetings with Qantas people and stakeholders of all varieties, absorbing a mother lode of data and feedback on one of the nation's most complex businesses. He also learned very quickly about Australians' particular fixation with the airline – he was accosted at the bottle shop by customers cursing Joyce, and petitioned by friends and associates over their frequent flyer statuses and Chairman's Lounge memberships.

As a Qantas outsider in 2022 and 2023, Mullen had closely observed the company's plight because 'a) it was interesting, and b) there were lessons for all of us in it', he tells me. As for his view of Joyce then, 'I probably had a bit more respect for Alan's considerable strengths, whereas most people didn't give him credit for anything.'

At Qantas, Mullen stepped into a play he'd seen before. His career as a company director began at Telstra in 2008, whose board he joined in the dying months of Sol Trujillo's reign – another infamously dominant CEO who lorded it over his board. Joyce's 'top-down' leadership had been exacerbated by the COVID crisis, Mullen acknowledges, but 'the reality is, if you look at the evidence, that "command and control" thing occurred much earlier. COVID just highlighted what was already there.'

Mullen is promising to drive further renewal of the Qantas board. 'To be fair, for those directors who were there, it was a very gruelling and damaging period. So we need fresh voices, fresh views, and people not burdened by the past.' Despite Saar's laundry list of changes to board processes, Mullen's solution is not elaborate: 'I think it's just got to be a regular, professional board.'

The huge changes of the past year have been even more shocking for Qantas people far more junior than its non-executive directors. 'But my reading of it internally is that people felt it had to be done,' Mullen says. 'It's good to clear the decks.' Another marine metaphor – and Mullen is quite the maritime historian – in an aviation story.

Mullen's appointment in February 2024 was tentatively construed as a positive for Hudson's own survival prospects. When he became chairman of Telstra, major investors were unconvinced by new CEO Andy Penn, but rather than move him on, Mullen chose to back him and drive him hard. His take on Hudson's performance to date supports that theory. 'Vanessa is a totally different person than Alan. I know people will say, Ah, but you were there for this whole period – which is fair comment, but I think she's her own person. And I wasn't sure about that, to be honest, when I started. The culture will change dramatically as she attracts different people around her and moves on from that legalistic, aggressive, combative culture of the past.' He looks at me for a moment. 'But so far, so good.'

Afterword

30 Sept 2023

Richard Goyder, like Alan Joyce, declined to speak to me for this book. In writing it, I often felt sadness for the immense damage Goyder has sustained to his public standing – something that is obviously very important to him. He is a nice man, and his mistakes were made I believe out of weakness, not malintent. But then I remember the victims of Qantas' 'low speak culture': the junior executives who went home from Mascot every night and cried themselves to sleep. There's more required in leadership than being nice.

The last time I saw Goyder was at the AFL grand final in 2023, when he appeared pale and shaken. In previous years, the speeches at the AFL's pre-match luncheon had been littered with gags about Goyder's chairmanship of Qantas, particularly given Virgin Australia's role as an official AFL sponsor. In one routine, MC Hamish McLachlan complained repeatedly to Goyder about not being offered membership of the Chairman's Lounge. There were certainly no Qantas jokes in 2023, although among the 600 guests, Goyder's manifestly terminal chairmanship of the airline was the topic of much furtive gossip.

Seeing the AFL chairman so diminished and humiliated at his own haute power event had a sobering effect on me. I keenly perceived my part in meting out his humiliation, and despite all the times I'd tried to warn him, I felt rotten about it.

Goyder and the prime minister were just two in a platoon of my Rear Window victims in the Olympic Room that day. Also present were former PwC CEO Luke Sayers (who was president of the Carlton Football Club); former Collingwood president Eddie McGuire; Virgin's Jayne Hrdlicka, and quite a few more.¹ Every time Port Adelaide president and former *Sunrise* host David Koch saw me, he capitulated into tears of laughter at the fact I was even there. I'd been buckling on my armour and swanning into these events for twelve years, but for the first time I felt the sheer weight of accumulated hostility and knew for certain it was time for me to move on with my life.

The Qantas story was the best of my career, and perhaps I learned something else from it: unlike Alan Joyce, Richard Goyder, and everyone else I'd harangued from high office over the years, I could seize my own 'vanishing window of opportunity' and go when they were begging me to stay, rather than stay when they were begging me to go. I tendered my resignation to the *AFR* seventy-two hours later.

Notes

Between January and August 2024, I conducted on the record interviews with the following people: Paul Scurrah, Josh Bornstein, Michael Kaine, Wayne Mader, Teri O'Toole, Steven Reed, Steve Purvinas, Tony Lucas, Sally McManus, Emeline Gaske, Michele Levine, Akbar Al Baker, Leigh Clifford, Sir Rod Eddington, Michael Stutchbury, Greg Hywood, James Chessell, Matt O'Sullivan, Kos Samaras, Tony Sheldon, John Sharp, John Mullen, Crispin Murray and Vanessa Hudson.

Introduction

1   That position had been vacated by Brendan Lyon (later of KPMG-TAHE notoriety), and the other candidate I somehow edged out was Matt Kean, future NSW treasurer, whose political destiny was scarcely affected by the minor setback.

2   It also didn't hurt that Australian troops were deployed to Al Minhad Air Base (aka 'Camp Mirage') just outside Dubai.

3   Qantas, Qantas-owned Jetstar, and Emirates were three of the four largest international carriers in the Australian market and yet the competition regulator has three times since 2012 granted them permission to operate as a cartel.

4   In 2021, Joyce appointed Parker Qantas' chief sustainability officer. He left the airline in September 2024.

5   Technically, the deal didn't need approval because APA was majority Australian-owned, but the consortium submitted itself to the foreign investment review process at the request of Treasurer Peter Costello.

6   Years later, Yates said that he'd assumed a lower profile during the APA bid after telling Allco boss David Coe (who died in 2013) that he was opposed to the deal – despite Yates having millions of his own money in it. 'There was too much leverage, and it was inappropriately timed because it was at the top of the market,' Yates said in 2017. But in December 2006, Yates had played down the deal's leverage, saying, 'There's $2 billion in cash on the balance sheet and effectively no banking covenants other than having to pay interest. [Privatised

Qantas] should be able to survive the most unexpected circumstances.' And if Yates knew in 2007 that 2007 was the top of the market, why didn't he mention that in 2007 instead of 2017? The value of that alleged insight had diminished 100 per cent after the fact.

7 Joyce totally reimagined Qantas headquarters by converting four old buildings into a modern campus which opened in 2014.

8 Holdforth resigned in 2015 after Qantas permanently injuncted her against publishing an insider's account of the Qantas grounding in 2011.

9 After several years in obscurity, Epstein re-emerged in February 2024 as principal private secretary to Prime Minister Anthony Albanese.

10 Unbeknownst to us, Dixon had granted this interview to *AFR* reporter James Chessell, my former colleague in Joe Hockey's office. Fifteen years later, as the *AFR*'s publisher, Chessell clashed with Qantas over its dramatic boycott of the newspaper.

11 The Hollywood film by the same name, starring Samuel L. Jackson, was released three years earlier.

12 The executive floor, known as QCA9, was another eccentricity of the company. While the dingy lower floors were laid out in an elementary, rectangular fashion, it is no exaggeration to say that QCA9 was configured as a maze. Even Qantas veterans would regularly find themselves lost without hope in its corridors. Panelled entirely in red mahogany, the hallways veered off at obtuse angles, before doubling back on themselves. Augmenting the labyrinth effect was the absence of any nameplates on the doors. The only signposts were the secretaries, who oftentimes had the temerity to leave their stations or to not have arrived yet. Company mythology attributed the design to Gary Toomey, the CFO of Australian Airlines (and later Qantas), who was said to be paranoid about kidnappers or other intruders. It sounded outlandish but then again not exponentially crazier than any other Qantas folklore I'd heard and adopted as fact. In researching this book, I checked the story with Toomey, who was amused by it but denied its veracity.

13 This was actually the only time I ever interviewed Joyce for a real publication, as opposed to Qantas News.

14 Annabelle left Qantas in January 2020 and joined United Airlines.

Eleven Weeks from Bankruptcy

1 As the name suggests, a share buy-back is where a company buys back its own shares to retire them. This reduces its number of shares on issue and increases the value of all remaining shares.

2 In 2017, Qantas was Australia's second most trusted brand.

3 A staunch republican (up to a point), Joyce accepted his decoration in that year's Queen's Birthday honours list.

4 The extension of Joyce's tenure was widely reported on 1 May 2019, the press having been briefed directly by Qantas. In 2023, Joyce attempted to write this out of history, but I'll deal with that later.

5 Joyce returned to Sydney permanently in 2024.

6 For the uninitiated, wide-bodies are planes with two aisles. Single-aisle aircraft are called narrow-bodies.

7 There was a loophole here: if Qantas could get customers to 'voluntarily' accept flight credits before Qantas had cancelled their flights, the customers would have effectively surrendered their refund rights, but this loophole was quickly closed by ACCC intervention, which I'll come to later.

8 Think of net debt as like your mortgage offset account. It is your total debt minus your cash.

9 In effect, the sell-off meant that Virgin noteholders doubted the airline's survival prospects. They preferred to crystallise 42 cents in the dollar on their four-month-old investment, even foregoing their first interest payment in May, over the risk of getting zero as unsecured creditors if Virgin fell into administration or receivership.

10 Indeed, HNA had already collapsed into the hands of the Chinese government.

11 Joyce quickly accepted an offer from Woolworths chief executive Brad Banducci to help redeploy Qantas staff to the supermarket giant, which with the entire population stuck at home had suddenly found itself in boom times.

12 Qantas erroneously told customers that only credits converted from flexible tickets were eligible for refunds. The wording of these emails was in flux, but on 24 March 2020, they read: 'Vouchers are valid until expiry date shown above. If not used before this expiry date, the voucher value will be forfeited unless the original fare conditions permitted a refund.'

13 None of Qantas' debts had financial covenants, which are usually triggered if a company's earnings or cashflow falls below a level sufficient to service its interest payments (or if its total debts rise above a certain percentage of its equity). Then the lender is entitled to exercise more control over the company, including by forcing it into receivership. In circumstances where Qantas' revenue was evaporating, this put Qantas in an enviable position.

14 Staying within a net debt target range (where the net debt balance is a low multiple of annual earnings) was how Qantas maintained an investment-grade credit rating, which was its passport to secure funding from international banks on attractive terms – i.e. without financial covenants.

15 Based on an annual wages bill of $4.3 billion, but these are necessarily inexact figures. Stood-down staff, particularly in operations, would've

been among the lower paid. The company also would've initially kept paying a significant proportion of stood-down staff in annual/long service leave.

16 As more workers were stood up later in the pandemic, the proportion of JobKeeper money Qantas got to keep as a direct subsidy increased to approximately 50 per cent.

17 Qantas withheld all landing charges from airports even though Qantas passengers had already paid them to Qantas via ticket surcharges.

18 Bear in mind that 'current trading conditions' meant almost total hibernation – even domestic travel was virtually grounded and Qantas was operating at around 5 per cent of its total pre-COVID seat capacity.

19 Regarding the $40 million per week burn rate, Joyce told Bloomberg in August 2020 that 'actually our operating businesses are covering their costs, it's actually just the working capital movements and [financing costs] that are making us negative, which are not damaging the balance sheet'.

20 Not that the financial media was any better, producing not a single instance of scrutiny of Joyce's claim before or since I called it 'a raging falsehood' in the *AFR* on 27 August 2023. Even I was admittedly slow to twig.

21 Qantas said in its 2002 annual report that 'in the domestic market ... Qantas was able to add the equivalent of about seven years' growth, virtually overnight'.

22 As Virgin Blue grew rapidly, Qantas enjoyed two years of 75 per cent market share, before settling at 65 per cent, which was the 'line in the sand' Joyce would defend at great cost the following decade in a domestic capacity war with Virgin's Borghetti.

23 Operating as an extension of ScoMo's press office was quite nakedly Benson's (and *The Australian*'s) business model – while it lasted – and was the subject of considerable derision (and professional jealousy).

24 At that time, Joyce was a member of the Business Council's board, which Westacott reported to.

25 On 15 March, an item in the *AFR*'s Street Talk column speculatively linked Virgin to corporate undertakers KordaMentha. Virgin flatly denied any communications with KordaMentha.

26 Another senior figure at BGH Capital was Terry Bowen, who had served as CFO of conglomerate Wesfarmers under its then CEO Richard Goyder, and as the very first CFO of Jetstar under its original CEO, Alan Joyce.

27 In the end, only $70.6 million was spent under the scheme, so Rex got three-quarters of it.

28 Using 19.4 per cent of financial 2019 turnover.

29 Approximately 60 per cent of Rex's shares were owned by Singaporean interests.

30   In the end, the final amount spent under that scheme was actually $226 million.

31   These were 737s that Virgin Australia shed in its voluntary administration, which we're coming to shortly.

32   While Treasury initially costed JobKeeper at $130 billion, it announced a hugely embarrassing 'significant error' of that costing on 22 May, revising it down to $70 billion over six months.

33   JobKeeper 2.0, with much tighter eligibility criteria (which Qantas met), operated for a second six months between October 2020 and March 2021, and cost a further $19 billion.

34   Munger said this in his 1995 Harvard address, 'The Psychology of Human Misjudgment'.

35   On account of Qantas' pre-COVID revenue being three times that of Virgin's.

Reality on an Underlying Basis

1   The SPP was originally slated to raise $500 million but was significantly under-subscribed. While it was announced on 25 June, it didn't complete until 10 August, during which time Qantas shares fell from $4.19 to $3.36, mainly because Victoria had been plunged into lockdown. Under the retail SPP, every member of the Qantas board, including Joyce, bought their full allocation of $30,000. This was only the second (and final) time Alan Joyce ever paid for Qantas shares. In the company's last equity raising in 2009, he'd bought $10,000 worth. After 12 years as CEO, he owned 3 million Qantas shares, 99.5 per cent of which were zero-priced performance shares.

2   The same thing, sadly, was happening overseas. The US Department of Transportation had just issued its second enforcement notice demanding US airlines provide prompt refunds to customers whose flights had been cancelled.

3   In those eligible for a refund, Qantas now included cases where 'you cancelled your flight (before we did)', closing the loophole I referred to earlier.

4   Capacity is shorthand for 'available seat kilometres', which is the number of seats operated multiplied by the distance flown.

5   La Spina had previously been chief financial officer, but was transferred into the Qantas International role in 2019 to, as chairman Richard Goyder said, 'give him the opportunity to run a business' and, implicitly, to prove his chops as a successor to Joyce. Ironically, that move enabled Vanessa Hudson to take La Spina's job as CFO, then succeed Joyce without ever having run a major division of the Qantas Group.

6   Out of the original 6,000 (voluntarily) redundant Qantas employees, 775 of those were ground handling employees.

7　Indeed, whenever those 2,500 staff had worked since 1 April, Qantas got to keep their JobKeeper payments as a corporate subsidy.

8　Not-so-fun fact: on Alan Joyce's executive leadership team, there were more men named Andrew than there were women.

9　Outside of its frequent flyer program, that is, which never stopped making money.

10　Airfares went nuts barely 18 months later.

11　The figure of 100,000 was an estimate of the Board of Airlines Representatives of Australia, of which Qantas was a member.

Transport Workers' Union v. Qantas

1　This document was produced in the trial but had been circulated widely among aviation workers years earlier.

2　In airline speak, 'above the wing' is airport customer services, like check-in and boarding, whereas 'below the wing' is ramp, baggage, and aircraft cleaning, catering, refuelling and towing.

3　Not all of this was wages suppression. Technology also drove vast productivity improvements (economist-speak for 'doing the same work with fewer workers'). For instance, new generation aircraft and engines needed far fewer maintenance hours than those they replaced. Check-in kiosks and automated bag-drop stations, introduced in 2010, rendered 50 per cent of airport customer service staff obsolete. The internet, particularly the shift to online bookings, did the same to Qantas call centres (even if, post-COVID, Qantas found itself critically short of humans manning the phones). Over the same period, Qantas' annual revenue failed to keep pace with inflation, as global competition intensified and Qantas' and Jetstar's combined market share of international passengers to/from Australia shrank from 31 per cent to 26 per cent.

4　In 2024, the Albanese government appointed Gibian vice president of the Fair Work Commission.

5　In that case, Justice Lee delivered the only judgment in Australian legal history whose citations included *Anchorman: The Legend of Ron Burgundy* (and its sequel *Anchorman 2: The Legend Continues*), after I had likened Stead to the film's weatherman Brick Tamlin, played by Steve Carrell, who Justice Lee characterised as 'a gaping moron'. Justice Lee now presides in the ongoing class action over Blue Sky's collapse. Stead was originally a respondent to that class action but she, along with seven other former Blue Sky directors and EY's two signing audit partners, were dropped from the claim in November 2022.

6　Qantas' GMC comprised Joyce and all of his direct reports – the heads of Qantas Domestic and International, QantasLink, Jetstar and Loyalty, plus specialists like CFO Vanessa Hudson, strategy head Rob Marcolina, general counsel Andrew Finch, and PR and government boss Andrew McGinnes.

7   Also in 1989, Ian's wife Justine Oldmeadow, an Australian Postal and Telecommunications Union official, was appointed to the Australian Industrial Relations Commission.

8   Fifty-one per cent of Jetstar ground handling staff voted in favour of the new agreement.

9   Enterprise agreements (EAs) are referred to interchangeably as enterprise bargaining agreements (EBAs).

10   These notes were only discovered for the court because a third executive, Colin Hughes, had scanned Jones' annotated document and emailed them to himself and Nicholas.

11   Approximately 500 airport customer service staff took voluntary redundancy, a quarter of that workforce.

12   By the time the case came before the court, Jones had left Qantas to assume the role of chief customer officer at Virgin Australia.

13   Justice Lee admitted the metadata into evidence, and in his judgment determined that: 1) a Freehills solicitor seconded to Qantas' industrial relations team, Jessica Light, emailed Doyle and Popple of Freehills, Matthew Follett (a barrister, now acting for Qantas in the trial) and Millen on the morning of 18 November; 2) Doyle had then emailed Finch, Follett, Millen, Light and Popple; 3) the draft RFA Word document had been emailed repeatedly among these recipients between 6:42pm and 7:11pm; 4) a final draft (last saved by Freehills) was emailed from Doyle to Finch, Follett, Millen, Light and Popple at 7:41pm; before 5) Finch, at 8:11pm, sent a final PDF version of the document to Andrew David.

14   Actually, there were no proceedings yet, though Follett's involvement even before the outsourcing decision was made suggested that Qantas fully expected litigation to ensue.

15   Qantas didn't sign contracts with third-party ground handling companies until late January 2021.

16   In cross-examination, Andrew David said he had only ever received Joyce's financial authority by delegation when Joyce was on leave, but that it had never involved a power of attorney. David agreed with the proposition put to him by TWU counsel that the outsourcing delegation was 'in a form that you had never before been party to or involved in, in your career at Qantas'. David further agreed that the usual course of approving a Qantas Domestic transaction was that he would sign the RFA and if the transaction value exceeded his financial authority, Alan Joyce would sign it.

17   Savings of $103 million per normal year (but even greater savings in 2021 during lockdowns) plus $80 million of capital expenditure on new equipment avoided.

Crossing the Rubicon

1   Some might say that's a bit rich coming from me ...

2   Sharp then immediately sent Rex chairman Kim Hai Lim a series of messages recounting the contents of his conversation with Joyce. I have seen those contemporaneous messages.

3   Based on available seat kilometres in the six months to 31 December 2020.

4   Cromwell paid $80 million (so you can only imagine what it charged Qantas in rent), while Qantas paid $50 million.

5   Virgin had been established in Brisbane 20 years earlier only because of the substantial subsidies (including payroll tax concessions) offered to it by the Beattie government.

6   By the time of publication, there were seven Qantas A380s flying, with one back out in scheduled maintenance and the final two yet to return from their COVID mothballs.

7   The Morrison government's timeline had been thrown into legitimate disarray on 8 April, when the obscure Australian Technical Advisory Group on Immunisation recommended against people aged under 50 receiving the AstraZeneca vaccine, which up to that point had been the backbone of Australia's vaccine program. The government also had a supply deal with Pfizer, but deliveries were heavily weighted to the back half of 2021, and even then there were only enough doses coming to vaccinate half the adult population. No deal had been struck with Moderna.

8   The 343,500 shares from his 2020 long-term award were also kept aside for a further year.

9   This figure includes 154,118 Qantas shares worth $607,225 which Joyce received in September 2020 as his deferred short-term bonus for 2018.

10 Twelve A380s went into storage in 2020 but the company announced in August 2021 that two weren't coming back.

11 Qantas started 2022 with a labour surplus, having stood up all of its crew ahead of demand, but COVID had created staff shortages by April.

12 This number was hugely inflated by the inclusion of pilots. Captains earned anything from $200,000 to $470,000.

13 In reality, it was even more than that, because the Qantas board calculated the number of shares granted to Joyce (698,000) based on the deflated share price on 30 June 2021 ($4.66), not on the price on the day the plan was announced ($5.18). By doing so, it gave Joyce 70,000 additional shares worth $362,000 on that day. The board – only naturally – did not calculate the share grants of frontline workers in this way.

14 There were also the 1,000 Qantas shares, to be granted to any contin-
    uing employee in August 2023 under the recovery and retention plan.
15 Qantas return airfares (all cabins) July 2019 versus July 2022.
16 The Full Court also heard (and dismissed) an appeal from the TWU
    against Justice Lee's rejection of its application for reinstatement of
    those outsourced employees. Both the original and appeal judges agreed
    that financial compensation was an adequate remedy. Justice Lee would
    determine the quantum of that remedy in 2024.
17 Incidentally, if Joyce's legal advice had been that Qantas' first appeal
    enjoyed a reasonable prospect of success, should he not, given its
    unambiguous failure, then have been moved to consult a different set
    of legal advisers on the prospects of the success of a second appeal?
18 Sonia Millen would depart Qantas in November 2023, one of the first
    senior executives to leave the company after Vanessa Hudson succeeded
    Joyce. She became a partner specialising in employment law at top-tier
    firm Allens Linklaters, where she continued to act for Qantas as a legal
    adviser.

Not Match Fit

1   In retrospect, this was a design flaw of the JobKeeper program. The
    same happened to the foreign-owned baggage handling companies
    Menzies, Swissport and dnata (owned by Emirates). Their difficulty
    replacing their pre-COVID workforces was one cause of the massive
    spike in mishandled baggage that bedevilled Qantas in 2022.
2   Mandatory self-isolation for close contacts ended for the entire commu-
    nity in NSW and Victoria on 22 April and in Queensland on 28 April.
3   These figures exclude regional flights.
4   All four flight attendants on Virgin Australia flights stayed onboard
    for the passenger boarding process.
5   Qantas didn't need to replace most of its redundant A380 captains
    yet because only six of the original twelve A380s (two of which were
    scrapped) returned to flying in 2022.
6   Those 787 and A330 captain positions could also be filled by 737 captains,
    but let's not complicate my hypothetical any more than we have to.
7   Qantas didn't need quite as many A330 captains as pre-COVID because
    it had reduced the passenger A330 fleet from 28 to 26 – sending two
    to be converted to freighters.
8   The 20 per cent who couldn't get a refund fitted into three baskets: 1)
    those who'd already partially used the value of their credit and had
    a remaining balance left over – though even those balances would
    eventually become eligible for refund after Qantas changed its rules
    in August 2023 in response to public outrage; 2) customers who had
    accepted inducements (like bonus Frequent Flyer points or status

credits) to transfer their flight credits into Qantas Passes and in doing so agreed to cede their refund rights; and 3) customers who converted their non-flexible tickets into COVID credits and whose flights Qantas didn't subsequently cancel.

9   In June 2022, Qantas added a pop-up disclaimer to the redemption (but not the original booking) process which read: 'If you use a payment method other than Flight Credit on qantas.com lower fares may be available.'

10 When lockdowns returned, on 7 July 2021, Qantas removed the condition, including retrospectively for credits issued since March (though that didn't help the customers who'd already redeemed them). Also, Qantas never informed these customers of the restored flexibility of their credits. Qantas again reintroduced the 'equal or higher' condition on 1 August, but by 26 August it was again removed (retrospectively) as Sydney and Melbourne entered marathon lockdowns and domestic flying was stone dead until November.

11 Qantas emailed customers virtually daily with relentless sales offers. 'Earn 50 bonus status credits at BP', 'Discover where 65,000 bonus points could take you', 'Earn up to 20,000 points through Qantas Car Insurance', 'Five days only: earn 50 bonus status credits by making a booking' and 'Final days to join the Qantas Club for less' was a typical week.

12 Jetstar's credits had much lower average balances, but the same principal applies because a smaller amount of money was (generally speaking) worth more to the average Jetstar customer than to a Qantas customer.

13 Except when airlines interfere with natural prices, which they often do; for instance, airlines drop prices to prioritise market share over profit.

14 Qantas says 2026 is the soonest it can get its heavy maintenance checks completed by booked-out offshore engineering facilities.

15 That was true even after Qantas received three 787-9s in 2023. A Qantas A380 has more than twice the number of seats of a Qantas 787-9.

16 According to aviation data provider, Cirium.

17 Qantas was even using a dodgy calculation for the mishandled bag rates it reported in 2022, using a metric of per 1,000 passengers instead of per 1,000 bags (which was the industry standard). Unsurprisingly, its method made the mishandled bag rate look much lower. I pointed this out in my column in 2022 and Qantas flatly denied that this was its effect. The airline has since reverted to measuring mishandled bags per 1,000 bags and also (to the credit of the new regime) given me those numbers for 2022, which I've used in this book in place of the figures they were peddling at the time.

18 Indeed, this was Qantas' submission in compensation hearings before Justice Lee in March 2024.
19 To meet the Morrison government's strict cap and align with the capacity of the states' hotel quarantine programs, almost all arriving international flights had fewer than 20 passengers on board.

The Best CEO in Australia

1 A regular victim of Joyce's grillings was Colin Hughes, a key figure in the illegal decision to outsource Qantas' baggage handling, and by now promoted to the position of Qantas chief operating officer. The previous year in the Federal Court, Justice Lee had had 'some difficulty in accepting that Mr Hughes was always doing his best to give candid answers'. Whether Alan Joyce formed the same view we'll never know. Hughes left Qantas in October 2023.
2 Slot hoarding was the common practice of Qantas and Virgin of cancelling, at the last minute, domestic flights they never intended to operate. By keeping those flights scheduled, it deprived any challenger airlines of access to those precious take-off and landing slots in peak times.
3 From 2014, Chanticleer had to share that prime real estate with my column, Rear Window.
4 Qantas had included a slide summarising its government subsidies in every financial result presentation since COVID began, but dropped it from this presentation even though Qantas still received $260 million from the Commonwealth in the second half of financial 2022.
5 The small 'margin' on the subsidies, readers may recall, was a rationalisation advanced by Jetstar CEO Gareth Evans 18 months earlier.
6 The Qantas board's remuneration committee, which sets the key performance indicators of the CEO's at-risk pay arrangements, was until 2021 chaired by Paul Rayner, a former Big Tobacco executive. In the relevant period, its other members were Maxine Brenner, Belinda Hutchinson, Michael L'Estrange and Todd Sampson.
7 In Australia, companies generally prefer dividends over buy-backs because, for shareholders, there are tax advantages attached to dividends. For reasons I won't bore you with, those tax advantages weren't at that time available to Qantas shareholders.
8 According to the Parliamentary Budget Office, $16 billion of JobKeeper was paid in 2020 to companies whose revenue *increased* in the period. In those cases, JobKeeper padded shareholder dividends and executive bonuses.
9 Full-time equivalent positions, not actual people. There had been 37,000 of those.
10 About 1,200 of these job losses were in businesses that were sold, such as Qantas Catering, Qantas Defence Services and Helloworld.

11 Sell-side research used to be funded by the fat brokerage fees paid by fund managers to the investment banks' trading desks. The rise of index funds, ETFs and industry super funds saw those fees collapse and the banks slash their spending on research.

12 McLachlan ended up retiring after the 2023 grand final.

13 Goyder claimed falsely, just as David had, that baggage handling 'had been wholly outsourced by Easter last year when our flying was back at 100 per cent and service levels were maintained'. Actually, Qantas' flying – that's domestic and international – at Easter 2021 was back at just 30 per cent of pre-COVID levels. It was also only 58 per cent of Easter 2022 levels. International flying for all airlines at Easter 2022 was 1,034 per cent of Easter 2021, and post Qantas' (illegal) outsourcing, all airlines were relying upon the same overwhelmed baggage handling companies.

Joyce 1.0

1 That date has since been pushed out to 2026.

2 ULR stands for 'ultra long-range'.

3 XLR stands for 'extra long-range'.

4 A purchase option locks in the price and delivery time but allows the airline to back out of the purchase up to a certain date. It is sadly not an instrument available to Qantas passengers when they book their flights.

5 Neo stands for 'new engine option'.

6 Another 11 had been slated for the new premium airline called 'RedQ' which Joyce was briefly proposing to establish in Singapore or Malaysia. RedQ was quietly killed weeks later.

7 The remaining 21 standard A320s had been converted to neos and deferred.

8 The A321LR was a stretch version of the A320neo. LR stands for 'long-range'.

9 In the end, Jetstar's first A321LR arrived in July 2022.

10 Alternatively, if Qantas had only proceeded with the full 787 order, it could've increased the group's wide-body seat capacity by 55 per cent.

11 Assuming a like-for-like seat configuration.

12 It was also because of Emirates' other commercial advantages, which Qantas used to bellyache about right up until it decided to partner with them.

13 Jetstar took eleven 787-8s between 2013 and 2015. The 787-9 was 6 metres longer and could fly slightly further than the 787-8. The -8 entered service globally in 2011 whereas the -9 entered service in 2014.

14 The 787-9s launched other new routes: Perth–Rome in 2022 and Perth–Paris in 2024.

15 The A330 fleet was reduced to twenty-six in 2022 after Qantas converted two to freighters.

16 While the 787 operated the marathon Melbourne–Dallas route, for instance, the A330 could operate non-stop to Los Angeles only from Brisbane and with severe payload restrictions (meaning Qantas couldn't sell all the seats on the plane or carry any freight).

17 To keep them going, Qantas said, the A330s scheduled to retire last would undergo (another) cabin refurbishment in 2025. The A330s had already gone through cabin upgrades between 2014 and 2016.

18 By comparison, Singapore Airlines retired the last of its A330s in 2020 (the oldest of them were aged 11) while Emirates retired its final A330s in 2016.

19 As a major Boeing customer, Qantas received an approximate 40 per cent discount on the list price, but that was just as true in 2005 as it was in 2023.

20 The original fifteen are now more than 22 years old.

21 That was $366 million of statutory pre-tax profits, of course. Joyce's *underlying* profits were much higher!

22 Even despite that scalding lesson, Joyce failed to heed it in 2019 when at the absolute top of Qantas' fortunes, he agreed to stay until at least 2022.

23 I vividly remember that gruesome day of the pink envelopes at Qantas headquarters.

24 By 2015, those shareholders owned 83 per cent of Virgin Australia.

25 As explained in the opening chapter, an investment grade credit rating gave Qantas access to the cheapest and most attractive terms for its borrowings. Equally, losing it triggered an increase in interest rates on any new borrowings.

26 It was a fairly consistent position for Abbott and Hockey to take, given they had just cut subsidies to auto-makers, leading to the closure of the Australian car manufacturing industry.

27 For instance, $430 million of redundancy costs were excluded from Qantas' underlying loss. Funny, because in the following years, Qantas sure as hell didn't exclude from its underlying profit the corresponding savings arising from a lower headcount.

28 Across those seven years, the few small profits had been more than cancelled out by the larger losses.

29 The equity, or net assets, in a company is its total assets minus its total liabilities.

30 Qantas and Jetstar had more than 300 aircraft.

31 Journalists were unwittingly letting Qantas deduct the $1.1 billion company tax credit its loss had generated.

32 That was an underlying half-year profit, of course. It was a statutory half-year profit of $289 million. Joyce had only once ever delivered an *annual* profit that large.

33 This was a slightly dodgy figure because it excluded the fleet of Network Aviation, a fly-in, fly-out charter business Qantas acquired in 2011. In 2015, Network's fleet of Fokker 100s was more than 15 years old. Today, the average age of the 32 aircraft in the Network fleet is 25 years.

34 'Earnings accretive' means to increase the company's earnings per share.

35 When Qantas' aging fleet became an issue in 2023, Qantas' treasurer, Greg Manning, told the media that aircraft age 'has always been a factor in our fleet planning process but it's definitely not the main factor and hasn't been for some time'.

36 The double benefit of not buying aircraft, of course, was that Qantas also 'saved' by not having to depreciate them.

37 Again, this excluded Network Aviation.

38 By 2024, twenty-four of Qantas' 737-800s were aged 20 years or older. The first of their A321XLR replacements will not arrive until 2025.

39 Having said that, Qantas was still a leaner organisation in 2008 than it had been 10 years before that. Joyce's predecessors Geoff Dixon and James Strong had both also inherited far more bloated organisations than they'd handed to their successors, and they'd done exactly what Joyce had to do, which was incrementally make the airline more efficient.

40 The job was soon split, with human resources shunted under corporate strategy chief Rob Marcolina, and industrial relations fatefully devolved to chief lawyer Andrew Finch.

Fighting the Facts

1 Adjusted for inflation, airfares were still lower in the 1990s and 2000s.

2 Qantas return airfares (across all cabins), December 2022 versus December 2019.

3 Svensson filled the vacancy left by Steph Tully's promotion to CEO of Jetstar. Svensson previously ran Qantas' all-powerful revenue management department.

4 It certainly happened in 2008, when I worked at Qantas, right after the QF30 and QF72 accidents.

5 It's unclear whether Joyce was saying that the fuel price had risen 65 per cent in the previous six months or 65 per cent versus pre-COVID. Based on the data, I suspect the latter.

6 As the price of fuel globally is denominated in US dollars, Qantas is additionally exposed to the exchange rate between the Australian and US dollars.

7 Unit costs and unit revenues are costs and revenues per available seat kilometre.

8   Joyce and McGinnes wanted no such discussion with me. To the best of my recollection and records, McGinnes had not contacted me in more than two years.

9   That was actually Joyce's pay for 2017.

10 In 2018, a political furore erupted when the ABC's then chief economics correspondent, Emma Alberici, (relying on disreputable research by the Australia Institute) launched a botched attack on large Australian companies, including Qantas, over their non-payment of company tax, failing to explain (or perhaps even understand) that Qantas was drawing on carried-forward tax losses.

11 Qantas only began breaking out its Australian and foreign income tax payments separately in 2017 (for 2016 onwards). Before that, we had to guess which was which.

12 In retrospect, it was unfair of me to mention AviationKeeper, given every cent of that money went directly to Qantas crew.

13 Indeed, Qantas' first-half accounts released the prior week included a deferred tax asset of $136 million, which meant that Qantas considered it had actually *overpaid* tax by that amount. If the ATO ultimately agreed, then Qantas certainly did not pay $411 million in tax.

14 Qantas, meanwhile, had paid just $10 million of fringe benefits tax in 2022 (and in the vicinity of this amount in any given year). It was a rounding error. But that wasn't the only reason it was inadvisable to mention it. FBT was, after all, the tax payable by Qantas on the non-cash perks of its board and executives – like the novated leases on their luxury cars and the free first class flights for their whole families. If this was Qantas' financial contribution to the nation, it might've been better left unacknowledged.

15 McGinnes had a template. Another tedious op-ed in Hudson's name in October 2019 bore an uncanny resemblance to this one. Steve Purvinas, it began, 'said the turnaround of the national carrier was relative only to the financial loss presided over by the same management. And, therefore, any performance pay based on that turnaround was misplaced. So, in a nutshell: if you're on deck when there's a problem – and you fix it – it was probably your fault to begin with.' Strawman punchline!

16 In her piece, Hudson was indignant that I had characterised the government's freight subsidy as 'juicy', yet in 2024, Qantas admitted to me that the profit margin it had generated on that subsidy was $60 million.

17 'The Shonky awards were a bit shonky,' Alan Joyce also complained in a sit-down interview with *Sydney Morning Herald* columnist (and grateful Chairman's Lounge member) Peter FitzSimons.

18 To Joyce's credit, much of that headcount reduction up to 2019 was enabled by improved productivity.

19   While Qantas management did undertake an internal piece of work around the 8,500 jobs figure, it was never released publicly and did not even go to the Qantas board.

20   The dollar value used here for Joyce's share-based awards is based on the closing price of Qantas shares on the day my column was published (29 March). The ultimate value of the awards would be based on the share price when they vested in August.

21   Joyce received no short-term bonuses in those three years, and in 2020 even forwent his base salary for four months, before taking a 35 per cent cut to his base salary for a further three months.

22   At least, there was no indication at this stage that he would be penalised.

23   Joyce succeeded in becoming a case study in management courses, just not for the reasons he might've hoped.

Simon the Likeable

1   Goyder was specifically exercised that I'd described Joyce as 'the most despised [CEO] in Australia'. I'd assumed this was a relatively uncontroversial statement of fact. Indeed, a fortnight later, Curtin Research Centre director Nick Dyrenfurth described Joyce in the *Sydney Morning Herald* as 'in contention with RBA Governor Philip Lowe for the title of Australia's most loathed public figure'. Not that Joyce was a public figure, of course.

2   Powerless, that is, in the absence of attitudinal or behavioural change on his part, and he was way past that.

3   Even as opposition leader during the election campaign, Albanese would've travelled on Defence's VIP jets.

4   I wrote more than 40 columns about Rio Tinto in that period, so really, Qantas was getting off lightly.

5   Qantas announced the following month that L'Estrange would retire from the board at the AGM in November.

6   The AFL Commission was just a highfalutin term for the AFL's board. Members of the governing body were called commissioners instead of directors.

7   Auld was appointed CEO of the Australian Grand Prix Corporation in 2023 while Rogers became CEO of the Victoria Racing Club in 2024. One of the other candidates Rogers edged out for that job was Kylie Watson-Wheeler.

8   That threat can't have been too serious, of course, since Goyder would've gladly consummated it.

9   Qantas Domestic NPS was 35 for April 2023. In 2021, it was consistently in the fifties. Svensson even presented a chart at Qantas' investor day four weeks later which showed Qantas Domestic NPS remained well below pre-COVID levels, seemingly contradicting Joyce's, Hudson's

and his own previous public statements. NPS for May 2023 was even lower again, at 30, the top of another rapid descent.

10 In the month of April 2023, Qantas (excluding QantasLink) on-time arrivals were 74 per cent, beating Virgin but still lagging the long-term industry average of 82 per cent.

11 Joyce was verballing Goyder here, who had not actually said Joyce would've retired a few years ago if not for COVID, only that Joyce agreed in 2020 to stay until the pandemic was over. It was a subtle but material difference.

12 *The Australian* reported that 'the Qantas board has asked Alan Joyce to stay on as CEO for another three years or more, meaning he's set to head the carrier until at least 2022', while the *Australian Financial Review* wrote, 'The Qantas board has asked Alan Joyce to stay on as boss for a further three years amid a leadership reshuffle.' The headline on the *AFR*'s Chanticleer column that day was 'Qantas' Joyce deserves another three years'. Soon after, in the *Sydney Morning Herald*, columnist Stephen Bartholomeusz noted 'some raised eyebrows last week when Qantas revealed that the tenure of its chief executive, Alan Joyce, had been extended by at least three years'. This wasn't just some wild and unsourced rumour being reported as fact by three major newspapers. It was directly briefed to the journalists by Joyce's enforcer Andrew McGinnes.

13 The deal put Qantas passengers behind *The Australian*'s and the *AFR*'s digital paywall. Physical copies of the newspapers were also made available for purchase in Qantas lounges.

14 Those newspapers, and the *AFR*, came under Nine ownership in 2018 through the merger between Nine and Fairfax Media.

15 O'Sullivan wrote a book about Qantas, *Mayday*, which was published in 2015.

16 The contract with Nine sat with Svensson, who, as chief customer officer, ran lounges and wi-fi.

Alan's Enchanted Spectacles

1 The pilot centre opened in August 2024.

2 For the second two and a half years, it would convert to a regular lease (or 'dry-lease') and the aircraft would be operated by Qantas crew.

3 Finnair's longstanding strategy was to hub traffic between Asia and Europe. Having to fly around Russia, its immediate and sprawling neighbour, was ruinous to Finnair's Asian network, adding 40 per cent to the length of most flights. Helsinki–Tokyo, for instance, went from a 9-hour to a 13-hour flight.

4 Qantas did place that order three months later, in August 2023, with the first replacements slated to arrive in 2027.

5   Qantas attempted a takeover of Alliance Airlines in 2022 but the trans-
     action was blocked by the ACCC. Qantas still owns 20 per cent of
     Alliance.

6   Every single Qantas A330 operated international routes. Qantas had a
     mix of A330-200s and A330-300s. The two -200s that were converted
     to freighters had no pilot rest facilities for the longest flights, but
     identical -200s underwent minor upgrades (basically the addition of a
     curtain) so they could operate flights of up to 8.5 hours. Other -200s
     (with further cabin modifications) commonly operated flights of up to
     12.5 hours. The Finnair planes were -300s, which cannot fly as far as
     -200s but can carry 30-40 more passengers.

7   The assertion was wacky enough as it was, but deteriorated further
     with age. It soon became public knowledge that spare Finnair cabin
     crew would not be operating the Qantas flights. Rather, Finnair was
     using cheap Thai and Singaporean flight attendants from Asian labour
     hire agencies. The Flight Attendants' Association was incensed. 'If the
     FAAA's position is that Qantas partners aren't allowed to source labour
     as they see fit,' Qantas responded, 'that feels a bit like overreach.' Here,
     again, was McGinnes' strawman debating trick. Actually, the FAAA's
     position was quite validly that 'we were briefed [by Qantas] earlier in
     the year and the information we were given about saving the jobs of
     Finnair crew is inconsistent with what's happening in practice'.

8   *Deceit and Self-Deception: Fooling Yourself the Better to Fool Others* by
     Robert Trivers, Penguin, 2011.

9   *The Power Paradox: How We Gain and Lose Influence* by Dacher Keltner,
     Penguin, 2016.

10   Aviation industry groups and consulting firms for hire produced all
     sorts of reports containing travel forecasts right out to 2050. You
     wouldn't want to have made any investment decisions based on their
     reports immediately preceding September 11, the GFC, the swine flu
     pandemic or COVID-19.

11   There was a sole sceptical question posed later by an (unnamed) online
     participant. It went: 'History suggests periods of abnormal profits in
     domestic or international across the aviation market globally are unsus-
     tainable. Why will this be any different?' David's answer was telling:
     'At the risk of being slightly cheeky I could say, "Were you listening
     to the last 20 minutes?!"' He was all but saying, Did you forget to
     drink from the large cup of Kool-Aid we placed in your arm rest? The
     in-person audience showed no such scepticism.

12   The two most common reasons given by a public company CEO selling
     shares were: 1) to satisfy a tax obligation (often on the shares them-
     selves) or 2) to pay for a divorce, the euphemism being 'pursuant to a
     Family Court settlement'.

13 In August 2016, Brambles announced the retirement of its CEO Tom
     Gorman and in the subsequent five days, Gorman sold 99 per cent of
     his shares in the company for $8.4 million. In January 2017, a month
     before Gorman retired, the company issued a profit downgrade. On
     the day he retired, the stock had fallen 26 per cent since his share sale.
14 This is a pre-tax figure.
15 Joyce and Lloyd also owned a house in Palm Beach, purchased in 2015
     for $5 million.
16 The shares had vested many years ago, so any income tax obligation
     had already been met. There would be a capital gains tax liability on
     the $17 million sale of up to $3 million, but that wouldn't be payable
     until April 2025, well after the Mosman property had settled.
17 Indeed, nobody would even know, because once Joyce ceased being a
     director of Qantas, the company no longer had to file a publicly avail-
     able change in his shareholding with the ASX. And after 1 July 2024,
     it would no longer be disclosed in Qantas' annual report.
18 Based on $6.75 share price.
19 In September 2017, Treasury Wine Estates halted its buy-back while
     its CEO Michael Clarke and other executives sold shares. In February
     2018, Domino's Pizza CEO Don Meij sold his shares into the compa-
     ny's buy-back. After I published a column about it, the board agreed
     to 'adjust its buy-back protocols to address this perceived conflict'.
20 The ACCC ultimately reduced the scope of its action to 8,000 flights
     by eliminating 2,000 flights where customers were advised of their
     cancellation within two working days.
21 The investment market was *mostly* still supportive of Joyce. Fund
     manager Perpetual, which bought a 1.2 per cent stake in Qantas in its
     2020 equity raising (then increased its holding to 2.4 per cent), sold
     out of the company in May 2023.
22 Andrew McGinnes joined Joyce at the meeting with King. These
     meetings only became public knowledge on 18 September 2023, when
     Qantas disclosed them to a Senate committee in response to questions
     on notice.
23 This briefing note was released by the department to another Senate
     inquiry in September 2023.
24 Even the office of Treasurer Jim Chalmers (who the ACCC reports
     to) told industry stakeholders that 'we have no in-principle objection
     to an extension, providing it is a priority of Minister King'.
25 In 2012, right after Joyce grounded the airline, Qantas fell to 15th. Up
     until then, it had consistently been rated in the top five airlines in the
     world. Post-2012 Qantas was consistently named in the top 10.
26 The number of Qatar's requested new flights per week was incor-
     rectly stated as 21 or 28 in every media report (including all of mine)

and even by Catherine King. It was 28 to Australia's four 'gateways' (Brisbane, Melbourne, Perth and Sydney), and another seven that could fly to a gateway as long as it also touched a 'regional' airport (under this proviso Qatar was already operating a daily Doha–Melbourne–Adelaide service). Outside of those 35 flights, Qatar could operate an unlimited number of flights to non-gateway airports, and in 2023 it already operated a daily direct Doha–Adelaide service, taking its weekly flights to/from Australia to 42.

27 Doing so would've been entirely in character for Qatar Airways, which also owned 25 per cent of British Airways and Spain's Iberia, 10 per cent of Hong Kong's Cathay Pacific and 10 per cent of South American airline LATAM.

28 The European Union had insisted on a similar guarantee from Qatar but in return for rights to unlimited flights.

29 The fact of these meetings would only become public on 13 October 2023, when a Senate committee released Qantas' answers to its questions on notice. Joyce was accompanied by Andrew McGinnes to both meetings with King, but Joyce met alone with Albanese.

30 The women relied on the international Montreal convention governing airlines' liability to injured passengers, to which both Australia and Qatar were signatories.

31 King also complained to Qatar that its flights to Canberra had not been reintroduced after COVID. But then neither had Singapore Airlines'. King, says one staffer close to the process, 'just threw that in there as a bullshit thing and of course it was never mentioned again'.

32 King wrote to Qatar on 14 July, but the airline only received the correspondence on 20 July.

33 https://m.sydneyairport.com.au/corporate/media/corporate-newsroom/sydney-airport-traffic-performance-june-2023.

34 'I wouldn't link the two' were King's precise words to *SMH* journalist Latika Bourke.

A Very Valued Benefit

1 Under John Borghetti, Virgin Australia would introduce its own version called The Club, since rebranded to the Beyond Lounge.

2 These include American Airlines' Concierge Key, British Airways' Premier, Delta's 360°, Emirates' iO and United's Global Services.

3 Virgin received $2.30 of every $10 spent on domestic travel by the Australian Public Service.

4 A less understood advantage of Chairman's Lounge membership for consultants, anyone in a selling occupation, or merely the socially ambitious was the opportunity to peddle their services (or themselves) to this elite cohort. These members spent their hours in the lounge looking

around – or pretending not to look around – for chance conversations to orchestrate.

5 Of course, it's possible that those MPs didn't receive any flight upgrades.

6 Qantas only operated its London flights via Dubai until 2017, when it rerouted Sydney–London back through Singapore and funnelled Melbourne passengers onto its new Perth–London service. 'When [Joyce] started doing okay himself, then he didn't need his friend,' says former Qatar Airways' CEO Akbar Al Baker. 'So he has no problem to dump anybody, regardless of how close you are to him.'

7 Additionally, in Albanese's capacity as shadow transport minister, Qantas invited him (along with three ministers in the Turnbull government) to travel on its inaugural Perth–London flight in March 2018, then provided him with three nights' accommodation and a free flight home.

8 'Space available' upgrades carry a negligible monetary value (to the company as opposed to the traveller) because the unsold premium seat was perished inventory once the flight closed. But firm upgrades have a real accounting cost to the company because those seats are taken off sale and the airline foregoes ticket revenue it could've otherwise earned (or lower loyalty points liability by offering those seats up for redemption or points upgrade).

9 MPs elected after 2017 only received a Chairman's Lounge membership for themselves (unless they became ministers or officeholders). MPs elected before this received one for themselves and their spouse.

10 By 2023, the ratio was generally one primary Chairman's Lounge membership per million dollars of travel spend, though some of the largest and longest-standing corporate customers did better.

11 The actual number of flights Catherine King blocked was 35 per week, not 21, so the amount of local spending by visitors foregone would've actually been higher.

12 Doha airport is just 380 kilometres from Dubai airport and 320 kilometres from Abu Dhabi airport.

13 Alan Joyce claimed in 2012 that 'what the Emirates partnership does for us to be honest is secure jobs in the medium to long term'. In 2012, Qantas had 33,600 employees. By the time COVID hit in March 2020, Joyce had reduced headcount by 13 per cent, to 29,400. Really, what the partnership did was allow Joyce to outsource a significant part of his international business.

14 Measured by available seat kilometres. Emirates was the largest non-US carrier in the world.

15 In 2017, Qatar Airways had tried to buy 10 per cent of American Airlines but backed down after its offer received a frosty reception. The

bid coincided with Qatar's diplomatic isolation by its Gulf neighbours and the Trump Administration.

16   Star Alliance was the leading global airline alliance, followed by oneworld and then the smallest, SkyTeam.

17   The position rotates between the CEOs of member airlines.

18   Gurney left in July 2023 and oneworld did not name his successor, Nat Piper, until February 2024.

19   Emirates was allowed a whopping 126 flights per week – 105 into Brisbane, Melbourne, Perth and Sydney, and 21 into Adelaide. In 2023, it was flying 63 to the major cities and none to Adelaide.

20   In 2008, one of Albanese's first moves as a new minister in the incoming Rudd government was to appoint Eddington as the first chairman of Infrastructure Australia.

21   Even as late as 2011, Qantas lobbyists were briefing federal MPs on human rights abuses in the UAE, in a shadow campaign against Emirates (and Etihad). The very next year, Qantas jumped into bed with Emirates and started flying to Dubai itself.

22   This meeting was revealed in November 2023 by an FOI request lodged by *The Guardian*.

23   Qantas initially nominated a different executive to go in Joyce's place, but the Senate committee responded with a summons for Joyce himself to appear. Qantas confirmed this in a statement: 'Despite no other company CEO being required to attend, the committee subsequently insisted that Alan appear, which he will do.'

24   It was actually King's fifth different reason, if you count her private conversations linking Qatar's bid for new flights to the Doha airport incident and to Qatar's withdrawal from the Canberra route.

25   By comparison, Australia's most distrusted brand, Optus, had fallen only 18 rankings after its customers' privacy was seriously breached in a major cyber-attack.

26   Roy Morgan was using the incorrect $2 billion total of COVID subsidies being peddled by Qantas.

27   Chenoweth and Tadros would sweep the top honours in journalism, including the Gold Walkley and the Graham Perkin Award.

28   After I put the particulars of the internship to the prime minister's press office, a spokesman responded by email, 'What you have suggested is incorrect,' but then refused to clarify what was incorrect and declined to answer or return my multiple phone calls. The story was correct, of course, and soon after my column was published, it was independently verified by the *Financial Times*, the world's pre-eminent business newspaper, which ran the story on its front page.

29   This was the subject of a *Herald Sun* investigation in 2021.

30 Qantas reported an extraordinary 104 per cent return on invested capital. What this meant was that Qantas' profit in one year was greater than all of the capital (equity and debt) in the business. It showed the depletion of invested capital in Qantas over many years, and it showed the unsustainability of Qantas' level of earnings. The company's ROIC in 2019 was 18 per cent.

31 Actually, it was more like $800 million of costs out. The $1 billion was based on 100 per cent of pre-COVID capacity, and Qantas was only back to 77 per cent. Funnily enough, Joyce didn't explain this.

32 Andrew McGinnes remonstrated with the *SMH* journalist after the press conference for asking the question.

33 It was $3 million whether based on the previous day's (23 August) closing price or the closing price on 30 June. Joyce's swathe of bonus shares would vest imminently and push him back over the minimum, but he had been below the minimum for the 12 weeks since he sold $17 million shares on 1 June.

34 That was about the least incendiary thing Aitken said. He also said, 'It is hard to think of a business in Australia that charges more for its products and provides as poor a service'; 'Part of getting paid as CEO of a public company is copping some negative heat – if you don't like it then don't accept tens of millions in salary and bonus[es] and go drive an Uber'; and 'You often find after a long-term, high-profile CEO leaves a business that the market loves, you look back a few years from now and think, "Why didn't I sell my shares when he/she left?"'

35 Hudson's 'not as good as it gets' diagnosis was fuller: 'And that's not just with the cost programs, it's also going to be about the new aircraft that are coming. They're more fuel efficient, they've got a better range [and] they're going to open up new networks … Also, the loyalty business is going to continue to grow.'

36 Indeed, it was Qantas' argument in the case that David's and Jones' motivations were identical, which Justice Lee accepted.

37 Joyce was more dismissive in the press conference that morning, saying, 'Now, there's a little bit of nonsense around this. We're doing more than any other airline in the world to get people their credits back.'

38 Qantas' announcement conceded begrudgingly that 80 per cent of the credit-holders were actually entitled to a refund. Qantas couldn't issue those refunds automatically, said Markus Svensson, because 'the credit cards used for the purchase as far back as 2019 may have expired'. Of course, this would not have been a major issue had Qantas issued the refunds in March 2020, which was Qantas' prima facie contractual obligation to those customers.

39 Customers had to know they had to pre-register to be eligible for the double points. Only 5,000 customers took up the offer.

Grand Theft Aero

1   In response, every member of the committee except Sheldon declared their Chairman's Lounge memberships.

2   Joyce also disputed the fact that airfares were 40 per cent higher than pre-COVID, preferring his own innovative construction: Qantas' international fares from April to June 2023 were up just 10 per cent compared to the same period in 2019 if you adjusted for inflation. The absurdity of this was twofold: firstly, Qantas customers didn't get to use inflation-adjusted dollars to pay those fares. Secondly, Qantas' prices were a leading cause of the rampant inflation in the first place.

3   Jones went on Sky News three days later and complained that his statement had been 'completely uncontroversial (and) misconstrued' – including, presumably, by the transport minister. In Jones' defence, he had also said, 'I'm not a defender of Qantas in any respect ... The real issue here is that Qantas and other carriers are treating their customers respectfully, ensuring they're providing on-time services, the lowest possible price(s), baggage handling services that actually work and when planes are cancelled, you can get a refund or a credit that you can actually use.'

4   Well, sort of. While the money would no longer expire, customers still had to claim it.

5   The $570 million consisted of $365 million owed to Australian-based Qantas customers, $90 million to Australian-based Jetstar customers, and $115 million to overseas Qantas and Jetstar customers.

6   I use a dollar value based on the closing price of Qantas shares ($6.22) the day before the grant (24 August).

7   Also based on the 24 August closing price.

8   For non-financial readers, I am extrapolating what Murray said here. He literally said that the 'rating' – or earnings multiple – of Qantas shares would've remained significantly higher even if earnings were lower. That would've meant a higher share price.

9   Germany took a 20 per cent stake in Lufthansa which it has since sold. Government ownership of Air France-KLM increased to 37 per cent while the Italian government renationalised Alitalia (now ITA).

10   And, in fact, that was in circumstances where Qantas didn't have the legal right.

Captain, You Must Listen!

1   Of course, the Queensland government via its investment arm QIC was a small shareholder in Virgin Australia, which stood to benefit from any additional Qatar flights.

2   Agriculture minister Murray Watt aped the same senseless lines: 'Qatar Airways can already fly as many planes as they want into the Gold

Coast and Cairns but have chosen not to. There is no limit to the size of the planes they can fly into Brisbane.' Deputy Prime Minister Richard Marles claimed, 'We obviously want those airlines, those countries, which have that access to use it to its fullest possible extent. Qatar is not doing that right now.'

3 The Harris review had been sitting on the desks of King's predecessors Michael McCormack and Barnaby Joyce for the 18 months before that election.

4 Before that, a dozen years as Wesfarmers CEO put him at the absolute heart of Western Australia's establishment but also one out, one back from the reputational problems at its portfolio companies like Coles, Target and Kmart; all of them had their own CEOs.

5 That figure included the $6.5 million of deferred bonuses from 2020, 2021 and 2022 which were granted to Joyce on 25 August 2023, and is based on the closing price ($6.20) of shares that day.

6 Qantas' main argument in the High Court – which had already been rejected by the Full Court of the Federal Court – was that Lee had mistakenly applied the Fair Work Act's prohibited reason of preventing the employees from exercising their workplace right to strike. Qantas argued the prohibited reason only applied when employees had actually commenced exercising that right, not when employers acted to prevent them from exercising it in the future.

7 O'Halloran's predecessor as CEO, John Cloney, stayed on as chairman for 12 years before Hutchinson replaced him, so QBE clearly had anti-quated ideas about what good corporate governance looked like.

8 Twenty times larger by market capitalisation, which is the total value of all shares on issue; rightly or wrongly, this is the measure by which company director pay is generally set.

9 The estimated value of those post-employment flights was already accounted for in the directors' remuneration disclosures – albeit at the discounted rate.

10 For instance, on a single SYD–LHR first class return ticket, the $18,000 fare plus full-freight FBT should've come out at $34,000, but Qantas was stating it as remuneration of just $13,000.

11 Also given the age profile of the board, most (though certainly not all) of the directors' children were older than twenty-six so ineligible for the benefits.

12 One of the answers revealed that six Qantas staff had passes to Parliament House, which were sponsored by Catherine King, Michael McCormack and Barnaby Joyce (all transport ministers), Simon Birmingham (a former tourism minister), Liberal MP Julian Leeser and Andrew Bragg, the Liberal senator who in 2022 said, 'There's no question there are far too many vested interests in this building and if

I had it my way, I would have it locked to (them).' The building was also swarming with hypocrites.

13   Though it was an easy benefit to give up for an ACT senator who lived a short drive from Parliament House.

14   ISS had recommended against Brenner's election to the Telstra board over her Qantas record, but confusingly, supported the re-election of Sampson to the Qantas board.

Feel the Difference?

1   Finch was at least stripped of responsibility for industrial relations, which was placed under Hudson's new chief people officer, Catherine Walsh, who was hired from PwC, of all places.

2   Qantas flew Australians from Tel Aviv to London, then back to Australia on its regular services. The RAAF air-lifted Australians from Tel Aviv to Dubai and then Qatar operated a special flight from Dubai.

3   Turkish Airlines' rights would increase to 28 weekly flights in 2024 and 35 flights in 2025, yet they would mostly go unused.

4   It's a fine line, of course. IR lawyers can advise a company whether its genuinely held reasons for a decision are legally sound. But they cannot advise a company how to sack union members by hiding behind permitted reasons that aren't legitimately the company's reasons for doing it (and I'm not suggesting Freehills was doing this).

5   Also because of Qantas' ticketing system limitations, from 1 January that remaining balance could only be refunded, not used for flights.

6   'Breakage' revenue on flight credits (when they expire after 12 months without having been redeemed) would continue to generate even more annually.

7   This was a misleading comparison because in many cases those airlines provided free residential accommodation to their cabin crew.

8   The media dutifully reported Qantas' 'underlying' profit of $2.1 billion, still 16 per cent lower than in 2023.

9   Commonwealth Bank CEO Ian Narev was stripped of his long-term incentive shares for 2018, but unlike Joyce he hadn't met the hurdles for those shares to be paid. In 2016, Rio Tinto suspended $30 million worth of former CEO Sam Walsh's LTI shares, but ultimately paid them in full in 2020 and 2021.

Afterword

1   Despite taking the same side of the Qatar debate, I had written savage columns about Hrdlicka – including one only six months earlier entitled 'Roll up, roll up, for Bain and Jayne's pea and thimble trick'.

Acknowledgements

I wish to acknowledge, foremost, my wife's immense efforts caring for our new son (and me) while I spent nearly ten months down this rabbit hole. And my mother for all her love and help. My profound thanks to Lance Reynolds, whose idea this book was and who – let's face it – tricked me into writing it. To Ben Ball at Simon & Schuster, my other obstetrician. I really have loved working with you but I pray this will be an only child. My thanks also to Meredith Rose, my meticulous and forgiving editor.

My huge appreciation to Leroy Lobo for keeping me on the field. To Michael Roddan and Lachlan Cartwright, whose excellent advice got me started. To Lucinda Holdforth, Leigh Sales and Pam Williams for talking me through the valleys of self-doubt. Adele Ferguson, Hedley Thomas and Kate McClymont for their generosity in reading early chapters. My former *AFR* colleagues, especially aviation reporters Lucas Baird and Ayesha de Kretser. Thanks also to Amelia McGuire at the *Sydney Morning Herald*.

Thank you to Danielle Keighery at Qantas, and Henry Budd, who got lumped with the unenviable task of being the airline's liaison officer with Satan.

To the multitude of Qantas people who trusted me with their stories, and various others who assisted me but quite understandably don't want their names anywhere near mine.

And to all of my friends whose messages I never returned and invitations I had to decline in 2024.

This is the page you're told to write thirty minutes before the print deadline. Thus, I apologise to whoever I've forgotten. I know there'll be someone.

Index

Abbott, Tony, 274
Abbott government, 156, 201
Aer Lingus, 259
ABC, 197, 200
  7:30, 246–9
  ABC News, 200
  ABC Radio, 278
  AM, 273
  Media Watch, 16, 204, 310
  Radio National, 258–9
The Age, 201, 276
Air New Zealand, 14, 42
  post-COVID seat sales, 129
  RepTrak rank, 180
  Virgin Australia stake, 155
Airbus, 150
  A220, 151
  A320, 93, 151, 320
  A320neo, 151, 161–2
  A321, 151
  A321LR, 151
  A321XLR, 151, 164
  A330, 12, 119, 129, 152,
    154–5, 161, 163, 206–8,
    239
  A350, 150, 154, 271
  A350-1000ULR, 19, 150
  A380, 11, 43, 94, 97, 119, 129,
    152–5, 161, 163, 170, 271
  non-aviation component
    manufacturing, 120
aircraft *see also by manufacturer*
  biggest unfulfilled order,
    150–2
  deferred defects, 120
  depreciation, 158–9
  fuel costs, 172
  major heavy maintenance
    checks schedule, 163
  'minimum equipment list', 120
Airline Partners Australia
  (APA), 7–8
Aitken, Angus, 245
Al Baker, Akbar, 219, 234–6,
  271, 291
Al Meer, Badr Mohammed, 311
Albanese, Anthony, 19, 61, 260
  Australian Open attendance,
    300
  big business, relationship with,
    300
  Dutton's criticism, 255

flight and club membership
  benefits, 229–31, 243–4,
  250
government stake in Virgin, 39
Hamad Airport incident,
  223, 273
Indigenous Voice to
  Parliament, 240–1
Joyce and, 61, 189, 216, 221–2,
  240, 257–8, 266–7, 272,
  286, 290–1, 300
King, support of, 242
net favourability rating, 241
Qantas, support of, 189–90,
  240, 270, 298
Qantas-Emirates tie-up,
  support of, 234
Qatar Airways air rights
  stance, 5, 221–2, 234,
  257–8, 270–2, 311
Rex, opinion on, 311
Albanese, Nathan, 225, 231, 240,
  242–4, 250
Albanese government, 108, 217,
  219, 224
  airline competition, approach
    to, 257, 271
  Aviation Green Paper, 257,
    272–3
  Qantas lobbying, 216, 272,
    285–6
  Qatar Airways decision, 219,
    298
  support of Qantas, 224, 260–1,
    267
Allco Finance, 7
Alliance Airlines, 207
Allsop, James, 297
Amadeus ticketing system, 306
American Airlines, 130, 154, 236
Andrews, Daniel, 89
Ansett, 31, 59, 82, 154
  Managers Lounge, 226
The Australian, 38, 199–200, 239
Australian Airlines, 10, 226
Australian and International
  Pilots Association (AIPA),
  94, 280
Australian Competition and
  Consumer Commission
  (ACCC)
  airfares, 169, 216

Airline Competition
  Taskforce, 215–17, 256–7
airline monitoring powers, 45,
  259–260
cartel conduct authorisation,
  233
complaints about Qantas,
  86, 224
COVID-19 flight credits, 249
domestic aviation industry,
  observations on, 216,
  224, 312
'ghost flight' lawsuit, 128, 214,
  258–60, 277, 293, 296–7,
  305–6
Joyce's opinion, 215
Qantas flight credit email,
  122
Virgin complaint, 34
Australian Council of
  Superannuation Investors
  (ACSI), 261, 275, 278, 293
Australian Council of Trade
  Unions (ACTU), 108–9
Australian Financial Review
  (*AFR*)
  AFR Magazine, 16, 20
  airline competition, 273
  Chairman's Lounge and, 20,
    204, 225, 315
  Chanticleer column, 21, 26,
    43, 95, 136–7
  Clark interview, 300
  commercial deal, 200
  complaint by Joyce and
    Goyder, 184, 190–1, 316
  corporate heads' contact, 173
  COVID-19 flight credit
    manipulation, 126, 249,
    252–4
  Goyder and, 145, 147
  Hudson and, 176–8, 182, 188,
    199, 246
  Joyce and, 143, 169–70, 259,
    261
  Oldmeadow interview, 59
  PwC tax leaks scandal, 242
  Qantas aging fleet, 163
  Qantas boycott, 200–4
  Qantas culture and
    management dynamic,
    315–16

Qantas customer complaints, 219
Qantas' opinion, 192
Qatar Airways air rights campaign, 223
Sharp's op ed, 84, 86
symbiosis with Qantas, 14–15
Tully and, 130–1
Australian Football League (AFL), 192–3
CEO candidates, 193–7
Gather Round, 190, 194
Australian Grand Prix, 21, 112
Australian Licensed Aircraft Engineers' Association, 89, 106
Australian Open, 299–300
Australian Securities Exchange (ASX), 26, 38, 82
Australian Services Union (ASU), 104, 115
Australian Shareholders' Association, 293
AviationKeeper, 117, 137, 175

Bailey, Fran, 5
Bain Capital, 40–1, 45, 82, 90, 220
Baird, Bruce, 3–5, 8
Baird, Lucas, 131
Barron, John, 204
Bates, Stephen, 291
Bensan, Sondal, 147
Benson, Simon, 31–2
Berejiklian government, 89
The Betoota Advocate, 174–5
BGH Capital, 35, 39–40
Biden, Joe, 266
bin Khalifa Al Thani, Sheikh Khalifa, 222
bin Rashid Al Maktoum, Sheikh Mohammed, 6
bin Saeed Al Maktoum, Sheikh Ahmed, 6–7
Birmingham, Simon, 90, 288
Bishop, Robin, 35, 39
Boeing
717, 151, 312
737, 117, 151, 154, 163–4, 170, 312
747, 12
747-400, 153
777, 271
777X, 19
787-9 Dreamliner, 16, 19, 24–5, 27–8, 97, 152–4, 161–3, 206
non-aviation component manufacturing, 120
Bonza, 217, 224, 311–12
Borden, Jenny, 59, 262
Borghetti, John
Qantas CEO candidate, 9–11, 22
resignation, 11
Virgin Blue CEO, 155, 202
Bornstein, Josh
Oldmeadow, impression of, 59, 62

outsourcing disputes, 78
Qantas, opinion of, 54
TWU v Qantas and, 63, 65, 70, 75, 77, 80
union representation, 54
Boyd, Tony, 136
Boyle, Jane, 14–15
Brandis, George, 56
Branson, Richard, 23, 155
Brenner, Maxine
Qantas directorship, 262, 282, 293
Qantas travel benefits, 284–5
questioning of Joyce, 283
retirement, 292
Telstra election, 293
British Airways, 132, 236, 238
Bromberg, Justice Mordy, 106–7
Bromwich, Justice Robert, 106–7
Bureau of Infrastructure and Transport Research Economics, 114
Burke, Tony, 109, 239
Business Council of Australia, 109–10
Byron, Stephen, 217, 256, 313

CAE, 94
Callachor, Damian, 220
Canavan, Matt, 239
Caon, David, 16
Carter, Colin, 314
Cass-Gottlieb, Gina
airline sector ombudsman, call for, 217
domestic aviation market description, 216, 224
Qantas ghost flight penalty, 258–9, 297, 305
Cathay Pacific, 129, 236–7
Certis, 112–13
Chalmers, Jim, 256–7, 260
Chenoweth, Neil, 242
Chessell, James, 200, 203, 243
Chief executive officer (CEO) see also by name
appointment practices, misconceived, 195–6
celebrity status, 18, 317
Fysh's guiding principles, 267–8
CHOICE
Shonky Award, 178
Civil Aviation Safety Authority, 120, 227
Clark, Tim, 7, 235–7, 300
Classic Reward redemptions, 30
Cleary, Andrew, 15
Clifford, Leigh
appointment of Joyce, 158
capital considerations, 162
Chairman's Lounge, appraisal of, 228
Joyce's share sale, 215
mentorship, 166
opinion of Joyce, 9, 19, 145, 158
ConnectionSaver software, 164
Cook, Roger, 270
Cormann, Mathias, 38, 40

Coronavirus pandemic
see COVID-19 pandemic
Corporate Confidence Index (CCI), 143–4, 148
Costello, Peter, 8, 11, 256
Cottee, Annabelle, 16
COVID-19 pandemic
'11 weeks' narrative, 27–9, 131–2
see also 'eleven weeks' narrative
airport security agents, 113
airport staff shortages, 113–14
aviation industry's recovery modelling, 42–3
AviationKeeper, 117, 137
baggage mishandling, 116, 128, 132, 135, 142
border closures, 23, 27, 82–3
border openings, 97–8
close contact rule exemption, 114
'eleven weeks' narrative, 27–9, 131–2
see also '11 weeks' narrative
engineering backlog, 120
European governments' support, 266
exploitation by Qantas, 43–4, 81
first confirmed Australian infection, 20
flight cancellations, 22, 24, 28, 30, 82, 86, 98, 114, 122–3, 126, 128, 132, 306
Great COVID Reopening of 2022, 30
impact on travel industry, 98, 264
infection rates, 97–8
international travel, resumption of, 134
JobKeeper scheme, 28, 36–40, 50–3, 83, 90, 113–17, 139, 175, 177, 266, 304
Joyce's observations on passengers, 113
Joyce's responses, 22, 46–7, 95–6, 98, 101, 135–6
lockdowns, 46, 96
mandatory testing for international travel, 101
Morrison government aviation industry support, 23, 83
on-time performance, 114–17, 127–8, 132, 142
passenger demand for flights, 98
Qantas brand, impact on, 130–1, 134, 136, 268
Qantas carriage contract, flight cancellations and, 22, 24
Qantas cash reserve, 27, 84–5, 99
Qantas domestic capacity, increase in, 133
Qantas executive bonuses, 21, 99
Qantas financial status, 96, 99, 127, 137

COVID-19 pandemic *continued*
Qantas flight credits, 24,
45–6, 82, 85, 122–7,
182, 245–53, 259, 306,
307
Qantas flight grounding, 21–2,
27, 42
Qantas GMC demeanour, 167
Qantas ground handling
layoff, 55
Qantas ground handling
outsourcing, 78, 133–4,
293
Qantas inflight service, 118
Qantas international flight
relaunch, 97
Qantas operational reliability,
113–15
Qantas recovery and retention
plan, 99–101
Qantas rescue flights, 20–1
Qantas seat cut, 22, 98
Qantas staff bonuses, 105
Qantas staff cuts, 101–2, 115,
139, 181
Qantas staff training, impact
on, 117–18
Qantas 'underlying/adjusted'
profit, 47–8
Qantas workforce stand-down,
23–4, 27–8, 96, 101, 184
Qatar Airways' flight
continuity, 220, 237,
258, 290
quarantine for overseas
passengers, 22
repatriation flights, 21, 51–2,
101, 103–4, 220
resumption of services, 95, 117
'revenge travel', 101, 129
Rex online refund portal, 85
seat capacity, recovery of,
128–30, 210
self-quarantine, 21–2
skilled labour loss, 117
tourism industry support
package, 83
United States governments
support, 266
vaccination rollout, 95–7
Virgin Australia
nationalisation proposal,
32–4
Virgin Australia seat cut, 98
WHO designation, 21
Cromwell Group, 88
Crosby, Lynton, 8
Culbert, Geoff
COVID-19 comment, 21
domestic airline competition,
224
post-COVID-19 travel chaos,
112–13
Qatar inquiry evidence, 277

Daily Mail, 319
Daily Telegraph
'CON AIR' headline, 260
COVID-19 flight credits, 255

David and, 25, 131–3
Qatar Airways, 234
'Re-Joyce' pun, 14, 263
Dash 8 Q-400 turboprops, 312
David, Andrew
criticism of Joyce and, 185
defence of COVID-19
operations, 25, 131–4
docking, 318
inflight incidents, 170
international travel conditions,
211
JobKeeper stance, 50
La Spina's duties, absorption
of, 49
Oldmeadow's relationship with
Qantas, 58
request to Joyce to shorten
trip, 135
sacking of staff, 318
TWU v Qantas evidence, 64,
66–7, 70–1, 75–8, 80,
107, 247
Davidson, Louise, 278, 294
de Kretser, Ayesha, 223
de Rome, Belinda, 11
Deloitte, 39–41, 45, 287
Delta, 164
Department of Foreign Affairs
and Trade (DFAT), 21, 103,
290, 298
Department of Infrastructure
and Transport, 221
Devine, Miranda, 15–16
Diamond Princess, 21
Dick, Cameron, 89
Dillon, Andrew, 190, 197
Dixon, Geoff
advertising, 52
AFR aviation reporters and, 15
aircraft orders, 152, 154
Baird and, 3
child, 9
Clark's recollection, 300
'constant shock syndrome', 21
engineers' pay increase, 11
meeting with Mullen, 302
politicians and, 3, 7–8
pre-tax profits, 155
privatisation and efficiency,
264
purchase of 737-800s, 154
Qantas leveraged buyout, 7
retirement, 14
Singapore Airlines' market
bid, 6
speechwriter, 10
succession and, 9
two-brand strategy, 313
Doyle, Rohan, 71–3, 304–5
Dubinsky, Rick, 60
Dutton, Peter, 255, 273, 313

Earnings Before Interest Tax
(EBIT), 210
Echo Law, 248–9, 259
Eddington, Rod, 237–8, 266
Elliott, Shayne, 256
Embraer, 207

Emirates, 6
A380 fleet, 153
Adelaide flights, 258
adviser, 7
event sponsorship, 6, 300
increased access grant, 299
in-flight wi-fi, 164
post-COVID seat sales, 129
Qantas alliance, 7, 156, 229,
233–7
Qatar Airways, relationship
with, 233, 236, 300
Wolgan Valley development,
6–7
Enterprise bargaining agreement
(EBA)
ground crew, 61–2
long-haul cabin crew, 101–5,
108, 110
pilot, 119
short-haul cabin crew, 110
Epstein, David, 11
Etihad Airways
cabin crew training facility
flight allocation use,
post-COVID, 277
Qatar Airways, competition
with, 233
seat sales, post-COVID, 129
state subsidisation, 220
UAE frequencies for use, 299
Virgin Australia alliance,
14–15, 23, 155
Evans, Gareth, 51
EY, 65–6

Fair Work Commission, 61, 65,
102, 110
Fairfax Media, 201–2
Farrell, Don, 224, 290
Farrow, John, 111
Ferguson, Adele, 201
Ferguson, Sarah, 246–9
Finch, Andrew
ACCCC claim, defence to,
296–7
allegation against TWU, 50
power of attorney delegation,
76, 303
Qatar inquiry, 285–9, 309
resignation, 309
Saar review, 318
TWU v Qantas evidence,
67–77, 104–8, 276, 309
Find My Credit online portal,
248
Finnair, 206–8, 239
Flanagan, Maurice, 6
Flight Attendants' Association of
Australia (FAAA), 101–3,
108–11
Flight Centre, 20, 128, 270
Follett, Matthew, 73
Forager Funds, 147
Freshwater Strategy, 241
Frydenberg, Josh
ACCC airline monitoring
power, 45
aviation support package, 23

domestic aviation market
    competition, 45, 215
JobKeeper announcement, 36
Rex support, 40, 83
Virgin takeover, 38–9
Future Fund, 293
Fysh, Hudson, 267–8, 307–8

Gaske, Emeline, 104, 115,
    121–2
Ghoshal, Sumantra, 165
Gibian, Mark
    TWU v Qantas hearing, 68–75
    union representation, 55
Gillard government, 61
Gissing, John, 79–80, 185, 262
Glass Lewis, 293
Global Financial Crisis, 155, 165
Goodwin, James, 60, 224
Goyder, Janine, 145
Goyder, Richard
    AFR op ed, 145–6
    AIPA assessment, 280
    CCI reference, 143, 148
    CEO naming gaffe, 200
    character, 19, 275, 315
    complaint against AFR, 184,
        187–91, 218, 316
    COVID-19 position, 96
    decision-making style, 192–4,
        196
    defence of Joyce, 187
    defence of Qantas, 278, 292,
        294
    dynamic with Joyce, 167, 186,
        189, 199
    exchanges with author, 190–1,
        218–19
    executive appointments, 34,
        144, 167, 193, 319
    Hudson, support for, 185–6
    investor relations, 278–9,
        291–2
    Joyce and, vii, 1, 143–5, 148,
        187, 262–3, 274, 317–19
    Joyce's bonus 'claw-back'
        claim, 277–8
    'mistakes were made'
        acknowledgement, 292–3
    'Over to you, Gil' nickname,
        193
    preservation of role, 274
    Qantas board 'fully engaged'
        claim, 261–2
    Qantas board tenure, 281
    Qantas reliability
        pronouncement, 169
    Qantas share buy-back,
        defence of, 146–7
    Qatar inquiry, 285, 288–9
    remuneration, 285
    reputational damage, 321
    response to criticism, 276
    retirement, 292, 319
    sale of Joyce shares, 214, 279
    scepticism of ability, 167
    Simon the Likeable
        comparison, 194
    successor, 292, 301

survivability of football codes
    and COVID-19, 34
travel benefits, 285
work without pay election, 21
GQ, 18
Grant, Martin, 16
Gray, Ben, 8, 35, 39–40
Gregg, Peter, 9, 11
Gregory, Sean, 242
The Guardian, 198, 245
Gurney, Rob, 236

Hamad International Airport
    (Doha), 222–5, 273
Harbison, Peter, 26
Harcourt, Tansy, 14–15
Harle, Simon, 8, 35
Harris, Peter, 224
Harris review, 256, 273
Haydon, Jodie, 231
Hazzard, Brad, 114
Hehir, Grant, 36
Henry, Ken, 256
Herald Sun, 260
Herbert Smith Freehills, 55–6,
    71–3, –7, 303
Hewitt, Angus, 245
Hey, Jacqueline, 282–3, 292, 301
HNA Group, 23
Hockey, Joe, 9, 11, 156
Hogan, James, 14
Hogg, Kate, 13
Holdforth, Lucinda, 10, 13–14
Howard, John, 11
Howard government, 5, 7–9
Howes, Paul, 15
Hrdlicka, Jayne, 322
    Qatar air rights concerns,
        221–3, 232–3, 255–6,
        270–1, 300
    resignation, 309
    Tennis Australia role,
        299–300
Hudson, Vanessa
    AFR tax op ed, 176–8, 182,
        188, 310
    apology to customers, 279,
        286, 306
    approach, 308–10
    bonus for cost reduction, 280
    booking and change fee
        amendment, 307
    commencement at Qantas, 59
    customer complaints, dismissal
        of, 199
    customer improvements, 264,
        279
    docking, 318
    domestic market, comment on,
        312–13
    'Feel the Difference' mantra,
        309
    flight credit manipulation,
        249
    flight credit rule change, 307
    investor presentation, 210–12
    Joyce's opinion, 182, 186
    Keighery hiring, 14
    loan arrangements, 24–7

'low speak up' culture and, 318
Marcolina appointment,
    309–10
media queries, responses to,
    197–8, 245
Mullen and, 320
promotion to chief financial
    officer, 19
Qantas board changes and,
    296
Qantas CEO appointment,
    197, 200
Qantas CEO candidacy,
    185–6
Qantas performance claims,
    244, 265
Qantas property footprint
    review, 87–91
Qatar inquiry, 285–90
scepticism, 309
trading update announcement,
    279–80
Yangoyan promotion, 104
Hughes, Colin, 63–6, 77
Hume, Jane, 250, 256
Hutchinson, Belinda, 282, 294
Hywood, Greg, 201–2, 204

'I Still Call Australia Home'
    commercial, 19, 52, 133
Iberia, 236
Indigenous Voice to Parliament,
    240–1, 260, 316–17
Industrial relations
    cabin crew pay deal, 102–3
    cabin crew reduction, 117,
        238–9
    EBAs see Enterprise
        bargaining agreement
        (EBA)
    industrial action, 59–62, 106,
        110–11
    Jetstar ground crew, 62
    Jobs and Skills Summit,
        changes arising from,
        108–9
    Joyce's stance, 18, 62, 109
    licensed aircraft engineers,
        11–12, 106, 121
    pilots' strike, 59
    Qantas' approach and attitude,
        12, 54, 104–10
    Qantas flight grounding,
        59–62, 110
    Qantas staff 'fragmentation',
        109
    right to strike, 63–4, 103, 105
    Seremetidis stand down,
        297–8, 315
    shutdown, 60–1
    TWU and see Transport
        Workers' Union (TWU)
    wage policies, 61–2, 105–6,
        184
International Air Transport
    Association (ATA), 43,
    211, 311
Isom, Robert, 236
ISS, 275, 293

Jackson, Margaret, 5–10
Jacques, Jean-Sébastien, 191
Jetstar
  '380 million airfares for under
    $100' claim, 253
  A320, 93, 151
  A320neo, 161
  COVID-19 flight credits, 22,
    122, 248, 252–4, 260
  domestic market capacity,
    82, 312
  fleet management, 43, 151–2
  forced divestment, 313
  flight cancellations, 22, 132
  government assistance, 51
  ground crew strike, 62
  growth, 55, 152–3
  head office consolidation, 87–8
  international market share,
    152, 156
  Joyce's role, 9, 55
  on-time performance, 114,
    116, 128, 132, 142, 169
  outsourcing, 49, 116
  pilot training, 206
  recruitment post-COVID-19,
    121
  resumption of domestic
    aircraft service, 95
  seat availability
    post-COVID-19, 129
  staff cuts, 50
  TWU pay deals, 60
  undercutting, 312
Jobs and Skills Summit, 108–9
Jones, Paul
  CEO candidacy, 309
  Lee J's findings, 247, 309
  TWU v Qantas evidence, 58,
    64, 71, 77, 81, 247, 309
Jones, Stephen, 257
Joyce, Alan
  7:30 interview, 246–9
  '11 weeks' narrative, 25–8
    see also 'eleven weeks'
      narrative
  787-9 Dreamliner inaugural
    flight, 16
  A330 freighter conversion,
    justification of, 207–8
  ACCC concerns, dismissal of,
    215, 217
  acknowledgement of criticism,
    169–70
  Aer Lingus flight booking
    model, 259
  AFR advertising boycott, 200,
    203–4
  AFR businessperson of the
    year, 18
  age at appointment, 166
  airfare prices, 171–3
  Albanese and, 61, 189, 216,
    221–2, 240, 257–8, 266–7,
    272, 286, 290–1, 300
  'announceables', 181–2
  annus mirabilis, 18
  apology to frequent flyers, 137
  argument with Devine, 15

The Betoota Advocate satire,
  174–5
  board supervision of, 317
  celebrity status, 18, 166
  CEO designate, naming as, 11
  CEO role, perception of, 140
  Chairman's Lounge and
    see Qantas Chairman's
    Lounge
  challenges to, 1, 19–20, 29,
    166–7, 283, 315–16
  character assessment, 87, 91,
    140–1, 158, 166–7, 185,
    192, 199–205, 208–10,
    215, 247, 251–2, 263, 268
  Clark's support, 300
  Clifford's opinion, 9, 19, 145,
    158
  'command-and-control
    structure', adoption of,
    167, 315, 320
  Companion of the Order of
    Australia, 18
  compartmental thinking, 205
  complaint against *AFR*, 184,
    187–8, 192, 316
  concession on decline in
    standards, 136
  cost reduction program, 44,
    121, 155, 217–18, 264
  COVID-19 situation,
    optimisation of, 43–4, 95
  criticism by corporate heads,
    136
  customer service, attitude
    towards, 169, 265–6, 268
  decision-making authority,
    69–70
  delayed capital expenditure,
    benefits of, 164–5
  delegation of authority, 70, 76,
    142, 303
  'democratisation of air travel'
    claim, 253
  depreciation of aircraft,
    interpretation of, 159
  'efficiency' rationale for record
    profit, 217
  egging of mansion, 131, 212
  'eleven weeks' narrative, 25–8
    see also '11 weeks' narrative
  email to staff on COVID-19
    'challenges', 135–6
  engineer recruitment
    announcement, 180–1
  Fairfax Media coverage, 201–2
  final financial results
    announcement, 244
  Finnair wet-lease, explanation
    of, 208
  fleet management, 150–5,
    160–4, 246, 264–5
  flight credit manipulation, 127,
    247–9, 259–60
  flight grounding, 21, 110
  flight training centre
    dedication, 206
  Fysh, comparison with,
    267–8

  'giant wave of international
    airline capacity' lament,
    156
  government assistance to
    Virgin Australia, stance
    on, 32–5
  Goyder and, vii, 1, 143–5, 148,
    187, 262–3, 274, 279,
    316–19
  GQ man of the year, 18
  growth of Jetstar, 152–3
  hiring, 9
  'holy trinity' achievement,
    148
  identity as CEO, 205
  illusory truth effect and, 26
  impact and influence, 10,
    91, 165–6, 263, 266–9,
    275, 315
  industrial relations stance, 18,
    62, 109–10
  investment minimisation
    tactic, 166
  investors and, 215, 275–6, 278
  JobKeeper scheme, 36–7
  King meeting, 221, 238
  'kitchen-sinking', 158
  leadership style, 1, 167, 185,
    315, 317, 320
  legacy mode, adoption of, 199
  liability, 184
  marriage, 18
  marriage equality campaign,
    18, 166, 316–17
  McManus' impression, 110,
    268
  media questioning, 344–5
  mentor, 166
  net favourability rating, 241
  O'Brien meeting, 263
  post-COVID holiday, 131,
    135, 140
  power, 19, 209–10
  praise for Hudson, 182, 186
  profit inflation, 155, 159–60
  property portfolio, 131,
    212–13
  public approval, value of, 205
  public figure, renunciation as,
    140–1, 181, 208
  public scrutiny, 204
  Qantas board, relationship
    with, 283
  Qantas financial status,
    assertions on, 26–9, 139,
    157–8, 244, 264–5
  Qantas headquarters
    relocation, 93
  Qantas post-COVID
    performance claims,
    145–6, 169, 171–2, 197
  Qantas share buy-back,
    motivation behind, 146–7
  Qantas shareholding, 45, 96,
    100, 137–8, 148, 160,
    212–13, 244–6, 261, 264
  Qantas workforce stand-
    down, 24
  Qatar inquiry, 286

relationship with Oldmeadow, 59, 62
remuneration and bonuses, 1, 18, 96, 100–1, 108, 137–8, 148, 159, 160, 183–4, 213, 246, 251–2, 261–3, 275–6, 277–8, 282, 293, 318
'reprioritisation of capital', 161
reputation, 19–20, 49, 179, 181, 215, 260–1, 265
resignation, 20, 261–2, 267, 272
resignation requests, 141, 143
retirement, 26, 213, 262
revenue optimisation practices, 259
review of media coverage, 185
Rex, opinion on, 84–7
sale of shares, 212–14, 244–5, 279, 316
Senate questioning *see* Senate inquiry into Qatar decision (Qatar inquiry; Senate Select Committee on the Cost of Living
shrinking of Qantas International fleet, 152–3
stripping of bonus, 1, 318
successor, 19, 185, 197
Sydney Theatre Company chair, 180
tenure, extension of, 45, 199
trade unions, opinion on, 142
TWU v Qantas response, 107–8
'very little government support' remark, 138–40
Virgin Australia complaint against, 34, 140
workforce rationalisation, 43, 142
zero-profit flights, promotion of, 51–2
Joyce, Anthony, 259
Joyce, Geoff, 8
'Joyced', 131
JWS Research, 18

Kaine, Michael
call for Joyce's resignation, 50
impression of EBA, 105
Joyce's industrial relations decision, 61–2
Oldmeadow advice, view on, 57
Oldmeadow's impression, 305
opinion of Oldmeadow, 58–60
outsourcing decision, advice on, 54–5
Qantas' reliability during COVID-19, 115
Sheldon briefing, 239
TWU v Qantas analysis, 65, 70, 73–4, 76, 80
Keighery, Danielle, 14
Keltner, Dacher, 209
Kidon, Filip, 292

King, Catherine, 36, 241–2, 257
ACCC monitoring of Qantas, 216
Qantas Chairman's Lounge and, 289
Qatar Airways air rights decision, 221–5, 238, 241, 250, 256–7, 271–3, 286, 298–9, 311
Qatar inquiry response, 276–7
slot system action, 312
Turner's labelling, 299
King & Wood Mallesons, 314
Kirkland, Alan, 256
KLM, 132
Knight, Elizabeth, 145
Koch, David, 322
KPMG, 157

La Spina, Tino, 49, 67, 92, 161
Labor Party, 36, 260–1
see also by politician name
Lane, Sabra, 273
Lee, Michael
appointment of mediator, 297
Brandis' esteem, 56
outsourcing proposal, characterisation of, 303
TWU case and *see* Transport Worker's Union of Australia v Qantas (*TWU v Qantas*)
Leigh, Andrew, 257
L'Estrange, Michael, 191, 281, 285
Levine, Michele, 179, 242, 265
Liberal Party, 8
see also by name
Littleproud, David, 313
Lloyd, Shane, 18, 212–13
LOGOS, 93–4
Lucas, Tony
facility ownership and control, view on, 94
Finnair wet-lease, opinion on, 207
Qantas decision-making, assessment of, 280–1
Qantas fleet purchase, opinion of, 154–5
Qantas pilot training, 119–20
Qantas staffing during COVID-19, concerns about, 116–18, 128
'raise' process analogy, 281
Lufthansa, 132

McCormack, Michael, 35–6, 40–1, 220, 271
Macquarie AirFinance, 39
Macquarie Bank, 7–8
McGinnes, Andrew
AFR advertising boycott, 203
AFR articles meeting, 187
air turn-backs and diversions letter, 171
description of author, 173
flight increase announcement, 206

Hudson and, 296
Joyce's resignation, 262
Qantas tax argument, 177
Qatar inquiry, 286
resignation, 309
Rex dispatch, 86–7
Saar review, 318
Senate inquiry responses, 250, 252, 254
tone of press releases, 91, 131, 146
McGowan, Mark, 98
McKenzie, Bridget
competition in aviation, 313
COVID-era bonus query, 261
Qatar inquiry role, 251, 286–8
McLachlan, Gillon, 144–5, 192–7, 276
McManus, Angela, 111
McManus, Sally
Joyce's legacy, opinion of, 260–1
Qantas job cuts, scrutiny of, 239
Qantas' role in law reform, 109–110
strength of Qantas brand, 268
Mader, Wayne, 61–2
Malinauskas, Peter, 190, 194, 258, 270
Marc Newson Skybeds, 161
Marcolina, Rob, 309–10
Marles, Richard, 260
Maurice Blackburn, 54
Miles, Steven, 270
Millen, Sonia
industrial negotiations and, 111
Reed's opinion, 104–5
TWU v Qantas evidence, 70–2, 104
Miller, Michael, 204
Minns, Stephen, 314
Minogue, Kylie, 189
Moody's, 156
Moore-Wilton, Max, 234
Morrison, Scott
Benson and, 31–2
domestic travel, promotion of, 83
Dreamliner reception, 19
Hamad Airport incident description, 222
Hawaiian holiday, 141
JobKeeper announcement, 36
predecessor, 3
self-appointment to ministries, 40
Virgin support, 38–40
Morrison government
COVID-19 management and *see* COVID-19 pandemic
job losses as threat, 83
Qatar flight doubling grant, 220–1
Movember, 317
Mullen, Jacqui, 300

Mullen, John
  chairman appointment, 301
  company directorships, 319–20
  corporate activism, take on,
    316–17
  Joyce, opinion on, 1, 318–19
  media approach, 310
  removal of *AFR*, opinion
    on, 315
  vision, 320
Munger, Charlie, 37, 285
Murdoch, Lachlan, 15, 145
Murdoch, Sarah, 15
Murray, Crispin *see also* Pendal
  conversations with Goyder,
    292
  Joyce, opinion of, 17–18,
    165–7, 265
  Joyce's share sale, 214–15
  Project Sunrise, view on, 18
  Qantas' focus, criticism of, 127
  Qantas investment, opinion
    of, 162
  Qantas share buy-back,
    support of, 148
  Rio Tinto analogy, 274–5,
    292

Nanshan Group, 23
National Party, 36, 40–1
National Press Club, 8, 300
Nationalisation, 32
Net promotor score (NPS), 198
News Corp Australia, 15, 200,
  204, 296
Newson, Marc, 16
Nicholas, Paul, 64, 77
Nine Entertainment Co., 200,
  203

O'Brien, Kerry, 263, 269
O'Connor, Brendan, 180
Offshoring
  heavy maintenance, 44, 94
Oldmeadow, Ian
  creation of QGS, 60
  industrial relations career,
    58–9
  Joyce and, 62
  O'Toole meeting, 110–11
  outsourcing advice, 58, 81,
    105, 303–5
  Qantas mass sacking concerns,
    62
  Qantas pay deals, 61
Oldmeadow, Justine, 58–9, 81,
  111, 303–4
Oldmeadow Consulting, 57–9
O'Neil, Michele, 239
O'Neill, Meg, 144, 193
oneworld alliance, 235–6
O'Sullivan, Matt, 201
O'Toole, Teri
  bargaining agreement
    negotiations, view on,
    102–3, 108–11
  Qantas outsourcing and
    sackings, opinion on,
    115, 121

Outsourcing
  call centres, impact on, 115,
    122
  flying, 207
  ground handling, 49–50,
    54–8, 65, 107, 133, 142,
    146, 293
  in-house bid (IHB), 65–7, 70
  Joyce's fight with unions, 142
  Lee J's summation, 303
  pilot training, 94, 206
  proposal meeting, 303
  risks, 304–5
  savings, 80
  TWU case *see Transport
    Workers' Union Of
    Australia v Qantas
    (TWU v Qantas)*
Ownership Matters, 293

Paatsch, Dean, 167, 209
Parker, Andrew, 7
Parker, Doug, 262, 281
Parker & Partners, 7
Payne, Marise, 222
Pendal *see also* Murray, Crispin
  Clifford, praise for, 166
  defence of Qantas, 147–8
  Goyder and, 274
  Joyce, view on, 17–18, 44, 166
  Joyce share sale, concern
    about, 214
  vote against Sampson, 294
Perrottet, Dominic, 89
Perry, Neil, 16, 189, 239
Pocock, Barbara, 291
Pocock, David, 289–91
Points Plus Pay option, 30
Popple, Brad, 72
Project Rubicon, 88
Project Sunrise, 18, 93, 150,
  163, 211
Project Winton, 151
Prostate Cancer Foundation, 317
Purvinas, Steve
  inflight incidents, 170
  Joyce, opinion of, 62
  parts availability, concern
    about, 120
  pay rise offer, characterisation
    of, 105–6
  Qantas heavy maintenance
    facility proposal, 89
  Qantas recruiting practice, 121
  'slow-bake' pledge, 60
PwC, 93, 242–3, 290

Qantas
  2023 AGM, 281, 292–5
  2023 annual report, 277–8
  ACCC actions *see Australian
    Competition and Consumer
    Commission (ACCC)*
  activism, 316–17
  advantage over Virgin,
    313–14
  advertising boycott, 202–4
  AFR feud, 200–4
  AFR symbiosis, 14–15

airfare pricing, 105, 127–9,
  168, 171–2, 210, 216–17,
  219, 233, 265, 283, 296
Albanese's praise, 189–90
anti-competitiveness, 6, 216,
  224, 268, 271, 300
app capabilities, 164
asset write-down, 157–9
Australian jobs and, 238–9
board member benefits, 284–5
booking fee changes, 307
brand damage, 130–1, 134,
  136, 268, 281, 296
call centres, 25, 115, 122,
  124, 164
capacity forecasts, 101, 110
capital expenditure, delayed,
  148, 160–5
capital-intensive business,
  161–2
Cass-Gottlieb's description,
  305
centenary celebrations, 189–90
CEO hiring practice, 9
commercial advantages, 32
commercial deals with media,
  200–2
commercial objective, 266
Commonwealth government
  spending, 227–8
communications to customers,
  136
company tax, 175–8, 284, 310
comparative adequacy mantra,
  133
compensation mentality, 92
complexity of company, 140
conflict-avoidance of board,
  316
connection time, management
  of, 164
contract execution policy, 68–9
'corporate welfare-seeking', 90
COVID-19, operations during
  see COVID-19 pandemic
credit rating downgrade, 156
culture, 10, 75, 91, 133, 166,
  205, 310, 315–17, 320–1
customer expectations,
  absolute, 127, 132–3
customer experience, 148, 164,
  198–9
customer improvements, 264,
  279–80
customer satisfaction, 44–6,
  123, 126, 130–1, 136,
  142–3, 147, 172, 182, 199,
  219, 224, 268, 308
customer loyalty strategies,
  307, 314
debt financing, 25, 29, 44–5
delivery of A380s, 11
delusion, 209
denialism, 115, 133
domestic market dominance,
  82, 216, 312–14
economic efficiency, 90
Emirates alliance, 7, 156,
  229–36

employees *see* Qantas staff
engineering and spare parts
  backlog, 120
executive versus staff, disparity
  of treatment, 104–5
external communications, tone
  of, 315, 318
'final frontier' of aviation, 18
financial interests,
  prioritisation of, 1, 30,
  127, 148, 178, 246, 315
financial liability, 30, 127
fleet *see* Qantas fleet
flight credit class action,
  248–9, 259
flight simulators, 91–5, 119
foreign ownership cap, 33
fuel costs, 172, 279–80
Fysh's ideals and guiding
  principles, 267–8, 307–8
'ghost flights' lawsuit *see*
  Australian Competition
  and Consumer
  Commission (ACCC)
government lobbying, 216,
  272, 285–6
government subsidies and
  support, 50–3, 89, 92–3,
  137, 139, 156, 174–8, 242,
  246, 256, 264, 266
head office, 10, 87, 88
'holy trinity', 17
Indigenous Voice to
  Parliament support, 240,
  260, 316–17
inflation rates, contribution
  to, 168
inflight catering, 28, 94, 130,
  169, 198–9
inflight incidents, 12–13,
  170–1
influence, 5
insolvency, 29, 31
institutional investors, 147–8
integrated operations centre
  (IOC), 12
international market share
  reduction, 152
investment inadequacies, 154,
  156, 161–4
investor sentiment, 278–9
Labor government support,
  260–1, 267
labour hire agencies and, 54,
  239
'lazy' capital, unlocking of,
  94
media influence, 310–11
Miller's criticism, 204
monopoly, 39, 314
national carrier status, 24, 105,
  127, 133, 141–3, 266,
  270, 290
national property footprint,
  review of, 87–93
nature pre-Joyce, 10
NPS, 198
on-time performance, 142,
  169, 198

'operational transformation'
  priorities, 63
powerlessness over price
  notion, 173
pre-tax annual loss record, 157
privatisation, 133, 264
'productivity improvement'
  rationalisation, 43
profit, 17, 106, 148–9, 157,
  159, 172, 174, 178, 210,
  217, 244, 280, 308
profitless revenue growth, 52
public sentiment, 134, 174,
  179, 189, 197, 204, 225,
  242, 247, 255, 260, 283,
  314–15
Qatar Airways, schism with,
  220–1, 233, 236
relativism, financial and moral,
  184
repayment of debt, 50, 128,
  177–8, 246, 256
RepTrak rankings, 136,
  179–80, 296, 308
reputational damage, 179,
  192, 198
request for approval (RFA),
  70–5
Rio Tinto analogy, 191, 274–5,
  281, 292
risk management policy, 67–8
Saar review, 314–18
safety reputation, 12, 91, 133
sale of surplus land, 93–4
share buy-back, 138, 146–8,
  159, 197, 210, 214
share prices, 17, 21, 25, 27, 95,
  147, 157–60, 213, 308
shareholder engagement,
  294–5
shareholder gratification
  'within reason', 162
shareholder presentation,
  210–12
Sharp's opinion, 84–5, 172,
  256
Shonky Award, 178
Singapore Airlines,
  competition with, 237
skirmish with Rex, 83–4
slot hoarding practice, 224,
  256, 260
'Spirit of Australia' tagline,
  133
'structural uplift' in domestic
  revenue, 218
sustainability credentials, 162
Sydney Airport tenancy, 92
technology spending, 164
trading updates, 97, 150, 159,
  210, 279–80
'transformation costs', 48
travel agent commission,
  slashing of, 95
TWU v Qantas decision,
  impact of, 276
'underlying/adjusted' profit,
  47–9, 53, 150, 306
undertakings, nature of, 93

Virgin Australia collapse,
  role in, 33, 38–40, 140
website problems, 164
wi-fi, in-flight, 164
Qantas Airports, 55
Qantas Airways Limited (QAL),
  59–65, 109
Qantas Cabin Crew Australia
  (QCCA), 102, 109
Qantas Chairman's Lounge,
  169, 260
  AFR courtesy copies, 200,
    204, 315
  benefits for Qantas, 227–9
  establishment, 226
  inducement, nature of, 232
  invitation-only status, 2
  Joyce's influence, 228, 231–2
  membership, 4, 227–8, 231–2,
    289, 291, 302
  Mullen and, 302
  network, 226
  opacity, 229
  perks, 226–7
  Pocock queries, 289
  politicians and, 4, 225,
    229–32, 242
  status credits, 228
  Sydney Morning Herald poll,
    291
  symbolism, 2, 204, 227
Qantas Domestic
  EBIT margin, 210
  fleet, 154
  market share, 155–6, 216
Qantas Drive, 89–92
Qantas fleet *see also by*
  manufacturer
  age, 154, 160, 163–4, 314
  capability gap, 207
  delivery post-Joyce, 165
  disinvestment, 163, 264–5
  extended retirement age claim,
    163
  flying hours, increase in,
    163–4
  Joyce's management, 150–5,
    160–4, 246, 264–5
  refurbishment, 314
  renewal, 149–55, 160–2
  selection, 152
  wet-lease, 206–7
Qantas Freight, 95, 207–8
Qantas Frequent Flyer program
  accrual on government travel,
    end of, 228
  apology, 137
  COVID-19 flight credit
    bookings, 248
  COVID-19 points balances,
    129
  major overhaul, 307
  membership, 139, 314
  redemption seats, 136, 198, 280
Qantas Ground Services (QGS)
  employment conditions, QAL
    compared, 63, 109
  limit on workforce, 61
  motive for establishment, 60

Qantas Group, 60, 152, 160–1, 252
Qantas Group Engineering Academy, 180
Qantas Group Management Committee (GMC)
'black hat'/chief challenger role, 167
Carter bonus inquiry, 314
Jones' cost savings document, 64
nature of, 80
Oldmeadow attendance, 58
'operational transformation' documents, 63
outsourcing decision, 67–70, 304
Qantas International
COVID-19 grounding, 42
EBIT margin, 210
fleet write-down, 159
pilot stand down, 118
post-COVID-19 fleet, 94, 129
relaunch, push back of, 95
shrinking, 152–3, 155
Qantas Loyalty, 95
'Qantas News', 14
Qantas Pass, 125–6
Qantas pilots
COVID-19 and, 118–19
EBA, 119
Finnair wet-leasing, 206–8, 239
Joyce's fleet management, impression of, 208
New Zealand, 239
preservation program, 118
promotion, 119
seniority by aircraft system, 119
training, 91, 94, 118–20
training centre, 91–5, 118, 206
Qantas staff
adequacy, insistence on, 121–2
baggage handlers, grounding of, 60–2
'bargaining chips' for subsidies, 91
condemnation of treatment, 64, 80, 107, 146–7, 211, 240, 247, 266, 279–80, 293, 297–8
cost reduction, 55, 60, 64, 80, 118, 121, 155–6, 172, 264
COVID-19 impact *see* COVID-19 pandemic
culture, 10
disaggregation, 59–60
'discretionary bonuses', exclusion of, 48
division strategy, 60
head office, 87–91
identity, 104
industrial relations issues *see* Industrial relations
JobKeeper payments, 37–8, 50–1, 139, 177, 304
legacy, 59–63, 102, 104

long-haul flight attendants, 101–4, 108, 110
loyalty, 104, 266
licensed aircraft mechanical engineers, 106, 121, 180–1
New Zealand cabin crew, 239
outsourcing *see* Outsourcing
part-time majority, 121
pilots *see* Qantas pilots
Qantas share offer, 100
Qantas' treatment, 104
QCCA *see* Qantas Cabin Crew Australia (QCCA)
QGS *see* Qantas Ground Services (QGS)
rationalisation, 43, 142, 181
recruitment post-COVID-19, 121, 135, 180–1, 238
redundancies and sacking, 43, 49, 62, 88, 95, 115–16, 121, 180, 184, 240, 247, 264, 297
relocation, 88, 92–3
short-haul crew, 110–11, 169
specialists, 88, 117
training, 117–18
QantasLink, 79, 104, 151, 207
Qatar Airways, 5, 42
Australian air rights campaign, 219, 220–4, 236–7, 241–2, 250, 255–60, 270–2, 290, 299, 311
continuity during COVID-19, 220, 237, 258, 290
economic benefits of increased flights, 233
'fair competition' lobbying, 220
fleet age and capability, 225
growth, 234–5
Hamad Airport incident and, 222–5, 273
Israel evacuation, 298
post-COVID seat sales, 129
profit, 241
Qantas' concerns, 220–1, 236
Senate inquiry *see* Senate inquiry into Qatar decision (Qatar inquiry)
Virgin Australia alliance, 220–1, 233, 311
QFuture, 155

Rangiah, Justice Darryl, 106–7
Reed, Steven, 102–5, 117
Regional Express (Rex)
administration, 311–12
expansion, 217
government support, 35–6, 83
Joyce's opinion, 86–7
National Party choice, 40
online refund portal, 85–6
Qantas size compared, 87
refund portal, 85–6
skirmish with Qantas, 83
slot hoarding, impact of, 224
RepTrak
advice to Qantas, 181–2

confidential briefing pack, 179–80
Qantas rankings, 136, 296, 308
Rio Tinto
Juukan Gorge disaster, 191, 274–5, 281, 292
Robb, Andrew, 256
Roy Morgan, 17, 136–7, 179, 242
Rudd, Kevin, 11
Russell, David, 298
Ryan, Monique, 291

Saar, Tom, 314
review, 314–18
Samaras, Kos, 241, 300
Same Job, Same Pay legislation, 109, 305
Sampson, Todd, 282, 293–4
Sams, Peter, 102
Sayers, Luke, 322
Scheinkestel, Nora, 301
Scherer, Christian, 150–1, 154, 163
Schneider, William, 292
Scriven, Jon, 167
Scurrah, Paul, 22, 31–4, 36, 38–40
Senate inquiry into Qatar decision (Qatar inquiry), 270, 276, 285–6
Finch's assertions, 287–8
Hrdlicka's evidence, 221, 223
Hudson's responses, 286–90
Joyce and, 258, 286
King's response, 276–7
outcome, 290
Qantas Chairman's Lounge queries, 289–90
Qantas' written responses, 289
Senate Select Committee on the Cost of Living, 239–40, 247, 250
COVID-19 flight credits, 251–5, 260
Joyce's remuneration and bonuses, 251
McGinnes responses, 252
parties, 250
Qantas' credibility, 255
Seremetidis, Theo, 297–8, 315
Sharp, John, 36, 83–6, 172, 256
Sheldon, Tony
evidence gathering, 249
Finch, impression of, 288–9
Joyce and, 205, 239–40, 302
'Joyced' reputation of Qantas, 131
meetings with Albanese, 61
Mullen, impression of, 301–2
Qantas, relationship with, 11–12
Qantas' progressive political stances, view on, 317
Sampson, opinion of, 294
Senate Select Committee questions, 250, 252–5
senator office, 110
Shorten, Bill, 239, 276

Sims, Rod
  competition policy review,
    256–7, 273
  COVID-19 flight credits, 46
  Virgin complaint against
    Qantas, 34–5
Singapore Airlines
  air rights request, 5, 7
  competition with Qantas, 237
  continuity during COVID-
    19, 42
  in-flight wi-fi, 164
  ownership, 5
  post-COVID seat sales, 129
  Qantas financial position
    compared, 139
  Skytrax ranking, 219
  Virgin Australia stake, 23, 155
Sky News, 27, 32–3, 219, 245,
  265
Skytrax World Airline Awards,
  219, 311
slot hoarding, 224, 256, 260, 312
Smith, Heather, 281
'Snakes on a Plane' incident,
  12–13
Sodhi, Gaurav, 147
Standard & Poor's, 156
Stefanovic, Karl, 218, 260
Strawbridge, Vaughan, 40
Strong, James, 59, 152, 264
Stutchbury, Michael
  AFR boycott, opinion on,
    202–4
  AFR coverage meeting, 173,
    187–8
  Albanese Chairman's Lounge
    membership, 231, 243
  Hudson op ed, publication
    of, 176
  Joyce's leadership, assessment
    of, 202–3
  Qatar Airways air rights
    campaign, 273
Sukkar, Michael, 35
Sumers, Brian, 19
Svensson, Markus, 169, 179, 198,
  203, 236
Swan, Wayne, 270
Swissport, 297, 304
Sydney Airport, 21, 88–9, 112,
  224
Sydney Gateway Project, 91
Sydney Morning Herald
  Goyder's 'best CEO in
    Australia' claim, 143
  Joyce op ed, 171
  Joyce share sale, questions on,
    244–5
  Joyce's extended tenure, 199
  Joyce's management, coverage
    of, 201–2
  Qantas AFR boycott article,
    200–1, 203
  Qantas Chairman's Lounge
    poll, 291
  Qantas headquarters, NSW
    government offer
    regarding, 93

Qatar Airways air rights
    campaign, 223–4
Sydney Night Patrol, 112
Sydney Theatre Company, 180

Tadros, Edmund, 242
Tanner, Lindsay, 228
Tebbutt, Carmel, 231
Telstra, 293
Texas Pacific Group (TPG),
  7–8
Tonagh, Peter, 15
Transport Workers' Union
    (TWU), 11–12, 50
  call for Joyce's resignation, 50
  flight attendants' pay deal,
    102–3
  ground handling pay deals, 60
  IHB for ground handling
    workforce, 65–7
  Joyce's impression, 76
  membership, 63
Transport Workers' Union of
    Australia v Qantas Airways
    Limited (TWU v Qantas)
  accounting implications, 108
  evidence and analysis, 62–79
  facts in dispute, 56
  Federal Court judgment, 78,
    106–7, 247, 276, 303–4,
    309
  High Court judgment, 276,
    293
  media coverage, 75–6
  mediation, 297, 302
  parties, 55–6
  Qantas appeal, 106, 108
  Qantas press releases, 78–80,
    107
  settlement, 297, 302–3
Treacher, Karl, 130
Trivers, Robert, 209
Troubled Asset Relief Program
    (TARP) (US), 35
Trump, Donald, 21, 79, 266
Tully, Stephanie, 130, 250, 252–4
Turkish Airlines, 299
Turner, Graham 'Skroo', 20, 223,
  256, 299
Tyler, Tony, 262

Ukraine invasion, 206–7
United Airlines, 5, 42, 60, 164
United Arab Emirates, 6, 234–5
Universal Air Travel Plan
    (UATP), 125–6

Vaile, Mark, 6–7
Velocity Frequent Flyer program,
  23
Virgin Australia
  administration, 42–3
  airline stakes, 155
  baggage handling, in-sourcing,
    134, 297
  baggage tracking, in-app, 164
  collapse, 31, 33, 38–41, 263–4
  Commonwealth government
    spending, 228

complaint against Qantas,
    34–5
corporate travel account loss,
    82
COVID-19 job losses, 83
COVID-19 seat cuts, 98
debt, 22–3
domestic ground handling,
    116
domestic market share, 155–6,
    216
Etihad Alliance, 14–15
Fairfax Media deal, 202
government support, 33–9, 90
Jetstar undercutting, 312
JobKeeper, impact of, 37–8
Joyce's view on nationalisation,
    32
loan proposal, 38
long-haul operation, 129
on-time performance, 114,
    116, 127–8, 142, 169, 198
  Qantas compared, 90, 313–14
Qatar alliance, 220–1, 233,
    311
rebranding, 155
redundancies, 50
RepTrak ranking, 308
restructuring, 41, 45
sale to Bain Capital, 40, 45, 82
slot hoarding practice, 224
unionised staff hire, 297
Virgin Beyond, 231, 291
Virgin Blue, 11, 60, 155
Virgin Group, 23, 155

Walker, Bret, 106
Wallace, Cam, 14
Waterhouse, Rachel, 295
Watson-Brown, Elizabeth, 291
Watson-Wheeler, Kylie, 194–6
Webber, Tony
  competition in aviation, 271
  government-funded airfares,
    opinion of, 83
  Qatar air rights campaign,
    233–4, 277
Webster, Alison, 19
The Weekend Australian, 139
Westacott, Jennifer, 32, 109–10
Western Sydney Airport, 87–8
White, Linda, 110
Whittaker, Paul, 15
Wirth, Olivia
  CEO candidate, 185, 200
  Frequent Flyer overhaul, 307
  Howes and, 15
  Joyce and, 11, 262
  Oldmeadow meeting, 59
  resignation, 296
Wong, Penny, 272
Wood, Danielle, 256–7
Woodward, Richard, 61
World Health Organization
    (WHO), 21

Yangoyan, Rachel, 104
Yates, Peter, 8
Young, Neil, 55–6, 67–8, 73

Joe Aston wrote the celebrated Rear Window column for the *Australian Financial Review* for twelve years. Prior to that he worked in corporate communications, including at Qantas. He lives in Sydney.